THE VICTORIANS AND OLD AGE

THE VICTORIANS AND OLD AGE

KAREN CHASE

OXFORD
UNIVERSITY PRESS

OXFORD
UNIVERSITY PRESS

Great Clarendon Street, Oxford OX2 6DP

Oxford University Press is a department of the University of Oxford.
It furthers the University's objective of excellence in research, scholarship,
and education by publishing worldwide in

Oxford New York

Auckland Cape Town Dar es Salaam Hong Kong Karachi
Kuala Lumpur Madrid Melbourne Mexico City Nairobi
New Delhi Shanghai Taipei Toronto

With offices in

Argentina Austria Brazil Chile Czech Republic France Greece
Guatemala Hungary Italy Japan Poland Portugal Singapore
South Korea Switzerland Thailand Turkey Ukraine Vietnam

Oxford is a registered trade mark of Oxford University Press
in the UK and in certain other countries

Published in the United States
by Oxford University Press Inc., New York

First published 2009

British Library Cataloguing in Publication Data
Data available

Library of Congress Cataloging in Publication Data
Chase, Karen, 1952–
The Victorians and old age / Karen Chase.
p. cm.
Includes index.
ISBN 978–0–19–956436–1 (acid-free paper)
1. English fiction – 19th century – History and criticism. 2. Old age in literature.
3. Aging in literature. 4. Old age – Great Britain – History – 19th century.
5. Older people – Great Britain – History – 19th century. I. Title.
PR878.A394C47 2009
823'.009'355—dc22 2009008812

Typeset by SPI Publisher Services, Pondicherry, India
Printed and bound in Great Britain
on acid-free paper by the
MPG Books Group, Bodmin and King's Lynn

ISBN 978–0–19–956436–1

1 3 5 7 9 10 8 6 4 2

For Michael

Acknowledgments

I thank the many friends and students who patiently allowed me to think out loud my ideas about aging and liberally contributed to them. To Caitlin Dallas I owe much gratitude for her hard work and ingenuity in checking notes, obtaining permissions, scanning images, and making excellent editorial suggestions. Michael Chase-Levenson, to whom I dedicate the book, is part of the spirit which brought it into being, and Alex and Sarah provided the support necessary for its completion. Theresa Mangum and Helen Small were more than colleagues working in the same area; their generosity and high standards have contributed much to my own research. The University of Virginia generously granted a timely sabbatical. Finally, it has been a particular pleasure to work with Andrew McNeillie at Oxford University Press.

Could it be, even for elderly people, that this was life?—startling, unexpected, unknown?

Virginia Woolf, *To the Lighthouse*

Contents

List of Illustrations

Abbreviations

A	Trollope, *Autobiography* (1883)
AW	Carroll, *Alice in Wonderland* (1865)
BH	Dickens, *Bleak House* (1853)
BR	Dickens, *Barnaby Rudge* (1841)
C	Trollope, *The Claverings* (1867)
CC	Dickens, *A Christmas Carol* (1843)
Cr	Gaskell, *Cranford* (1853)
CYFH?	Trollope, *Can You Forgive Her?* (1865)
DC	Dickens, *David Copperfield* (1850)
DG	Wilde, *The Picture of Dorian Gray* (1891)
DS	Dickens, *Dombey and Son* (1848)
FP	Trollope, *The Fixed Period* (1882)
GE	Dickens, *Great Expectations* (1861)
H	Oliphant, *Hester* (1883)
HKHWR	Trollope, *He Knew He Was Right* (1869)
LCB	Trollope, *The Last Chronicle of Barset* (1867)
LD	Dickens, *Little Dorrit* (1857)
MC	Dickens, *Martin Chuzzlewit* (1844)
MED	Dickens, *The Mystery of Edwin Drood* (1870)
NN	Dickens, *Nicholas Nickleby* (1839)
NN	Morris, *News from Nowhere* (1891)
OCS	Dickens, *The Old Curiosity Shop* (1841)
OMF	Dickens, *Our Mutual Friend* (1865)
OML	Trollope, *An Old Man's Love* (1884)
OWT	Bennett, *The Old Wives' Tale* (1908)
PM	Trollope, *The Prime Minister* (1876)
S&B	Carroll, *Sylvie and Bruno* (1889)
Sketches	Dickens, *Sketches by "Boz"* (1836)
TDC	Trollope, *The Duke's Children* (1880)

TW	Trollope, *The Warden* (1855)
UT	Dickens, *The Uncommercial Traveller* (1860)
V	Brontë, *Villette* (1853)
WW	Collins, *The Woman in White* (1860)

Introduction

In the first decade of the twentieth century, 'senescence' entered the vocabulary as a distinct phase of human existence, as did 'adolescence.'[1] The act of naming may be the beginning of professional life for a subject, but it is the culmination of a process through which a culture newly designs and shapes human experience. This book traces that lived experience of old age through the Victorian epoch to the time when it becomes an established 'category' of scientific and political discourse. Old age has a social and cultural life long before it incites a professionalism. In this study, I examine nodal moments of intersection between narrative and cultural experience which increasingly bring 'senescence' from the private into the public sphere. All analyses of old age are indebted to the rich historical investigations undertaken by Peter Laslett, Michael Anderson, Pat Thane, and Jill Quagdano. And the conceptual framework upon which I draw is inconceivable without the contributions by Kathleen Woodward, Pat Jallands, Pat Thane, Simone de Beauvoir, and Helen Small, to name just a few of the people whose work has inspired my own. What I offer here is neither a comprehensive history nor a theoretical appraisal: rather, I have attempted to provide a contextually rich account of threshold moments and landmark events, and an analysis of the leading cultural manifestations of old age which both defined and reflected the aging experience in Britain. I look to interpret its complex and variable forms, as they become conspicuous from roughly the middle of the nineteenth century until the passing of the Pension Bill in 1908.

Darwin demonstrated that nature favors those best able to adapt; their reward is survival. Civilization attempts to correct for nature's indifference, creating conditions whereby adaptation, and thus longer survival, is accessible to greater numbers of people. What better mark is there of civilized progress than an extension of life for the common person, the opening of a period that demographers now call the "fourth estate," more typically known simply as "old age"? But civilization's rewards are too often distributed no more fairly than nature's. Civilization also rewards those best able to manipulate their own environment, but physical capacity is closely bound to economic and social power, and frequently those whose biological constitution suggests an early demise are instead supported well into advancing years. Throughout history there have been individuals whose lives extend beyond eighty years; in the few cultures which exhibit high regard for the elderly, there may even be a sizable portion of the population who enter old age. However, within the western tradition, old age as a distinct phase of life only seizes public attention when the numbers of people living well past the years in which they can support themselves by their own labor (or their own income) require provision (housing, medicine, food), advice, and expertise from the social body. In this sense, old age—not as a lived experience, but as a phenomenon provoking legislation in the social arena and noticeable publications in the literary arena—is an event of the eighteenth and nineteenth centuries. In fact, until the nineteenth century the attempt to define 'old age' specifically by years was limited and variable.[1] Old age might be determined by looks, experience, feeling, or by the inability to bear arms or to work. Not surprisingly, it is the last—the capacity for work—which lent increasing value to the chronological definition of old age.

Lynn Botelho has usefully charted attempts to find an adequate nomenclature for aging. In 1607, Henry Cuffe (*The Differences of the Ages of Man*, London, 1607) distinguished two stages, the first from fifty to sixty-five, in which diminished strength counters "a will and readinesse to be doing," and the second, "decrepit old age," when both "abilitie" and "all wilingenesse" are extinguished. Botelho then quotes the famous passage from John Smith's mid-seventeenth-century study, *The Pourtract of Old Age* (London, 1666) in which old age is divided into three stages:

> First, crude, green, and while it is yet in the beginning, while men are able to do business, and go about their employments, and this is but one little remove from manhood and doth immediately border upon it. The second is full mature, or ripe age; when men begin to leave off their employments and betake themselves to retiredness; when God hath no work for them, and they have no strength for him; or lastly, extream sickly decripit, overgrown old age; in which it may be truly said old age is perished; when their breath is corrupt, when their daies are extinct, and the grave is ready for them.[2]

1. See Janet Roebuck, "When Does 'Old Age' Begin? The Evolution of the English Definition," *Journal of Social History*, 12 (spring 1979), 417; and Pat Thane, *Old Age in English History: Past Experiences, Present Issues* (Oxford: Oxford University Press, 2000), 24.
2. Lynn Botelho, "Old Age and Menopause in Rural Women of Early Modern Suffolk," in *Women and Ageing in British Society since 1500*, ed. Lynn Botelho and Pat Thane (London: Longman, 2001), 44.

Botelho summarizes the rough distinctions between those definitions which stress chronology, function (the ability to support oneself and participate in the world), and culture (which assigns traits or characteristics to age), but she is careful to point out that "all three ageing processes can function simultaneously, and yet not be of equal importance or occur at equal speed."[3] Lived experience rarely provides the precision which later generations would seek, and as Pat Thane reminds us,

> In all times there have been competing optimistic and pessimistic, paradigms of old age and we cannot readily determine whether one or the other was culturally dominant. All cultures have a variety of images of ageing available to them from which individuals and groups shape their expectations. These images shift and compete and if any one of them gains hegemony it does not necessarily do so for long.[4]

My aim is to illuminate the cluster of signs upon which the Victorians drew in order to derive meaning from the experience of growing old within a society and culture only just beginning to take age into full account. The pictures of old age generated through fiction, journalism, science, and the fine arts reflected and shaped the quality of life for older people; they provided words and images which helped to form a conceptual basis for understanding 'senescence' as an integral phase of existence. As pressures for legislation became increasingly insistent, new legal forms for thinking about age were assimilated into the rich narrative variety already at hand. Like most births, the emergence of images and a language for old age came out of struggle. Rather than think in terms of success and failure, we should consider the successive attempts to provide more satisfactory accommodation to those who faced age as a challenge to the times in which they lived. In this way, we can understand our own position in time as part of an ongoing process, always requiring adjustment and invention. We are tinkers in time; and age is the condition and the subject of our work.

In her study of old age in the eighteenth century, Susannah Ottaway points to the effort to sustain subtle distinctions by separating the 'young-old' from the extreme old: phases between the conventionally named "green" and "decrepit" were carefully articulated.[5] By the nineteenth century, concepts

3. Ibid. 44. 4. Thane, *Old Age in English History*, 6.

5. Susannah Ottaway, *The Decline of Life: Old Age in Eighteenth-Century England* (Cambridge: Cambridge University Press, 2004), 69–70.

familiar to modern analysts were widely discussed, though without the terminology we append today. The author of an 1881 essay for *Fraser's* on the cheerfulness of the old asks "who are the Old?", and with some frustration settles for the chronological description, "For the present, let it be accepted that a man between forty and fifty is growing old. Between fifty and sixty he is somewhat advanced in life. Between sixty and seventy he is old. Between seventy and eighty he is aged. Above eighty he is venerable, or patriarchal," and then rejects the chronological premise by concluding "But here idiosyncracy is everything. It all depends on the individual man."[6] Indeed, Lewis Carroll's infant fairy Bruno innocently puts the case vividly when, in response to the question "You would guess me to be an *old* man, wouldn't you?" he answers "I don't know if oo're an *old* man...I thinks oo're *eighty-three*."[7] This work hopes to show that although 'age' and 'old' do come together, the meeting is frequently unpredictable and as often unstable.

It is easy enough to recognize the ambiguities of definition and to see how chronological, functional, and cultural conceptions of age each capture some nuances while ignoring others. In addition to these ways of thinking about age we must include the individual subject's estimate of its own condition. This does not make experience or maturity necessarily a synonym for old age, but neither can we dismiss individual report or the perception of 'agedness' in others. A person may call herself (or be called) aged though she is only 40, fit and with no physical manifestations of decline. In some instances age may be a transient rather than a permanent condition. Is it fair to consider these instances in an experience of "senescence"? It seems right to do so when the periods between 'feeling' old and 'being' old are more or less continuous, when they are not broken by lengthy periods of interruption, and when the passage of time only results in a confirmation of old age as established by other standards as well.

Modernization did not greatly extend the age of mortality: that shifted only by a few years well into the twentieth century. But, as has often been noted, the decline of mortality rates in childhood and in youth swelled the numbers at the other end. The population doubled between 1740 and 1840, and then again between 1840 and 1900.[8] With the greater number of

6. "Concerning the Cheerfulness of the Old" *Fraser's Magazine* NS 23 (February 1881), 250.
7. Lewis Carroll, *Sylvie and Bruno Concluded*, in *The Complete Works of Lewis Carroll* (London: Chadwyck-Healey, 1994), 613.
8. See Jill Quadagno, *Aging in Early Industrial Society: Work, Family, and Social Policy in Nineteenth-Century England* (New York: Academic Press, div. of Harcourt Brace Jovanovich, 1982), 22, 29.

people moving to cities, it is no surprise that in London one out of three people living in the workhouses was elderly by 1851; by 1891 that figure had become one of every two, and throughout Britain one of every three.[9] Through the 1840s it was adequate for each guild to define old age according to the period at which one became unfit to perform the tasks associated with the particular work: a glass worker might retire at 40, while a carpenter waited until 50, and an engineer until 55.[10] Philanthropic Friendly Societies located the onset of old age at 50 in the 1870s and 1880s. Pressure to make economic provision for the growing number of needy elderly people prompted the government to affix responsibility first on the immediate family, and when that proved inadequate a Royal Commission, established in 1895, set 65 as the age at which one was eligible to retire with a state pension.[11] By 1908, the age for retirement was moved to 70, for economic rather than qualitative or biological reasons.

The numbers tell one story, and it is a fascinating narrative with its own dramatic turns. But there are competing stories which make the experience of old age in the nineteenth century dense, rich, and often confusing. Alongside the demographics of aging, other definitions persist. The lifecycle has its own permutations which differ among individuals, but fall roughly into types of experiences which become socially and psychologically recognizable. Teresa Mangum argues that Victorians were taught to "perform their old age" in specific forms which are then reflected in the images reproduced artistically through narrative or illustration.[12] My own analysis places the Victorian construction of agedness into signal clusters of related phenomena from the social and literary cultures in which it was developed. The governing principle of this study is that frictions inevitably arose between elderly people whose numbers and needs taxed the state which sought to identify, classify and—somehow—provide for them. It is my purpose to interpret the volatility of these relations as they appear in narrative form, social policy, or cultural attitudes. Furthermore, I suggest that the terrors, anxieties, and yearnings of old age as well as its pleasures and humors not only exceed, but often challenge, the emerging conventions.

9. David Thomson, "Workhouse to Nursing Home: Residential Care of Elderly People in England since 1840," *Ageing and Society*, 3 (1983), 47.

10. Roebuck, "When Does 'Old Age' Begin?", 421.

11. Ibid. 420.

12. Theresa Mangum, "Little Women: The Aging Female Character in Nineteenth Century British Children's Literature," in *Figuring Age: Women, Bodies, Generations*, ed. Kathleen Woodward (Bloomington: Indiana University Press, 1999), 59.

The landmark events in Victorian old age unfolded as no coherent historical movement, nor as a continuous public concern. The problem of the elderly flared and faded before it settled into sustained focus in the last twenty years of the century. The method of the book is, accordingly, the method of cases and contexts. Illuminating moments in the history—especially as presented in complex narratives—are located within the widely changing circumstances of the elderly. Throughout a set of intersecting problems provide the framework of my account:

- The elusiveness of senescence as an experience and a social performance; the indeterminacy of old age and the struggle within imaginative and political life to bring it clarity; the continuing resonance of the Ciceronian ideal of old age as a period of dignity, serenity, wisdom, respect and self-respect, alongside growing and inescapable instances of old age as misery, bewilderment, solitude, dispossession.
- The central place of institutions—the workhouse, the hospital, the asylum, and the almshouse—in the conditions of Victorian old age; the massing of the urban elderly poor in these administrative spaces; the imaginative life of institutions; and the competing zones of private life, at once a refuge from officialdom and a site of stress within the family.
- The power and powerlessness of age; the spreading deprivation at the bottom of the social scale, only slowly recognized through the course of the century; but also the prominence of elderly figures of power, above all Queen Victoria, but also leading politicians such as Gladstone, Disraeli, and Palmerston, who exerted "gray power" in the face of emergent modernity.
- Cross-generational relationships as an abiding preoccupation of imaginative life and a resource within the social history of old age, but also generational division as an emerging and conspicuous episode towards the end of the nineteenth century, when partisans of the New contested the iconography of the Old, especially at the moment of the Queen's Jubilees and the retrospection of the fin-de-siècle.
- The creation of the "elderly subject" as a category in medical and sociological research, a late-century effect of the developing discipline of gerontology, as well as a response to the work of novelists, painters, and journalists; the elderly subject as the newly focused point of attention and as marking a new phase of understanding and self-understanding.
- The halting movement towards public provision for old age through a system of universal pensions; the pension movement not only as a legislative political episode, but also as a documentary resource and a

crystallization of images, attitudes, intentions, and fantasies; the doubleness of age as a social category and as a lived experience, age as the condition for others before it is one's own life.

The chapters are organized around major literary works set alongside episodes and artifacts, diaries and memoirs, images and inscriptions, that produced (and now illuminate) the construction of old age through Victoria's long reign. I begin with Charles Dickens, whose panoply of aged figures begins with his earliest 'sketches' of the thirties and ends only with his death in 1870. But in addition to the notable figures, whose individual stories create a dynamic narrative of possibilities for the enactment of aging, is the city itself, which locates youth and age within the physical contexts of modernity. Central here are the portraits of institutions which largely determine the quality of life in its final stages. The workhouse and the asylum become animated forces representing both the care and indifference of society to the casualties of time. Dickens places the rural within an urban context as delicately as old age figures within a robust youth. In this way he gives visual representation to what historians today refer to as the 'graying of the countryside,' a consequence of modernization which encouraged a marked progression of young people to the urban centers.

The chapter on Anthony Trollope examines another fault line within the cherished picture of old age that the Victorians appropriated from the Ciceronean ideal, in which substitution of one capacity for another and a diminishing desire corresponding to weakening competencies ensure a smooth and happy old age. The premise underlying Trollope's startling farce entitled *The Fixed Period* is that a culture of youth may not only secretly desire the passing of the generation before; it may take steps to ensure a timely death in order to prevent the pain, awkwardness, and expense of senility and to provide a more prosperous future for those left behind. The contest between children and their aging parents in Trollope's fiction generates new perspectives on the place of age imperialism and colonization. And through other novels which study the housing and tending of the aged, we glimpse the important (but ultimately inadequate) attempt to care for the aged through a system of almshousing. The almshouse movement (if such it can be called) is largely a forgotten story, overshadowed by the larger governmental institutions which dealt with old age formally—and officially. Trollope helps us revive these important attempts to aid the growing numbers of old people through private means and through smaller, often improvised, arrangements.

Government itself has a private and a public face, and the two chapters which follow study their intersection. The aging Queen Victoria has her own story and the story of a century to tell: her long life and reign produced a dense body of images by which the century could understand its own aging. Lewis Carroll's *Alice* books uncannily prefigure this phenomena of age-looking-at-youth-looking-at-age. Written in the 1860s, the books could not anticipate what would be thirty years hence. But since Victoria prematurely appropriated old age from the moment of Prince Albert's death in 1861, the insights of the Oxford don are half-dreamed and half-confirmed by glimpses of the Queen readily available through the proliferation of images in the new media. Suddenly there are queens everywhere: Margaret Oliphant was one who made them frequent in her fiction. Here I am most concerned with narratives of age retaining or relinquishing power. The history of the monarchy in the nineteenth century is a study of the diminishment of power, and here too Victoria's experience of aging becomes exemplary. But the chapter also discusses the resources of imaginative expression for age, especially the strain against conventions of realist plausibility. Gothic, sensation, mystery, magic—these are familiar ways for literature to convey moments of extreme crisis. In public life there are also extraordinary occasions which require special forms for representation before they can be adequately apprehended: war is just the most obvious example, but I will argue that aging is another. The witchcraft trials of the sixteenth and seventeenth centuries may well have been in part a collective expression of fears about aging. Certainly these events intrigued the Victorians as much as they have preoccupied ages before and after. What brings these ideas together is the predominance of old women who were figured as witches both in life and in literature. Although Victoria herself was not one to use or even appreciate sensation literature, her grasp of the mundane was both a resource and a limit to her in times of need. Margaret Oliphant's ability to straddle the two extremes—the supernatural and the mundane—again makes her a fine figure for capturing elements both within the purview of the Queen and without, in what we might call the purview of a world inhabited but ignored. Paradoxically, it is through the very concrete economic crises occasioned by speculation that we can find congress between the 'real' and the supernatural, between fantasies and actualities of aging in the nineteenth century. In very different ways, Elizabeth Gaskell and Margaret Oliphant both make old age a resource when economic vagaries tilt downwards due to uncertain speculation: their older heroines assume the function and often the aspect of royalty within the small communities at their command. At the end of the century we find a plentitude of Queens, and if Victoria's image takes precedence, she by no means dominates the market.

In the closing decades of the century the elderly became newly visible, and in the final two chapters of the book we consider attempts to portray age through varieties of portraiture—visual, statistical and literary. Diverse media generated images that brought age to the forefront of political engagement and cultural preoccupation. The chapter begins with Oscar Wilde, whose novel *The Picture of Dorian Gray* reminds us that aging is a verb, and that its meaning is inconstant, as are its actions. Dorian Gray has a terror of growing old, and this terror is expressed through one of those supernatural conceits articulated in Chapter 3. In this chapter, I will discuss Wilde's aesthetic of age, his attempt to see the movement through generations as capable of dignity and passion. Cicero offered a model for the art of aging, but despite his admiration for the classics, Wilde's characters cannot find the harmony that Cato describes. In Wilde's novel, there is a science of aging and an art of staying young: it is the failure of Dorian's Faustian bargain which makes us realize the necessity for some exchange between the two. An art which petrifies the image, or, to put it another way, an art which doesn't age, is not only supernatural: it is unnatural. It engenders dispositions that cannot be sustained, because they have no life in time. But Wilde reflects the impulse to join science with art, as equal partners in the effort to admit age within the portals of aesthetic glory. If the critic is artist, as Wilde claims, then aging is not only inevitable, it is a desirable part of all aesthetic activity. The chapter turns then to pictorial representation, with attention falling chiefly upon the works of Herbert von Herkomer in order to glimpse the status of old age within the fine arts. Herbert von Herkomer is not the only artist for whom old people register, but in his pictures the elderly 'speak' with a resonance not found elsewhere. By bringing his work into focus, and associating it with the literature of the period, we can see how each contributes to the aesthetic of old age which was consolidated by the time of Victoria's Diamond Jubilee, in 1897.

The next chapter begins with William Morris's *News From Nowhere*, a novel in which age is the sensitive litmus which measures the health or illness of a society. Within the compass of this political fiction, age and aging appear as products of errant social policy produced under the distortions of nineteenth-century life. Only a 'new age' could produce a new kind of old age: Morris imagines the transformation of the aging body as an index of social justice. From Morris's utopic fiction the account moves to another late-century perspective on aging generations: the efforts of social scientists and political reformers to produce systematic description that might lead to systematic (though not revolutionary) change. The furore around construction and passage of an Old Age Pension Bill serves as a radiant center and agitating catalyst for consideration of the forms of social portraiture which gave age its contemporary features. The chapter moves to conclusion through an encounter with the social work of Charles Booth and Beatrice Webb, whose statistical surveys and descriptions greatly influenced the fin-de-siècle discourse of aging, and finally we turn—in a kind of personal appendix to the statistical report—to the aging lives of the social scientists themselves, the anguished experience of Herbert Spencer and Webb.

Finally, we glance at the way old age is figured after death. By the end of the century it became more common to associate death with old age since mortality among the young had been so greatly relieved. But this is not a study of death; my interest here is to examine some manners in which Victorian culture inscribed old age within its figuration of life history. A last chapter considers the function of 'inscriptive narratives' to assess how these final perspectives illuminate the representations of the aged. There is no happy ending to the narrative of old age because there is no ending at all. We are still in the process of defining the fourth estate, even as the experience of aging itself is already evolving into something new.

Inevitably there are limits to set, exclusions to be made. Innumerable other characters, texts, pictures, and events could have earned consideration here. The most glaring exclusion is that of poetry, where, except for occasional salutes, the excision has been deliberate. The loss is regrettable, but there is compensation in examining the narrative convergence of fiction and journalism, and the social and cultural milieu in which these forms thrived; and there is coherence in the balance offered between the interpretation of novels and the novelizing responses in political and social life. There remains a poetry of old age whose story may be told by someone else.

A Note on Texts: The great length of the novels and easy access to many fine editions make references to Dickens's works by chapter more convenient for readers. Unless stated otherwise, I used Oxford editions when quoting from Dickens's work. References to all other authors will indicate edition and page number.

I

Faces and Spaces: Locating Age in the Dickens World

> He was past the prime of life, but Father Time is not always a hard parent, and, though he tarries for none of his children, often lays his hand lightly upon those who have used him well; making them old men and women inexorably enough, but leaving their hearts and spirits young and in full vigour. With such people the grey head is but the impression of the old fellow's hand in giving them his blessing, and every wrinkle but a notch in the quiet calendar of a well-spent life.
>
> *BR*, ch. 2

The epigraph describes the genial locksmith Gabriel Varden from Dickens's early novel of misguided riot, *Barnaby Rudge*. In so doing, it blandly introduces a complex attitude towards age under the feint of simplicity. We are each responsible for our own old age, for though age we must, we drive the cart which carries us forward. But how does one 'use time well'; and what is "a well-spent life"? With unequal amounts of change in our pockets, how can we choose to spend life as we would, and what happens when intention and desire, determination and wish occur in the plural and in contradiction? With one hand Dickens sternly demands acceptance of moral agency and responsibility, while with the other (which designs the rest of the narrative) he discloses a convoluted path of obstacles and complications. Pickwick and his friend Mr. Wardle, the brothers Cheeryble, of *Nicholas Nickleby,* the benign Garlands of *Old Curiosity Shop*, Dr. Strong, and the Peggottys (Daniel or Mary) in *David Copperfield*, Wemmick's Aged P in *Great Expectations*, Mr. Lorry from *A Tale of Two Cities*, Betty Higden from *Our Mutual Friend*, or Mr. Grewgious, from the last, unfinished novel, *The Mystery of Edwin Drood*, are fortunate to have achieved the distinction of age without experiencing a tarnish to their virtue. To be sure, their goodness is inextricably woven with surrounding evil, much as the youthful innocence of Oliver Twist and Little Nell requires for effect the evil of Fagin and Sikes, the malignity of Quilp, and the weakness of Grandfather Trent. More often, though, the aged in Dickens carry the "streaky bacon" of mixed traits, usually seen as marks of their encounters with fate, chance, and other characters.[1] Anthony Chuzzlewitt and the inimitable Sairey Gamp; Mrs. Skewton and Miss Tox; Mr. Dick, Mr. Wickfield, and Aunt Betsey Trotwood; Miss Flite, Sir Leicester Dedlock, and Mr. Gridley; Mr. F's Aunt and Mrs. Clennam along with the brothers Dorrit and Old Nandy; Dr. Manette; Miss Havisham; the Boffins, Twemlow, Riah, and Silas Wegg are all cases in point, elderly characters who bear stains and spots of age. Although it comes inexorably to all, age often comes in fits and starts, and through means other than that of time passing. Here, for instance, is the scheming Jonas Chuzzlewitt, introducing "Our clerk...Old Chuffy":

> "Is he deaf?" inquired one of the young ladies.
> "No, I don't know that he is. He an't deaf, is he, father?"
> "I never heard him say he was," replied the old man.
> "Blind?" inquired the young ladies.
> "N—no. I never understood that he was at all blind," said Jonas carelessly.
> "You don't consider him so, do you, father?"
> "Certainly not," replied Anthony.
> "What is he, then?"
> "Why, I'll tell you what he is," said Mr. Jonas, apart to the young ladies, "he's precious old, for one thing; and I an't best pleased with him for that, for I think my father must have caught it of him." (*MC*, ch. 11)

The tone is only half comic, since images can be as infectious as trouble or care, and any of these might achieve the effects of age more dramatically than the time of clock or calendar. As specters of possible decay through age, the bitter and obsessive Mrs. Steerforth (*DC*) and Miss Havisham (*GE*) pose the dangerous threat of infection to their younger companions (Rosa Dartle and Estella).

That age might come too soon, that it might come through either social failure or psychic trauma, that "Agitation and anxiety of mind" might produce "wrinkles and grey hairs with no unsparing hand" (*BR*, ch. 81)—these are Dickensian axioms of life history. The haunting images of Ignorance and Want in *A Christmas Carol* are only the most striking examples among many others: "Where graceful youth should have filled their features out, and

1. Dickens uses the phrase at the start of ch. 17 in *Oliver Twist*, as a reference to the alteration of comic and tragic scenes in melodrama.

touched them with its freshest tints, a stale and shrivelled hand, like that of age, had pinched, and twisted them, and pulled them into shreds" (*CC*, stave III). This confusion of youth and old age is a recurring and unstable feature. Paul Dombey, like his predecessor Little Nell, is "old in adversity and trial" though still a child (*OCS*, ch. 2). Alternatively, Tim Linkinwater is only one of several old men who gets "younger every birthday than he was the year before" (*NN*, ch. 37). No one forgets Scrooge's delighted refrain at the close of *A Christmas Carol*, when the old man embraces his recovered humanity with the happy squeal that "I'm quite a baby" (*CC*, stave V) More frighteningly, Jonas Chuzzlewitt imagines a terrifying assault by "some infant in an hour grown old, or old man in an hour grown young" (*MC*, ch. 51). One even finds age and youth confusing their connotations, as in the description of the church into which Little Nell and her grandfather wander towards the close of her short life: "even change was old in that old place" (*OCS*, ch. 52). Age has its agitations and excitements, its restlessness and rages, just as youth sometimes appears lethargic, calm, mature or at ease. Rather than settle characters along the spectrum of chronology, Dickens sifts and shifts relations between physical and social age. In this he consistently uses age to produce singularities of character: the behavior of young Paul Dombey or old Mr. Gride seems grotesque *because of their age*; similarly the pathos of Oliver Twist or Little Nell, Mrs. Skewton or Lady Tippins is intelligible because of *their* age; and age makes pronounced the noisy humor of Mr. Micawber or the quiet humor of Augustus Twemlow. If youth is tormented by the question, 'Who am I?,' Dickens's characters at any age can be bewildered by their place in the temporal measure of life.

In the final section to this chapter, we will see that the most subtle and probing portraits of age are not limited to elderly characters, or to 'character' at all; in characteristic Dickensian fashion, age is an attribute which comes and goes, affixes to things and places as well as to names and faces. "The year was old that day" intones *The Chimes*, and (as in this case) New Year's or Christmas Day often figure *as* Age, so too does memory, the affective counterpart to these festive occasions (ch. 2, The Second Quarter). The passage of time marks the environment no less than it does character. Not surprisingly, the city becomes a landscape for narratives of age, both by way of contrast to rural surroundings, and also through the incorporation of those contrasts within its own precincts. Dickens's London is an archeological wonder, grafting old with new, selective memory with equally selective reality. Claiming that urban growth "enters only in the form of resistance to it," Richard Altick reminds us, when reading Dickens, to conjure London as it looked in the 1820s. Perhaps so, but we see the twenties filtered through eyes which lived through and amid the upheavals culminating in the sixties, which, as Altick himself describes, witnessed "massive excavations for arterial sewers and the first underground railway, the building of huge new railway terminals (Broad Street, Cannon Street, Holborn Viaduct, St. Pancras, Charing Cross, Victoria) and the lines leading to them, and the cutting through of broad thoroughfares like Queen Victoria Street and Holborn Viaduct."[2] And this, we might add, is for starters. Critics such as Welsh and Schwarzbach explore the niceties of Dickensian 'resistance' to urban development, for 'resistance' is a usefully ambiguous term, capable of enfolding such various and contradictory expressions as denial, bemusement, and excitement. The face of the city became a map charting the advance of the young under the name of modernity. Dickens understood the change not simply as a matter of new constructions replacing the old, but also in the spread of city life, the pressure to extend which, it will be my pleasure to show, Dickens depicts in generational terms, sometimes as an encroachment of youth on age, at other times as the stubborn fixity of age blocking the entrance of youth, or the reassurance of age set against the tempests of youth. The variations are endless and constantly shifting: no single attitude remains permanent, and neither 'youth,' nor 'age' play hero or villain. Unlike the moral dichotomy between good and evil, in which Dickens might argue that while good is better, evil is 'necessary,' in the contrast between youth and age the valuations shift to compelling effect. Dickens is no more sentimental towards the young than the aged, and though he prefers the intense vitality more typical of youth, he inclines towards the perspectival distance and comprehensive gaze which age affords. Typically, he wants it all.

Shutting up old women: age, gender, and institutions

A cartoon in *Punch's Comic Almanac* of 1854 depicts Lord Aberdeen, the Prime Minister, as an old lady awaiting deportation. Covered in Scottish plaid, she sits by the docks with the smoke from steamships behind her, substantial baggage alongside, and her hands firmly grasping an upright missile as if armed with umbrella and pattens. A chessboard decorates her

2. Richard Altick, *The Presence of the Present: Topics of the Day in the Victorian Novel* (Columbus: Ohio State University Press, 1991), 414.

handbag, signifying the intractable puzzle of the British adventure in the Crimea, where the scale of mismanagement was becoming clear, not only on the battlefield but also in the military hospitals, whose failures had been vividly exposed by Florence Nightingale. A sign referring to Nurses deployed in the East and a stub marked 'Aberdeen' protruding from the box on her lap suggest her identity (the Scottish Aberdeen kept an estate north of the border) as well as her destination. The caption reads "How to Get Rid of an Old Woman," and the choice of phrase is symptomatic. The vacillating leader, the Scottish outsider, the Ottoman exotic, and the acts of banishment and exile—these images cluster around the figure of an aged woman. They also suggest how this figure attracts associations from a distance and serves as the deposit for a wide range of negations.

Punch's Comic Almanac for 1854 reflects popular worry that Britain is being overtaken by 'outsiders,' and frustration with what appeared to be unwarranted pacifism by Lord Aberdeen and his coalition government. Aberdeen *was* old (he was 70), and *Punch*, in figuring his seeming eagerness to capitulate to foreign pressures, transforms him from old man to old woman. Indeed, in a companion illustration earlier that year, Aberdeen and Russell (serving in a fragile coalition government) are *both* figured as old women, old washerwomen, who in angry but futile postures stand with the water between them—the contested space of the Crimean War reduced to a mere barrel (see Figs. 1 and 2). The xenophobia derives from a perceptible fear of scarcity during the wartime debacle. "All Up With England" intones *Punch*: "Sincerely do we congratulate our readers on the extreme distress and misery in which the English are involved by reason of the impious war which they have dared to wage against our August Lord and Master, Nicholas. We have the happiness to assure the subjects of His Imperial Majesty that those wicked islanders are in a state of absolute starvation."[3] England is ruled by and overrun with 'outsiders,' and age usefully provides an image for an outsider demanding goods belonging to others. There is one more thread to unravel in this densely textured cartoon. According to *Punch*, the women of England, comically and consciously, repudiate age itself. A short squib entitled "The Perpetual Youth of the Women of England," exposes another futile war, women fighting the onset of old age:

> It appears from the Census, that the people of Great Britain are the youngest people in the World. We are not surprised by this result, and indeed we only

3. *Punch's Comic Almanac for 1854*, 47.

Figure 1 *Punch's Comic Almanac* of 1854:
"How to Get Rid of an Old Woman"

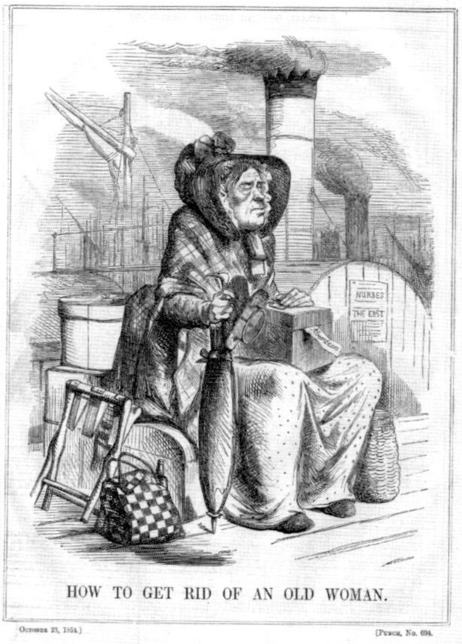

Figure 2 *Punch's Comic Almanac* of 1854:
"A Home and Foreign Question"

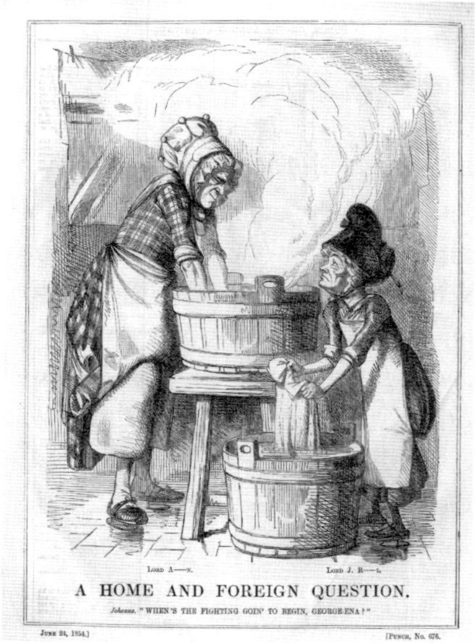

> wonder that there is any woman in England above the age of 30, which we are convinced would have been impossible had the ladies been left to make their own returns.... We verily believe that if the women had their own way, they would never adopt the epithet "old," should they even live to be a hundred, and that they would class themselves in the category of "second childhood" rather than admit their arrival at the stage of anility. Such is the female horror of the vale of years, that a woman would sooner declare herself to be in her dot-age, than to have reached that "certain age" which any figure above thirty is supposed to indicate.[4]

The heavy humor rhymes with Dickens's scathing image of the notorious Mrs. Skewton, known as "Cleopatra," who sedulously impersonates youth, even while she tries to peddle her daughter to Mr. Dombey in the novel that bears his name. At bedtime Mrs. Skewton's repression of age comes undone in a chamber of horrors.

> Thus they remained for a long hour, without a word, until Mrs. Skewton's maid appeared, according to custom, to prepare her gradually for night. At night, she should have been a skeleton, with dart and hour-glass, rather than a woman, this attendant; for her touch was as the touch of Death. The painted object shrivelled underneath her hand; the form collapsed, the hair dropped off, the arched dark eyebrows changed to scanty tufts of grey; the pale lips shrunk, the skin became cadaverous and loose; an old, worn, yellow, nodding woman, with red eyes, alone remained in Cleopatra's place, huddled up, like a slovenly bundle, in a greasy flannel gown. (*DS*, ch. 27)

Old age, and particularly 'old women,' are vulnerable to these tones of corrosive portraiture that recurred through most of the century. Fantasies of banishment—"How to Get Rid of an Old Woman"—accompany a readmission in the form of a scapegoat. Dickens's famous Podsnapian solution for sweeping away all unpleasantness with the wave of an arm is enacted repeatedly in the refusal of old women. Nevertheless, although shunted to the social margins, the old woman remained figuratively pervasive. She is the outsider who stays the strong British arm, the ghost who depletes resources, the phantom whose growing numbers ominously swell census reports and warn of a great social problem in the making. In this guise she plays a leading role in the practice of institutionalization that occupied a central place in the Victorian encounter with age and that will be a sustained concern for us in this study.

Driving impatiently through crowded London streets, the "ancient" youngster Mr. Bailey, clerk for Montague Tigg, exasperated by the "elderly

4. *Punch's Comic Almanac for 69.*

ladies who wanted to cross, and ran back again," asks peremptorily "Why they didn't go to the workhouse and get an order to be buried?" (*MC*, ch. 27). To many elderly people who qualified for admission, going to the workhouse seemed to be a direct order *to be buried*, and in a most humiliating, undignified fashion. It is fitting to begin with the workhouse, because it casts an ominous shadow over the mid-nineteenth century landscape, for most standing as a symbol of the problems rather than an image of the solutions for the various frailties which beset those least able to overcome them. Notoriously, the 'reform' of the Poor Laws, which passed in 1834, transformed the idea of community or governmental support from an obligation to provide and a right to receive, into a debt always growing, never shrinking, and, at the other end, a privilege unwanted and dreaded. With mounting numbers of people in need of assistance and no prospect of balancing funds with requirements, it seemed rational to the utilitarian ethics of the planning committee, to demand 'proof' that inmates were 'deserving' of parish support. Part of the proof consisted in the willingness to reside within the workhouse instead of accepting modest payments permitting one to live and, when possible, to continue to work, outside.

Such attempts to curb or abolish out-door (outside the workhouse) relief had a devastating effect on the aging population whose ties to the community were already tenuous, often confirming a sense of thorough social superfluity. Enforcement of the central tenets was lax, however, and in most parishes (especially in the countryside) there were alternative forms of relief available to the aged at least until the 1870s and beyond, when new restrictions and tighter enforcement were imposed. But the aged poor were caught in an unsteady space between legislative fiat and the unpredictabilities of actual social practice. The very uncertainty of legal application—susceptible to change according to local parish custom and the temperament of the beadle—was itself a stimulus to the cultural imagination. Dickens's Betty Higden, long anathematized by contemporary moderns who find her portrait sentimental and her obsession with the workhouse melodramatic, is neither of these things when placed, or replaced, in her historical/institutional moment. Betty's plot suggests both the predicaments and the makeshifts available to aging women, who struggled to maintain independence despite physical deterioration and economic hardship.

Sarah Gamp, on the other hand, cherished by early and later readers, has never suffered from the charge of sentimentality. We may agree with only the second half of Pecksniff's evaluation—"She is respectable, but not sentimental" (*MC*, ch. 24), but the undertaker's estimate is more precise—"That's a woman who observes and reflects in an uncommon manner" (*MC*, ch. 25). Her excesses fall within recognizable channels, so that we find them humorous if not endearing: she makes us laugh. Sarah has no fear of the workhouse, and every confidence in her own abilities to give service to her community into and through the last years of her life. Though the differences between Betty Higden and Sarah Gamp are as great as the near twenty years that separate them in Dickens's *oeuvre*, there is good reason to place them in mirror relation. Both women are old, though Sarah is closer to three rather than Betty's four score years. But Betty is not what Sarah would have become, for 'Sairey' is complete already, and though 'softened' slightly by the close of the novel, she remains just barely within the circle of good which emanates from old Martin Chuzzlewit. I bring together these two characters because they demonstrate a range of experience available to aging women who struggled to support themselves independently. One possibility is to live *within* (but not necessarily *in*) the institutional framework society offers; the other is to maintain oneself, in however makeshift or morally suspect a fashion, *outside* the system. These are seeming alternatives only: the provoking fact is that both characters could be described in either position. This is why I introduce them as 'mirrored' images despite the great differences between them. As we will see, one remains outside not by rejecting but by imitating institutionalized protocols: both Betty Higden and Sarah Gamp are entirely separate characters drawn inevitably, and in similar fashion, to the institutional life which was at the heart of attempts to provide for the aged in the Victorian period.

At first glance, Betty Higden's ambitions do not promise much narrative satisfaction: "Patiently to earn a spare bare living, and quietly to die, untouched by workhouse hands—this was her highest sublunary hope" (*OMF*, III, ch. 5). Initially, the words seem to summon what Helen Small has described as the "exposed manipulativeness of Dickens's narrative in its engagement with old age. The old recall and speak when the novel's moral schema dictates."[5] But Betty Higden is no mere vessel for platitudes; complexity attaches, not to her 'character' as such, but to her deeply agitated social situation. 'Patient' and 'quiet' exist in narrative tension with those intrusive "workhouse hands"

5. "The Unquiet Limit: Old Age and Memory in Victorian Narrative," in *Memory and Memorials: 1789–1914, Matthew Campbell,* ed. Jacqueline M. Labbe, and Sally Shuttleworth (London: Routledge, 2000), 72.

and this is precisely the issue which creates the drama of her life. Until she approaches her eightieth year, Betty Higden has maintained self-sufficiency despite the deaths of husband, children, and grandchildren. She enters the narrative, however, only when independence is threatened. Her vulnerability is the condition of her visibility. Fearing the troubling episodes in which numbness and dumbness overcome her, Betty agrees to relinquish her one surviving relative, a great-grandson, to the protection of the benevolent Boffins, who are themselves old, though one generation younger than her. Given the prospect of increasing frailty, she projects a future in which either the workhouse looms, or she allows the Boffins to adopt her little Johnny, so that she can support herself by selling portable goods in country villages. The 'choice,' however, is itself a fiction, given Betty's near-hysterical repudiation of the workhouse ethos. When John Harmon notices that she shrinks from the mere mention of the word—workhouse—she replies:

> "Dislike mention of it?...Kill me sooner than take me there. Throw this pretty child under cart-horses feet and a loaded waggon sooner than take him there. Come to us and find us all a-dying, and set a light to us all where we lie and let us all blaze away with the house into a heap of cinders, sooner than move a corpse of us there!" (*OMF*, I, ch. 16)

It is difficult for contemporary readers to appreciate Betty's dread of the workhouse. And yet Peter Laslett detects the same attitude "still rumbling on the historical horizon for the British poor," and Stephen Hussey provides ample evidence that fear of the workhouse continued to dominate the imaginative life of many poor older women between 1918 and 1950.[6] And with good reason. Certainly readers in the 1860s and those who followed in the next few decades would recognize that ending life in a workhouse was more of a probability than a possibility for women in Higden's position.

It is suggestive to any research on the cultural imagination that Betty's understanding of the workhouse derives from no personal experience: she is precise in attributing her knowledge to journalism. Suddenly her early enthusiastic endorsement ("I do love a newspaper") and her appreciation of the workhouse orphan Sloppy as a reader ("He do the police in different voices") appear more complicated.

6. Peter Laslett, *A Fresh Map of Life: The Emergence of the Third Age*, 2nd edn (London: Macmillan, 1966), 23; also see Stephen Hussey, "'An Inheritance of Fear': Older Women in the Twentieth Century Countryside," in *Women and Aging in British Society since 1500*, ed. Lynn Botelho and Pat Thane (Harlow, Essex: Pearson Education, 2001), 186–206.

> "Do I never read in the newspapers...how the worn out people...are put off, put off, put off—how they are grudged, grudged, grudged, the shelter, or the doctor, or the drop of physic, or the bit of bread? Do I never read how they grow heartsick of it and give it up, after having let themselves drop so low, and how they after all die out for want of help?" (*OMF*, I, ch. 16).

Information is itself the novel's great currency, circulating like so many shares, passing in this instance from the newspapers, by way of Sloppy's dramatic rendition, through old Betty Higden's horror, and finally into the narrator's wrath, and, in principle, the reader's engagement. Testimony from newspapers, journals, broadsides, and ballads was often without a doubt 'sentimental.' But it was such information that brought the question of age out of the obscurity of private life and into a public realm. Old age—as an emergent modern concept—was an effect of public opinion, and it was only through the mediations of discourse that Victorian old age received a definition, a number—65 and older—a body of imagery, and the ambiguous dignity of a medical/institutional category.

Though Betty Higden relied on print for her information, her creator was himself a central purveyor in the discourse of old age. As early as the 1830s, in his "Meditations in Monmouth Street," Dickens finds himself imagining

> some metropolitan workhouse, situated in the midst of crowded streets and alleys, filled with noxious vapours, and ringing with boisterous cries, where an old and feeble woman, imploring pardon for her son, lay dying in a close dark room, with no child to clasp her hand, and no pure air from heaven to fan her brow. A stranger closed the eyes that settled into a cold unmeaning glare, and strange ears received the words that murmured from the white and half-closed lips. (*Sketches*, 77–8)

This is the image haunting old Betty Higden as she makes her plans to run away and keep moving in order to avoid the paralysis that revives her phobic horror of the workhouse. The 'deadness' which steals over her is an internalization of the workhouse condition.

At stake is something other than a dread of institutional power. The Children's Hospital which tends her great-grandson cannot always prevent death, but it encourages life. Betty's admiration for the Great Ormond Street Hospital for Sick Children and her terror of the workhouse make clear that her objection to the latter is no simple rejection of institutional relief. It is the *particular* institution which rouses her horror, the institutionalization of the elderly that has neither the intention nor the effect of stimulating life. Betty is spared the workhouse experience, but unlike her fears of the hospital, which quickly change to admiration once she visits the actual place, her nightmarish fantasies of the workhouse are nowhere refuted.

Dickens did not set out to investigate or describe the situation of the aged, but they intrude, awkwardly and revealingly, in his accounts. In his visit to the Sunday chapel service of a "large Metropolitan Workhouse" he encounters "longer and longer groves of old people" who "were there, in every variety."

> Mumbling, blear-eyed, spectacled, stupid, deaf, lame; vacantly winking in the gleams of sun that now and then crept in through the open doors, from the paved yard; shading their listening ears, or blinking eyes, with their withered hands; poring over their books, leering at nothing, going to sleep, crouching and drooping in corners. There were weird old women, all skeleton within, all bonnet and cloak without, continually wiping their eyes with dirty dusters of pocket-handkerchiefs; and there were ugly old crones, both male and female, with a ghastly kind of contentment upon them which was not at all comforting to see. Upon the whole, it was the dragon, Pauperism, in a very weak and impotent condition; toothless, fangless, drawing his breath heavily enough, and hardly worth chaining up.

These elderly inmates are well-off compared to those elsewhere in the workhouse, where in one room we find "several ugly old women crouching, witch-like, round a hearth, and chattering and nodding, after the manner of the monkeys." The worst problem is tedium:

> In all of these Long Walks of aged and infirm, some old people were bedridden, and had been for a long time; some were sitting on their beds half-naked; some dying in their beds; some out of bed, and sitting at a table near the fire. A sullen or lethargic indifference to what was asked, a blunted sensibility to everything but warmth and food, a moody absence of complaint as being of no use, a dogged silence and resentful desire to be left alone again, I thought were generally apparent.[7]

Emma Sheppard's staid accounts of visiting the elderly in the London workhouses of the fifties confirm Dickens's impressions and make Betty's imagined terrors seem like reasonable apprehensions. "I never can forget my first sensation," Sheppard relays, "when I sat down among them in the

7. "A Walk in a Workhouse," *Selected Journalism*, 239, 242, 239, 240, 242. The editors of the Pilgrim edition of Dickens's letters identify this as "possibly the Wandsworth and Clapham Union."

Hospital Wards, where the old and infirm where [*sic*] located; the listless look—the dull vacuity—the lack of all interest, except for the petty details of tea versus gruel—potatoes versus rice!" Sheppard confirms her own dismay in the responses of visiting clergymen. Thus the Reverend Wh. H. regrets the absence of tasks to occupy the inmates, while the Bishop Armstrong protests against their being treated "as if they were so much waste material."[8] Visiting one workhouse, Sheppard is told "how the aged often longed for a bit to eat between meals, and were sometimes so exhausted when their food came that they could scarcely touch it." She calls for a suspension of the rule prohibiting an older person from saving food from one meal in order to eat it later. The crude formulation of the workhouse—"all that remains is put into the soup"—is a cost-saving solution which ignores the dietary needs of older people, who often can't eat according to fixed times and schedules, and need to be able to eat when they can.[9]

I quote at length because it is important for us to see what 'Betty' saw, what Dickens saw, and what his contemporaries saw The images which confronted them and provoked their sympathy as well as their outrage offer alternative understandings to those drawn from legislative documents, parish records, or census reports. For example, under the Brabazon Scheme operating in the Kensington and Tonbridge workhouses, elderly women were encouraged to sew small goods for sale.[10] The scheme may have been inadequate, but it at least marked a difference from the lethargy just described. Other discrepancies are equally worth noting since they contribute to both a wider and more close-grained picture than that offered by official discourse, either complacent or reformist. Emma Sheppard agitated for a varied diet, increased visitation, and gifts in the shape of tea, sugar, snuff, some of the "homely comforts," the "trifles" which make all the difference. She reports favorably of the Master of the Union Workhouse at Kingston-on-Thames, a Mr. Hogg, who tells her that "All inmates over sixty years of age have tea, sugar, butter, and one pint of beer daily" and that each is given a clean plate at meals, a tin tea-can and tea-pot, a soup can, knife, fork, and spoon.[11] And yet, technically, these provisions should have

8. Emma Sheppard, *Sunshine in the Workhouse* (London: Nisbet & Co, 1858), 7, 18–19, 21–2. 9. Ibid. 36, 35, 36.

10. See Theresa Deane, "Old and Incapable? Louisa Twining and Elderly Women in Victorian Britain," in Kelho Thane, *Women and Aging in British Society since 1500,* 181.

11. Sheppard, *Sunshine in the Workhouse*, 27, 24, 51.

been no exception: regulations at this time stipulated just such adjustments for the care of the elderly within the workhouse.[12]

We find a similar disparity with regard to the accommodation of elderly couples. In the later 1840s it was possible for elderly married couples to avoid the inevitable separation which was one of the infamous disciplinary rules of workhouse admittance. Few older people apparently requested such accommodation, but whether they did or not (and whether or not they acted under coercion), the fact was that within the workhouse inmates were characteristically seen as single. In fact, according to available records in 1853, there were only 873 aged couples in the 624 institutions. Of these, only about one-third shared a room. Explanations for choosing separation vary, but they are uniformly vague: 'wife in infirmary,' 'female in sick ward,' 'husband ill and in infirmary,' 'on account of illness,' 'haven't lived together for twenty years,' 'on own request,' 'from choice,' 'refuse to live together,' 'request to be separated,' and 'not lived together several years.'[13] Such indeterminate phrases register the indeterminacies of elderly life in the workhouse. If only one of the pair was aged 60 or over, the decision as to their accommodations was left to the provider rather than to the couple. And 'choice' or 'request' can be evasive characterizations of actual conversation. I do not mean to suggest that couples were prevented from choosing to cohabit, or that their wishes were misrepresented, only that it is very difficult to convey motives, intentions, and explanations in documents not intended for this purpose.

Partly due to the representational vocation of Dickens, a horror and distaste of the workhouse became an incontestable social datum. But the degree to which actual conditions justified such dread has been the subject of sustained investigation for several decades now. To a significant

12. According to the Report of the Committee on the Poor Law Amendment Act of 1838, "paupers in the workhouse who exceeded sixty years of age should be allowed to substitute tea, butter, and sugar for certain other less desirable items in their diet if they wished to do so." Roebuck details many instances in which older people were granted "small luxuries" such as tobacco, snuff, tea, sugar, butter, even gin in addition to ale. Janet Roebuck, "When Does 'Old Age' Begin? The Evolution of the English Definition" *Journal of Social History*, 12 (Spring 1979), 419. And David Thomson warns us that some inmates may well have exaggerated their age upon admission, since after 60, inmates were granted "exemptions from numerous rules governing diet, medical attention, uniforms, work, alcohol, snuff, tobacco and permits for leave." David Thomson, "Workhouse to Nursing Home: Residential Care of Elderly People in England since 1840," *Ageing and Society*, 3 (March 1983), 55. Susannah Ottaway's work demonstrates that many of those exceptions were already adopted by some eighteenth-century workhouses. Susannah Ottaway, *The Decline of Life: Old Age in Eighteenth Century England* (Cambridge: Cambridge University Press, 2004), 270–2.

13. Quoted in Thomson, "Workhouse to Nursing Home," 57.

extent new research has rehabilitated the status of institutional support throughout the nineteenth century, helping us to revise an earlier unrelenting focus on its failures. Peter Laslett and the Cambridge Group for the History of Population and Social Structure have persuasively exposed myths of idyllic family relations in which large extended families provided generational support top down and bottom up. Their work demonstrates that there was no abrupt shift from familial to institutional reliance in the nineteenth century, because the nuclear family never adequately addressed generational needs. It is not then as if society began to care for the elderly when family relations broke down. Rather, public assistance of some form had been long established, and only when the disparity between need and provision became too great was there an attempt to write or enforce existing legislation requiring families to take greater responsibility for their aging members. Even so, all statistical accounts—from the national census to the record books of individual workhouses—show a dramatic increase in the number of old people, especially older women, who depended on institutional support of some kind in the last third of the nineteenth century. If at mid-century about one in seven people living in a workhouse was over 65, by the last decade of the century the ratio was one in every three. The figures were highest for women, and especially for older women living in London, who represented one of every two workhouse inmates. Dickens's observation of 'groves' of old women gives imagery to the colorless data.

While Laslett and his cohorts show decisively how important community support was throughout the period, David Thomson goes much farther in his revisionism. His work calls for a radical reconsideration of the effectiveness of the Poor Laws to address the problems of poverty and old age in the period. Thomson claims that well over half the elderly population at mid-century received some kind of financial support, but that "workhouses played a minor part in the actual day-to-day provision for an elderly population, though an infinitely greater one in the minds of people affected by them."[14] Even he acknowledges, however, that London posed special problems for the elderly; his evidence shows that

14. David Thomson, "The Welfare of the Elderly in the Past: A Family or Community Responsibility," in *Life, Death, and the Elderly: Historical Perspectives*, ed. Margaret Pelling and Richard Smith (London: Routledge, 1991), 202, 208.

> In 1851...one of three of London's 20,000 workhouse inmates was past the age of sixty-five, while in the rest of the country the numbers were about 15,000 out of total of around 100,000 inmates, a ratio of about one to seven....by 1891 one in every three workhouse inmates in England and Wales (including London) was aged 65 or more: in London the figure was closer to one in two, and a number of the metropolitan workhouses had been given over entirely to the care of the old.

The figures were especially high for women living in London: "In 1851...12.4% or one in eight of all women past the age of seventy-five and living in London lived in a workhouse. This meant that the elderly women in London were six times as likely to be in a workhouse as were women elsewhere."[15] Thomson interprets these figures as proof of effective legislation; available forms of relief, including the workhouse unions, were accommodating the need for assistance. But several critics have taken brisk issue with Thomson; they suggest that his optimism derives from the peculiarity of the particular workhouses upon which his studies are based. Located in Suffolk, his chosen field provided a higher standard of care than that offered in metropolitan centers.[16] For my purposes, the significant factor is that even in David Thomson's own words "a number of metropolitan workhouses had been given over entirely to the care of the old."[17] So in fact his historical revision—in part intended to break the link between the workhouse and the aged—has actually had the effect of showing that, at least in the exception that was London, the link was tight and growing ever tighter. In this respect, Dickens's Betty Higden had every reason to shiver in horror.

So far I have argued that the dread which old people often felt at the prospect of the workhouse derived in large part from popular publications, journalistic and fictional, which only partially digested the social facts. But then the intended effect of the New Poor Law, its notorious stroke of social engineering—to discourage the able-bodied poor from reliance on public support—depended on circulating images of the stringent conditions of institutional life, including well-known regulations for eating, drinking,

15. Thomson, "Workhouse to Nursing Home," 47, 51.
16. Pat Thane, "Old People and their Families in the English Past," in *Charity, Self-Interest and Welfare in the English Past*, ed. Martin Daunton, (London: UCL Press, 1996), 117–21; Richard M. Smith, "Ageing and Well-being in Early Modern England: Pension trends and gender preferences under the English Old Poor Law c.1650–1800," in *Old Age from Antiquity to Post-Modernity*, ed. Paul Johnson and Pat Thane (London: Routledge, 1998), 69; E. H. Hunt, "Paupers and Pensioners, Past and Present" *Ageing and Society*, 9 (1989), 407–30.
17. Thomson, "Workhouse to Nursing Home," 47.

dressing, working, socializing, or obtaining permission to get 'out.' In practice, however, the application of this principle was wildly erratic, and this because the New Poor Law permitted so much local interpretation. It was not only that each district board could decide to continue out-door relief; it was also—as Charles Booth later put it—that "Each Board is free to give any sum it may think fit as out relief; free to construe 'destitution' as it pleases, free to make what arrangements it thinks right for the maintenance and comfort of the inmates of the workhouse."[18] In fact then, until tighter restrictions were placed on out-relief in the early 1870s, many older people continued to receive assistance both on a regular basis and in times of particular need. Richard Smith, for example, points out that

> in the early 1840s perhaps two-thirds of women of the age of seventy and one-half of the men of that age, one-half of the women aged sixty-five to sixty-nine and a significant minority of women fifty-five to sixty and men in their sixties received a weekly pension that bore a very close relationship to the wages received by labourers.... In addition extra payments were not infrequently granted for quite extensive periods of need, for special diets, medicine, the employment of nurses or home-helps, the purchase of alcoholic beverages, shoes and clothing.[19]

What this means, of course, is that any effort to reconstruct the lives of the elderly poor has to begin with extreme variation according to site. Holding to that perception, we must recall the great population shift in the nineteenth century, which resulted in the movement of the young and middle-aged toward London and other growing cities. And as these groups streamed toward the metropolis, seeking opportunity and excitement, they left behind the old. The effect was to create a graying of the countryside, and indeed it was in rural England that the aged poor received the most attentive support, while in the countryside they were regularly given out-door weekly pensions. In the 1890s Booth put the point with terse power: "Industrial migration is always of the same character; the young and vigorous move; the old stay behind and are reinforced by those who, as they become old, drift back."[20] It is not, of course, as if London had few old people. It had more

18. Charles Booth, *The Aged Poor in England and Wales* (London: Macmillan, 1894), p. vi.
19. Richard M. Smith, "Ageing and Well-being in Early Modern England: Pension Trends and Gender Preferences Under the English Old Poor Law c.1650–1800," in *Old Age from Antiquity to Post-Modernity*, ed. Paul Johnson and Pat Thane (London: Routledge, 1998), 69.
20. Booth, *The Aged Poor*, 12.

of almost everything, including the elderly, and increasingly more of them, as the century wore on and the population of aged citizens increased. The key point, though, is that the many London aged were far exceeded by the young. And it is this demographic convergence that seems so important to the life of the old in the nineteenth-century metropolis: the aging elderly in the midst of a great, surging, young population. A large number of the old, but a smaller number proportionally, this is the unstable mix, and the result is conspicuous: far more indoor relief of the old in London, a pronounced institutionalization of care in the metropolis. In the countryside, where the proportion of the aged was greater, they enjoyed higher levels of weekly support, and, decisively, they were commonly allowed to stay out of the workhouse. In London the tendency is the reverse: the aging poor were so often institutionalized by the comfortable middle-aged. As time passed, the country aged began to suffer from the same problems of institutionalization that those in the city had experienced earlier. At the end of the century, John Hutton sponsored a bill to provide cottage homes for the aged instead of forcing them into workhouses. After visiting twenty-one workhouses in the North Riding Unions of Yorkshire, he reports that 40 percent of the inmates were over the age of 65, and that the condition of "these poor old things" is execrable:

> they have to pass the closing days of their life in the daily and hourly company of the very lowest and most degraded of their kind; men and women they would never have associated with in their village homes; and now, with generally grievous bodily infirmities requiring constant attention, they have to pass their time huddled up in a chair listening to the foul talk of those around them, or lying bedridden, often alone in neglected misery, attended occasionally by some rough paupers who take no pains to conceal the wish that the poor sufferer was dead.[21]

By the end of the century it was clear that, for the purposes of estimating distress among the aged population, the city—country divide was becoming negligible, and that the elderly were a problem nationwide. The idea of a national pension plan gained momentum, and it is a subject with its own complex narrative which I will consider in more detail in the last chapter.

At present we remain concerned with Betty Higden's plight, and, against the tide I have just described, we will turn with her from the city and

21. John Hutton, "Cottage Homes for the Aged Poor," *Nineteenth Century*, 43 (January–June 1898), 634. Even so, we should keep in mind that at the same period, the percentage of elderly in metropolitan workhouses was still far greater.

towards the country. It is a turn in tone as well as direction, for if in the city Betty's voice is both melodramatic and sentimental, in the country it becomes a quiet murmur. Country life is far from idyllic, but the agitations produce no shrill or excessive emotionalism. Betty follows the Thames, passing through Chertsey, Walton, Kingston, Staines and beyond, stopping to sell from her basket on market-days in town, or in the great houses along the way. The deadness which she hoped movement and activity would allay actually worsens, but it is no longer associated with workhouse numbness; now it is "in accordance with the laws of the physical world," which 'naturally' foretell her coming death. Betty articulates the contrast in her thoughts, to which Dickens gives these words. She imagines the Thames beckoning her, and to the impoverished elderly more generally "Come to me, come to me! When the cruel shame and terror you have so long fled from, most beset you, come to me! I am the Relieving Officer appointed by eternal ordinance to do my work...My breast is softer than the pauper-nurse's; death in my arms is peacefuller than among the pauper-wards" (*OMF*, III, ch. 15). The institution continues to influence the images and phrases available to her, but at least she imagines a kinder, softer institutionalization. And before she succumbs to the call beckoning her ever more strongly, she busies herself in the active pursuit of trade.

Once again contemporary readers, misled by the tone, may find this sequence as sentimental as her urban experience. But original readers had another context in which to place Betty Higden as she made her way up the Thames, with her basket of goods, an aged figure pursuing her trade vigorously and alone, in and about small market towns. In her study of *Victorian Countrywomen*, Pamela Horn charts the diminishment of crafts and trades in rural communities throughout the nineteenth century. These once flourishing industries had provided opportunities for women to work at home, and to contribute substantially to the household or to their own support. These opportunities dwindled for a variety of reasons including new production methods making it unnecessary to outsource labor, importation of materials, higher wages in factory work, commercial industries taking on what were once domestic trades, and increasing unavailability of training in these fields for younger girls. Thus the description of the trades in the latter half of the century tends increasingly to focus on the accounts of older women or the memories of those who knew them. Lace making, straw plaiting, glove and button making, netmaking, thatching mats, and hosiery work were tasks which older women continued to perform until they could no longer work at all. Often, these trades involved a great deal of physical exertion including arduous travel. For example, in order to gather the wool necessary for knitting stockings, "many of the women searched hedgerows and hillsides for the wisps left behind by the flocks of grazing sheep. They often spent several days on their travels, each party of about six women carrying with them sufficient provisions to last for a week or a fortnight, together with sacks to carry home their booty." Once the goods were produced, they had to be collected and brought to a place where they could be consigned to someone employed by the manufacturer buying the goods. Laundresses often had to carry water and then the clothes some distance. Horn tells the story of Mrs. Caroline Irons, who "eked out a tiny living by walking to Oxford and back each week with a handcart to collect meat for sale among the villagers—a journey of over twenty miles.... Her last trip was made in November 1898, when she was already in her early seventies."[22] Betty Higden should be placed within the context of those whose economic position were precarious at best, who made the most of the resources at hand in order to support herself and others dependent on her. Like many old women, single or widowed, she combined several low-paying occupations in order to preserve a meager survival. Initially she operates her mangle, with the help of the poor workhouse dependent Sloppy, and she offers herself as a 'child-minder.' If these occupations seem more fitting, and less bizarre than her decision to roam the countryside as a one-woman shop, it is only because we are unacquainted with what was, after all, an increasingly familiar sight in the second half of the nineteenth century: the elderly woman making her solitary way from village to village, asking for little, offering little, while hoping desperately to avoid the dread prospect of the workhouse. Moreover, by placing her among the stalwart survivors of the novel, we maintain the connection between Betty and the other characters who resourcefully find ways to earn a living out of unimaginable materials (including corpses and recyclable trash) and impoverished circumstances. Dickens in no way softens the hardness of her life, but he grants her what she wished for, the dignity of self-reliance and, at the end, the kind solicitation of a friend instead of the attendance—or not—of a pauper-nurse.

Sarah Gamp is another scavenger whose ties to the community seem strong only because they are complex and manifold. In fact, she is deeply

22. Pamela Horn, *Victorian Countrywomen* (Oxford: Basil Blackwell, 1991), 166, 183, 190–1.

reliant on others. Sairey flourishes, but without the bourgeois assurances of a bank account or family and friends who are willing to provide for her. Her position is sensitive to every current; her entire income relies on sustaining employment. She offers attendance on those occasions for which everyone stands in need of service—birth, illness, incapacity, death—and so she remains confident of continuing in her trade. Even so she is aware of the constant need to maintain the support and good will of those, like Mr. Mould, the undertaker, or "fellow-labourer" Mrs. Prig, who has some connection to a hospital, and upon whose recommendations she relies (*MC*, ch. 29). Anne Summers provides data which allows us to see how competitive the situation was. For example, she points out that in the 1841 census, Holborn, Sarah's district, contained the highest concentration of nurses in the city, with a total of 1,062 (out of 4,687 in London).[23] It is the precariousness of Sarah's economic situation that keeps her as morally uncertain as she is socially unestablished. At one point Dickens describes how she "had kept two-thirds of herself behind the door, ready for escape, and one-third in the room, ready for siding with the strongest party" (*MC*, ch. 51). She will forever pause in the doorway, hesitating whether to advance or retreat, depending on where power lies and how much it will be to her advantage to enter or retreat.

Readers may have adored Sairey Gamp the character, but they feared 'Sarah Gamp,' the embodiment of a domiciliary nurse. Catherine Judd points out that her age "accurately represents the dominant presence of older women within institutional nursing. The 1851 census records that of the 25,466 institutional nurses working in Great Britain, 19,325 were beyond their mid-forties."[24] Within the workhouse, nurses were typically among the eldest residents. Elizabeth Twining who, like Emma Sheppard, was a dedicated 'visitor' to the workhouses, accounted for seventy salaried nurses and 500 pauper-nurses or nursing assistants who "were over fifty years of age, one-quarter were over sixty and some even over eighty years old."[25] Until the 1860s and beyond, the image of a nurse mixed with images of aging women. Judd explores the negative effect Gamp's example either confirmed or released, and drawing on Foucault's concept of the "carceral continuum," identifies the principal cause of the fear she inspired: "Rather than being cruel workers in corrupt asy-

23. Anne Summers, "The Mysterious Demise of Sarah Gamp: The Domicilliary Nurse and her Detractors, c.1830–1860," *Victorian Studies*, 32 (Spring 1989), 369.
24. Catherine Judd, *Bedside Seductions: Nursing and the Victorian Imagination, 1830–1880* (London: Macmillan, 1998), 35.
25. Quoted in Deane, "Old and Incapable?", 170.

lums, workhouses, or jails, domiciliary nurses...bring the taint of degenerate institutions into the domestic realm, thereby transforming private homes into metaphoric prisons."[26] The inspectatorial aura of the attending nurse seems clear in the case of Brontë's Mrs. Horsfall, who, in *Shirley*, guards Robert Moore like a ferocious soldier, preserves the doctor's interests, and 'protects' him from all visitors. Sarah, however, intimidates not through imposition of a strict regimen, but through her callous disregard of the patient's needs. Both Summers and Judd identify Gamp's nursing style with older women who never experienced institutional training and were not associated with reforms in nursing techniques.[27] Sarah is best seen as a symptom of the disease rather than as part of a failed cure. Her ability to extract self-advantage from each encounter is distinguished from the conduct of other, more villainous scavengers by her good humor, by her willingness to share the takings with others (so long as her own share isn't compromised), and above all by our recognition of the vulnerability that underlies her appetite.

Just here we need to distinguish between Gamp the predatory nurse and Gamp the shrewd aging woman. Summers, Judd, and Poovey properly emphasize the negative effects of her example for the public estimation of domiciliary nurses. And yet the complex cultural meanings of Sarah Gamp include the eruptive agency that she seizes for herself. Her transgressions are large only in their inventiveness; they are small and petty in their kind. In one exemplary scene, Sarah's preparations for eating and sleeping clash with her night-watch of the fevered Mr. Lewisham. While he lies unconscious on the bed, she orders a maid to provide her with all the delicacies (and drink) she can imagine, enjoys her feast thoroughly ("I don't believe a finer cowcumber was ever grow'd"), only then remembers her nursing duties, and so "administer[s] the patient's medicine, by the simple process of clutching his windpipe to make him gasp, and immediately pouring it down his throat" and finally thinks "'I a'most forgot the piller, I declare!' said Mrs. Gamp, drawing it away. 'There! Now he's comfortable as he can be, I'm sure! I must try to make myself as much so as I can.'" Having stolen his pillow for herself (he can't be comfortable with or without it), she removes "a row of

26. Judd, *Bedside Seductions*, 72. In a footnote she refers to Foucault's notion of the "carceral continuum" [*Discipline and Punish: The Birth of the Prison*, trans. Alan Sheridan, (New York: Vintage, 1979), 303], by which he means the association between workhouses, hospitals, insane asylums, and jails. She writes: "Within this conflation or continuum, the nurse becomes an exchangeable worker: at once teacher, prison-guard, surrogate mother, and nurse" (Judd, p.170, n. 16 to ch. 3).

27. Ibid. 69–70; Summers, 365.

bald old curls that could scarcely be called false, they were so very innocent of anything approaching to deception," and prepares herself for sleep (*MC*, ch. 25). Who in this scene thinks of Mr. Lewisham? In *Oliver Twist* the pauper-nurses are old harridans more grotesque than evil, and less comic only because they are vultures to the dying Agnes (Oliver's unfortunate mother). And Mrs. Bangham, charwoman and messenger who performs the task of nursing assistant to Doctor Haggage in *Little Dorrit*, is not harsh to Mrs. Dorrit in the event of Amy's birth. She is, like Sarah Gamp, simply practical, unsentimental and 'thirsty.'

As late as 1899, G. J. Shaw Lefevre was still calling loudly for "competent nurses" rather than pauper inmates to serve within the workhouse.[28] Soon, trained and untrained nurses competed for work, but in the 1840s, 'professional' standards were not yet established. Sarah Gamp, in any case, is not a professional but a performer, and what she performs is the resourcefulness of age within tightly constrained circumstances. Whether she assists at a lying-in or a laying-out, her behavior is always cheerfully *open*. There is nothing surreptitious, under cover, not even anything discreet about Sarah Gamp. She performs her wrong-doing as one might an act of selflessness. She has no thought of concealment: indeed, publicity is her preference. In *Dickens, Women and Language*, Patricia Ingham refers to the theatricality of syntax in such old ladies as Mrs. Skewton and Sairey Gamp, and this fondness for self presentation extends beyond language.[29] Mrs. Skewton affects to be Cleopatra, while Sairey Gamp—unscrupulous, unsavory, and unreliable—re-creates herself as a *sui generis* theatrical subject, whose only precedent is herself. In both cases, the extravagant egotism, the hunger for sensation, and the showy self-dramatization attract moral condemnation, but they must also be seen as the precipitates of age, and especially as the radically ambiguous and radically theatrical responses of aging women.

Sairey Gamp, an unrepentant appetite and an extravagant fantasist, enacts the provocations of age from within the mode of Dickensian comedy, while Betty Higden, upright, earnest and self-chastening, lives within the ethical mode and offers the challenge of a besieged subjectivity that still demands acknowledgment. The two women live within the limits of meager income

28. G. J. Shaw Lefevre, "The Treatment of the Aged Poor in Workhouses," paper read at the Hampshire Poor Law Conference held at Winchester, June 1, 1899. MS F.W.A. 84, University of London, special collections.
29. Patricia Ingham, *Dickens, Women and Language* (New York: Harvester Wheatsheaf, 1992), 76–7.

and unyielding institutions; these conditions are rigid and inflexible; but, as I have been suggesting, they are compatible with styles of enterprising agency. Indeed Sairey and Betty share a notable gift. Even inside their severe social and material constraint, they both cultivate an imaginative alter ego who richly extends their range of experience. Sarah's friend Mrs. Harris accompanies her everywhere, as a voluble (though invisible) presence. Mrs. Harris too is old, and she possesses a complicated genealogy that frequently verges on breaking through the narrative of *Martin Chuzzlewitt* with its own urgent claims. Only her dedication to the task of praising Sarah Gamp—or Sarah's dedication to the same—keeps her within the fold of this voluminous novel. Moreover, although we tend to think of Mrs. Harris as Sarah Gamp's invention, in a manner of speaking, *Sarah Gamp is Mrs. Harris's invention.* Mrs. Harris's Sarah is not an old woman living on the edge, perpetually straining to maintain an uncertain position and depending often on the misfortunes of others for her own well-being. The ever-faithful, ever-admiring imaginary friend proclaims Sarah's erudition on all subjects and her superiority on all occasions: "you best of hard-working and industrious creeturs as ever was underpaid at any price, which unerpaid you are" she exclaims at an opportune moment (*MC*, ch. 46). So crucial to her own identity is Mrs. Harris, that Sarah angrily renounces her partner Mrs. Prig, when that lady presumes to doubt her existence:

> "What!" said Mrs. Gamp, "you bage creetur, have I know'd Mrs. Harris five and thirty year, to be told at last that there ain't no sech a person livin'!...But well you mayn't believe there's no sech a creetur, for she wouldn't demean herself to look at you, and often has she said, when I have made mention of your name, which, to my sinful sorrow, I have done, 'What, Sairey Gamp! debage yourself to *her*!' Go along with you!" (*MC*, ch. 49)

The invention of Mrs. Harris is the means by which Sarah Gamp secures the (comic) dignity of age. With Mrs. Harris to accompany and to exalt her, she does not become an accomplished professional, an ethical paragon, not even a different person. No one's opinion alters because of information gleaned from Mrs. Harris. And yet the effect of the exuberant invention is to display Sarah Gamp as a vigorous imaginative fecundity, which in her old age keeps her "green."

Mrs. Harris has a significant late analogy in the figure of Sloppy, the 'half-wit' whom Betty Higden rescued from the workhouse and more or less adopted as her own. Betty does not invent Sloppy, but it is only through her inexhaustibly attentive care that his genius is called into being. Sloppy resumes a thread originally stitched in the relations between the half-wit Barnaby Rudge and his self-sacrificing mother. If it is Betty's patronage that summons virtues that would otherwise have lain fallow, he reciprocates through devotion to the elderly lady. He operates the mangle and helps Betty to oversee the three children she 'minds'; more importantly, as I have noted, "he do the policeman in different voices"—that is, he reads the newspaper to her, opening the world and helping her to 'hear' and see through his creative lens. Like Mrs. Harris, Sloppy's devotion to Betty is a large part of the narrative he relates. When he sees her distress, his wail ignites a similar response in the children too young to understand the causes of her anxiety. And when Mrs. Boffin offers Sloppy a place in her own household he responds:

> "There's Mrs. Higden. Mrs. Higden goes before all. None can ever be better friends to me than Mrs. Higden's been. And she must be turned for, must Mrs. Higden. Where would Mrs. Higden be if she warn't turned for!" At the mere thought of Mrs. Higden in this inconceivable affliction, Mr. Sloppy's countenance became pale, and manifested the most distressful emotions. (*OMF*, II, ch. 10)

The witnessing of the elderly will be central to their place in Victorian representation. As vulnerable agents, they often depend on the observation of others—real or imaginary—who will lend them due acknowledgment. In the visual arts too, as we will see later in this study, the aged assume the role of witnessed subjects, threatened agents, whose dignity requires a gaze of interest.

Where Sairey speaks her own encomia through the voice of Mrs. Harris, Sloppy expresses the same for Betty Higden, whom we might otherwise dismiss. He saves her from the two-dimensionality of a thoroughly good creature, not by telling us something about her that we couldn't learn elsewhere, but by demonstrating in his own person the effects of aged dignity. *He* is the testament of her worth more than the words he speaks about her. Before she sets off on her last journey, Betty secures a future for her loyal page: "He would have made a wonderful cabinet-maker…if there had been the money to put him to it" Betty informs Rokesmith/Harmon, who is acting secretary for the wealthy Boffins (*OMF*, II, ch. 14). And thus it is no surprise that when she dies, Sloppy is put in the way of this trade, through which he finds his path to the novel's other artist, the lame Jenny Wren, by crafting for her a beautiful cane.

Betty Higden and Sairey Gamp take their place in the foreground of this first chapter because they embody so many intersecting contingencies within the Victorian conundrum of aging: terror of abandonment and dread of institutional confinement, material deprivation and intellectual bewilderment, the unsortable mixture of responsibility and dependency. But through representing their extremity, Dickens uncovers a stubborn and surprising resilience. In significant measure, theirs is the resilience of the elderly bricoleuse, reduced to the most exiguous circumstances—the odd scraps and instruments in an invalid's room, or the "trifling stock" in a basket (*OMF*, III, ch. 8)—who nevertheless discovers the tactics of persistence. Comic or sentimental, shrewd or innocent, these aging women retain a generative power that belongs to the composite image of the Victorian elderly and that should not be overlooked within simpler narratives, smoother trajectories.

Incarceration of the mind: lunacy and old age

The elderly often appear as a kind of fiction in Dickens—a kind of specter—fading into impalpability. The very, very old fill the spaces of the workhouses; they flit about the edges of the plot, scurrying mice; they become comic props; stick figures deployed to balance an image. This is often how other characters see them. What may be an active inner life can appear a complete vacancy, and what is called imagination in younger people may seem dementia among the aged. And yet it is worth opposing the "ghastly kind of contentment" of the institutionalized elderly to the old who still walk on the streets. What is distinctive in the portraits of Miss Flite, Krook, or Old Smallweed in *Bleak House*, of the pathetic Mr. Cleaver and Wegg (*OMF*), of the old man David Copperfield meets on the Dover Road, or Nell's grandfather in *Old Curiosity Shop*, is the unsettled energy of age. In Mayhew, too, the misery of old age in the streets often appears as a fitful excitement—overwrought, frantic, sometimes raving or seething—a terrible recklessness.

The aging of bodies is not just an individual trial; it is a formidable social challenge that reveals itself whenever the aging body intersects with the unrepentant youthfulness of London. The movement of the elderly through the city is always an evocative passage. *Little Dorrit* records the struggles of old Nandy when he leaves the workhouse to visit William Dorrit in the Marshalsea prison and traverses a risky path—especially risky for the elderly—through the center of London.

> Anybody may pass, any day, in the thronged thoroughfares of the metropolis, some meagre, wrinkled, yellow old man (who might be supposed to have dropped from the stars, if there were any star in the Heavens dull enough to be suspected of casting off so feeble a spark), creeping along with a scared air,

> as though bewildered and a little frightened by the noise and bustle. This old man is always a little old man. If he were ever a big old man, he has shrunk into a little old man; if he were always a little old man, he has dwindled into a less old man.... And so, like the country mouse in the second year of a famine, come to see the town mouse, and timidly threading his way to the town-mouse's lodging through a city of cats, this old man passes in the streets. (LD, I, ch. 31)

The old man—exposed to traffic, noise, the swarm of boys, the hooting, predatory modern city—the old man threading his way through London becomes a sign of the past, a past that has been forgotten within the coursing modernity of the city. London is a city of cats, ready to pounce on any elderly mouse scurrying by the way—and not just any old mouse, but an old country mouse. Frail antique Nandy, the country mouse, chased and harried by metropolitan modernity, secures the Dickensian link between age and the countryside. The elderly person and the rural pasture are linked as vestiges, relics, remnants.

When the aging body walks abroad in the metropolis, we have, in effect, a reversal of that modern emergency in which we see London going out of town, the march of brick and mortar, the restless, rapid encroachment on the countryside—this is countered by the passage of the aged self stubbornly alive within the city, the country mouse, moving with halting steps, but still preserving the rags and shards of the past. Nandy, as we see later, serenades his daughter in her Happy Cottage. This figure of the singing father who rejoins his daughter in their urban oasis makes an epitome of the seal between generations. Morever, as the one who is set free from the workhouse even for a brief moment, the wrinkled yellow old Nandy becomes an unlikely figure of liberation, an image of escape from institutional paralysis, the meager life of discipline and surveillance. For just the space of an afternoon and under threat of the predatory cats, he performs the gesture that eludes Betty Higden and that will loom among the debates of the next decades: to be old and yet to belong in a web of sociality—to be old and still to sing in London.

Dickensian London is a complicated machine. It flattens the past, induces homogeneity, and ravages tradition. But crucially, it fails to complete its project. London is not the Coketown of *Hard Times*, where the discipline of industry simply obliterates difference, enforcing unity until objects, people and architecture, meet in nightmare conformity. London is rather the pleated city, the city of folds, the creased metropolis. Even as it endures the simplifications of modernity, it carefully allows spaces for the obsolete, the endangered, and the elderly.[30] The seeding of the metropolis with human relics and with the remnants of its rural past, its bygone beauty is a refusal of the false present tense—the falsity of monied respectability, and the cream stucco covering the truth of brick. In the face of such shams, Dickens offers a hope that amid London's pleats and folds there might grow a garden: the bearer of age in a time of false youth. This is a hope and a promise we will pursue in the final section of this chapter.

***

If the Workhouse was intended to curb the agitations caused by poverty and hunger, Asylums were the institutional means for subduing the emotional agitations often associated with old age. In this connection, the minutes of the Directors of the Poor for St. Pancras in north London describe a small but revelatory incident of 1860. It seems that the District Surgeon, a Mr. Jeffreys, had issued an order to put in the Workhouse an old man named Henry Hart as one suffering from "mental excitement and needing restraint." The problem was that Jeffreys had never gone to see Hart—had simply heard a story and ordered the confinement. The Directors of the Poor first voted to fire the surgeon and then decided only to censure him. Here is just one case, but it leaps out of the archive as suggesting the conditions of local power and the terms of normalization. Henry Hart was "mentally excited," and so Jeffreys, feeling secure within prevailing assumptions, made a perfunctory decision to restrain the mentally excited man in the Workhouse without bothering to have a consultation. So many stories resemble this one that the outline of a distinctive conversion narrative begins to emerge. It is a tale of transformation: the agitated, overly excited, aged poor of the streets converted into the docile inmates of the workhouse. And what gives sharp edge to this narrative is an issue I can come at by returning once again to Dickens's 1850 essay, where he describes the workhouse scene as "Groves of babies in arms; groves of mothers and other sick women in bed; groves of lunatics...groves of old people." The easy movement from lunatics to old people becomes an all too familiar association which persists today, and to which the medicalization of old age in the nineteenth century contributed even though it did not create it.

30. This section incorporates work from lectures and an essay co-authored with Michael Levenson entitled "Green Dickens," in *Contemporary Dickens: Essays in Honor of Steven Marcus*, ed. Eileen Gillooly and Deirdre David (Athens: Ohio State University Press, 2008).

Here I want to invoke Peter Bartlett's fine study of the treatment of madness among the poor—focused, specifically, on the growth of public asylums during the nineteenth century. *The Poor Law of Lunacy* argues that the new asylum system, instead of becoming an independent network of hospitals, entered the workings of the poor law. Overwhelmingly, it became the poor who filled the new institutions. What this meant, according to Bartlett, is that the workhouse and the madhouse became two faces of one system, and that we can only understand the function of the Victorian asylum if we see it not as a strictly medical institution dominated by doctors but more fundamentally as part of the general institutional treatment of poverty. Local officials and the workhouse staff had extraordinary powers to direct the relief-seeking poor to one place or another—to permit them to stay out-of-doors with some small weekly pension, or else to be confined in one of two institutions: the workhouse or the asylum.[31] And it is striking that many of those diagnosed as mentally deranged were not sent to the county asylums at all, but were kept in the workhouse, and this despite the fact that there was ample room in the asylums. In their Eleventh Annual Report of 1857, the governing body for the asylums, the evocatively named Commissioners in Lunacy, complained of the reluctance of local authorities to deliver up their insane: there were several cases where the commission staff entered the workhouse, demanding the immediate transfer of certain inmates.[32] Bartlett is uninterested in age; madness is the category that guides his research. And yet my claim is that a reconsideration of Victorian madness has everything to do with a new study of Victorian age. I said earlier that what separated London from the rest of the country was the institutionalization of pauperism, which brought many more of the aged poor into the workhouse, and the archival documents give us strong reason to believe that workhouse life, both its diet and discipline, often created the conversion of temperament that I've been describing: the shift from elderly agitation to docility and vacantness. But it is exactly this transformation that makes the poor, aging man or woman resemble the figure of the imbecile. That object of workhouse fascination, the mental defective, is stupefied into dullness, and located, diagnostically, between the congenital idiot and the dangerous lunatic.

Again Old Nandy, who lives within the interstices of *Little Dorrit*, is a case in point. Although no scene depicts his life within the workhouse, we do

31. Peter Bartlett, *The Poor Law of Lunacy: The Administration of Pauper-Lunatics in mid-Nineteenth-Century England* (London: Leicester University Press, 1999), 21, 41, 55, 91–5.

32. Ibid. 55.

see him as a visitor to the Marshalsea Prison, where William Dorrit enjoys pointing out his deficiencies (mental and physical) to Arthur Clennam. As he appears in this setting, Nandy is fully passive, yielding to institutional pressures to perform as an aged object. Abject submission is the price he is willing to pay, because he fears he will be a drain on his daughter and her struggling family if he is expelled from the workhouse. But when he is free to join the Plornish family in their Happy Cottage, he enlivens the party as its festive center. His lightly sketched career traces the arc of 'conversion': from activity to passivity, ebullience to lethargy.

A recurrent preoccupation among poor law officials, what might fairly be called an institutional obsession, was the task technically named "classification," a word circulating through the official hearings and reports. It refers to the perpetual work of distinguishing the kinds of paupers—the drunk, the sick, the old, the married, the unfortunate, the undeserving—and then, in a second act, placing them (or, more strikingly, choosing not to place them) in different physical compartments of the House. Because of the unique institutionalization of the London poor and the sheer size of the workhouses, the pressures to classify were heavy. Local authorities sorted the human mass that streamed their way, enjoying the "full power to subdivide the inmates as they choose."[33] During the hearings of the Royal Commission a question was put to a Guardian of the Poor, again from St. Pancras: "Do you attempt any classification in your workhouse?" "The classification at the present time consists in this, that they are classified into infirm, healthy and imbeciles."[34] And yet, of course, exactly the point to which I've been aiming is the unsettling confusion between age and imbecility—a confusion richly demonstrated in an exchange involving Hugh Owen, permanent secretary to the Local Government Board. "As to imbeciles, what becomes of those whose cases are not sufficiently decided to send them to the county asylum?" Owen's answer is blunt: "They are retained in the Workhouse; there is no other provision."

Even more notable is the next remark buried in the records of the Commission. To the question, "How do you treat lunatics and imbeciles?" this answer was given: "In 1883 an inquiry was held by order of the Local Government Board concerning harmless lunatics; the majority of aged persons receiving relief were certified as imbeciles. There were then over 500 imbeciles [in our union]: at the present time there are only 13; of those 13

33. *Royal Commission on the Aged Poor, Parliamentary Papers*, xiv–xv, 1895, 75. 34. Ibid. 124.

the majority are young people living with their parents"[35] Could there be a more striking example of the powers of classification, especially when these powers are enacted on the small scale among a few local officials? An account of the early 1880s turned up those groves of imbecility that Dickens found, such large groves because so many weaknesses of old age passed for mental derangement. But a new count of the 1890s gave an entirely different picture, because under pressure from central administration, the elderly were suddenly placed in a new class, if not always a new space, of their own.

Here, of course, is why lunacy and imbecility cannot be studied apart from the treatment, or maltreatment, of old age. We have seen how the acts of power, the classification and representation, convert the old into institutional objects to be named and placed. But there is another dimension to the subject, one which helps to explain why classification of the elderly with the imbecilic seemed to reflect a 'natural' association. One of the most influential models depicting the life curve as it was conceived in the nineteenth century reflected the belief that as the body degenerates, so does the mind:

> Human old age, with the great dependence of the mind on the body for its expression of activity, is characterized by a gradual intensive and extensive decline in psychic strength...There also occurs a disorder of the mind, the madness of old age...This illness...arises in those elderly persons who were never mentally disturbed previously and also possess no disposition towards it.[36]

From this perspective, the Dickensian ideal of a green old age was a defiant position. It is not simply that he advocates *retention* of youth throughout the older years, it is that he describes a condition of age in which the mind continues to be flexible and elastic in its own manner (not in the manner of youth) and in pursuit of its own aims and objects. Is this a 'second childhood'? If so, it has its own logic and justification, its own rewards, and is in no way a grotesque or diminished acting out of the first. As we have seen, one of the most severe and visible consequences of institutionalization was the 'unnatural' suppression of mental agility. The lack of mental stimulation and not the passing years led to the degeneration of mental faculties.

35. Ibid. ii. 163.
36. Quoted from *Enzyclopädisches Handbuch der Gerichtlichen Arzneikunde*, ed. Sie Benhaar (1838), i. 643–4 in Hans-Joachim von Kondratowitz, "The Medicalization of Old Age: Continuity and Change in Germany From the Late 18th to the early 20th Century," *Life, Death, and the Elderly: Historical Perspectives*, ed. Margaret Pelling and Richard Smith (London: Routledge, 1991), 150.

If conditions within the workhouse varied markedly from one to the next, so too did conditions of workhouses, asylums, and almshouses. The almshouses will be of interest in the next chapter, but here it is worth dwelling a little more on the place of the aged in asylums. In his essay "The Welfare of the Elderly in the Past," David Thomson writes that "Hospitals and lunatic asylums can be overlooked in the present context: nineteenth century records suggest that only small numbers of the elderly then found their way into such places." But in "Workhouse to Nursing Home," he reports that "The use of asylums to house the aged was essentially a late-century development. In 1871 lunatic asylums housed 35 per 10,000 and 44 per 10,000 of men and women aged 65–74 years, at a time when hospitals included a mere 8 per 10,000 of the same groups."[37] The context for the first remark concerns total sums over a long span of time. The second remark indicates the great change that occurred in the last three decades of the nineteenth century.

The numbers are small in terms of the total population, but in relation to the number of old people placed in hospitals the percentage of people placed in asylums is striking. And if we dip below the figure of 65, and cast the net a little wider, the statistics are even more telling, since all records show that the greatest number of people admitted to such institutions were in the 40+ age group. Forty had an ambiguity for the Victorians, comparable to its place for us. But for women the threshold has particular relevance to the onset of old age since typically, when menopause began, a woman was considered to have entered both the portals of old age and mental instability. Lynn Botelho puts the case tersely: "Menopause played a critical role in early modern England's cultural definition of old age, but it was its symptoms, rather than its primary biological feature of infertility, which marked women's point of entry into old age."[38] Elaine Showalter's work in this area has amply documented the association between menopause and the classification of insanity, and she shows how institutionalization often created the conditions it then described.[39]

Until the 1845 Lunatic Asylums Act, there were only nine such accommodations available to paupers who otherwise languished in the workhouses or

37. Thomson, "The Welfare of the Elderly in the Past," 207; "Workhouse to Nursing Home," 52.
38. Lynn Botelho, "Old Age and Menopause in Rural Women of Early Modern Suffolk," in *Women and Ageing in British Society since 1500*, ed. Lynn Bothelo and Pat Thane (Harlow, Essex: Pearson Educational), 53.
39. Elaine Showalter, "Victorian Women and Insanity," repr. in *Madhouses, mad-Doctors, and Madmen: The Social History of Psychiatry in the Victorian Era,* ed. Andrew Scull (London: Athlone Press, 1981), 333.

without any care whatsoever. As the number of asylums grew and classifications of insanity began to determine the assignment of paupers, the problems which beset workhouses began to overcome the asylums. For example, John Walton explains that in the Lancaster Asylum, the increased number of people aged 60 and above between 1851 and 1971 led to the return of many inmates to the workhouse: "the rise [in percentage of admission in the elderly] took place in spite of anxious attempts by the asylum authorities to return chronic patients of quiet demeanour to the workhouses [though] experience showed that many patients lost their tranquillity after transfer, and had to be returned to the asylum in a worse state than before."[40] Andrew Scull claims that the rise in numbers is due in part to the classificatory nomenclature, and in part to the growth in the number of such institutions. Following Foucault, he concludes that asylums cultivated the kind of culture that required the services they provided:

> The very existence of the institution not only provides a means of dispensing with all sorts of disorderly, disturbing, and disruptive individuals; it also, by offering another means of coping, affects the degree to which people are prepared to put up with those who persistently create havoc, discord, and disarray, as well as with those whose extreme helplessness and dependency creates extraordinary burdens for others....the asylum inevitably operated to reduce family and community tolerance.[41]

Indeed, as the century came to a close, one common argument in favor of institutionalization was that the old, their friends, and the community would all be better served. In *On Boarding-Out Deserving Aged Workhouse Inmates* (1897), S. D. Fuller argued that such a release of the old from workhouse confinement would be a wound to family life. The presence of old people disrupts households and communities. As examples he cites the negative consequences of "causing the children's voices to be hushed for their sakes" and the necessary relinquishment of privacy (!) in the move from the workhouse to a home. The elderly would be "exposed to the dangers of drink," and caretakers would find it impossible to provide acceptable food to suit their tastes.[42] Some historians have focused on the attempts to rationalize public service through institutional means, while others often

40. John Walton, "The Treatment of Pauper Lunatics in Victorian England: The Case of Lancaster Asylum, 1816–1870," *Madhouses, Mad-Doctors, and Madmen*, 189–90.
41. Andrew Scull, *The Most Solitary of Afflictions: Madness and Society in Britain 1700–1900* (New Haven: Yale UP, 1993), 382–3.
42. S. D. Fuller, "On Boarding-Out Deserving Aged Workhouse Inmates," (London: H. G. Saunders & Son, 1897), 6–7.

take note of alternative movements, including efforts to re-assimilate the elderly within the communities in which they previously lived or to find ways to avoid initial institutionalization. In its early stages there was a wide path towards the welfare state, and efforts to centralize were regularly supplemented if not countered by attempts to maintain local oversight.

Once admitted to an asylum, patients frequently suffered from the same lack of occupation that inmates of the workhouse endured. In his exhaustive report on the conditions of asylums, conducted during the period 1875–8, Mortimer Granville seized on this as a particular evil: "I am very far from thinking the superintendent of a pauper establishment would be justified in leaving his patients without suitable occupation. The considerations which appear to me conclusive as to the evil of allowing lunatics to be alone with the ogre of their disease tell with equal force against idleness." The conditions in some of the institutions he evaluated were so appalling that Granville admitted, "It would require the pen of the author of 'Pickwick'... to place the facts in their true light, to colour them with natural hues, inspire them with realistic force," and by the time he gets to Hampstead, in London, he writes despairingly

> if asylums for the incurably insane are to be made depositories for the troublesome old people who throng the 'infirm wards' of poor-houses, we fear there will be reason to regret their existence.... They may be weak, dirty, troublesome, but they are certainly no more affected with mental disease than persons whose powers of mind have always been small, or are almost spent, can be said to be the subjects of morbid processes.[43]

The 1875 *Report of Commissioners in Lunacy* came to a similar conclusion, which Granville acknowledges:

> There is, also, a considerable class of aged persons suffering...from mere loss of memory and the dementia consequent upon old age, who, there is no doubt, might be properly taken care of in the infirmary wards of any well-managed workhouse.... Having regard to the...number of persons at present in the asylum, either labouring under feebleness of mind or body arising only from old age, or whose impairment of mind is only connected with partial paralysis, we cannot but think that many might have been kept in the infirmaries of the metropolitan workhouses...By calling the aged and peevish paupers of both sexes insane, and removing them to an institution where the requisite care-taking can be done in the lump, they save expense, and, if the transfer be accomplished cleverly, they may also take some credit for humanity.[44]

43. J. Mortimer Granville, *The Care and Cure of the Insane: Being the Reports of the Lancet Commission on Lunatic Asylums, 1875-6-7, For Middlesex, the City of London and Surrey*, 2 vols. (London: Hardwicke & Bogue, 1877), i. 33, 146.

44. Quoted ibid. 264–5.

We see vividly what has happened: depending on the admitting supervisors, aged people might be identified as paupers or lunatics. You to the right; you to the left: workhouse or asylum. Often conditions were much better in the latter, sometimes not. Certainly the cost of care was doubled.[45] Although treatment in the worst was far less shocking than the horrors of eighteenth-century misery in large institutions like Bedlam, frightening images persisted in popular fantasy. "Moral management" gradually replaced more coercive restraints, but many inmates suffered from 'treatment' as well as neglect.[46] And although the aged poor were vulnerable in greater numbers and to greater degrees than those who possessed sufficient income, age sometimes made wealth alone irrelevant. In 1883 Louisa Lowe, the secretary to the Lunacy Law Reform Association, published a book with the inflammatory title: *The Bastilles of England; or, The Lunacy Laws at Work*. The gauntlet is thrown down on the very first page: "Few analogies can be more striking than those between our English houses licensed for lunatics, and the Bastilles of pre-revolutionised France, between the English medical certificates of lunacy with their concomitant 'order' of incarceration, and the French *lettre de cachet*."[47] Dickens's Dr. Manette was jailed in the Bastille as a young man, and though many years passed before he was freed, we are also invited to see his incarceration itself as the 'treatment' which accelerated, even which caused, the peculiar manifestations of insanity associated with his old age. When he is released Dr. Manette is inattentive, absent and absent-minded, 'vacant,' absorbed in inward meditation, confused, and difficult to rouse. In *A Tale of Two Cities* there is a political context in which to place his disorders, but in fact he differs very little from the old in other novels, whose only 'crime' has been the unfortunate association with institutions, and like them, re-invigoration requires renewed attachment to family and friends.

Neither the workhouse nor the public asylum sought inmates, but neither did they rely solely on self-admission. And if terrifying stories circulated about workhouses discouraging entry or even turning away those in need,

45. See Marelene A. Arieno, *Victorian Lunatics: A Social Epidemiology of Mental Illness in Mid-Nineteenth-Century England* (London: Susquehanna University Press, 1989), 27.

46. See ibid. 71; Vieda Sultans, *Madness and Morals: Ideas on Insanity in the Nineteenth Century* (London: Routledge & Kegan Paul, 1975); Akihito Suzuki, *Madness at Home: The Psychiatrist, the Patient, and the Family in England 1820–1860* (Berkeley: University of California Press, 2006); Joseph Melling and Bill Forsythe, *The Politics of Madness: The State, Insanity and Society in England 1845–1914* (London: Routledge, 2006).

47. Louisa Lowe, *The Bastilles of England; or, The Lunacy Laws at Work* (London: Crookenden & Co., 1883), 1.

there were still more frightening tales of those who were forced into lunatic asylums, private or public, against their wills. The certificate of lunacy to which Lowe referred was obtainable by securing the signature of obliging medical 'authorities.' She describes several instances of abuse, including one old lady who was kidnapped on a trip to Bath, after a scheming nephew obtained the signatures of two doctors who saw her just long enough to complete the form. She was incarcerated for two months and released only after agreeing to grant power of attorney to her nephew, allowing him to oversee all of her affairs, and accepting readmittance if she failed to conform to his requirements. And though older women were more vulnerable to such schemes, Lowe describes cases in which men were victims as well.[48] Even public figures were subject to such scares: Bulwer Lytton had his wife Rosina incarcerated when she was 55, after she had caused him great and visible embarrassment. The doctor Hale Thomson, sent to observe her initially, reported that he had "never found a clearer head, or a more logical mind, or sounder flesh and blood, than Lady Lytton's." Nevertheless, as her grandson describes, "When she arrived at Mr. Hale Thomson's house by appointment in the afternoon of June 23, Lady Lytton was informed that arrangements had been made for her removal to Inverness Lodge as person of unsound mind, on the medical certificate of Mr. Thomson and Mr. Ross [an apothecary]." In this case public outrage (and, apparently, some maneuvering on the part of the Queen herself), caused Lord Lytton to permit her release after twenty-four days.[49] The temptation to incarcerate someone who might otherwise be an inconvenience or impediment was a topic that Wilkie Collins, among others, keenly pursued. His narratives concentrate on the most dramatic instances or possibilities, and younger people tend to be the focus: Anne Catherick, Laura Fairlie in Collins's *The Woman in White*, and Helen Malden/Talboys (Lucy Graham/Audley), in Braddon's *Lady Audley's Secret* are the most famous examples. But the problem had special implications for older people, whose vulnerabilities may have been enhanced instead of mitigated by their privileged position.

Privilege, however slight, could clearly result in better care. There is no better example than in cases when the older person seems to have indeed

48. Louisa Lowe, 13–16; 46–8.
49. Reported in David Lytton Cobbold, *A Blighted Marriage: The Life of Rosina Bulwer Lytton; Irish Beauty, Satirist and Tormented Victorian Wife 1802–1882* (Knebworth, Hertfordshire: Knebworth House Education & Preservation Trust, 1999), 8–10.

suffered from some mental instability and had the good fortune to find tender care from those who could afford to extend it. Mary Lamb was 34 at the start of the nineteenth century, and thus began Victoria's reign as an old woman in her early seventies. She died in 1847 at the age of 82. 'Madness' ran in the family—her brother Charles was resident briefly in an asylum in Hoxton—though because of her bizarre murder of her mother in September of 1796 only Mary's madness is well known. Charles objected when his older brother put Mary in an asylum after the murder, and by Christmas of 1797 the brother and sister become co-resident, each caring for the other as well as possible. When she was in her sixties, Charles would write "When she is not violent her rambling chat is better to me than the sense and sanity of this world."[50] Dorothy Wordsworth also relied on the devotion of her brother to ensure domiciliary care in their own home when she suffered severe mental disorientation in the last two decades of her long life. "Only be a loving child to me in my age, and bear with my whims and fancies," Aunt Betsey asks of David when he questions the wisdom of her laying out so much money for his training to become a Proctor (*DC*, ch. 23). 'Whims and fancies' belong to those who can afford private or home care. As Lord George Gordon says (and who should know better) in *Barnaby Rudge*, "we must not construe any trifling peculiarity into madness" (*BR*, ch. 48). Betsey Trotwood also knows of the horrors of dementia, having saved Richard Babley, more familiarly remembered as Mr. Dick, from incarceration by his own brother, by agreeing to care for him herself. Her explanation assumes acquaintance with the historical contexts I have analyzed:

> He has been *called* mad...And nice people they were, who had the audacity to call him mad....Because his brother [Mr. Dick] was a little eccentric—though he is not half so eccentric as a good many people—he didn't like to have him visible about his house, and sent him away to some private asylum-place, though he had been left to his especial care by their deceased father, who thought him almost a natural. And a wise man *he* must have been to think so! Mad himself, no doubt!...I am ready to take care of him, and shall not ill-treat him as some people (besides the asylum folks) have done (*DC*, ch. 14).

Mr. Dick's 'madness' is, like Miss Flite's, not only benign but beneficial. When Mr. Woodcourt offers his medical attention and friendship to Miss Flite, and Mr. Jarndyce sees to it that she receives small, but regular payments,

50. Helen Ashton and Katharine Davies, *I Had a Sister: A Study of Mary Lamb, Dorothy Wordsworth, Caroline Herschel, Cassandra Austen* (London: Lovat Dickson, 1937), 76.

she too transcends the spiral of madness and becomes involved and helpful in her little community. Custodial care takes many forms outside of the institution, but all of them rely on a certain privilege, and not all of the recipients are as admirable or likeable as Mr. Dick or Miss Flite. The insane neighbor who flagrantly admires first Mrs. Nickleby and then little Miss La Creevy, is said (by his private keeper) to have been "the cruellest, wickedest, out-and-outerest old flint that ever dared breath" (*NN*, ch. 41) until he became simply (and comically) depraved in his madness. Grandfather and Grandmother Smallweed have made a madness of capitalism (or is it the other way around?); their grandchildren would not provide for them, but they can provide for themselves, prolonging both madness and survival. And the madman of unspecific age, though associated with aging, who inhabits David Copperfield's old room when David returns as a man to visit the graves of his parents is likewise a silent testimony to the privilege of private care against a background of institutional privation.

The aged in Dickens, like their counterparts in Victorian society, are at once everywhere and overlooked. Once seen, they are pervasive in the plenitude. And yet it is clear that for Dickens, as for early nineteenth-century officialdom, there was no systematic or coherent understanding of the place of age. Much of the importance of his fiction to a study like mine is that it generates the elderly manifold, its rich plurality, precisely because it offers no schemata for the aged. The elderly are irreducibly various, which is not to say that they are a formless abundance. Even as Dickens displays their diversity, he instinctively generates figures of age who through their very extremity—extremities of demand and resourcefulness, victimage and recovery, abjection and power—establish the provocation that the later nineteenth century will struggle to comprehend.

Much of that struggle, as Dickens also lets us see, depended on transactions between the elderly and institutions—especially workhouse and asylum—that were no more transparent than they were. The aged as a category developed alongside, often within, a social apparatus developed to address other challenges, particularly those of the poor and the lunatic. As the last two sections have shown, the increasing visibility of age was in large part an effect of the expanding prominence of institutional response. A growth in population was matched by the growth in social administration. Placed within the dense gatherings of these new spaces, the elderly slowly assumed the shape of a social mass and a clinical object, and they become susceptible to a new language of care and control. Moreover, as this language became dominant in the second half of the century, it altered the image of need and the possibilities for provision. Dickens's Betty Higden, a creation of the 1860s, marks a moment when a literary self-consciousness of age meets a maturing self-consciousness in the generational ideology of officialdom: her dread of the workhouse is a testament to the spread of its powers. It is fair to claim that old age became institutionalized in the nineteenth century, even when it managed to avoid institutionalization.

London through the ages: aging in the Dickensian city

From the earliest phases of his career, Dickens recorded an audaciously transforming London, the metropolis as an apparatus that inexorably produces modernity. What makes this issue resonant here is that the march of the modern city intersects with the problem of human aging. London is a vessel for individual senescence, but it is also itself a protagonist that performs its own aging. The task of this section is to widen the field of our problem, to place the instabilities of generational life within the unstable milieu—physical as well as social—of the modernizing city.

The vignette "Scotland Yard," one of the early *Sketches by Boz,* evokes a metropolitan neighborhood on the verge of its disappearance. For generations it had survived as a closed, nearly unknown community, whose original inhabitants were "a tailor, a publican, two eating-house keepers, and a fruit-pie maker." These were joined by "a race of strong and bulky men" who heaved and carted coal, thereby bringing money into the micro-economy of Scotland-yard (*Sketches,* 64). The settlers and the traders achieved a simple collective equilibrium anchored at a public-house, where they gathered to recall "old legends of what the Thames was in ancient times," only "to meet again in the same room, and to say and do precisely the same things on the following evening at the same hour" (*Sketches,* 65). This is economy as ecology, a self-contained system of human exchange (narrative as well as material) that exists in organic relation to the natural world. The river brings ships; the ships deliver coal, which the traders carry into the country; and when coal has been exchanged for cash, they return to convert it into food and drink and clothes. The smooth ancient circuit finally breaks when the modernizing world intrudes to disrupt the flow between nature and culture. The new London Bridge appears, and then a new Hungerford market and a police headquarters. Outsiders begin to pass through the secluded streets, until Scotland Yard is thrown open to novelty. In the midst of this "change, and restlessness, and innovation," the shopkeepers now compete with one another: the fruit-pie maker calls himself a pastry-cook, and the eating-house keeper solicits customers "among a new class of people;" a boot-maker arrives, and then a dress-maker: "The old heavers still assembled round the ancient fireplace, but their talk was mournful: and the loud song and the joyous shout were heard no more" (*Sketches,* 66–7).

Here, at the beginning of his career, Dickens secures a firm link between modernization and social trauma. At the end of the piece, he suddenly introduces one more figure, that of a very old man, who offers a potential overlooked by the busy young, advancing recklessly into the future without caution or restraint:

> Amidst all this change, and restlessness, and innovation, there remains but one old man, who seems to mourn the downfall of this ancient place. He holds no converse with human kind, but, seated on a wooden bench at the angle of the wall which fronts the crossing from Whitehall Place, watches in silence the gambols of his sleek and well-fed dogs. He is the presiding genius of Scotland Yard. Years and years have rolled over his head; but in fine weather or in foul, hot or cold, wet or dry, hail, rain, or snow, he is still in his accustomed spot. Misery and want are depicted in his countenance; his form is bent by age, his head is grey with length of trial, but there he sits from day to day, brooding over the past; and thither he will continue to drag his feeble limbs, until his eyes have closed upon Scotland Yard, and upon the world together (*Sketches*, 67–8).

We can take this man as a figure of Father Time, but also as an icon of pastness brought into the peculiar conditions of Victorian modernity. To grow old is not only to lament the loss of youth, but also the disappearance of the ancient city. Here and elsewhere, nostalgia is often a dominant tone, which in its warmest moments renders the city as a benevolent elder and a source of consolation.

In an essay of 1852 co-authored with Henry Morley, Dickens celebrates London as "a fine old oak" whose age capably supports the precarious lives of infants through the foundation of the Great Ormond Street Hospital for Children in Queen's Square. "Great Ormond Street," we are informed, "belonged to our great-grandfathers; it was a bit of London full of sap a great number of years ago," its age being fundamental to its capacity to nurture the young. The street "is cut off, now, from the life of the town—in London but not of it—a suburb left between the New Road and High Holborn." The Square includes a number of "spectral streets," where elderly inhabitants reside in even older houses.[51] The juxtaposition of living ancients with the care of seriously ill or dying children casts aged London as guardian—the weak tended by the forgotten.

"We marked the advance of civilisation, and beheld it with a sigh" (*Sketches*, 66)—the remark captures the unstable tonality in Dickens's early thinking about the irresistible loss of generational equilibrium. It is clear enough that he regrets the disappearance of the past and that he mourns the waning of "old customs" and "ancient simplicity." But the wistfulness of the "sigh" and the staginess of the emotion suggest the unsettled attitudes. The word "improvement"—as in, "Improvement began to march with rapid strides to the very threshold of Scotland Yard" (*Sketches*, 66)—is Dickens's name for modernization, and it is of course not his alone. It stood generally to describe renovations of the built and the natural environment; within the context of London it came to refer to the ambitious urban transformations conducted by John Nash under the patronage of the Prince Regent. In *Metropolitan Improvements* (1828), James Elmes had prepared engravings to celebrate the changes, including the cutting of Regent's Street, the laying out of Trafalgar Square, the renovation of Buckingham Palace and the Mall, and the creation of Regent's Park and the villas that encircle it. Nash's projects often involved the destruction of closed urban spaces (like Scotland Yard) in favor of broad avenues and open squares. Dickens, who knew these precincts well, faced uncertainty in establishing a perspective on the change.

He walked incessantly, becoming "of the streets, streety" (*LD*, ch. 6); he knew their past as well as his own. The solitary streets draw Dickens in the way that Chancery draws its various suitors in the novel *Bleak House*. For example, the pretext for "Arcadian London" is the mass evacuation of Londoners during the 'long vacation' of September 1860, and the setting is Bond Street, itself divided in the eighteenth century into an 'old' and a 'new.' "It is pastoral to feel the freshness of the air in the uninhabited town" reports the narrator, almost overcome: "The Arcadian simplicity of

51. Charles Dickens and Henry Morley, "Drooping Buds," from *Household Words* (April 3, 1852), in *Uncollected Writings from Household Words*, 1850–1859, ii, ed. Harry Stone (Bloomington: Indiana University Press, 1968), 404.

the metropolis altogether, and the primitive ways into which it has fallen in this autumnal Golden Age, make it entirely new to me" (*UT*, 183).[52] The pleasure of the piece derives from the "repose" found throughout the streets as the narrator rambles through "deserted Westminster" without seeing or hearing anything about "the Ozone" ("Arcadian London," 187). Accompanying, perhaps heightening the present bliss is the recognition that the impression of a "happy Golden Age" will fade: "The iron age will return; London will come back to town" ('ibid,' 189). The Arcadian vision was produced under the aegis of the aging season and elaborated by a recording consciousness eager for recollection. Dickens's street narratives commonly rescue the old and retrieve the ancient past; they preserve in memory what modern construction destroys materially, and in doing so, offer continuity between the vanishing past and the nascent future. Instead of imagining rural excursions, Dickens describes the pleasures of finding urban solitude. At night, he prowls the city streets, hungering for periods in which the crowds are within doors or away from the city. At these times age is a palpable presence. "The City of the Absent," is the title of one essay of the early 1860s which explains that exploration of the city's "deserted nooks and corners...should be made in summer-time, for then the retired spots that I love to haunt are at their idlest and dullest."[53] Unlike 'Dullborough Town,' however, which is characterized by the sleepy boredom of routine and a lack of variety, the deserted city is as fascinating to the observant stroller as the bustle he more typically finds. And significantly, where Dullborough Town is associated with the stroller's childhood, the deserted city offers the variety of sensations produced by old streets persisting through all changes into the present. When the roar of the busy present, always growing, recedes, the quiet of past ages resonates.

A favorite formulation is to explain how something 'was once...but now' has altered. The new does not supplant the old so much as it grafts itself on to it, thus creating the image of a complexly textured age, in which modernizing purposes surround and penetrate old appearances, creating uncanny contrasts. Here, for example, is the famous rooftop at Todger's, from *Martin Chuzzlewit*: "There was a sort of terrace on the roof, with posts and fragments of rotten lines, once intended to dry clothes upon; and

52. Dickens's Journalism, 4: *The Uncommercial Traveller and Other Papers 1859–1870*, ed. Michael Slater and John Drew (London: J. M. Dent, 2000).

53. Ibid. 262.

there were two or three tea-chests out there, full of earth, with forgotten plants in them, like old walking sticks," but now the terrace serves no better purpose than to offer a perspective of the city from a height, the height, or distance suggested by age (*MC*, ch. 9). Like the area in which the Clennam house now rots in *Little Dorrit*, this area too has changed from the "ancient doorway of carved oak, from which, of old, the sounds of revelry and feasting often came; but now these mansions, only used for storehouses, were dark and dull, and, being filled with wool, and cotton, and the like... had an air of palpable deadness about them which, added to their silence and desertion, made them very grim" (*MC*, ch. 9).

In *David Copperfield* Millbank enacts a peculiar kind of obsolescence. It is not simply that the space has succumbed naturally to the effects of time; rather, it has been forced into obsolescence through the careless disregard of the present. David and Mr. Peggotty follow the prostitute Martha through the city streets, into the "narrow water-side street by Millbank." Here the street ends, leaving only houses along the riverside, and "an obsolete old ferry-house" (*DC*, ch. 47). It might be at the edge of the mythical River Styx, or it could be the noxious refuse of industrial development. We seem to be at the divide between nature and civilization. Dickens describes the decay of the place through the accumulation of things, like so many deposits in the primordial mud. As he would come to imagine London's muddy streets in *Bleak House,* so too in this earlier novel Dickens dismisses the thousands of years between the earth's beginnings and the present day:

> The neighbourhood was a dreary one at that time; as oppressive, sad, and solitary by night, as any about London. There were neither wharves nor houses on the melancholy waste of road near the great blank Prison. A sluggish ditch deposited its mud at the prison walls. Coarse grass and rank weeds straggled over all the marshy land in the vicinity. In one part, carcases of houses, inauspiciously begun and never finished, rotted away. In another, the ground was cumbered with rusty iron monsters of steam-boilers, wheels, cranks, pipes, furnaces, paddles, anchors, diving-bells, windmill-sails, and I know not what strange objects, accumulated by some speculator, and grovelling in the dust, underneath which—having sunk into the soil of their own weight in wet weather—they had the appearance of vainly trying to hide themselves. (DC, ch. 47)

It is here, in this repellent atmosphere, that Martha comes to put an end to an intolerable existence. But "here" consists of age upon age, from the earliest infancy of time to the early efforts of industrial manufacture and speculation. Martha momentarily wishes to fling herself into the age, mixing with all ages and becoming part of the gruesome deposit of age itself.

In *Our Mutual Friend* this area is slightly more respectable, but its decay points to the irrelevance of old age rather than to its threatening and festering draw.

> In this region are a certain little street called Church Street, and a certain little blind square, called Smith Square, in the centre of which last retreat is a very hideous church with four towers at the four corners, generally resembling some petrified monster, frightful and gigantic, on its back with its legs in the air. They found a tree near by in a corner, and a blacksmith's forge, and a timber yard, and a dealer's in old iron. What a rusty portion of a boiler and a great iron wheel or so meant by lying half-buried in the dealer's fore-court, nobody seemed to know or want to know...After making the round of this place, and noting that there was a deadly kind of repose on it, more as though it had taken laudanum than fallen into a natural rest, they stopped at the point where the street and the square joined, and where there were some little quiet houses in a row. (*OMF*, II, ch. 1)

No impoverished victim from the 'oldest' profession leads us or the characters here: the place is not deserted but a seething grave. Surprisingly, however, it houses the novel's artist and social critic Jenny Wren along with her friend, and the novel's heroine, Lizzie Hexam. The area is disreputable and grotesque, but its age is consequent upon neglect rather than malign intention; furthermore, it can generate a living rather than an ending. The point is not to associate the area with death, but with the processes of living in and through time, the processes of aging.

Something analogous to "once...but now" is at work in Dickens's use of the phrase "old-fashioned." Whether applied to people, places, or things, the phrase suggests age, but often it describes youth. Little Paul Dombey is old before his time, and thus his quality of being "old-fashioned" makes him a grotesque. But Esther Summerson's old-fashioned ways signify her most modern acquisition of the role of domestic angel. Similarly, in *A Tale of Two Cities*, Tellson's Bank (in the city) and Mr. Lorry (of Clerkenwell) are both old and old-fashioned, but they represent the best hope (future) for settling the revolutionary potential which exploded in the past and threatens the present. In more humorous fashion, Guppy, the aspiring legal clerk in *Bleak House*, is a classic comic fop who appears superannuated when compared to his friend, the younger (but eternally aged) Smallweed. In *Our Mutual Friend* Mrs. Boffin's love of fashion is made quaint when contrasted with Bella Wilfer's initial materialism and Mrs. Lammle's lively trade in the marriage market. Against these examples of modernity, Mrs. Boffin's garish taste appears hopelessly outmoded and therefore hopeful. These rich examples of the inter-mixing of past and present register the complexity of Dickens's syntax of age which extends possibilities for contact between young and old by sifting the traits which might have been assigned only to one or the other. In the jumble of 'old-fashioned' and 'once was' we find a multi-valent response to old age and modernity.

Dickens's treatment of the railway in *Dombey and Son* in the later 1840s demonstrates that a simple regret for lost histories cannot do justice to a more complicated modern temporality: the past now felt as obsolescent, a tumultuous present, and an unknown future. The iron monster brings chaos to Staggs's Garden in Camden Town. Houses are "knocked down; streets broken through and stopped; deep pits and trenches dug in the ground; enormous heaps of earth and clay thrown up..." The passage is a climactic account of the incoherence of modernization. Space has lost its intelligibility: "Everywhere were bridges that led nowhere; thoroughfares that were wholly impassable." Where there once stood a knowable community, however poor, now there is physical upheaval and also social convulsion: the coming of the railways has "wholly changed the law and custom of the neighbourhood." This tableau of disorder in *Dombey and Son* is a *locus classicus* of the emergency of modernity. But it is also the place where Dickens perfects the irony corresponding to his own unstable perspective. The railway derangement is rendered as overwhelming and violent, but it is also misinterpreted by those who endure its first effects. The citizens of Staggs's Gardens take up an "uncommonly incredulous" perspective; they see their wretched homes as making a "sacred grove not to be withered by railroads" (*DS* ch. 6). Transfixed by the originating violence of modernity, they miss its redemptive telos.

The pattern of irony, here and in many other places, depends on first registering the shock of modernity, and then assuming (in order to surpass) the standpoint of the benighted local traditionalists. The railway in chapter 6 of *Dombey and Son* is brutally destructive, but this is because it is "unfinished and unopened." By the time we reach chapter 15, all has changed. The deprivation of Staggs's Gardens has given way to a carnival of prosperity:

> The old by-streets now swarmed with passengers and vehicles of every kind: the new streets that had stopped disheartened in the mud and wagon-ruts, formed towns within themselves, originating wholesome comforts and conveniences belonging to themselves, and never tried nor thought of until they sprung into existence. Bridges that had led to nothing, led to villas, gardens, churches, healthy public walks.

The once skeptical inhabitants now boast of their connection to their new employer, the railway (*DS*, ch. 15). The critique of modernization had been vivid, but in light of Dickens's radical ambivalence, the critique is identified with the ignorant traditionalists and loses force as time and progress unfold. Once irony has exposed the limits of resistance, the railway has launched "upon its mighty course of civilisation and improvement" (*DS*, ch. 15) and *Dombey and Son* warns us not to stand in the way of the Juggernauht.[54]

And yet a telling development in the later fiction is the preservation of aging spaces that will offer the elderly a refuge from young modernity. We have glimpsed this already in the journalism from the 1860s, in which the craving for urban repose counters the appetite for urban unrest. Dr. Manette's London lodgings are exemplary in this regard. He lives off Soho Square, which had been designed in the late seventeenth century, "a quainter corner...was not to be found in London." Manette's corner of Soho assumes the aspect of pastoral:

> There was no way through it, and the front windows of the Doctor's lodgings commanded a pleasant little vista of street that had a congenial air of retirement on it. There were few buildings then, north of the Oxford-road, and forest-trees flourished, and wild flowers grew, and the hawthorn blossomed, in the now vanished fields. As a consequence, country airs circulated in Soho...It was a cool spot, staid but cheerful, a wonderful place for echoes, and a very harbour from the raging streets. (*TTC*, ch. 6)

Critics have too hastily dismissed the importance of the pastoral to later Dickens, though Derek Johnson does demonstrate that throughout his career, Dickens "would constantly relapse into pastoral habits of thought," however occasional and casual they might be.[55] There is no progressive elimination

54. There is a like argument applied to the figure of Carker, the novel's villain. He seems to represent the young generation, plotting to overthrow and usurp the wealth and power of the old. But typically, Dickens complicates the simplicity he introduces: Carker's desire to possess exactly what Dombey owns indicates the limitations of his own modernity. On the other hand, Walter's loyalty to his old Uncle Sol—including his affection for Sol's ways, his friends, and his shop—initially inhibits his understanding of the commercial world into which he is cast. He brings no prior (old) expectations or knowledge with him and thus learns from scratch how to manage a business. Carker's methods may have brought about the commercial bust; it is through *Walter's* expert guidance—a youth tied emotionally but not bound practically—that the firm of Dombey and Son flourishes once again at the novel's end.
55. Derek Johnson, *Pastoral in the Work of Charles Dickens* (Berne: Peter Lang, 1992), 265. See also Northrop Frye, "Dickens: The Comedy of Humors," in *Experience and the Novel*, ed. Roy H. Pearce (New York: Columbia University Press, 1963), 73; Steven Marcus, *From Pickwick to Dombey* (London: Chatto & Windus, 1965), 253; Andrew Sanders, *Dickens and the Spirit of the Age* (Oxford: Clarendon, 1999), 151; Michael Squires, *The Pastoral Novel: Studies in George Eliot, Thomas Hardy, and D. H. Lawrence* (Charlottesville: University Press of Virginia, 1975), 12; Herbert Sussman, *Victorians and the Machine: The Literary Response to Technology* (Cambridge, Mass.: Harvard University Press, 1968), 43.

of the pastoral from the metropolis, only greater fluctuation in the images of aging pockets, some rotting, some pastoral, and many variations of each, contending, thwarting or encouraging intergenerational sympathy and connection. We must take these moments seriously. Dickens fashions an urban pastoral of small scale and limited temporal reach. But despite—or because of—its diminutive size and short span, it serves a crucial narrative function. Metropolitan pastoral does not banish what challenges it; whether by choice or necessity, it incorporates the severities against which it stands and takes pleasure in the contact. It offers no permanence; indeed, its pleasure is sharp in part because we know that this pastoral will be revised, transferred, or even demolished in the next turn of plot. The dimensions of the natural world may be reduced, but its power to kindle the larger world around is undiminished. Thus as a repository for the irritations and anxieties of city life or as the generator of new energies, the urban pastoral, a figure for age, contributes to the revitalization of youthfulness, necessary for urban dwelling.

Mr. Tartar's "garden in the air" (*MED*, ch. 21) replete with runners, mignonette, and wallflower, adorns the staid but somewhat lonely and isolated building in which we find the elderly Mr. Grewgious tucked away:

> Behind the most ancient part of Holborn, London, where certain gabled houses some centuries of age still stand looking on the public way, as if disconsolately looking for the Old Bourne that has long run dry, is a little nook composed of two irregular quadrangles, called Staple Inn. It is one of those nooks, the turning into which out of the clashing street, imparts to the relieved pedestrian the sensation of having put cotton in his ears, and velvet soles on his boots. It is one of those nooks where a few smoky sparrows titter in smoky trees, as though they called to one another, "Let us play at country," and where a few feet of garden mould and a few yards of gravel enable them to do that refreshing violence to their tiny understandings. (*MED*, ch. 11)

Decisive to the force of this image is that the scene of rural peace is hard by the "clashing street," the noise of novelty, the clamor of the brazenly young city. "Let us play at country" is in one sense what Betty Higden resolved, moving outward to avoid the network of urban institutions—workhouse, asylum—prepared to entrap her. Driven back to an old countryside suitable for her great age, she is lucky to have a graceful death. But part of what I mean to suggest is that Dickens, like others at mid-century, tried to imagine a solution other than death for the elderly, and in a place other than the countryside. The importance of Dickens here is that before there could be a public policy for the elderly of the kind that would be sedulously promoted by Charles Booth, there needed to be an imagery to legislate by, and images of flourishing not failing.

In this connection, an evocative passage from *Little Dorrit* deserves to be quoted at length.

> Mrs. Plornish's shop-parlor had been decorated under her own eye, and presented, on the side towards the shop, a little fiction in which Mrs. Plornish unspeakably rejoiced. This poetical heightening of the parlor consisted in the wall being painted to represent the exterior of a thatched cottage; the artist having introduced (in as effective a manner as he found compatible with their highly disproportionate dimensions) the real door and window. The modest sun-flower and holly-hock were depicted as flourishing with great luxuriance on this rustic dwelling, while a quantity of dense smoke issuing from the chimney indicated good cheer within, and also, perhaps that it had not been lately swept. A faithful dog was represented as flying at the legs of the friendly visitor, from the threshold; and a circular pigeon-house, enveloped in a cloud of pigeons, arose from behind the garden-paling. On the door (when it was shut), appeared the semblance of a brass plate, presenting the inscription, Happy Cottage, T. and M. Plornish; the partnership expressing man and wife. No Poetry and no Art ever charmed the imagination more than the union of the two in this counterfeit cottage charmed Mrs. Plornish. It was nothing to her that Plornish had a habit of leaning against it as he smoked his pipe after work, when his hat blotted out the pigeon-house and all the pigeons, when his back swallowed up the dwelling, when his hands in his pockets uprooted the blooming garden and laid waste the adjacent country. To Mrs. Plornish, it was still a most beautiful cottage, a most wonderful deception; and it made no difference that Mr. Plornish's eye was some inches above the level of the gable bedroom in the thatch. To come out into the shop after it was shut, and hear her father sing a song inside this cottage, was a perfect Pastoral to Mrs. Plornish, the Golden Age revived. And truly if that famous period had been revived, or had ever been at all, it may be doubted whether it would have produced many more heartily admiring daughters than the poor woman. (*LD*, II, ch. 13).

In all its whimsy and absurdity, Mrs. Plornish's Happy Cottage celebrates the persistence of pastoral in the midst of urban hardship. The portrait of rural simplicity—thatched cottage, faithful dog, pigeon-house, all enhanced by the ancient song of her aged father—preserves a relic of what London has devoured. The city saturates space and fills in emptiness, but then, improbably, back inside a house within the metropolitan center, there flourishes an Arcadian ritual, the ceremonies of a bygone age.

In a similar light I invoke a luminous moment from *Our Mutual Friend*: the garden lovingly planted on the rooftop of Fledgeby's counting house in the midst of financial London: a garden composed of just a "humble creeper," "a few boxes" of flowers and evergreens within the "encompassing wilderness of dowager old chimneys" (*OMF*, II, ch. 5). In this lineage belongs Miss Flite's threatened flock of birds in *Bleak House*, which grows in *Our Mutual Friend* into the marvelous tropical aviary inside the Harmon house off somber Cavendish Square, an aviary within the phantasmagoria of "gold and silver fish, and mosses, and water-lilies, and a fountain" (*OMF*, IV, ch. 12). Wemmick's Castle in *Great Expectations*, perched defiantly against the creeping metropolis, is another strangely prodigious act of pastoral invention. Squeezed within a spread of "back lanes and ditches," the Castle is a working farm: with its pigs, its fowls, its rabbits, its cucumbers (*Great Expectations*, II, ch. 6). What completes the recovery, of course, the Aged P himself, preserved as if in aspic, at the very margin of life, as a kind of trophy of longevity. These are all sites of deep investment in Dickens, scenes of flourishing where the green world returns to the gray of London.

These places are associated with the past, but they are very much *of* the present. They differ from the Cloisterham of *Edwin Drood* or the Canterbury of *David Copperfield*, both ancient cathedral towns upholding tradition against the tide of modernity. Similarly, they differ from the rural retreats outside of London, like Pickwick's small collective gathered in Dulwich, the similar retirement chosen by the Maylies and Mr. Brownlow at the conclusion of *Oliver Twist*, or even David's birthplace, Blunderstone. Rather, these London 'nooks' represent a creative grafting of new onto old. The 'architects' of these gardens are undistinguished, ordinary citizens whose engagement with their environment encourages the intersection of youth with age, which, for Dickens, is crucial for individual and social health and vitality.

In the novels of the fifties and sixties there are few lyric effusions; more often the pastoral exerts tacit pressure on the narrative and erupts in surprising places. Almost without exception, these sites are associated with old age. The urban pastoral, so emblematic in late Dickens, offers a rejoinder to the raw youth of the present tense, but also a solace to modernity. These settings in the heart of raging, thrusting, uproarious London represent a quite serious "play at country." What I presented earlier as the Betty Higden problem is the problem of a baffled old age, stymied by institutional impasse, driven out of the youth of London in an attempt to die in a manner of its own choosing. The urban pastoral suggests an alternative to impasse, and it does so by presenting an attachment across generations. Miss Flite showing her birds to the young wards of Chancery, Lizzie Hexam and the tiny broken Jenny Wren sitting in the rooftop bower with ancient Riah; Pip and Wemmick tending the Aged P in his garden—in such moments and in such improbable sites we find an affective circuitry between youth and age, which stands precisely as the alternative to classification and institutionalization.[56]

The self-consciously fictive quality to these images of pastoral recovery makes them vulnerable to crass distortion. On the one hand, the novels offer the preservation, in effect, of exhibition spaces—strange inner places where the green past can be rehearsed and performed. But it is after all a short though telling step, from the make-believe of the Plornishes to the grotesque pretensions of the elderly Mrs. Skewton or Lady Tippins. Happy Cottage is a "counterfeit cottage" and the other cases also depend on "poetical heightening" to achieve their peculiar force. If these are examples of the Dickensian conceit of the "pious fraud," we should not forget that the fraudulence is founded on something sacred, here associated with the integrity of endurance through time, or old age. The self-consciousness of Dickensian urban pastoral derives from a distanced perspective associated

56. Notably, these moments of radiant refuge alternate with impostures, when the pastoral is recruited for fraudulent purposes. The sham nature of old Mrs. Skewton, Edith Dombey's mother, is once again a case in point. A synthetic creation herself, nothing more than a mix of cosmetics and wasting bone, Mrs. Skewton is unsparingly satirized for her affectation of green thoughts about green spaces. ("I assure you, Mr Dombey, Nature intended me for an Arcadian. I am thrown away in society. Cows are my passion. What I have ever sighed for, has been to retreat to a Swiss farm, and live entirely surrounded by cows - and china" (*DS*, ch. 21).) Caught within this counterfeit discourse, the pastoral ceases to offer the genial benefit of ancient repose. "Nature" is left as a debased token of fashion, a privileged currency in polite conversation, but lacking any purchase as alternative to the failures of modernization.

Later novels pursue similar terms of satire: Harold Skimpole in *Bleak House* is another elderly person who poses and parades in synthetic pastoral as one who "loves to see the sun shine, loves to hear the wind blow, loves to watch the changing lights and shadows, loves to hear the birds, those choristers in Nature's great cathedral" but who never breaks from the aesthetic frame that converts nature into style. Skimpole, is "very fond of nature, very fond of art," which is exactly the problem (*BH,* ch. 6). The Nature-cult now appears as a sterile aestheticism, a tease and a social ploy, and finally as an attempt to deny the boundaries of age which insist on giving way to the generation below and assuming a different role in the panorama of life's stages the city provides. Mrs. Merdle in *Little Dorrit* brings the absurdity to its highest pitch. "If we were in a more primitive state," she daintily says," if we lived under roofs of leaves, and kept cows and sheep and creatures instead of banker's accounts (which would be delicious; my dear, I am pastoral to a degree, by nature), well and good. But we don't live under leaves, and keep cows and sheep and creatures" (*LD*, ch. 33). Her proviso gives away the truth, without giving away the game. When the old, then, make nature itself an artifice, hoping to prolong youth in a world in which youth is the only currency, we can only wonder at these distortions and look beyond narrative for solutions which might right these wrongs.

with age, and the pleasure it produces relies on its intentional fictionality. 'Harsh reality' is not banished because Dickens's pastoral refuses to retreat or be defeated by it. It is in this way that age becomes a resource against the abrasions of industrialism.

One last tableau belongs in this concluding phase of discussion. We have seen the elderly as beset and encircled, caught within an institutionalizing public world that nevertheless allows narrow maneuvering for those who can devise a "pastoral" resistance to modernity. But at telling and opportune moments a more confirming vision breaks through. The frailty of the aged is suddenly overcome; strength is recovered; the specter regains blood and body. The rousing of the old is a charged and passionate event in the novels. The revival of the failing body, the sudden surprising return of force, the flaring of a fading ember—this is a recurrent and evocative scene. Old Martin Chuzzlewit throws off his weakness, becomes "strong and vigorous" (*MC*, LII) and blazes with moral fury. The frail Dr. Manette returns to Paris and recovers "the kindled eyes, the resolute face, the calm strong look" (*TTC*, III, ch. 4) In the same novel, Jarvis Lorry reanimates his ancient body when he faces the extremes which love and loyalty demand. In *Little Dorrit* Frederick Dorrit suddenly breaks out of his dotage and defends his niece Amy with passionate eloquence; Mrs. Clennam dramatically sheds her hysterical paralysis and moves for the first time in decades. In the last paragraphs of *Our Mutual Friend*, little old Twemlow, timid, inoffensive, and overlooked, rouses himself to support the scandalous marriage of Eugene Wrayburn and Lizzie Hexam. He insists on calling Eugene a gentleman "in the sense in which the degree may be attained by any man" (*OMF*, IV, ch. 17). In the teeth of contempt, Twemlow recalls the old language of gentility in order to make a contemporary demand. These are all luminous incidents within the career of aging, in which Dickens no longer leaves the elderly within their tight circumscription, but ponders the power of the marginal and the resources of the weak.

That his last completed novel ends with the sudden heightening of the long-bent Twemlow suggests just how important the pattern was to Dickens. But it will be equally important to the history that follows. The elderly did not simply recede from view. Although they were often confined to dark spaces and shunted to the margins of life, they continued to exert a pressure on a society that often preferred to ignore them. Then in scenes of great moment, increasing as the century wore on, the elderly rise as they do in the work of Dickens, reminding the young of their continuing force and their unmet claims.

2

Almshouse to Empire: What is 'Enough' for Old Age?

It is a truth universally acknowledged, that Trollope's novels host a more extensive range of characters middle-aged and beyond than other nineteenth-century bodies of fiction. Bradford Allen Booth, for instance, has written that, "It is instructive of Trollope's real interest and genius that it is through his older characters—the Proudies, Archbishop Grantly, Septimus Harding, and Josiah Crawley,—not his young lovers, that he is known," and David Skilton (editor of most of Trollope's novels for the Oxford World's Classics) says what might be applied more generally to the fiction: "With this emphasis on maturity, it is not surprising that Trollope enjoys writing about the middle-aged and the elderly."[1] Famously, Trollope describes his own interest in the aging of characters in the Palliser novels in chapter 10 of the *Autobiography*: "In conducting these characters from one story to another I realised the necessity, not only of consistency...but also of those changes which time always produces....It was my study that these people, as they grew in years, should encounter the changes which come upon us all" (*A*, 154). Altering proportions of 'consistency' and 'change' ensures the versatility of age, which will resist the lure of cliché. In his attentiveness to the elderly Trollope resembles Rembrandt, whom Shaw perceptively characterized as "a fellow who would paint a hag of seventy with as much enjoyment as a Venus of twenty."[2] Trollope does not try to make scarlet from gray, but he does endow grayness with multiple shades. Consider for instance the distance between Monica Thorn, sister to the 50-year-old Wilfred Thorne

1. Anthony Trollope, *An Autobiography* (Berkeley: University of California Press, 1947), p. xi; Anthony Trollope, *Orley Farm* (London: Oxford University Press, 1950), p. xv.
2. G. B. Shaw, *Man and Superman* (1946; repr. Harmondsworth: Penguin, 2000), III, 171.

of Ullathorne, whose greatest "follies" were to exaggerate her brother's nostalgic "foibles," but whose youth remains in the "roseate hue" left on her 60-year-old face, and the "nimble" widow Mrs. Van Siever, "a ghastly old woman" who, at almost 80 years old, tries to manipulate the future even to the extent of marrying the unscrupulous man she tried first to force upon her daughter.[3] Along with Dickens, and each of the figures whose works are analyzed in this study, Trollope demonstrates a heightened awareness of the fact that age, like youth, comes only once to each, but every day may alter the experience of it.

Age is further complicated by the typical distance Trollope's narrators assume from all characters, young and old. As in Dickens, and often elsewhere, narratorial distance achieves the effect of age, since it suggests a comprehensive (and often sympathetic) view of the 'follies and foibles' enacted by the erring characters. And yet Trollope's narrator often ages alongside the characters whose life course he records, and he too is troubled by the sentiments of the elderly. As the narrator observes at the conclusion of *The Last Chronicle of Barset*: "I have been induced to wander among [the inhabitants of Barset] too long by my love of old friendships, and by the sweetness of old faces" (*LCB*, 891), and though he makes no such plea for the reader's generous understanding at the close of the Palliser series, we readily acknowledge a similar emotion and grant the same pardon. Jerome Buckley entitled his classic study of the *Bildungsroman* 'Season of Youth': there is no novelistic form specifically devoted to the growth and development of seniority, but Trollope's fiction suggests that there is a narrative 'season' of age which, if less visible than the main currents, is all the more likely to persist in the undercurrent, quietly agitating from below.

The attitudes of age

Though aging is the common lot, in Trollope's world women generally grow old much sooner than men. Julia Brabazon tries to explain this to Harry Clavering, "Our ages by the register are the same, but I am ten years older than you by the world."[4] In *The Duke's Children* Lady Mab considers becoming the wife of the recently elected House member, Lord Silverbridge, heir to

3. Anthony Trollope, *Barchester Towers*, (Oxford: Oxford University Press, 1962), P196, 194, 196; Anthony Trollope, *The Last Chronicle of Barset* (Oxford: Oxford University Press, 1981), 245, 380.
4. Anthony Trollope, *The Claverings* (New York: Dover, 1977), 2.

the Duke of Omnium. Though they are the same age (he is older by 'weeks'), she wonders "How was it that she was so old a woman, while he was so little more than a child?"[5] She knows it would be expedient to marry him, and he is willing enough, but "He is such a boy. I should always treat him like a boy,—spoiling him and petting him, but never respecting him" (*TDC*, 242). He is aware of her estimate: "Mabel Grex when most sweet to him, when most loving, always made him feel that he was her inferior. She took no trouble to hide her conviction of his youthfulness" (*TDC*, 250). Trollope's *oeuvre* is filled with women—young and old—making paths for young men and helping them to find marital and vocational success, often at their own expense. It is not that this work makes them old, or keeps the men young (although in some instances this may well be so); more important is that it places women in a condition of age and men in the condition of youth. No explicit rule associates women with a particular age, but concerning men, Trollope is less cautious, declaring (in the voice of the bold American young lady Isabel Boncassen): "Indeed there is no such thing as a young man, for a man is not really a man till he is middle-aged" (*TDC*, 260).

Though he is intellectually and rhetorically no match for his famous father, Silverbridge nonetheless manages to "arrive at something near the truth in his inward delineation" of the two women who would marry him. The manner in which he distinguishes between Isabel and Lady Mabel goes some distance in the effort to separate youth from age: "Lady Mabel with all her grace, with all her beauty, with all her talent, was a creature of efforts, or, as it might be called, a manufactured article. She strove to be graceful, to be lovely, to be agreeable and clever. Isabel was all this and infinitely more without any struggle." He elaborates, making clear that the process by which the raw material of British girlhood becomes the product of a mature British woman is itself best characterized as *age*:

> When he was most fond of Mabel, most anxious to make her his wife, there had always been present to him a feeling that she was old. Though he knew her age to a day,—and knew her to be younger than himself, yet she was old. Something had gone of her native bloom, something had been scratched and chipped from the first fair surface, and this had been repaired by varnish and veneering. (*DC*, 544)

Both women are quick, articulate, imaginative and agile, but whereas the American girl is natural and spontaneous, the British woman is labored,

5. Anthony Trollope, *The Duke's Children* (Oxford: Oxford University Press, 1974), ch. 16, 128.

self-crafted. Like James or, for that matter, George Bush's notion of "old" Europe, Trollope adheres to the conventions of his day, which associate degrees of age, first with the continental European cities, then successively, England, Ireland, and America. This is complicated by the sexual typology which classifies women as old as soon as they confront the harshness of their vulnerability in a powerfully masculine society. Marie 'Max' Goesler is 'old,' when she comes to London from Belgium in *Phineas Finn*; English Lady Laura becomes old when she refuses romance in favor of expedience; the Irish Mary Flood Jones (Phineas Finn's first wife) is very young in years and constitutionally. On the other hand, the equable Mrs. Dale (in *A Small House at Allington*) is no longer young in years, though she "could have been as young in heart" as the youths around her for "Women at forty do not become ancient misanthropes; or stern Rhadamanthine moralists, indifferent to the world's pleasures—no, not even though they be widows.…It is not that a woman should call herself in years younger than her father's family Bible will have her to be. Let her who is forty call herself forty; but if she can be young in spirit at forty, let her show that she is so."[6] In other words, if the plot allows her a measure of stability (though poor, Mrs. Dale has managed to maintain her dignity and a home for her family), and her own character is 'willing,' a woman may escape the onset of premature old age.

As we shall see, age is related to the rhythms of plot as much as to calendar time or to traits of character. And since age is subject to narrative vagaries, its manifestation may not accord with the usual process which marks small alterations in the course of time. Frequently, aging eschews process and comes about as the consequence of a sudden occurrence in response to some deeply moving event. Arthur Fletcher realizes that his love for Emily Wharton is not only rejected, but also that his suit can have no favor in the future once she signifies her intention to marry the unworthy Ferdinand Lopez. Trollope registers the intensity of Fletcher's shock by announcing, "He became old in that half hour."[7] And Lady Mary (*The Duke's Children*), forbidden by her father to marry the man she loves, considers: "She had a strong idea that she would ultimately prevail,—an idea also that 'ultimately' should not be postponed to some undefined middle-aged period of her life" (*TDC*, 86). Just as 'ultimately' can be manipulated so that it is (nearly)

6. Anthony Trollope, *A Small House in Allington* (Oxford: Oxford University Press, 1981), 24.
7. Anthony Trollope, *The Prime Minister* (Oxford: Oxford University Press, 1983), I, 155.

at hand, age too can descend or be imposed long before biology would warrant. The demands of narrative, the endowments of character, the biology of time, may each instigate a change in age, and often enough the three are asynchronous. Throughout *An Old Man's Love* (1882), Trollope vacillates when describing what it means for William Whittlestaff to be 50 years old. "You ain't a young man—nor you ain't an old un" his housekeeper, Dorothy Baggett, reminds him.[8] The narrator puts the case more pointedly, though less vividly: "He was not a young man, because he was fifty; but he was not quite an old man, because he was only fifty" (*OML*, 16). Whittlestaff's middle age gravitates towards old age both in his own conception and in that of those around him. Just after he has proposed to her, Mary Lawrie observes him from her window: "she thought that he appeared older than she had ever remarked him to be before" (*OML*, 43). He seems transformed before her eyes: "As she looked at him, he seemed to be older than before" (*OML*, 49). Whittlestaff makes it his purpose to study how he might "make my advanced years fit for your younger life," but she only thinks of him as "not now...so old," before her youthful lover returns to England to claim her hand in marriage (*OML*, 53, 54). In a moment of revealing bafflement, Mary's recently returned lover asks a friend about Whittlestaff: "'Why do you call him old?' said John Gordon. 'Well; I don't know. He is old.' 'Just turned fifty.' 'Fifty is old.'" (*OML*, 98). Trollope is deliberate and self-conscious here; Whittlestaff's personality ages well beyond his years, so that eventually "he knew that he was old of his age" (*OML*, 153) even though he remains 'just fifty.' Similarly, there is no contradiction when we read in *Phineas Redux* that "Mr. Maule was now something about fifty-five years of age, and almost considered himself young."[9] 'Just' and 'almost' qualify the assertions without reversing them, and by shaking their stability make the possibility of counterclaims always possible.

'Fixed' is perhaps the most charged word in Trollopian diction: as a condition or a trait it migrates towards old age. Circumstances which restrict the field of action or habits of thought predictably coincide with aging. For example, the crux of "Why Frau Frohmann Raised her Prices" (1877) hinges on the title character's resistance to change. She wants no departure from the "old ways" and refuses to raise the fee for staying at her inn. Adhering to a "fixed price" becomes an idée fixe, and yet in doing

8. Anthony Trollope, *An Old Man's Love* (Oxford: Oxford University Press, 1991), 5.
9. Anthony Trollope, *Phineas Redux* (Harmondsworth: Penguin, 2003), I, 184.

so, she allows the quality of her service to deteriorate while guests and employees are alike dissatisfied. In the end, Frau Frohmann submits to inevitable change. When she accepts the butcher's sage advice to 'swim with the stream,' the inn thrives and everyone adjusts. "She still felt that the old times were good, and that no other times could be so good as the old times," but she is nonetheless "quite satisfied that she had done the right thing in raising her prices."[10] Just as a 'fixed price' is pernicious, so too a "fixed income" is an evil. Frau Frohmann asks how two elderly women will be able to continue visiting the inn if she raises the fee and is counseled by one of her guests, a Mr. Cartwright:

> "But what of those poor Fraulein Tendels?" she said.
> "Ah, yes," said Mr. Cartwright. "There you come to fixed incomes."
> "To what?"
> "To people with fixed incomes. They must suffer, Frau Frohmann. There is an old saying that in making laws you cannot look after all the little things. The people who work and earn their living are the multitude and to them these matters adjust themselves. The few who live upon what they have saved or others have saved for them must go to the wall." ("Frau Frohmann," 344–5)

Surrendering her own fixity, she raises the price but not for the women who must live with their 'fixed income'; similarly, her daughter can now marry her suitor because, as he tells her, Frau Frohmann agreed to settle "the amount now fixed" for her 'mitgift' (dowry) ("Frau Frohmann," 347).

In *He Knew He Was Right* (1868–9) Trollope pursues the association between age and fixity in both of the novel's plots. Miss Stanbury is almost 60, a fierce Tory whose habits are as entrenched as her opinions are decided. Like Frau Frohmann, she is a landlady who will neither raise nor lower her rents though the economy requires such shifts. And yet the prospect of a future without familial relations prompts her to change: "Now, thus late in life, she was going to make another venture, to try an altogether new mode of living" which will entail having a niece live with her.[11] Louis Trevelyan is still in his twenties, but at the start he becomes fixed in an attitude of jealousy from which he cannot extricate himself. As we have seen, this emotional fixation causes him to 'age' dramatically, though not in terms of the calendar. 'Swimming with the stream' captures the movement of youth just

10. Anthony Trollope, "Frau Frohmann," *The Complete Short Stories*, ii (London: W. Pickering, 1990), 338–9, 348, 353.
11. Anthony Trollope, *He Knew He Was Right* (London: Oxford University Press, 1948), 74.

as fixity implies the paralysis associated with age. A deep and persistent goal in Trollope—at once ethical, political, and psychological—is to maintain the motions of an ongoing life current. The aim is not the preservation of youth, so much as a youth that flows without stoppage toward age, and an age that sustains a mobility that allows for flexible and resilient responses to inevitable change.

If to be old then typically risks fixity, Trollope works to restore variability to this 'fixed period,' by showing how elastic is the terminology of age, and how loosely bound it is to specific traits. The 'fixed period' isn't fixed at all, and 'old' itself differs greatly depending on its modifier, its context, and its referent: 'old enough,' 'too old,' 'old-fashioned,' 'old-hand'—these are just some of the ways that Trollope extends the range and amplifies the density of age.

The most radical consequence of an age-conscious prose is the heightened awareness of the kinds of intimacies exchanged between older characters, or between an older and a younger character. The story in *An Old Man's Love* turns on Mr. Whittlestaff's attempt to marry the daughter whom he has taken into custody for her own protection after the death of "his best beloved friend, Captain Patrick Lawrie" (*OML*, 3). This initiating factor, the death of the friend, is all but buried beneath the matrimonial desires it generates, but we might well say that Whittlestaff mistakes the course which his friend's death precipitates. Because he is just at that unstable age of 50—not yet old but not young—Whittlestaff identifies with the conventions of both novel and culture when he thinks it is marriage that will best suit him. Unable to consult his only friend, and unwilling to address the question with the housekeeper who, but for class, could have served in the Captain's stead, Whittlestaff ineffectually 'discusses' the matter with himself:

> If he can be imagined to have talked to a friend as he talked to himself, that friend would have averred that he spoke more frequently against marriage…than in favour of it. "After all it will never do," he would have said to this friend; "I am an old man, and an old man shouldn't ask a young girl to sacrifice herself." (*OML*, 19)

He does propose to Mary Lawrie nonetheless, and paradoxically it is the unsuccessful proposal to the girl that tips the scale, so that at 50 Whittlestaff becomes the 'old' man of the title. The prospect of marriage ages him, because it is not after all what he most needs. "A quiet life with my book is all that I care for;—with just one other thing" (*OML*, 234) he tells her. But he mistakes the 'other thing' for which he longs. "He was a man who had thought much of love"; he has read Petrarch and medieval romance to find examples, but these are not the models best suited to him (*OML*, 220). He thinks he wants a wife and adheres blindly to this conventional formulation of desire, but what the novel shows throughout is that his need for friendship exceeds romantic desire.

This friendship he obtains in an indirect but illuminating manner. When he releases Mary Lawrie from her promise to marry and tells her young lover that he will not stand in their way, he becomes the elderly 'friend' who becomes the confirming *supplement* to the romance of the young. John Gordon, the proper suitor, writes to Mary of Whittlestaff: "Next to me,—yes, Mary, next to myself, he should be the dearest to you of human beings.... Would that I could look forward to a life in which I would be regarded as his friend" (*OML*, 244). Mary's response to the letter is revealing: "The letter she thought was perfect, but not so perfect as was Mr. Whittlestaff.... When Mary had said to herself that he was of all human beings surely the best, it was to Mr. Whittlestaff and not to John Gordon that she made allusion" (*OML*, 246). Despite her relief, she is determined "to evince a regard for Mr. Whittlestaff, not similar at all to the regard for which she would feel for her husband, but almost equal in its depth" (*OML*, 255), and in replying to her lover, she everywhere indicates her devotion to Whittlestaff (*OML*, 256). In short, an 'old man's love' turns out to be a rival plot, "almost equal" to the marriage plot, and quite as romantic. Moreover, this love from 'above,' this supplement, suggests an insufficiency in the passion of the young, as if youthful love can only fulfill itself when it escapes confinement and diverts some of the affective current to the receptive and sanctioning perspective of age.

In *The Way We Live Now*, Roger Carbury, "not much short of forty," longs to marry his cousin Henrietta, who in turn loves Roger's intimate friend, Paul Montague.[12] Despite his unworthiness, the younger Montague marries the girl, whereupon Carbury decides to leave his entire fortune, including the family estate, to Henrietta and to devote the rest of his life to her happiness. In all the ways we have noted, his fixity becomes the vehicle for his aging, and despite his middle years, he is the oldest character in the novel. Frequently, critics object to the flatness of the two lovers, but if

12. Anthony Trollope, *The Way We Live Now* (London: Oxford University Press, 1951), 47.

their romance is without fire, the friendship between the two men is tense, agitated, ardent. Roger's anger and Paul's remorse give the charged circuit of desire, and Henrietta finds her importance not through marrying either man, but in securing their friendship across a generational divide.

Even in his non-fiction prose Trollope looks everywhere for such friendships. The memoir of Palmerston, for example, records virtually nothing of Palmerston's marital life, but it lingers over the friendship with Lord Melbourne, where again even a small difference in age invites a distinctive style of intimacy:

> In the summer of 1845 Lord Melbourne went out of office, never to come back again, and Lord Palmerston, of course, went with him, having still before him twenty-four years of active official life. Lord Melbourne was only six years his senior, but he died at Brocket Hall in 1848. Lord Melbourne and Lord Palmerston had remained together since 1827, when Lord Melbourne, as William Lamb, was Secretary for Ireland. They had been united in a peculiar manner, each trusting the other, and believing in the other, not simply as Cabinet Ministers, but as friends whose ideas in politics were the same. Though Whig statesmen, they were at heart Conservatives. They afterwards became brothers-in-law.[13]

The most successful attachments in Trollope's fiction, marital or otherwise, are characterized as partnerships in which friendliness is eroticized so that we see it as the object of desire and the motive for relation. The effect is to draw emphasis from the conventional heterosexual youthful couple, and make possible the foregrounding of other types of relations, including that between older people and between people of widely different ages.

Older women frequently perform the office of mentor to younger women, and this, either in addition to, or in place of, the more familiar office of friend, familiar, chaperone, or even mother. In *The Duke's Children*, Miss Cassewary enjoys the vague charge of "looking after Lady Mab" (*TDC*, 72), although here the young woman is so mature that the two often appear to be tending one another. Miss Cass, as she is affectionately called, is a "positive old lady" (*TDC*, 124), who speaks her mind without hesitation or undue modesty, and who allows her charge a great deal of discretion in arranging private conferences with men. The generational difference creates an asymmetry that opens narrative possibilities, even as it permits reciproc-

13. Anthony Trollope, *Lord Palmerston* (1882; repr. New York: Arno Press, 1981), 80. Palmerston married Melbourne's sister.

ity across the markers of age. Repeatedly Trollope presses the implications of age differences, large and small, in order to create the productive uncertainties around root issue of acknowledgment, attachment, and responsibility.

Lady Milborough, in *He Knew He Was Right*, appears a bothersome busybody to Emily and Nora Rowley, but at the close of that novel Nora will have great reason to be thankful for her unselfish regard. With a married daughter living elsewhere, Lady Milborough is alone in London, but throughout the crises of the Rowland sisters, and despite their rather obvious disdain for her, she remains a generous and forgiving friend, whose conservative principle regarding young girls—"Young ladies, according to her views of life, were fragile plants that wanted much nursing before they could be allowed to be planted out in the gardens of the world as married women"—demands her solicitude. Nora may have been rude, "But to Lady Milborough it had seemed to be quite terrible that a young girl should be left alone in the world, without anybody to take care of her" (*HKHWR*, 888). But of course the prospect of an older woman "left alone in the world, without anybody to take care of her" surely is "quite terrible" as well. This is an ethical paradox created by the mix of generational difference alongside mutuality and reciprocity. Giving but not taking, and conspicuous in both acts, Lady Milborough lays bare the conundrum of an old age that is, and is not, within the net of human sociality.

In one of the major plot lines of the novel, Aunt Stanbury self-consciously attempts to conduct her life on the unsteady field of generational paradox. A "little woman, now nearly sixty years of age," she searches out a younger person for whom she might care and find in return a regard for herself. But this pursuit provokes visible conflict between old and young(er). "I suppose young women always think it best when they can get their own ways. An old woman like me has only got to do what she is bid" (*HKHWR*, 64, 774–5), she tells her niece, but the plot declines to follow the simple dictum. In fact, Priscilla insists on her ways and becomes 'old' (but not decrepit) because of it, whereas Aunt Stanbury *is* old, but becomes, not young, but youthful in her resistance and resourcefulness. The community marks the change, but mistakes the name which best characterizes it: "Miss Stanbury at this time was known all through Exeter to be very much altered from the Miss Stanbury of old;—or even from the Miss Stanbury of two years since.... Some said that she was becoming old, and that she was going out like the snuff of a candle" (*HKHWR*, 838). But her earlier insistence on 'her own way' is another way of referring to the fixity of years, whereas her new flexibility and pliancy ensure a future of open and evolving relations. What she perceives as failure the novel parades as success.

> She would sit thinking of the circumstances of her own life and tell herself that with her everything had failed. She had loved, but had quarrelled with her lover; and her love had come to nothing—but barren wealth. She had fought for the wealth and had conquered;—and had become hard in the fight, and was conscious of her own hardness. In the early days of her riches and power she had taken her nephew by the hand,—and had thrown him away from her because he would not dress himself in her mirror. . . . Now she was seeking to appease her self-accusations by sacrificing everything for the happiness of her niece and her chosen hero; but as she went on with the work she felt that all would be in vain, unless she could sweep herself altogether from off the scene. (*HKHWR*, 839)

She offers her house to the newlyweds and prepares either to move away or live with them as a guest. But then, out of affection rather than ineptitude, Dorothy returns the household keys to her aunt and insists that she will be content to let her continue to 'rule' the house.

In a similar fashion, Lady Milborough finds a more-than-daughter in Nora, who swears "a solemn silent vow of friendship for the dear old woman," and whose marriage palls next to the satisfactions of this tie: "It was astonishing how enthusiastic and how loving the elder and the younger lady were together" (*HKHWR*, 890). Nora's sister Emily (wife of Louis Trevelyan), and Dorothy's sister Priscilla, both live out the less happy scenario. By the end of the novel, Emily is but a shadow of the young girl she was two years earlier. When her dying husband suggests that, being still young, she may remarry, Emily's denial speaks not of love but of age: "'Never,' she said, with a shudder" (*HKHWR*, 921); and after his death, when she is endowed with enough money to ensure her comfort, she again rejects the possibility of remarriage "Anything but that!" The narrator confirms her attitude "We all know that widows' practices in this matter do not always tally with wives' vows; but, as regards Mrs. Trevelyan, we are disposed to think that the promise will be kept" (*HKHWR*, 928). She will be a mother, a sister, and a friend, but she is 'old' before her time and will remain so until the years catch up to her experience.

Unlike the other younger women, Priscilla Stanbury is associated with age from the start and is never a candidate for marriage. She is introduced as "the elder daughter" (the younger is 26), even "older" than her brother

Hugh (28), and the words adhere to her, though she cannot have reached an age to justify them (*HKHWR*, 71). Priscilla anticipates the strength to live on "forty years, perhaps, and probably the greater portion of that absolutely alone" after the death of her mother. But when her younger sister Dorothy protests, "'No;—you'll be with us then,'" inviting her to live with the family she is just then starting, Priscilla refuses, preferring "a hole of my own" to the shared company of well-wishers (*HKHWR*, 913–14). Trollope speaks only half in jest when he salutes Priscilla at the close, saying "something should be at least attempted for Priscilla Stanbury, who from the first has been intended to be the real heroine of these pages" (*HKHWR*, 826). Something *has* been done for her: she has been allowed to choose an independent spinsterhood and the courage to face old age without fear or loneliness. She will be alone, but not lonely. Thus without explicitly taxing the conventional representation of relations between young and old women, the novel manages to address the reversal *as if* it had specifically set out to study the problem.

Of course the most celebrated friendship in Trollope's fiction is that between Mr. Harding and the Bishop, who "loved each other warmly," and were in fact "all in all to each other." That it exists at all is notable, but that Trollope takes pains to show its small kindnesses, its gentle pressure and finely wrought generosities is what makes this remarkable friendship more memorable than the marital romances which dominate the plots of his novels. Furthermore, the narrator's distance from the romances results in a characteristic blend of irony and sympathy, even sentimentality, whereas the narratorial tone typical of the friendships between two older people or between an older and a younger person may be slightly wistful, but rarely ironic. Here is the penultimate paragraph of *The Warden*:

> Every other day a message is brought to [Mr. Harding] from the bishop. "The bishop's compliments, and his lordship is not very well to-day, and he hopes Mr. Harding will dine with him." This bulletin as to the old man's health is a myth; for though he is over eighty he is never ill, and will probably die some day, as a spark goes out, gradually and without a struggle. Mr. Harding does dine with him very often, which means going to the palace at three and remaining till ten; and whenever he does not the bishop whines, and says that the port wine is corked, and complains that nobody attends to him, and frets himself off to bed an hour before his time.[14]

14. Anthony Trollope, *The Warden* (London: Oxford University Press, 1969), 37, 283–4.

The simple rhythms and unornamented diction, the spare action and slight dissimulation all work towards the elegance of transparency: in this case, age permits the luxury of unwinding the knots of both embroiled youth and complex plotting. Like the marriage plot, this happy union produces closure in the novel, but unlike the former, from which issues an impermeable membrane (the couple, or at most the family), such friendships generate the possibility of continued sociality until 'death do us part.' In such modest and unpretentious fashion Trollope radically revises the protocols of narrative. He offers a change in plot—from the romance of courtship and marriage to the romance of cross-generational friendship—and this change transforms a fictional design, by altering the rhythms of plot and the terms of finality.

Enough is enough

Being old seems a far cry from becoming 'old enough,' but Trollope entwines the two, and from the entanglement there issues a thick description of generational conflict indispensable to understanding the condition of the Victorian elderly. In *Mr. Scarborough's Family*, old Mr. Scarborough corrects the young Harry Annesley's naive assertion that "there is enough" family fortune for father and sons to share: "There is no such word in the language as enough," he admonishes.[15] As *The Claverings* opens, Julia Brabazon tells her erstwhile lover that her honesty ought to be 'enough' for him, but he briskly repudiates the suggestion: "Enough! Indeed it is not. From what you know of me, do you think it likely that that will be enough?" (*C*, 2). "Enough" is another charged word in Trollopian semantics, and its particular relevance to age extracts an additional nuance. 'Old enough' may imply criticism: a person's age ought to have taught some useful rule or principle which the character has failed to absorb. Trollope also uses the word to imply entitlement, as in 'old enough' to drink or dance or drive. In a similar vein, the phrase sometimes indicates the necessary amount before something else can obtain; more might be better, but less would be too little. Reflecting on her own past, and comparing it to her daughter's present, Lady Glencora is said to be "old enough now to see all this and to appreciate it" (*DC*, 20). Age which is 'old enough' permits vision, comprehension, and sympathy; it is not at all the same thing as simply being old. For most characters, the achievement of this condition is temporary, since living in

15. Anthony Trollope, *Mr. Scarborough's Family* (London: Dover, 1988), 74.

time always imposes new imperatives which unsteady any equilibrium. When death comes, characters are caught somewhere in the dense midst of living.

Septimus Harding is the exception: in his old age he manages to reach a poise, where he becomes 'old enough' to achieve reconciliation, equilibrium, and even a joy mixed with gentle resignation. He is not waiting to die, but when death comes, he is prepared. Nowhere is the distinction between the emotions of character and reader more clearly marked than in the portrait of Harding's old age. "It was sometimes sad enough to watch him as he sat alone" (*LCB*, 512), Trollope intones, and indeed the images of Harding's gradual loss of faculty, his consciousness of increasing incapacity, and his refusal of dependency all make for sadness enough—enough to fill the eyes and then some. But Harding experiences no such sentiment. The reader may be "sad enough," but Harding is 'old enough,' old enough to prefer solitude rather than to suffer the sympathy of others, old enough not to dwell on loss, incapacity, restriction, but instead to ask "What was there left to him now in the world?" (*LCB*, 520), and to search until he found images which could answer:

> What was there left to him now in the world? Posy [his granddaughter] and cat's-cradle! Then, in the midst of his regrets, as he sat with his back bent in his old easy-chair, with one arm over the shoulder of the chair, and the other hanging loose by his side, on a sudden there came across his face a smile as sweet as ever brightened the face of man or woman. He had been able to tell himself that he had no ground for complaint,—great ground rather for rejoicing and gratitude.

Harding's son-in-law, the Archdeacon Grantly, puts the case in typically blunt fashion: "As the bodily strength fails and the power of control becomes lessened, the natural aptitude of the man pronounces itself more clearly" (*LCB*, 829). Aging here involves a distillation of character, an essence revealed through the disencumbering of other capacities. Although he achieves the rare distinction which being 'old enough' can endow, Harding is no more heroic in death than he was when, in the first of the Barsetshire novels, he eschewed rank, position, and income out of an instinctive moral reflex. Trollope reminds us of this earlier episode at the moment of his death as a warning not to make of this exemplary man's experience a pattern or guide to conduct. The Archbishop Grantly, who had vigorously opposed Harding's resignation in *The Warden*, now replies to his wife's query, "But he was right?" with qualified approval: "'As Septimus Harding he was, I think, right; but it would have been wrong in any other man'" (*LCB*, 861). Harding dies quietly, as he had lived. He tells his favorite daughter Eleanor not to weep when he dies since he is "full of years,—full of hope." Attended by the grandchild and children whom he has loved, his last words are a reinscription of the concept 'enough': "There is nothing left for me to wish, my dears;—nothing" (*LCB*, 834). He says it to his daughters and repeats it, verbatim, to his sons-in-law. Nothing is not emptiness; it is rather "full," or, in the language of age, 'enough.' The widow Mrs. Greenow, of *Can You Forgive Her?* sagely advises her younger niece that "enough is as good as a feast" (*CYFH?*, 664).

How are we to understand this new paradox? In the same way that he juxtaposes political antipathies in order to arrive at some equilibrium in his political convictions—he calls himself an "advanced conservative-liberal"—so Trollope disrupts the contrast between nothing and everything in order to arrive at the notion of 'enough.' This is no sleight of hand. Trollope wants to capture the long range of age and locate it on the short scale of fulfillment. Excess seems desirable from the youthful position of want. Had the old men in Hiram's Hospital been 'old enough,' they would have seen that their meager weekly sixpence was, like Harding's annual £800, 'enough.' But inspired by the young and fiery John Bold, they are encouraged to demand more. As Dickens puts it in "Titbull's Alms-Houses": "to get a little help is to get a notion of being defrauded of more" (*UT*, 289–90). The principle of fairness cannot provide 'enough' for the old pensioners, and so they die or live miserably. The point is not that old age requires resignation, so much as it demands a clear-sighted response to the question "What was there left for him now?" What is there *now*—now in the present, now at hand, now at this age and in these circumstances—that can satisfy? The characters for whom old age is most rewarding do not fix their hopes on a revival of past pleasures or on the promise of eternity: for them, even as they are about to depart, it is 'enough' to experience the satisfactions right before them, to dedicate themselves to whatever flourishing this world allows.

Age, we have seen, always raises questions of category and concept in Trollope, questions of vocabulary and syntax. It incites a verbal play that registers the plasticity in his view of aging. For example, Lord Nidderdale is described as "a middle-aged young man" and Adolphus Longstaff is "a young man of about thirty-five years of age" in *The Duke's Children* (*TDC*, 51, 93). Lord Ongar, in *The Claverings*, is small, bald, weak and thin, "The Peerage said that he was thirty-six...but any one would have declared him to be ten years older" (*DC*, 26), and by Trollope's descriptions, we easily might add another few decades. He is a young man who is old. Clearly the aim is not to produce idle verbal paradox, so much as to excavate new meanings for life in time.

"It seems to me that age does not go by years," Emily Wharton advises her persistent suitor, Arthur Fletcher, who is five years older than her, but still "quite young" in her estimation, though "It is long since I have felt myself to be an old woman" (*PM*, II, 292). Chronology is patently too restrictive, but when numerical and descriptive reports meet, a more subtle and flexible account of age is possible. In this way we can appreciate the full import of Silverbridge's estimate of his father. When Lady Mab offers hope that in time he may become an energetic public servant like his famously hard-working father, the boy is honest enough to reject youth and age as the terms of his development. "As far as I can learn," he confesses, "he was just as he is now at my age" (*TDC*, 125). What better way to characterize Plantagent Palliser than to say that he has been 'old' in manifold ways since he was a young man?

Almshouses and the aged

The instability of age, its unpredictable arrival, its uncertain measure, its deep ambiguity in individual lives, and its charged semantic ambiguities in the notion of 'enough'—all have a social counterpart in the almshouse movement which gathered fresh impetus in the nineteenth century. Established as early as the fourteenth century, Almshouses had been chiefly associated either with the Church or with particular guilds. But only in the seventeenth century was a secure link forged between the houses and the elderly.[16] In 1601 the Statute of Charitable Uses placed the old first in its description of those for whom charitable trusts were intended—"For the relief of aged, impotent and poor people"—and such preference was now marked in the individual trusts.[17] The first private charity to endow almshouses after the Reformation was Queen Elizabeth's College in Greenwich, whose charter indicated that "He who is become aged and which having before time been a labourer is now past work and labour shall first and before any other be chosen. After the aged in order the disabled, either by sickness or war—service or accident, the blind, the victims of robbery, fire or shipwreck, the continually sick or anyone over charged with a burden of children."[18] In time, separate institutions for the poor, the sick, the insane, and the elderly were established, though a prospective candidate frequently qualified in more

16. Jane Ellis, *The London Almshouses: Six Centuries of Housing for the Aged* (London: The Housing Centre, 1945), 2.
17. Neil Burton, *The Geffrye Almshouses* (London: Inner London Education Authority, 1979), 11.
18. Ellis, *The London Almshouses*, 3–4.

than one category, and, as we saw in the last chapter, assignment to institutions was often less determined by individual need than by official convenience.

In their nineteenth-century incarnation, almshouses occupied a transitional (and especially illuminating) place between the large institution and the domestic unit. They stand in the position of 'good enough,' providing a sufficiency of care outside the framework of family or workhouse. Neither private homes nor (for the most part) vast public institutions, they were administered largely by private charities. Moreover, they were most often explicitly founded *for the sake of the beneficiaries* rather than for the salvation of the souls who stipulated that their names be said in daily prayer by the bedesmen who received rooms on condition of this service. Of course, once emphasis falls on the recipients, and when the number of possible candidates exceeds the numbers of places available, the question of admittance becomes paramount. Here we should recall that although the political economists who devised the New Poor Law in 1834 are often held accountable for the notorious principles that attempted to separate 'deserving' from 'undeserving' poor, the distinction had a longstanding tradition. In one original charter we find the exhortation that help was to be available to "the brethren and sisteren if [their distress was] caused by fyr or water, the ves or sycknesse or any other hap so it be not on himselfe along ne through his own wretchedness."[19] But though similar in structure, these earlier notions of compensatory aid never encountered the dispossessed masses, whose need resulted in part from accelerated industrialization and from slight improvements in mortality rates. By the mid-nineteenth century, the question of desert was crucial, whether or not it was associated with the causes of economic distress. There were all too many poor old men and women, but how poor and how old were shifting criteria. Most almshouses named 50, 55, or 60 as the earliest age for occupancy, and their charters included instructions on the right to dismiss spouses and (if applicable) the children of pensioners who died. Establishing economic criteria was more difficult. In fact, as the century progressed, many almshouses became domiciles for those whose gentle status was threatened by economic distress, rather than for those who belonged to the under- and working classes. Beginning in the 1840s the Geffrye Almshouses required that all candidates for admission had claim to at least five shillings a week, a stipulation leading Neil Burton to note that "This regulation had a significant effect on the social composition of

19. Ellis, *The London Almshouses*, 1.

the Foundation, bringing in an increasing number of occupants who could be loosely described as genteel." Indeed, Burton argues that "an increasing number of the applicants for charity were women of genteel upbringing and of the same social class as the members of the Committee [of overseers and administrators] themselves."[20] When the age and social status of the givers became even remotely connected to that of the almsfolk, then the paradox of the situation is exposed most radically.

In *The Warden* the expression of this paradox takes another form. The income of the almshouse derived from the founding estate unexpectedly flourishes. I have referred already to John Bold's incitement of the bedesmen, giving them reason to hope that in light of the rising income each might be granted as much as a hundred pounds a year, and, as importantly, giving them grounds to criticize the Warden's claim to his annual eight hundred pounds rather than to a more modest two to three hundred. When the original donors no longer control the provision, the recipients see an opening for questioning not only the amount, but also the very basis of charity. Mrs. Mitts, a "tidy widow" who plays informer to the narrator of "Titbull's Alms-Houses," explains the cause for irritability among her fellow pensioners:

> "Well, whether the gentlemen really do deprive us of any little matters which ought to be ours by rights, I cannot say for certain; but the opinion of the old ones is they do. And Mr. Battens he do even go so far as to doubt whether credit is due to the Founder. For Mr. Battens he do say, anyhow he got his name up by it and he done it cheap." (*UT*, 293)

Dickens often probes the motivations behind charity—even Mr. Jarndyce's charitable impulses are submitted to a fairly severe scrutiny. But here we see how the fantasy of gratitude is replaced by the plausibility of suspicion once provision is exposed as fluid, unfixed, and variable. What is a fair income for the administrators and pensioners? To put the question in such terms is to conjoin classes on a horizontal rather than a vertical axis, which threatens both an established social hierarchy and the hierarchy of donor and recipient. Recast in this manner, who is to say that the trustees, or even the bequestor himself or herself, might not be closely related to the classes and types of people from whom they believed themselves to be disassociated? We learn of egregious transgressions committed by high officiators: the malefactions associated with clerics from St. Rochester's Cathedral and Winchester Hospital of St. Cross were the exciting

20. Burton, *The Geffrye Almshouses*, 38, 37.

germs of Trollope's story, but those were only the highly publicized, sensational incidents. When, partially in response to these infamous and exceptional scandals, the Charitable Trusts Act was passed in 1853, followed by the appointment of Charity Commissioners whose task it was to monitor the administration of charities, the problem remained unresolved. The Commissioners could ensure that those at the top didn't exploit those for whom the charities were intended, but could they also ensure some measure of fairness among the houses and their variously provisioned inmates? In his study *Almshouses*, Brian Bailey relates the case of one hospital at York which "had so much income in relation to its number of inmates that each of them received £94 a year around 1849, which was deemed by Lord Brougham's committee 'an income unnecessarily and mischievously large for persons in that station of life.'" Bailey argues that "The Charity Commission...[did] its best to bring some order to the chaos of private charity, which had inevitably resulted in some old folk living in relative luxury while others barely had the means of subsistence," but we might also note that in ensuring greater equality among recipients of all charities, the Commission also reinscribed the familiar class distinctions which such charitable institutions had threatened to subvert.[21] The Geffrye Almshouse Charter stipulated an annual payment of £6 which was increased in 1810 to a maximum of £16, but "As the nineteenth century progressed the basic pension was improved by a series of small bequests, until, by the end of the century, free inmates received an average of £2719.*s.* 3*d* per year, and the non-free inmates £29 2*s* 2*d*."[22] To be sure, these figures represent tightly constrained incomes, but they do begin to approach the margins of bare respectability. Indeed, after mid-century it was not uncommon to find among the 'inmates' retired governesses, schoolmistresses, and others of respectable professions alongside the trades which conventionally provided for their own.[23] Burton quotes one Matron who reported to a public enquiry in 1908 that "the great majority [of pensioners] are persons who have been accustomed to refinement either in homes of their own or in some other capacity in the houses of others."[24]

One of the vexing issues surrounding admission came to be the proportion of inmates who were "free" or "non-free" (bound by trade). Furthermore, whatever their experience of work had been in the past, pensioners usually were encouraged to supplement their income by any means which did not involve trade within the confines of their quarters. The truly destitute

21. Brian Bailey, *Almshouses* (London: Robert Hale, 1988), 183.
22. Burton, *The Geffrye Almshouses*, 37–8. 23. Ibid. 24. Ibid. 38.

found no hospitality from the almshouses: many regulations stipulated that candidates must never have accepted parish aid and that they must have contributed to the parish coffers themselves for some period of time. The London Almshouses were established "to afford a permanent asylum to aged and decayed freemen and householders of London and its environs...whose circumstances have become reduced, not through their own extravagance, idleness, or wilful default"; their protocol stipulated that applicants must provide "a certificate testifying character and general good conduct" which was signed either by the parish Clergyman or Churchwarden, by a "dissenting Minister and two substantial householders of the parish," by the "Alderman and two householders of the Ward where he or she shall have resided for two whole years, or by four substantial householders."[25] In addition, some almshouses required supplementary forms of verification, such as a signed letter confirming that the parish would readmit the pensioner in the case of death (for burial fees) or expulsion. The persistent attempt was to reward and sustain the barest respectability, rather than to create the conditions for achieving it.

Of course even these carefully delineated goals were not always attained. The stigma of the Workhouse transferred to the Almshouse despite efforts to maintain a strict line of social distinction between them. Dickens's Mr. Mell is an illuminating case in point. His mother's situation as a pensioner is made public through David Copperfield's indiscretion, the revelation becoming the grounds for dismissal of her son, a lowly schoolmaster at Mr. Creakle's Salem School. Mell's questionable respectability is decisively compromised by his mother's dependence, despite the fact that his miserable wages make it impossible for him to care for her himself. In the exposure scene, the malign headmaster and school proprietor Mr. Creakle pretends that the respectability of his school would be sullied by employing the son of an almswoman. When Mell concedes the truth of Steerforth's charge—that his mother "lives on charity in an alms-house"—Creakle demands that the poor schoolmaster announce publicly that this disgrace was never reported to himself.

> "I believe not directly," [Mr. Mell replies, but] "I apprehend you never supposed my worldly circumstances to be very good...You know what my position is, and always has been, here."
>
> "I apprehend, if you come to that," said Mr. Creakle, with his veins swelling again bigger than ever, "that you've been in a wrong position altogether, and mistook this for a charity school. Mr. Mell, we'll part if you please. The sooner the better." (Dickens, *DC*, ch. 7)

25. *The Institution of the London Almshouses. Instituted 1832* (London: W. Marchant, 1833).

At this moment, most readers feel as indignant as Tommy Traddles and as sorry as David Copperfield, but a characteristic edge sharpens Dickens's sentimentality in his rendering of almshouse life. It is only when the young David, just come to London on his way to Salem House, admits to Mr. Mell that he is about to collapse from sheer hunger and exhaustion that the latter decides to bring him to his mother's, so that the boy might eat a quiet meal while he himself steals the chance for a visit. Though David professes confusion and weariness "beyond description," he nonetheless astutely takes note that the house "was part of some alms-houses, as I knew by their look, and by an inscription on a stone over the gate, which said that they were established for twenty-five poor women" (*DC*, ch. 5). The old age of the pensioner is coupled with the diminutive stature of her surroundings: the "little black doors" and "little diamond-paned window(s)" that welcome the guests to the "little house." A revealing likeness to Mr. Peggotty's 'little' boat grows when one finds inside a Mrs. Fibbitson, whose irascible disposition and selfish claim to the fire evokes the portrait of the elderly Mrs. Gummidge who depends on Mr. Peggotty's generosity. But this is no Yarmouth romance for the young David: it is a London education. Mrs. Mell lovingly dotes upon her son as, at her request, he attempts (unsuccessfully) to play the flute while the over-tired boy absorbs the scene as if a dream. But compared to the respectable old age and poverty of Mrs. Gummidge this scene appears tawdry and even macabre, despite the genuine emotions exchanged between mother and son. It is as if in such a context—institutional charity instead of privately preserved independence—even Dickens's treasured domestic affections lose their glow. Whereas the Peggotty boat-house is not only new to David, but an original even within its type, Mrs. Mell and her situation are metynomically represented in the singular, even as they are understood to be samples repeated twenty-five times. Mrs. Mell herself is just "one of these poor old women," and David knows they have arrived at their destination when Mr. Mell "lifted the latch of one of a number of little black doors that were all alike, and had each a little diamond-paned window on one side, and another little diamond-paned widow above" (*DC*, ch. 5). Mrs. Gummidge complains, but Mrs. Fibbitson shakes her fist angrily at David, presaging the rage of Mr. F's aunt more fully than reminding us of Mrs. Gummidge's pitiable querulousness. The decline into charity here makes even love sound 'off-key,' and makes generosity appear weak before the strength of self-interest.

Some trades, it is true, assured a notably higher quality of almshouses than one could find through local parishes. Even so, the houses shared with other institutions the problem of providing care beyond the shelter of walls and beyond the ground of mere subsistence. Bold's incitement of the bedesmen in *The Warden* throws into relief Harding's involvement in their lives, his concern for them and his efforts to provide what comfort he can in the form of conversation, sympathy, and musical entertainment. These are the small ways in which he can give something to the men. The economic perspective that Bold introduces to the bedesmen initially makes these efforts seem pitiful at best, deceptive at worst. Knowingly or unknowingly, Harding's little generosities have served only to divert the men from understanding their larger 'rights.' But for Trollope the new irony quickly gives way to another, as the narrative takes pain to suggest that Harding's gift of culture surpasses the merely material gain offered by Bold. Trollope bestows on Harding a humility that makes him unable even to see how exceptional a 'warden' he has been, and that far from being undeserving of the income he has received, his small acts of good—seen by few though felt by many—amount to something more precious than his salary. Some of the pensioners eventually realize this; some do not. Harding never *feels* vindicated, though certainly Trollope vindicates him in no uncertain terms.

Left to themselves, as most pensioners were (apart from whatever tasks they were expected to perform), many of the beneficiaries, it is clear, fell into a kind of petty squabbling that stood for 'society' in these communities. In one resonant instance, the program of a London almshouse found the need to specify the prohibition of "blasphemous words, or any railing, bitter or uncharitable expressions to any other of the Almsmen or Almswomen, or any other person; nor shall any of them give any blow, or otherwise assault another."[26] In the case of Harding, although he never consciously intended to instill fellow-feeling among his constituents, Trollope clearly means this to be the effect of his benevolent presence upon the old men in Hiram's Hospital. Without him, their little community quickly falls apart. The residents in Dickens's Titbull's Almshouse similarly quarrel, spy on one another, gossip, and divide.

With little pleasing society near at hand, and with even less access to a wider sociality, pensioners could suffer from the lack of stimulation found in other, more austere forms of elder care. Of course this lack of stimula-

26. See *The Rules and Orders made by the Worshipful Company of Armourers and Brasiers, To Be Observed By All Persons admitted into, and inhabiting, the Company's Almshouses, situated in Bishopsgate Street Without, London* (London: Waterlow & Sons, 1879), 7–8.

tion manifests itself in quite different ways. Among the uneducated or illiterate, it often appeared in the form of listlessness, indifference, or lethargy. And in those who had exercised their intellectual capacities before entry, life in the almshouse often encouraged dissatisfaction, brooding reflection, jealousies, regrets. These reactions take many nuanced forms both in the records of actual almspeople and in literature. Augusta Webster's dramatic monologist "In An Almshouse" begins in an elegiac mood which starts to disintegrate even by the close of the initial stanza. The beauty of a summer evening, with which he opens, is clearly something apart from himself, which is where he 'ends.' The natural beauty makes him grateful for what he once had and hopeful for what might be after death, but in the 'here and now' of the summer evening in a small country almshouse, he positions himself apart from, outside of, shut out from, maybe even in opposition to, the beneficent world that stretches well beyond him. Overcome too soon by "swift decrepitude," the retired teacher is now "the grey-haired palsied man" who suffers from partial blindness, deafness, and feeble limbs. "That far world…my world once" becomes the subject for lament: he regrets that he didn't make more of his chances: "Ah, why was I too weak for such a life, | which once I might have chosen?" he asks (stanza 8). Having wasted his time in "Dreams, dreams!" (stanza 10), he missed the "days | I should have lived in: I came out of date" and now recognizes that "he who is thrown out in a fierce race | can hardly chide," if "the others ran too fast. | And if, as for me, if I grow old alone, | hid out of memory of springtime peers, | and have my roof and food by dead men's alms" he has only himself to blame. Self-castigation or the recriminations of others are the frequently twinned possibilities left to those who have no action beyond self-reflection.

The cultural representation of age and charity has its own twinning and doubleness. It moves between the critical force of documentation and a tonally unsteady affirmation of alternative practices of treating the elderly. The physical separation of the aged—whether in private rooms or institutional enclosures—meant that images circulated only erratically. It also meant that novels had significant effects on the social understanding of the problems epitomized by almshouse philanthropy. Dickens's Mrs. Gummidge, the irascible old lady whose presence seems dissonant in Mr. Peggotty's household, deserves more attention within this context. We have seen that, like Mrs. Fibbitson, Mrs. Gummidge appropriates the best place by the fire when David Copperfield comes to visit and that she complains bitterly about her sufferings which are deep and many. David wonders about her presence in the house, as well might many readers. But the force of her example is to show that, within the circle of domesticity, even the provocations of age can be muted and then healed. Mr. Peggotty endures her irascibility by remembering her loss, and he responds to her complaints with an unbroken, even relentless, sympathy. Mrs. Gummidge's conversion is one of the most encouraging comic reversals the novel offers: in the face of the 'real' tragedy of Emily and Steerforth, and with the prospect of breaking up the self-constituted 'family,' Mrs. Gummidge sheds her bad humor like a long-worn cloak and emerges altogether lighter, brighter, and full of energy. In a charged phrase she warns Mr. Peggotty that "I shall go into the House and die, if I am not took" (*DC*, ch. 51). The moment not only stands as a reminder of Mrs. Gummidge's fated end in the Workhouse if Mr. Peggotty had not absorbed her within his domestic world, but it also suggests how part of the work of the mid-century novel was to generate a counter-world to institutional degradation of the kind suffered by Mrs. Fibbitson in the almshouse. When Emily's emergency supervenes, Mrs. Gummidge, who had been emotionally sustained by close affection, flings her selfishness aside and assumes the strenuous burden of new responsibilities. Now, "Mrs. Gummidge was happy" (*DC*, ch. 51). Indeed, having been introduced in the gloomy tones of personal tragedy, as the perpetually grieving widow, she experiences the regeneration of comedy. Reports of her new life in Australia produce gales of laughter in David, and even in Agnes when, at the close, Mr. Peggotty explains how she upturns a bucket on a poor ship's cook who dared to propose to her. Less comically and more earnestly, the narrative records that, despite the hardships of emigration, Mrs. Gummidge has never been anything but "the willingest, the trewest, the honestest-helping woman…as ever draw'd the breath of life" (*DC*, ch. 63). The force of Mr. Peggotty's influence is such that all in the orbit of need may be included—even, in this case, Mr. Mell, who ends up with his aged mother, flourishing in Australia as they never could in England. "Australia" in *David Copperfield* functions as a space of open possibility, and for the aged it serves as counterpart and complement to the affective labor of the family circle. The declining Mrs. Gummidge remained open to recovery only because of the ample Peggotty-resources of personal acknowledgment and the repeated rituals of sympathy and care. The sheer narrative work involved in noticing her, healing her, and then freeing her to enjoy the regenerative power of Australia suggests the difficulty in imagining an alternative curve of age. The anti-institutional critique of *David Copperfield* depends on a massive emotional (and literary) attention to the individual case with all its intractable singularities. Indeed the work not only of this novel, but of many others at mid-century, is to suggest that a flourishing old age depends on such sustained attention to the particularity of individual lives.

For the Victorians, however, aging now occurred as a mass event that could scarcely be solved one case at a time. Here we return to the question of admission (and exclusion) in an institutional setting such as the almshouse. The degree of care was decided in large part by the capacity of the donor(s) to give, but it was complicated by the diverse social positions of the inmates. As we have seen, any fair appraisal of the conditions of poverty must include a wide social tranche from chronic dispossession to the fringes of respectability, and when people from such diverse positions were brought together in one space, temptations for discord opened. Furthermore, since many almshouses were affiliated with professions and guilds, the varying work-status of the candidates also became a source of potential friction. And then there were the social (and legal) ambiguities created by historically obsolete categories of selection. In *The Warden*, John Hiram's fifteenth-century bequest stipulated that recipients should be wool-carders but by the nineteenth century there were no longer any such in the area. Trollope's bedesmen thus comprise a general population of indigents: "Wool-carding in Barchester there was no longer any; so the bishop, dean, and warden, who took it in turn to put in the old men, generally appointed some hangers-on of their own; worn-out gardeners, decrepit grave-diggers, or octogenarian sextons" (*TW*, 3–4). Such difficulties were common. In London, for instance, the Framework Knitters' Almshouses in Shoreditch were established near the company from which candidates were chosen. But by the turn of the century, the company had moved to Nottingham and Leicester: there were no framework knitters to be found within a five-mile radius in London (as the founding constitution stipulated). Legal action was necessary before the almshouses could be sold so that new structures could be built nearer the present facilities. Trollope's story accentuates the social, as well as biological and physical, instability that inheres in the aging of all things: the attempt to provide for the future is at best only possible temporarily; it is always risky. Fluctuations in the price of real estate, in the income gathered through subscriptions, in the maintenance of buildings and other costs of upkeep and provision—all of this made the almshouse venture at once unpredictable and open to critique.

Attempts to govern the admittance of inmates were reflected in the terms of engagement and the regulations of conduct. From our perspective the rules no doubt appear excessive and intrusive: most almshouses dictated the number of days one could be absent and the time at night when one must return. Some included a prohibition against foul language or required attendance at church services. The Company of Armourers and Brasiers stipulated that each pensioner was responsible not only for his own behavior, but also for reporting the transgressions of others.[27] Sometimes clothing uniforms were required, although in other cases a small amount of money might be designated for clothing allowance. These disciplinary measures were usually regarded as means to preserve the respectability of the inmates as well as that of the trust which provided for them. Describing the London almshouses in 1920, Charles White emphasizes their dignity against the degraded cityscape:

> Ofttimes an almshouse, with its little garden, lends a touch of the picturesque to the mean streets, and in its neatness forms a contrast with the squalid habitations surrounding it. . . . Amid the few household treasures preserved from the days of their prosperity the old folk find a real home in the almshouse, and, free from the stigma of pauperism, preserve their freedom and individuality during the evening of their days.[28]

Certainly compared with other forms of institutional life, the almshouses were less intrusive and pensioners could enjoy more privacy here than elsewhere. At the turn of the century, when the drift towards a national pension was stronger, George Sims could say of the poor "It's legislation that is wanted, not almsgiving."[29] But charitable provision through almshouses was an attempt to provide for the elderly when there were no comparable alternatives in view and the likely movement was downwards, to the asylum or the workhouse, for the number of Mr. Peggottys must have been as few as the need was great.

Furthermore, we ought to acknowledge that donors, administrators, and even trustees were expected to observe certain regulations and (after 1853) to submit to inspections as well. Rules for pensioners were printed and distributed just as were rules for membership to the charity itself. A requisite donation could buy a vote or entitle a donor to nominate a candidate; a larger

27. Charles White, *Hospitals and Almshouses of London* (London: London General Omnibus Company, 1920), appendix.
28. Ibid. 2–3.
29. *How the Poor Live*, quoted in Brian Bailey, *Almshouses* (London: Robert Hale, 1988), 184.

donation could secure a place on a governing committee or on a board. Lists of donors and donations were published, making charity a public rather than a private act, and encouraging those of means to engage in the social life of their locality. Whole communities might be shamed into productive action. In St. Pancras, for example, it was an acknowledged "reproach that so large and populous a parish should be without an institution where those of the more respectable and industrious parishioners, who in their old age might be overtaken by misfortune, could find a refuge from penury and want."[30] And in 1850 the St. Pancras Almshouses opened in Southampton Road, admitting thirteen married couples and forty-one single men and women.

These last numbers point to the socially transitional character of the Victorian almshouse, namely its general willingness to accommodate the individual in his or her familial complex. Unlike other more specialized institutions (insane asylums or hospitals), and contrary to the practice of workhouses, almshouses assumed that couples and even families would remain together in the house. Architecturally the design acknowledged the desirability of privacy. Most almshouses were designed as small two-storied houses often grouped around a rectangle, but even when the buildings were larger, pensioners were housed in separate rooms rather than in wards (as in the workhouses). Writing in the 1860s, a cynical Dickens takes note of the sometimes ornate exteriors, charging that "the question how prosperous and promising the buildings can be made to look...usually supersedes the lesser question how they can be turned to the best account for the inmates" ("Titbull's Almshouses," *UT*, 289). But one might just as well take pleasure in the attempt to provide beauty and grace in the construction of dwellings for the aged. The interior spaces were small, and frequently enough unfurnished, without plumbing or cooking facilities in individual rooms. In other instances, accommodations were more spacious—larger single rooms or two rooms—and improvements in plumbing, heating, and cooking kept company with the passing years. The regulations required pensioners to keep the outside neat: passages had to be swept and gardens tended. And as an alternative to surveillance by officials (in the form of reporting absences, requesting leaves, etc.) there emerged a system of shared responsibility, which was encouraged informally and often enough formally as well. Pensioners helped to tend each other through illness or indisposi-

30. As cited in Ellis, *The London Almshouses*, 7.

tion, and this involvement often extended into other forms of reciprocal interactions. Towards the end of the century many almshouses had some system of nursing care and medical advice, but even so pensioners were expected to participate in caring for one another, as well as in maintaining the cleanliness and nicety of the place. This 1833 description of the London Almshouses erected in honor of the passage of the First Reform Bill sounds very much like Charles White's eulogistic nostalgia noted above:

> Each house consists of a sitting room, bedroom and kitchen leading off a central passage, together with coal cupboard and lavatory; a bath forming part of and hidden under the kitchen table is also provided, the water being heated from the kitchener. A small garden is attached to each house and these are nearly all cultivated by the residents. The houses are sited round rectangular grounds which are the care of a gardener and include a bowling green. Excellent shopping facilities are available nearby. The residents receive a pension and two-and-a-half tons of coal per annum. A Warden, who is in charge of the houses and general welfare of the inhabitants, is one of their number appointed by the Committee of Management and for this service he receives an additional allowance. A nurse who lives near calls daily and gives attention to any who need her services under the direction of a doctor who also visits daily and provides any necessary medicines. The Clerk to the Committee of Management calls monthly to pay the allowances and to watch the welfare of the inhabitants.[31]

The picturesque description evokes a rosy ideal, but it accurately captures the way many almshouses appeared like bucolic enclosures nestled within the dirty city. By the end of the century there were almshouses in almost all sections of London, and one of the earliest modern sources of information as well as one of the curiosities of research are the pamphlets printed in the early years of the twentieth century which were devoted to almshouses and which include transport information for visiting each residence. Almshouses became part of the tourist circuit; some remain so today. Along with the National Heritage plaques denoting residences of the famous on London streets, one frequently sees plaques or stone insets indicating the site of almshouses for the aged (see Fig. 3).

The fate of Trollope's bedesmen and of their almshouse was similarly pathetic: indeed, from the start of the novel the narrator commiserates: "Poor old men! Whoever may be righted or wronged by this inquiry, they at any rate will assuredly be only injured: to them it can only be an unmixed evil!" (*TW*, 43). Indeed, in just a few years they move from a tableau of comfort—in

31. Ibid. 5–6.

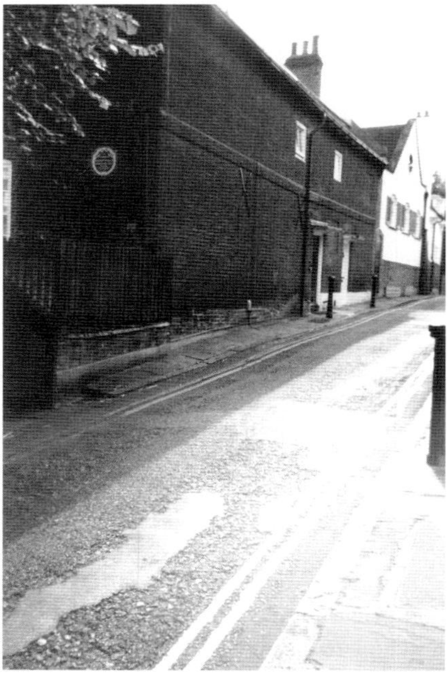

Figure 3 Victorian Almshouse. Photo courtesy of Karen Chase

which "all their wants are supplied; every comfort is administered; they have warm houses, good clothes, plentiful diet, and rest after a life of labour; and above all, that treasure so inestimable in declining years, a true and kind friend to listen to their sorrows, watch over their sickness, and administer comfort as regards this world, and the world to come!" (*TW*, 4, 43)—to the misery of an alienated and unkempt independence. Six of the twelve men have died "with no kind friend to solace their last moments" (*TW*, 280), while the remaining six feud amongst themselves in the now "disordered and ugly" building. The once lovely garden "is a wretched wilderness" though "a very few years since it was the prettiest spot in Barchester, and now it is a disgrace to the city" (*TW*, 281). In one respect, this scenario plays out the aging of the almshouses themselves, which were often built in nice areas, and which contributed to the freshness of their surroundings. In time, those areas often became overrun, over-populated, and untended. For example, Shoreditch was home to a handful of desirable almshouses, and yet by the 1860s it had become one of the poorest sections of London.[32] But in other respects, the salient trajectory of age is from a paternal notion of charity to a more modern, corporate notion,

32. See Neil Burton, *The Geffrye Almshouses*, 59.

in which the intimacy achieved by the Warden is replaced by the impersonality of a 'board.' Unlike Mr. Harding's interpretation of his role as 'warden,' most almshouses had a disciplinary overseer whose first task was to see that the rules were observed and whose concern for the comfort of the pensioners was not a formal priority. For Trollope, this too is a condition of age, a symptom of age and the tragedy of age.

The mental perturbations of old age

We have seen that responsibility for the aged becomes increasingly important with the growing number of elderly living beyond their capacity to support themselves. Legislation, however, crept well behind the pace of need. Had it not, the almshouse movement—if so it can be called—would never have flourished as it did. Private, religious, and professional charity were each stimulated precisely because of inadequate social provision. Moreover, the very efforts to rely on local support were countered by demands to return responsibility to individuals (relatives).[33] We saw earlier that in the second half of the century an emphasis in social policy was to charge the family with the responsibility for supporting its elderly; only in the late eighties and nineties did reaction set in firmly and a major effort in support of viable public pensions begin. During those crucial decades before the century's end, the notion of 'moral responsibility' replaced that of a strictly 'legal responsibility,' even as the burden of elder care became an issue for more than just the elderly person's children. In this manner the definition of 'family' itself is enlarged, including both a wider range of relatives, as well as other "friends" who may have been involved in the old person's life.[34]

We have also seen how, throughout the period in which legislative activity was sluggish, it became especially tempting to classify an elderly person as 'insane' rather than simply 'old.' Age reclassified as mental agitation or insufficiency was a condition which the community could address and the family could understand. With all its threatening and unsettling characteristics, insanity was a condition one could hope to avoid whereas aging was inexorable so long as life persisted. Trollope often juxtaposes age and lunacy, leaving the reader the task of forging the links between them. *He Knew He Was Right* contains a

33. See David Thomson, "'I am not my father's keeper': Families and the Elderly in Nineteenth Century England," *Law and History Review*, 2 (Spring 1984), 265–86. 34. Ibid. 278–9.

characteristically elliptical example. The young Mr. Glascock has been dividing his time in Italy between preparing for his wedding in Florence and visiting his old and dying father in Naples. Rather suddenly he realizes that he is the most appropriate person to attempt to secure the child held by the 'insane' Louis Trevelyan in Siena, despite the fact that the two have only a slight acquaintance. In the figure of Glascock the distance between old age and insanity begins to vanish. Perceived by a young girl to be "as old as Methuselah," he is in fact only in his thirties or forties (*HKHWR*, 711), and despite the fact that he is to be married in two days, he justifies his difficult role as emissary to Trevelyan on the grounds that "I am a little old, I sometimes think, for this philandering" (*HKHWR*, 798). Although Glascock does not succeed in retrieving the young child, he is nonetheless one of the few people whom Trevelyan trusts. A natural affinity grows between the 'old' Glascock and the 'insane' Trevelyan, though the former isn't old and the latter is only questionably 'insane.'

A more direct association between age and insanity occurs in Trollope's fantasy entitled *The Fixed Period*, in which old people retire to a College for a year before they die. During this interval they are free to do as they please, the only constraint being that they remain on the spacious grounds. Such enforced retirement exists on the cusp of the dreaded and the desirable and helps us to press the question of retirement in relation to the problem of lunacy. As studies by Donald Cowgill and Jill Quadagno show, early references to formal retirement were more often than not negative, or as Quadagno concisely puts it: "retirement is initiated as a social substitute for death."[35] Surely it is notable that in the 1881 census, 73 percent of British men 65 years or older still had some occupation. (Though the point will be expanded later, it is also worth observing here that, although by far the greatest number of elderly people in need of income support were women, discussions about pensions focused overwhelmingly on the requirements of working men.) Yet, even as the elderly, especially the elderly poor, clung to their work, its changing conditions created changing states of mind. As infant mortality rates dropped, more young people were in need of work, and as new technologies changed the workplace, a greater number of jobs depended on agility rather than experience. The image of someone working until death lost its practical appeal, even before its moral force disappeared. The complaint of hearty, able-bodied men became

35. *Aging in Early Industrial Society: Work, Family and Social Policy in Nineteenth-Century England* (New York: Academic Press, division of Harcourt Brace Jovanovich, 1982), 5. See also Donald Cowgill, "The Aging Populations and Societies," *Annals of the American Academy of Political and Social Sciences*, 415 (1972), 12.

the lament of the rapidly aging, and a body of literature began to represent the agitations of each group. George Sims's poem "Christmas in a Workhouse" describes a young man's desperate anger when asked to express gratitude to the workhouse system which had denied provision to help his starving wife, while W. Hazlitt Roberts was moved to write a ballad about an old man who commits suicide when forced to yield his job to a younger man. One difference between the two pieces is that Roberts based his ballad on a genuine suicide note, written by James Watson just before "hanging himself from the kitchen door of 1, E Block, Peabody's Buildings, Southwark Street, S.E.":

> Forever the young come crowding,
> Hustling the old away,
> Driving us into the gutter,
> As soon as our hair shows grey!
> Experience counts for nothing,
> Fidelity gets no chance,
> The tune is set by the engine
> And we have only to dance.[36]

The fact that there *was* a James Watson, who hanged himself from the kitchen door at 1, E Block, Peabody's Buildings, a large philanthropic residence built to house the 'deserving' poor, is a chilling reminder that behind the images, often generalized and more or less rhetorical, stood raw individual experience. Asking "What to Do with our Old People," one author concludes: "There is a time to be young and there is a time to be old. Our modern society is out of gear because that lesson of nature is not obeyed. To die in harness has become the ideal of almost every old man. But what might be the right ideal for a cab-horse is not necessarily the right ideal for a human being."[37] Tell that to James Watson. The question, 'what to do with our old people?' had no easy answers, for the 'humane' solution may have seemed anything but to the recipients. Thomas Mackay, of the Charity Organisation Society, put the question bluntly in 1895, "Ought old age to be a public or a private charge? That is the issue which the country is being asked to try."[38] Trollope's 'farce' in *The Fixed Period* offers a whimsical answer to this serious question, but the whimsy shouldn't mask the deep concerns his story exposes.

36. "A Paraphrase of a Letter Recently Addressed to a London Coroner" (Westminster Palace Press, 1896), University of London Special Collections, 4784 L123 4(41): L184.
37. F. Max Müller, "What to Do with our Old People," in *Old Age Pensions*, I, Fabian Tracts 1889–1900, University of London Special Collections, 4765 L123.4.
38. Thomas Mackay, "Old Age Pensions and the State," *Quarterly Review*, 182 (July 1895), 254.

President Neverbend, author and prime advocate of the "fixed period," the new law stipulating mandatory retirement and then execution, willfully disrupts contemporary sentiments about work and retirement. His vision is of a retirement short enough to remain pleasant and dignified. But the farmer Crasweller, slated to be the first inhabitant of the College, confesses, "I should have gone mad up in that College," and insists "That College will become a madhouse" (*FP*, 157). The implication here follows from arguments put forth in the last chapter. Insanity is an effect of non-productivity, and as the old have lost hope of significant productive work, they are particularly liable to its ravages. It is a fear Trollope himself possessed, a terror of idleness and its resulting infirmity, which might be diagnosed equally as age or insanity. In fact, while he was writing *The Fixed Period*, he wrote to his son that "Nothing really frightens me but the idea of enforced idleness. As long as I can write books, even though they be not published, I think that I can be happy."[39] Surely the unhappy figure of his father, unable to work and paralyzed by depression, haunts the writer and appears here and there in the fiction: Mr. Crawley is only one notorious example. Trollope's greatest admiration is reserved for those who work vigorously throughout their lives. In his memoir of Palmerston, for example, the length of Palmerston's indefatigable service is what rouses Trollope's intense admiration:

> He was in office altogether forty-nine years and some odd months;—all but fifty years! No other Englishman has, I believe, ever served so long.... But this man did so. He lived in all eighty-one years. Of these, twenty-two were those of boyhood and education; he enjoyed nine of enforced rest, though during those nine he was, with the exception of a month or two, an active member of Parliament; the remaining fifty saw him always in Parliament, always in office, always at the oar.[40]

Trollope is a careful observer not only of the work, but of the age and energy of the worker. After quoting a letter where Palmerston mentions that on a short hunting trip he returned before the rest of his party each afternoon, so that he could be sure to work, Trollope (an enthusiastic hunter himself) can barely restrain his approbation:

> Let gentlemen of sixty-seven who habitually go out hunting and shooting... bethink themselves of the manner in which they pass the remainder of the day after they have come home. Are they tired, and do they sleep, or sit over their tea? Do they congratulate themselves that at sixty-seven they have been

39. Quoted in Skilton, "*The Fixed Period*," *Studies in the Literary Imagination*, 6 (Fall 1973), 46–7.
40. *Lord Palmerston*, 1882; repr. (New York, Arno Press, 1981), 8.

> still able to perform so well many of the feats of their youth? I think I may say that they, none of them, betake themselves to the hard thoughtful work of their lives; and that, if such work still falls to their lot, it has to be done before they go out hunting or shooting. (*LP*, 131)

In Trollope's late story "Why Frau Frohmann Raised her Prices," Frau Frohmann briefly considers retirement as an alternative to change. But she renounces the possibility vehemently: "what did retirement mean? Would it not be to her simply a beginning of dying? A man, or a woman, should retire when no longer able to do the work of the world" (p. 343). Dying or insanity are the twin possibilities consequent upon retirement. If such fears seem distant from the contemporary belief in the restful well-earned peace, that is in part because work and pleasure were mutually constitutive for Trollope. Employing the mind was the only defense against the emptiness and depression which early claimed his father. But the association was far from unique to Trollope; it was culturally validated in many diverse ways. The most visible examples are drawn from the workhouses, since poverty gave sight to old age, and in the last chapter we repeatedly saw the confusion of boundaries between the effects of institutionalization and the manifestations of old age. Emma Sheppard had contrasted the tenderness of an almshouse with the brutality of the workhouse, but both contexts of impoverished age demonstrate the pressures toward the quiet mind and the docile body. Emile Souvestre's popular *Pleasures of Old Age* begins with familiar affirmations of "the occupations of a still active mind" and the insistence that old age, like all other ages, requires mental agility, without which deterioration accelerates.[41] But in fact an activity that looked like 'over-excitement' or 'mania' could look quickly to the confinements of an institution. We have already seen the power of nomenclature and seen too the effects of confusion between 'old age,' 'lunacy,' and imbecility. Given the dire alternatives, the twelve old bedesmen in the Almshouse established by John Hiram's will in *The Warden* are all the more reckless in their hasty endorsement of John Bold's call to rebellion. It is only through great good fortune that in their old age they have escaped the paired threats of workhouse and lunatic asylum.

Part of what distinguishes Trollope's contribution to this difficult tableau is that he is so responsive to the multiple corrosions of age, and especially the intersection of mental and physical debility. Enfeebled by marital strife,

41. Emile Souvestre, *The Pleasures of Old Age* (London: George Routledge and Sons, 1868), 6.

Robert Kennedy seems to his wife "insane" and "mad" (*Phineas Redux*, I, 172, 173); elsewhere his nervous fatigue is marked through the calendar: "He was still under fifty, but he looked as though he were seventy" (*Phineas Redux* I, 86). The conjunction of mental and physical decline appears in phrases such as "worn out," which the novels apply equally to the elderly and the deranged. For example, though only in his fifties, the monomaniacal narrator of *The Fixed Period* describes himself as "a worn out old man" (*TFP*, 7) as he begins to compose his narrative. In *He Knew He Was Right* Dr. Nevill describes the dying Louis Trevelyan as one who "has worn himself out...and there is nothing left in him by which he can lay hold of life again" (*HKHWR*, 924). Trevelyan's illness is equally a "malady of the mind or of the body" (*HKHWR*, 861) and, in two short years, is responsible for transforming him from "a remarkably handsome young man, who was well connected, who had been ninth wrangler at Cambridge, who had already published a volume of poems, and who possessed £3,000 a year of his own" (*HKHWR*, 1) to an old man:

> He seemed to be withering away. His hand was mere skin and bone. His hair and beard so covered his thin long cheeks, that there was nothing left of his face but his bright, large, melancholy eyes. His legs had become so frail and weak that they would hardly bear his weight as he walked; and his clothes...hung so loose about him that they seemed as though they would fall from him. (*HKHWR*, 854)[42]

Soon he will be carried "like a child" because he cannot walk, nor can he eat any solid foods. "Worn out" also serves an ironic function in this novel when it is applied to Miss Stanbury, who is elderly but anything but wasted in vitality. She self-consciously adopts the image of old age which Trevelyan can't help but perform as a young man: "Miss Stanbury...persevered, speaking of herself as a worn-out old woman, with one foot in the grave, who would soon be carried away and put out of sight." But whereas Trevelyan does "nothing,—nothing,—nothing," Miss Stanbury resumes her narrative dynamism by wielding her power in the house and in the community (*HKHWR*, 920, 930, 868). As in *The Fixed Period*, the elderly are not always so obliging or capable of performing to the

42. Compare this description with Septimus Harding: "He was a little, withered shambling old man, with bent shoulders, dressed in knee-breeches and long black gaiters, which hung rather loosely about his poor old legs,—rubbing his hands one against the other as he went" [the last movement refers to his silent violoncello playing which he did to soothe his nerves]. In both cases, it is isolation (largely self-imposed) rather than institutionalization which gives this picture to old age. Anthony Trollope, *The Small House at Allington* (Oxford: Oxford University Press, 1985), 170.

social expectations of old age. But those who possess questionable sanity, like Louis Trevelyan here, or Josiah Crawley (in *The Last Chronicle of Barset*), those whose mental deterioration causes a premature aging, enact the role and stand in the place of old age in Trollope's fiction.

Notably, it is the fear of incarceration that exacerbates Trevelyan's suspicion of those who care for him. In a fit of rage his father-in-law accuses him of insanity and threatens to persecute him on these grounds; Louis, dreading the asylum, clings to his miserable life in Siena rather than return to England.

> "Why are you afraid of going to England?" Stanbury asked.
> "Because they have threatened to put me—in a madhouse."
> "Nobody ever thought of so treating you," said his wife.
> "Your father did,—and your mother. They told me so." (*HKHWR*, 876)

Earlier, he describes his fear graphically: "'They can do nothing to me here; but they would entice me home because there they have friends, and can fee doctors,—with my own money,—and suborn lawyers, and put me away,—somewhere in the dark, where I shall be no more heard of among men!'" (*HKHWR*, 807). As we have seen, his fears are not unwarranted. London was precisely the place where his condition, his physical deterioration and mental confusion which paint him in the *image* of old age, might well have been diagnosed as lunacy.

Josiah Crawley, in *The Last Chronicle of Barset*, unable to account for the possession of a twenty pound check, becomes legally/morally suspect and seems to grow old and insane simultaneously. Almost 50 (that magic age for Trollope, as 17 was for Dickens), "he was morose, sometimes almost to insanity. There had been days in which even his wife had found it impossible to deal with him otherwise than as with an acknowledged lunatic" (*LCB*, 5). Throughout the novel, Mrs. Crawley suffers the dilemma of allowing others to believe her husband is either "a thief or a madman" (*LCB*, 36), when in fact his confusion is that of a morbid sensibility brooding over the common strains of work and poverty. Crawley persistently submits himself to an anxious and self-regarding scrutiny which finds him wanting; he accuses himself of insanity (*LCB*, 192–3), and confesses to his wife, "I know that I am weak where you are strong; that I am crazed where you are clear-witted" (*LCB*, 314). But at the close, when his possession of the check has been explained, the explanation cannot restore youth, agility, or lucidity. To be sure, he is relieved, but the canker of age will not disappear. Crawley's senescence cannot turn 'green;' it has been irreversibly cast as autumnal, with only winter to follow. However sweetly the old Bishop passes away, or however naturally the good old warden faces his end, Trollope maintains a flinty attitude towards 'decrepit' old age. Sooner or later, and under whatever particular circumstances we face, each of us will need to pass from old age to death. Along the way, we may confront madness, incapacity, or, more hopefully, only gently insistent warning. For some, old age may even be robust and vigorous. But eventually the end is common to each. This is the subject of Trollope's least 'characteristic' narrative, though his treatment of the topic is itself within recognizable conceits. I have referred in passing to *The Fixed Period*, and now it is time to consider it in more depth. The novel startles one, like a deliberate misplay at cards: it is curious and exceptional, and thus well worth special attention.

What to do with the old?

Although it was not published until 1882, I turn my focus to *The Fixed Period* now, because it grows directly out of the concerns and sensibilities charted so far, namely: subscription or resistance to the association of old age with fixity and insanity, and the attempts to configure 'enough' provision for (housing, care, and stimulation) for the elderly. To these we add the uneasy realization that ultimately longevity is finite and death poses its own housing problems. Furthermore, like the almshouses, which I characterized as 'transitional spaces' between home and institutional dwelling, this novel stands between our consideration of the institutional forms for old age and several notable social and artistic representations which follow. Trollope's fanciful narrative is best introduced by situating it against contemporary social and scientific currents, some of which we have met before, and some of which will now be elucidated.

Tone is not usually ambiguous or provocative in Trollope's fiction. His narrators often employ light irony when they wish to chide, without denouncing, some character or conduct. In a few instances, however, the narrative adopts a more extreme satiric posture in an effort to rebuke a personality, a social disposition, a political failure, and even a literary rival. In *The Warden* Trollope assails Dickensian satire by subjecting it to his own satirical treatment. In such a case the tone moves indeterminately: if satire is the object of critique, then what shall we make of its use as the critical instrument? Such tonal uncertainty is the condition, even the *donnée*, of *The Fixed Period*, which has generated many confusions since it was published. Even so, apart from a brief moment in 1905, when some in America took seriously the 'modest proposal' for universal euthanasia at the age of 67½, most readers had no difficulty in assigning a persuasive mode to the novel's design.[43] The difficulty lay in determining the target: was the work merely a comic reflection on the burden of the aged? Was its concern with euthanasia purely fanciful? Or was it an exercise in mode and tone without significant concern for its ostensible content? *The Spectator*'s review complained that the satire became too 'extravagant', while *The Times* appreciated only the "lively" cricket match described in chapter 5.[44] Twentieth-century critics have expressed dissatisfaction as well. Bradford Booth dismissed the work as "a very dull novel" and observed that "Abundant as was his gift for satire on conduct and manners—that is, people—he had no talent for satire on ideas." David Skilton found more to appreciate, but even in his generous estimation the novel is a "failure." Within Trollope's *oeuvre* the novel has usually taken the place of a rather slight anomaly. Robert Tracy, an exception here, associates it with Trollope's other works in its interest in showing how reality undermines theory and how the individual case will always disrupt smooth generalization. The risk in such an estimate is that only the reformer and the nature of reform seem important; the particular content—old age, euthanasia and cremation—are irrelevant.[45]

Trollope did not set out to write a social tract in *The Fixed Period*, but the novel has a particular resonance within his canon and a sharp social valence within the culture of aging. Composed in the winter of 1880–1, when Trollope was in ill health (he died in December of 1882), the novel's unstable narrator John Neverbend describes the failure of his attempt to found his Presidency and establish the independence of Britannula, on the rigid principle of enforced euthanasia and cremation before the age of 68. The 'now' of the story is thirty years after independence from Britain—in the year 1980—when a person has finally approached Neverbend's impartial and universal law. The attempt to mark the onset of old age is acknowledged

43. See Harvey Cushing, *The Life of Sir William Osler*, 2 vols. (Oxford: Clarendon Press, 1935), i. 664–72.
44. The *Spectator* review appeared March 18, 1882, p. 361; the *Times* review appeared April 12, 1882, p. 4.
45. Bradford Booth, *Anthony Trollope: Aspects of his Life and Art* (London: Edward Hulton, 1958), 130; David Skilton, "*The Fixed Period*: AT's Novel of 1980," *Studies in the Literary Imagination*, 6 (Fall 1973), 49; Robert Tracy, *Trollope's Later Novels* (Berkeley: University of California Press, 1978), 292–4.

as relative, even arbitrary, but the President argues that no evasions should compromise the power of the audacious reform.

At the time Trollope was writing, life expectancy for men was 44.2 years and for women 47.5 years. The proportion of people over 60 years old was 6.9% for men and 7.8% for women.[46] So while the choice of 67 ½ (a compromise between those who wanted 65 and those who preferred 70) was not outlandishly low; neither was it entirely generous. Within the frame of *The Fixed Period*, the stated motive for the law was to ensure economic prosperity through the untrammeled passage of youth to maturity and the removal of those who are or soon will be 'unproductive.' The old will no longer drain the economy; the young will now refresh it. Most importantly, the law ensures that since people will die before they decline, they will retain full dignity, and the young will feel the reverence due to those who have completed a full circuit of life.

The simple plot involves the destruction of the state largely through the efforts of the President's son, who loves the daughter of the very healthy man who is to be the first 'victim' of the new system. What makes the narrative more than farce or mere whimsy is neither its subject (the law which demands the death of those deemed 'old') nor its outcome (the failure of the law of the 'fixed period'). Rather, it is the complex location of old age within a thematic circuit involving generation, cremation, and the expansion of empire. The book raises a sharp question: Why is an energetic fantasy of age played out within the spaces of empire? John Neverbend, narrator and president, considers Britannula younger 'sister' to New Zealand, Australia, and North America. Like a jealous child, however, Britannula keeps its parent country constantly in mind, first through its eponymous name, but also through its institutions and pre-occupations. It stands as 'youth' to the 'age' of "the old mother country," and the law of the 'fixed period' undoubtedly marks the bid for youthful identity. The bold reform for a 'fixed period' of life is at one with the resistance to imperial authority.

The novel has been taken most often as simply a satire of reformism. Neverbend is the never-bending absolutist, the one who blindly commits to an absurd principle while missing the contingencies of life. He wants his

46. Peter Laslett, "Necessary Knowledge: Age and Aging in the Societies of the Past," in David I. Kertzer and Peter Laslett, eds., *Aging in the Past: Demography, Society and Old Age* (Berkeley: University California Press, 1995), 19.

friend Crasweller to march off to death, even though he remains hale, healthy, and unwilling. Neverbend holds to the supremacy of Law while bringing confusion and misery to the living. In his obstinate refusal to consider any exception to the 'rule,' he misses the claims of real individuals with immediate needs: his friend, his wife, his son. This is indeed the satirical structure of the book. And yet what makes *The Fixed Period* at once unsteady and important is that the absurd reformer has identified a genuine need—the entirely fanciful solution responds to real and urgent problems. One problem is the catastrophe of age; another is the disposal of dead bodies; and a third is the oppression of empire.

Trollope's story is framed by England's revocation of the island's independence. As the narrative opens, Britannula has once again been "absorbed by the mother country among the Crown Colonies" (*FP*, 6). In the *reading* experience, then, independence has been revealed as "fanciful" and contained, an image of rogue liberty. The story that the narrator/President *wants* to tell—the middle-age triumph over both impetuous youth (in the shape of his son) and imperious age (in the form of the British government)—is undone by a narrative of power in old age, the ancient power of the imperial state that can easily trounce the upstart colonials. On one side, then, the novel is a coy unmasking of the gerontocracy that dominated modern British politics. Within the fictive world, Neverbend reports that "The Prime Minister in Downing Street was seventy-two when we were debarred from carrying out our project, and the Secretary for the Colonies was sixty-nine. Had they been among us, and had we been allowed to use our wisdom without interference from effete old age, where would they have been?" (*FP*, 6). Where indeed, but long since deposited in the College of death. In the world outside the novel, as we know, gerontocracy was just as fully established. At 72, Gladstone succeeded Disraeli as Prime Minister in April 1880. A year later, Disraeli died at 77. In 1881, the Queen was 62. We designate the period an age of iron and steel, but we might also refer to the iron and steel of age. In the 1980s there was no effective challenge to the grey rule of power established by an aging Queen, cabinet, and parliament. As Charles Dilke apparently told Joseph Chamberlain in 1885, "it is in old age that power comes."[47]

47. Quoted in Colin Ford and Brian Harrison, *A Hundred Years Ago: Britain in the 1880s in Words and Photographs* (Cambridge, Mass.: Harvard University Press, 1983), 279.

In fact, of course for most people in Britain, old age brought vulnerability rather than power. If there was gerontocracy above, there were abuse and neglect of the elderly down below. We saw earlier how, as the catastrophe of old age became increasingly apparent, there was a movement to shift responsibility from the parish to the family. From the 1860s through the 1880s, public officials repeatedly tried to make children contribute to the financial support (though not necessarily the care) of their parents. At the same time the first movement for old age pensions exposed the extent of the need. And perhaps most strikingly, the problem of mass death in the cities made clear that the grave was no resting place for the elderly: coffins rose through the ground, corpses shared their poisons, noxious vapors circulated—all as signs of the degradation of the body.

We can fairly say that the last third of the nineteenth century saw the invention of the elderly subject, just as it constructed figures of the homosexual and the adolescent. Here the emergence of gerontology, as a medical subdiscipline, was decisive. Before his association with Freud, Jean-Martin Charcot had already established himself as the first modern gerontologist in Europe, the one who saw that the aged had largely escaped the eye of medicine. When his *Clinical Lectures on Senile and Chronic Diseases* were translated into English in 1881, the book created a new domain for late Victorian medicine; it also generated a discourse, requiring new concepts and a new lexicon. The very indices of the major journals—the *Lancet* and the *British Medical Journal*—register the provocation. Will "Old Age" be a category in the index? Is it distinct from "Longevity" or "Senility" or "Decrepitude"? Who were the aged? and how old exactly were they? These are the questions that we have begun pursuing in Dickens and in Trollope, but here cultural and scientific representation need to be brought more closely together. The development of a medical gerontology, and the invention of the decrepit subject, required more than a series of private devastations. It required a research project that emerged out of the massing of the elderly within institutions. Charcot had thousands of bodies in his Parisian hospital, and we have seen that in England not only the hospitals, but also the workhouses and asylums, furnished specimen-bodies.

What one finds throughout the last third of the century is an uncanny exercise in description. A subject is delimited, a vocabulary is articulated, and a research mission defined. In the mid-eighties, one of London's first self-conscious gerontologists, George Humphry, led a team from the Collective

Investigation Committee. The group cut, prodded, weighed, and compared, the corpses of the very aged. The result was a scientific delineation resembling William Dorrit's rehearsal of Old Nandy's failures to Arthur Clennam, which we examined in the first chapter. For Humphry and his colleagues, the senescent body was revealed as a congress of organs, each aging at its own rate, fluttering and failing. A striking contrast, for instance, is found between "the wasting of the spleen," the "shrinking of the brain" and the "enlargement of the heart."[48] It cannot have been easy to read these passages; it's not easy now, never easy to be an aging spleen reading about an aging spleen, or to read how the fatty heart still pumps erratically while the blood-making organs sputter and fail. Mentally, the decline was similarly and starkly depressing. Like other organs, the brain suffered from the use and abuse of years, and the medical literature is dense with accounts of mental failure.

What to do with the broken pieces, the failing bodies, the jellied minds? Part of the concern with accommodating the old (housing, feeding, and tending them) included an implicit directive to provide for them in such a way that their disintegrations will not offend or terrify others. This is not to deny the genuine concern in social legislation and charitable activity. But as the literary works pervasively demonstrate, motives were mixed, ambivalence was marked, and seldom were emotions pure. Inevitably, the question 'how to house the old' led to an accompanying thought, lingering as half question/half answer: 'how to bury them'? In this light I turn to a controversy that erupted in 1874. It began with the publication of an essay by the Queen's physician, Sir Henry Thompson, entitled "The Treatment of the Body after Death," and incited the public by its praise of cremation.[49] The Cremation Society was formed in the same year at a meeting in Thomson's home where sixteen figures, including Trollope, Tenniel, and Millais, drafted the founding statement. The sheer mass of death in the cities had put public health at risk; cremation was a response

48. George Murray Humphry, "Post-Mortem Examinations of Centenarians: With Remarks," *British Medical Journal* (March 19, 1887), 612–13.

49. *Contemporary Review*, 23 (1874), 319–28. See also Thompson's succeeding essays, "A Reply to Critics and an Exposition of the Process," *Contemporary Review*, 23 (1874), 553–71; and "The Progress of Cremation," *Nineteenth Century*, 23 (1888), 1–17. For several illuminating overviews of the importance of the cremation movement, see Brian Parsons, *Committed to the Cleansing Flame: The Development of Cremation in Nineteenth-Century England* (Reading: Spire Books, 2006) and Peter Jupp, *From Dust to Ashes: Cremation and the British Way of Death: 1820–1997* (Basingstoke: Palgrave Macmillan, 2006).

of unsentimental reformers to the horrors of the graveyard. A favorite story in the newspapers was the catastrophe of the cemeteries: coffins stacked on one another, bodies washed up to the surface of the ground, poisonous fluids circulating in streams, vile effluvia released into the air. The measured proposal of the Cremation Society was to permit cremation as the clean alternative to toxic death.

It is striking that until the 1870s the word 'cremation' was reserved for taboo practices in India, the habits of a subject population held guilty of mutiny in 1857.[50] No doubt, this was part of the reason that the campaign excited such horrified reaction. The notorious practice of a benighted people was now being coolly proposed as the ceremonial end of a British life—or as the *Times* noticed at the end of the decade: "The cry of 'cremation in our midst' is raised just as that of cannibals in our midst might be, and with the same signs of intense and unaffected horror."[51]

Beyond the imperial recoil, there remained the shock to the religious mind. The Bishop of Lincoln was appalled by the proposals. Preaching in Westminster Abbey, he declared that nothing was "more barbarous and unnatural" than cremation, and that "one of the very first fruits of its adoption would be to undermine the faith of mankind in the resurrection of the body, and so bring about a most disastrous social revolution." On the other hand, Canon Liddon of St. Paul's took the view that it was no greater miracle to imagine a resurrection from ash than from the "unburnt body." Cremation, said Canon Liddon, "could have made no difference except in the sphere of imagination."[52] Just so, Trollope would have said.

These high pronouncements excited a post-Darwinian contest that persisted to the end of the century. Its effect was to create a remarkable imaginative project which, once begun, took on a strange life of its own. For partisans on both sides of the question, the leading tactic was to evoke the dead and decaying body, buried or burnt, moldering or ashen. There was a kind of competition of imagery, a contest in fear, because, once out of the box, the body entered and anxious reverie that made it impossible not to think about the future of the aging carcass. Those who defended the rational virtues of cremation painted pictures of the clean urns arranged in

50. See Peter Jupp and Glennys Howarth, "Hindu Cremations in Britain," in Stephen White, *The Changing Face of Death and Disposal* (London: Macmillan, 1997), 135–48.

51. Editorial/Leader *The Times*, January 15, 1879.

52. *The Times*, Monday, July 6, 1874, p. 8; issue 28047, col. C; *The Times*, Friday, April 24, 1885, 10; issue 31429, col. D.

space-saving cabinets, and at the same time they pointed to the vile fluids of the decomposing bodies, mixing their miasma with others'. Thompson stated the case with simple elegance: "The aim of Cremation is to prevent the process of putrefaction." After witnessing the process in the late 1880s, he elaborates: "the complete incineration is accomplished without escape of smoke or other offensive product, and with extreme ease and rapidity. The ashes, which weigh about three pounds, are placed at the disposal of the friends, and are removed. Or, if desired, they may be restored at once to the soil, being now perfectly innocuous."[53] Imagine the change if the body were burnt while the service was conducted. Then by the time of the final hymn, there would be "the silvery-white, pure ash, which, after one short hour, was all that remained of a purified body, perfectly inoffensive to the living, might be left unchanged for centuries in any such cinerary urn as might be seen in the British Museum, beautiful in form." It was all an argument about how to dispose of the multiplying dead, but it inevitably became a discussion of living flesh, its parts and their names. The *Times* pleaded that "there are some matters which it is not well or wholesome to consider too curiously," confessing that "The affair has certainly its horrible as well as its attractive side. The preliminaries of cremation, the removal of the intended subject's liver and stomach, to be duly fastened up in a jar and ticketed with date and name…it seems to need something like the courage of a Bentham to face the prospect of this."[54] The cremation campaign intended to remove the blight of the stinking, oozing mortal body, only cast it in brighter, harsher light.

Trollope's membership in the Cremation Society in the years leading up to his writing of this novel indicates his commitment to a rational, enlightened solution to the evils of the cemetery. All those decomposing bodies that released poisons into the city air might be burned cleanly and swiftly, if only the public could get over its superstitions. The advocates of cremation were in the midst of their struggle when Trollope wrote *The Fixed Period* and, as John Neverbend describes his plans for ending human life by age 68, he relies on pictures of the clean and graceful technology of the crematorium.

53. Henry Thompson, "A Reply to Critics and an Exposition of the Process," *Contemporary Review*, 23 (March 1874), 571; "The Progress of Cremation," *Nineteenth Century*, 23 (Jan–June 1888), 7.

54. Editorial/Leader *The Times*, January 15, 1879.

I propose here that what happens within the novel is that the rationalism of cremation is brought to this side of the grave. The treatment of the corpse becomes—uncannily—the treatment of the aging body. Just as those in the Cremation Society imagined a death that avoided dissolution and toxic decay, so John Neverbend imagines an old age that escapes the indignity of shambling decline, shameful debility. We know that Trollope dreaded his own decay, the loss of mental power, the descent into helplessness. And there is also another difficult biographical datum. When Trollope was teased about the joke of *The Fixed Period*,—the very *idea* of such a law—he's reported to have said, "It's all true—I *mean* every word of it."[55] It should be clear that the category 'satire' cannot do justice to the provocations of the novel. We need another way to think about it, and I argue that the novel suggests another way to think about age in the nineteenth century.

Neverbend's law is a reaction against the social and legislative imperatives attempting to rationalize treatment of the elderly in England during the last third of the century. Where relatives were asked to take more responsibility in Britain, Neverbend peremptorily usurps all control for the state. Instead of providing income, shelter, work, or food, however, he ingeniously spares the public coffers all but minimal cost by abbreviating the time old age will be either endured or enjoyed. Like his law, which obliterates the problems of old age by obliterating old age, so too, the problems of generational discord are not solved so much as summarily pre-empted. Working, however, against Neverbend's schemes as well as the current of his own narrative, Trollope gives fictive shape to a shadow narrative, in which alternatives to extreme positions appear in viable, non-political guise.

First, conventional analogies between empire and its colonies, and between parents and children, are disturbed by the repeated failure of Neverbend's calculations. In the novel's asymmetry between family struggle (in Britannula) and imperial conflict (with Britain), we see that the interplay between 'parent' and 'child' can hardly be contained by anything so simple as 'rebellion' and 'repression.' Generational discord at home makes a parody of the similar tensions between imperial authority and the independent colony. Jack Neverbend, the President's son, becomes a man precisely by opposing the rule of *his* father: "I soon found that the one opponent whom I had most to fear in Britannula was my own son" (*FP*, 42). One of the ways in which

55. John Hall, *Trollope: A Biography* (Oxford: Clarendon, 1991), 487; see also David Skilton, *The Fixed Period* (Oxford: Oxford University Press, 1993), introduction, p. xiv.

Jack resists his father is by waging his own, rather different, competition with the British. President Neverbend is so preoccupied by the impending date of deposition—the time when his old friend Crasweller is to leave his thriving farm and his loving daughter and make his residence in the College which is to be home during the final months of his life—that he is surprised by the impending cricket match between Britain and Britannula that so fully engages his son.

The match stands at the center of the novel. The English have come across the ocean to play the natives, and the event occupies the entire fifth chapter; furthermore, it represents a turning point in generational and imperial relations. Here Ian Baucom's splendid study of the cricket field as a site on which English identity might be performed helps us to understand this seemingly anomalous pause in the story's progression. Baucom identifies the central functions of the sport in the construction of Englishness throughout the empire, among which is the sporting knowledge transmitted from one generation to the next; the transmission of English values which constituted 'gentlemanliness' (as well as fitness for military service); and the celebration of the green field as the locus of nostalgic images associated with a rural past in the form of the old village green. In the context of the charged image of the cricket lawn, we can understand why in a novel so concerned with generational passage, such an interlude is of great importance.[56]

In the last third of the nineteenth century, the Marylebone Club "ruled over the Cricket world in much the same fashion that Whitehall ruled over the empire."[57] In Trollope's story, the Marquis of Marylebone is himself the leader of the English team, and his stay in the Neverbend home brings the center of Englishness to Britannula where imperial 'fathers' and colonized 'sons' appear ready to play out the generational tensions that inhere in empire. But nothing of the sort happens, either in the game or in the house. The chapter is structured much as the famous garden-party chapter of *The Warden*, the event narrated in mock-epic and the warring parties rendered equally humorous. The English team is composed of "thoroughly old-fashioned, prejudiced, aristocratic young Englishmen" (*FP*, 53) along with eight professional players, whereas the Britannulans are all amateurs, untitled, modern, and, apparently, unprejudiced. But there is no neat dichotomy: the Britannulan team includes one player who is "much too old for

56. Ian Baucom, *Out of Place: Englishness, Empire, and the Locations of Identity* (Princeton: Princeton UP, 1999), 146–51. 57. Ibid. 150.

the game" but proves to be "the best man they had" (*FP*, 64, 65); and each team resists the new 'standardization' in favor of the older 'vernacular' which Baucom associates with the appeal of the early years of the game (*FP*, 151). Ironically, we see the vernacular through the introduction of new ('young') inventions which serve each side respectively. The English possess the "new catapult," but Jack is certain "that our steam-bowler will beat their catapult hollow" (*FP*, 50). And Jack's personal invention is the "Neverbend spring-bat" which helps him achieve the amazing feat of scoring 1,275 runs when W. C. Grace, England's greatest cricketer, himself set the record of 400 runs in a single match only in 1895![58]

Everyone realizes the high stakes at risk on the symbolic field of sport. Will 'old' England defeat the upstart child, or will youth defend its autonomy? Indeed, as John Neverbend observes the British preparing for the match, he muses "that England must be sending out another army to take another Sebastopol" (*FP*, 53). On the final day of the match "feelings were carried to a pitch which was more befitting the last battle of a great war, some Waterloo of other ages, than the finishing of a prolonged game of cricket" (*FP*, 66). Expecting war, preparing for battle, and anticipating fury, we find instead co-operation, friendly competition, and general good-will. The British refuse the colonialist challenge: they will not define the situation in the imperialist terms which might lead to loss of authority. "We don't call you foreigners" Lord Marylebone insists. "'If we be not foreigners, what are we, my lord?' 'Englishmen of course,' said he. 'What else?'" (*FP*, 59–60).

David Cannadine's study *Ornamentalism* (2001) offers an adjustment to prevailing theories of Empire. From the perspective of subject peoples, race has been the distinguishing feature of any analysis of imperialism, and this for conspicuous reasons: the designation of 'other' was cast so pervasively within terms of color, ethnicity, tribe. Cannadine's suggestion is that *from the perspective of the British*, race was subordinate to class. Settlers, travelers, and government officials alike desired to recreate the textured hierarchy characteristic of British society: "the British Empire was about the familiar and domestic, as well as the different and the exotic: indeed, it was in large part about the domestication of the exotic": "Far from wishing to reject the stratified society of the mother country, these pundits and politicians strenuously recommended its replication in the colonies." Furthermore, "in

58. Ian Baucom, *Out of Place: Englishness, Empire, and the Locations of Identity* (Princeton: Princeton UP, 1999), 153.

that enterprise, the colour of a person's skin was less significant than their position in the local social hierarchy."[59] Referring specifically to Trollope's two-volume study *Australia and New Zealand*, Cannadine writes:

> In 1873 Anthony Trollope had contrasted the social structure of Britain, which he thought to be traditional-hierarchical, with that of the United States, which he considered democratic-egalitarian. And from this starting point, he concluded (with relief) that "the colonies are rather a repetition of England than an imitation of America."[60]

What Trollope saw, and Cannadine stresses, is the appropriative habit of empire—the exploitation not of racial difference but social similarity. This is the power of imperial gerontocracy, the power to put the colony in the position of youth and to enforce repetition. *The Fixed Period* emphasizes the deep generational structure within the imperial dynamic: no matter how young the Englishman abroad, he was always in the role of parent and tutor, always an emblem of the seniority of Empire.

Furthermore, when confronted with those of common national origin, the response of the British state will be to assert the dominance of the head of family. In Britannula the collapse of distinctions is the *solution which the British impose* rather than the condition which they find. John Neverbend wants to be thought of as 'other'; he yearns to be 'foreign,' he glories in difference—or so at least he thinks.

> "We separated from the old mother country with no quarrel, with no ill-will;—but with the mutual friendly wishes of both," he tells Lord Marylebone, "If there be a trace of the feeling of antagonism in the word foreigners, I will not use it; but British subjects we are not, and never can be again" (*FP*, 61).

Nowhere is the difference between the two countries more marked than in the constitution of the very legislature which passed the law of the fixed period. In Britannula, there is only one assembly consisting of eighty-five elected members: there are no lords, and this difference gives the crux of the matter. Within the single legislative body, passage of the law of euthanasia had been temporarily obstructed by those who stubbornly maintained "the prejudices of the Old World," who belonged to the "old party" (*FP*, 39, 40), but who were then finally overwhelmed by the party of "youthful"

59. David Cannadine, *Ornamentalism: How the British Saw their Empire* (London: Allen Lane, 2001), pp. xix, 30, 124. 60. Ibid. 39.

reform, in a vote so overwhelming that it appeared "the old country... could not interfere" (*FP*, 40). And yet, despite the legislative act of independence, the 'old country' rejects the methods and manners of the young upstart, the insurgent colony. After the match, when the underlying political struggle stands revealed, the terms of imperial refusal are made clear. Sir Ferdinando Brown—the quintessential British-mannered colonialist who is sent to Britannula to rule after Neverbend is deposed—notes that "You have only one House in your Constitution...you will admit that a second chamber is not there to guard against the sudden action of the first" (*FP*, 124). Brown's assertion receives an official stamp from the Minister for the Crown Colonies, the Duke of Hatfield, who roundly regrets that "in their selection of a Constitution the Britannulists have unfortunately allowed themselves but one deliberative assembly, and hence have sprung their present difficulties" (*FP*, 127).

Here is the climactic instance of the displacement of generational life to political/imperial contexts. The 'young' country would abolish the 'old' system, which ruthlessly reasserts its uncompromising power. An independent liberal democracy, once set free from the weight of aristocratic privilege, would show its impetuous political youth and would dare to pass a law so audacious that it would transform the conditions of age. Neverbend wants to "protect the human race from the imbecility, the weakness, the discontent and the extravagance of old age," and his greatest fear is exactly what comes to pass, "that England should be again asked to annex us, so as to save our old people from the wise decision to which our own Assembly had come" (*FP*, 61). The British, it becomes plain, champion the old not out of solicitous concern—they propose no mechanisms, institutions, or plans for caring for the elderly themselves, and refuse to allow their namesakes the authority to regulate the course of senescence—but because they are themselves an 'old' people, intent to retain the prerogatives of national age.

A biology undergirds the politics. Old England, with its ancient upper house and aristocracy, insists on its own preservation in the face of the encroachments of an "insane democracy."[61] In this aspect the struggle appears as a Darwinian contest involving strength and fitness on the one hand, and the ability to adapt on the other. Trollope separates and braids two strands of Darwin's theory, making the struggle to survive and the ability to adapt alternative strategies, rather than conditions of a single species.

61. Trollope uses the phrase in the *Autobiography,* ch. 16, p. 245.

Neverbend himself casts his role in openly Darwinian terms, regarding adaptation as the process by which civilization advances from the fixity (of entrenched belief) to the flexibility (of pragmatic politics). He will "assist others in their struggle upwards in humanity" out of a desire to be "known as one who had benefitted my species" (*FP*, 105) and made it possible that "the race might from age to age be improved"(*FP*, 106). But instead of yielding to a natural evolution, he exerts an aggressive political will, and moving from the framework of Darwin to that of social Darwinism, he projects glory for the species, which will become at once more productive and no longer stained by generational conflict. But there is a Darwinian surprise for him: he learns that natural selection depends on more than one exception before a new rule can overcome. Instead of the triumph he anticipates, he must witness the "extinction" of his plans: "it is necessary that a whole age should be carried up to some proximity to the reformer before there is a space sufficiently large for his operations. Had the telegraph been invented in the days of ancient Rome would the Romans have accepted it or have stoned Wheatstone?" (*FP*, 118). His visionary reform must "necessarily be postponed to an age prepared for it."

John Neverbend never bends. He holds tenaciously to his unthinkable reform. But when his son, the cricket hero, alerts the British to the imminent deposition of his soon-to-be father-in-law—then gentle appropriation gives way to the threat of violence. Even as Neverbend escorts the candidate up the hill toward the College, a British warship sails into the harbor. The transaction is swift. The ceremony of deposition is halted; Neverbend is taken in custody; the independence of Britannula is revoked; a new governor is installed. When Neverbend asks how the naked assertion of power can be justified, Ferdinando Brown blandly replies that "you will generally find that the highest respect is paid to the greatest battalions." This is precisely the attitude that had appalled Trollope during his trip to South Africa, just before he undertook *The Fixed Period*; and when the Zulu War broke out in 1879, he blamed British provocation, asking "Have we not stretched our arms far enough?"[62] Within the fiction the cold imperial brutality has the effect of recuperating Neverbend, who takes on the melancholy aspect of a reformer without a reform.

The animating fantasy—which fully survives the satire—is a dream of age as glory, as triumph and dignity. Suppose it were possible to overcome

62. From the abridged, one-volume edition of *South Africa* (London: Chapman & Hall, 1879); quoted in Hall, *Trollope: A Biography*, 434.

the shameful debility of age. Suppose we were strong enough to accept a 'fixed period' of life, in return for self-respect. This is the historically well-motivated query of the novel. As we have seen, the afflictions of the elderly were now conspicuous in Britain, and if forced euthanasia is no solution, neither is its repeal. Neverbend's impossible vision haunts the novel, as it was meant to haunt his readers.

> During the last years of their lives they were to be saved from any of the horrors of poverty. How many now lack the comforts they cannot earn for themselves? And to them there would be no degraded feeling that they were the recipients of charity. They would be prepared for their departure, for the benefit of their country, surrounded by all the comforts to which, at their time of life, they would be susceptible, in a college maintained at the public expense; and each, as he drew nearer to the happy day, would be treated with still increasing honour. (*FP*, 3)

If this novel locates a response at the far limits of empire, it is because the insurgent colony represents a kind of play space necessary to the fictive labor. What has been difficult about *The Fixed Period* is precisely what is difficult about age, and indeed about empire. The liminal condition of bodily decline mirrors the liminal condition of the colony: both exist at the borders of experience, and both invite and require radical imagination. Death is a Not Yet, just as the colony is a Not Here.

The English repression and absorption of Britannula ends the utopic absurdist project of John Neverbend. But it does not, and cannot, cancel the problems of age, burial spaces, or the conditions of imperial power. To take seriously Trollope's claim that he meant what he said in *The Fixed Period* is not to assume that he would countenance the never-bending law of death. But it is indeed to say that the unthinkable proposal, placed in the testing-ground of the far colony, was meant as part of a conversation difficult to hold: a conversation about the ability of civic life to turn its face to age and to ask the question frankly, What should we do with the aged and failing, the distracted and exhausted, the dependent and dying? That such questions could now be posed, even within the strained forms of Trollope's fable; that the scandal of age could be represented as a central issue of public debate, deliberate policy, and legislative will—this marked a new scene of age, which will change its aspect rapidly and which it will be our purpose to encounter as it changes, and remains the same.

3

Creases and Crevices, Heights and Depths: Narrative Extremities and Age

The elderly are not alone in the keen, often desperate, pursuit of a bearable life. Still, there are forms of extremity characteristic of old age, just as there are for children, youths, and those in the long middle ages. The principal figures in the next two chapters—Elizabeth Gaskell, Margaret Oliphant, Lewis Carroll, and Queen Victoria—have little enough in common, but each contributes in related ways to the common lot from which an aging sensibility might be drawn. When avenues for meaningful attachments to others or to work are blocked, when passage to them is difficult, or when the young feel thwarted by the success of generations above, then age employs tactics of expression that can violate norms of propriety or even become radically transgressive. In this chapter, we encounter a range of literary and non-literary acts that attempt to represent the extremities of age.

In what follows I begin by bringing together the supernatural, the gothic, witches, and madness, because in their often surprising relations to one another they cast the circumstances of mid-Victorian aging into sharp relief. Each of these conditions is characterized by desperation, each invites the risk of psychic possession. Sometimes the old person is the possessor, sometimes the subject possessed; at other times age is the nurse which either relieves or inflames. Often the elderly narrator is the midwife to the gothic/supernatural, controlling youth through acts of storytelling and by providing tones that frame the meaning of narrative events. An old witch may frighten the young listener, but from the perspective of the elderly she might instead reveal the misery of age; alternatively, she can suggest energies that remain within the aging body and intensities of experience often banished from prevailing social discourse. From a gothic or supernatural perspective, youth frequently looms large in the succession of events: the young may exhibit aggressive desires to attack or obliterate their elders. But this portrait can also disclose the rage and fear of older people, who see youths as demons, eager to be rid of their elders.

In the second half of the chapter I follow a shift in mode that both Gaskell and Oliphant enacted: a displacement from supernatural to verisimilar modes, from forms of excess to styles of everyday life. The arrival at old age appeared to these writers both as an uncanniness, an anomaly, a strangeness, and as the most intractable reality, when hard truths of experience—frailty, dependency, mortality—showed themselves most vividly. My structure of argument here is to see the improbable and probable narratives of age, not as sharply contrasting, but as mutually implied. The gothic and supernatural representation of age discloses circumstances of quotidian social reality, but the verisimilar realisms consistently turn up forms of excess that make daily reality strange again. The chapter concludes with readings of Gaskell's *Cranford* and Oliphant's *Hester*, two works that take 'speculation' as a narrative resource for thinking about age.

All fantasy, from the mild daydream to supernatural intervention, depends on a habit of mind we might call 'speculation.' But of course there is another, more determinate use of the word which associates it with risky financial ventures. I intend to exploit the play between the meanings in order to engage narratives of age which illuminate the private corners which the elderly do not typically share with other generations and which youth does not typically explore. I mean to expose the risk involved in such exposure: for visibility forces an acknowledgment of extremity and brings private emergency into the public world. Moreover, the works of Gaskell and Oliphant, which together mark a short but distinct historical span, take up opposing attitudes toward speculation that will help to frame the late-century agitation charted in the last two chapters. Common parlance aligned financial speculation with modernity because the scale of economic gains and losses became increasingly grand: governments scrambled to meet the urgencies of rapid industrialization, competing markets (at home and abroad), and increasingly fluid economic and social conditions. Imaginative speculation, on the other hand, had no more claim on one period than another. It captured the mind as it wandered freely between all epochs of individual life or collective history; alternatively, it yielded 'speculative fiction,' like fairy or folk tales and parables, and, as the century advanced, utopian and futuristic fiction. All these forms become fables of generation.

The eeriness of age

Lewis Carroll's forays into the fantastic provide a good entry to the field, because of their disarmingly mild insistence that we look closely—occasionally more closely than we might find comfortable—at the universe of old age. Carroll's works generally separate 'real' from 'dream.' But the distinctions between the two are sometimes disturbingly and productively confused. The pairing of youth and age is a common trope in his work, provoking some of his deepest imaginative impulses, and in the two *Sylvie and Bruno* books their encounters are persistent and resonant. The story loosely follows the paths of two fairy children as they search for their elderly father, who has left his kingdom in the hands of a 'speculating' relative who hopes to seize the kingdom as his own. At the same time, the ailing narrator, who belongs to the human world, visits a physician-friend in the country, in order to recuperate. He enters into his friend's social world, but also meets and mixes with the fairy children on their excursions: the alternating movements generate an intricate reflection on age.

From the start, the aging narrator looks to find images for the coupling of young and old. It "was a pretty sight," he notes at one point, "to see the mutual love with which the two faces—one in the Spring of Life, the other in its late Autumn—were gazing on each other."[1] In the *Alice* books, which we will consider in the following chapter, a few significant creatures are marked 'old,' set within a frame clearly intended to suggest age wrapped around youth. But in these two later works, the number of elders increases until it encompasses a mass of figures. The narrator's old age and precarious health make him susceptible to the "eerie" condition required for the perception of the fairy world and other heightened mental and sensory experiences.[2] An aging beggar transforms into the old Fairy King; Sylvie and her old father find their complements in the 'real' world in Lady Muriel and the Earl of Ainslie, a "genial old man" and a loving father. Among the world of creatures age also signifies: for example, an "ancient crab" (*S&B*,

1. Lewis Carroll, *Sylvie and Bruno, The Complete Works of Lewis Carroll* (London: Chadwyck-Healey Ltd, 1994), 291.
2. Carroll describes the condition of "eerieness," which he considers a pre-requisite for access to the worlds of fancy, in his 1893 Preface to *Sylvie and Bruno Concluded*. Unlike the "ordinary state" which precludes perception of other worlds, or a "trance," in which *only* the extraordinary world is perceived, "the 'eerie' state" maintains awareness of both the actual and the fantastic (*Complete Works*, 512).

342) recalls the 'crabby' but good-hearted aged Gardener. Age is not only part of the world; it is a significant feature *of* the world. Creatures, fairies and characters do not double one another so much as they provide shadow or echo, adding the dimension which comes with age, and making that the norm, so that characters without it seem thin and insubstantial. "[H]ave you ever happened to notice another Professor, something like me, but different?" asks the elderly Professor at one point (*S&B*, 375). The two professors go simply by the names 'the Professor' and 'the Other Professor.' There are no distinct outlines among the aging figures: all remain slightly out of focus, slightly blurred, as if youth cannot quite see them clearly, or they themselves are visually impaired. The blurring brings new opportunities as well: where we lose the sense of integral character, we gain the possibility for diverse characterization, not so much multiple characters as shades and echoes all sharing the likenesses of age. If in the 'real' world, age is invisible through its own superfluity, in Carroll's fiction it is essential, and thus visible.

Carroll's aged figures cannot always see *with* youth, and the disparity causes regret on both sides: the children yearn to reach the fairy kingdom where their father now dwells, but obstacles separate them. From the opposite direction, the narrator repeatedly finds himself shut out from the genial world he would inhabit with the youth he finds so appealing: "I knew it would be impossible for *me* to follow. I could but stand outside, and take a last look at the two sweet children, ere they disappeared within, and the golden gate closed with a bang" (*S&B*, 383). The attractive condition of "eeriness" permits the transformation from one form into another, just as it assists in the movement from one place or condition into another. Family likeness similarly makes reciprocity a norm. Characters who are 'like' are not necessarily like-minded; rather, they are sympathetically inclined, emotionally disposed towards each other. This state enhances relations between old and young even while it respects the integrity of each. Still, the separations between youth and age are permanent, and transformations typically are horizontal rather than vertical. That is, young characters and old characters find complements within their own age groups.

Carroll's strategy departs from that often found in fairy tales, where young and old may exchange places. Consider, for example, the fairy queen in Jean Ingelow's *Mopsa the Fairy* (1869), whose bondage takes the form of enslavement within senescence. Her release from slavery and old age depends on finding someone willing to offer his most valuable coin in exchange for her. Notably, in Ingelow's tale, it is precisely a young boy rather than a young man who is the willing party. The old lady attracts the boy Jack by her gentle engagement with *his* needs rather than through the seductions of beauty or youth. But her attentions to him have little dramatic force: it is her transformation *back* into a beautiful young lady which transfixes both boy and reader:

> She had a little knot of soft grey hair, and she let it down and began to comb. And as she combed the hair got much longer and thicker, till it fell in waves all about her throat. Then she combed again, and it all turned gold colour, and came tumbling down to her waist...she was so covered with it that you could not see one bit of her, excepting her eyes, which peeped out, and looked bright and full of tears.
>
> Then she began to gather up her lovely locks; and when she had dried her eyes with them, she said: 'Master, do you know what you have done? Look at me now!' So she threw back the hair from her face, and it was a beautiful young face.[3]

But her recovery of youth—the conventional trope—only incites the tale to look back again toward age. Within moments of regaining her identity and after countless years spent as an old lady, the Queen refers to another ancient, known as "the apple-woman," who inspires the fairies' love because she relieves the tedium of their happiness by making them cry. She also evokes her own "old mother Fate," who is most powerful since her dictates prevail despite all efforts to counter them. Old Mother Fate does not appear, except as the plot itself, as if the old storyteller and the stories she tells are one and the same. The elderly, especially women, frequently figure in fairy tales, but Auerbach and Knoepflmacher point out the peculiar abundance of old women in Victorian fairy tales, and their various impersonations as the tale 'spinner,' and the nurturer, guide or impediment to immature youth.[4]

In Carroll's works the source of imaginative interest in old age does not derive from a dread (or fascination) with becoming old or retaining youth. Characters may change size and shape, and even gain a few years—as do Sylvie and Bruno when they appear as youths visible to humans—but the chronological divide which is loose around proximate edges keeps firm at the extremes. This is because Carroll is less interested in the intrapsychic dynamic of a single consciousness living through time than in the psy-

3. *Forbidden Journeys*, ed. Nina Auerbach and U. C. Knoepflmacher (Chicago: University of Chicago Press, 1992), 254. 4. Ibid. 13–14.

cho-social interchange between generations. *Each* age is dense and fraught, but Carroll maintains strict boundaries between them. Though old age enters the youthful universe only as an outsider, it remains a privileged standpoint from which to comprehend the world: "I stood in the midst of the group, as unconcernedly as a ghost, seeing but unseen," says the narrator of *Sylvie and Bruno* (*S&B*, 430). The young fairies can see beyond their realm, and they are aware that often they are unperceived. But though they register, they have no capacity to interpret the difference. The older consciousness (and body), detached from his own world through frailty, illness, neglect, or leisure, possesses the mental concentration necessary to explain the distances in terms more or less critical. Sometimes the distance produces discontent, as when the young and beautiful Lady Muriel first appears, and the narrator comments "with some bitterness... *She* is the heroine. And I am one of those subordinate characters that only turn up when needed for the development of her destiny" (*S&B*, 295). But the regret is more affectation than bitterness, since the tale centrally depends on the supervening mind of Age. These first instances let us broach the connection between Victorian supernaturalism and the circuit of generations. Following Carroll, we notice a willingness to suspend the trajectory of individual aging in favor of the phantasmogoria of encounters across the ages. Within the modalities of the unreal universe, characters become absorbed in their generational antonyms, deeply curious about the strange figures who half-resemble them, even as their closest bonds remain within their own group. Youth continues to enjoy the prerogatives of agency, cavorting through a world of rich incident. But age possesses the privilege and power of narration: the clarity of distance and the resources of comparison, interpretation, comprehension. It is, after all, a marked feature of the narrative act that it so comfortably stands in a condition of seniority. When it speaks at any distance of retrospection, as it does in almost all but epistolary fiction, the narrative voice—third or first person—is always in the posture of the elderly, *no matter how young it may be*, towards the earlier events that it recounts. In this respect, narrative is itself the performance of aging.

In narratives with a greater reliance on realistic conventions, the occasional turn to the supernatural exposes frightening aspects of old age. Consider, for instance, Lucy Snowe's uncanny encounter with the old woman she designates 'Malevola,' a.k.a. Madame Walravens, in Charlotte Brontë's novel *Villette*. Employed by Madame Beck on the pedestrian task of conveying through Brussels a "pretty basket, filled with fine hothouse fruit, rosy, perfect and tempting, reposing amongst the dark green wax-like leaves, and pale yellow stars of, I know not what, exotic plant" to Madame Walravens, Lucy finds herself on a deserted "no street at all," where "Antiquity brooded" not the least within the ancient church, "whose dark, half-ruinous turrets overlooked the square." A sudden downpour drenches her and nothing living meets her eye except for one "infirm old priest, who went past, bending and propped on a staff—the type of eld and decay."[5] The "very old woman" who opens the door leads her to a "desolate" room, where, as she gazes at a picture on the wall, Lucy finds "to my bewilderment, it shook, it sunk, it rolled back into nothing; its vanishing left an opening arched, leading into an arched passage, with a mystic winding stair; both passage and stair were of cold stone, uncarpeted and unpainted. Down this donjon stair descended a tap, tap, like a stick; soon, there fell on the steps a shadow, and last of all, I was aware of a substance" (*V*, 388). The 'substance' is none other than "Malevola, the evil fairy" who possessed "a hundred years in her features, and more perhaps in her eyes—her malign, unfriendly eyes, with thick grey brows above, and livid lids all round. How severely they viewed me, with a sort of dull displeasure!" (*V*, 389). The tiny skeletal figure is decked in the brightest colors and glittering jewels. "Hunchbacked, dwarfish, and doting, she was adorned like a barbarian queen," and she speaks "with the voice rather of male than of female old age" (*V*, 389). Lucy enters the fairy tale as an impartial, unknowing agent, but she turns out to be the central figure, who *to the very figures she portrays as threatening* she is the greatest threat of all. Her youthful ambition to maintain a school of her own, and her romantic passion for the man upon whom these two women (and the old priest) depend, make her a menace to the hopes of an older generation. Of course the reader sees through Lucy's eyes, but the older, narrating Lucy makes it possible for us to see past her younger self, and to see what, as a character, she cannot see. The social dimensions of narratives of age become dense with the private fears and fantasies that youth and age project onto the other: part of the instability of such narratives derives from the volatility of the subject/object position, and the fluctuating affective condition of each. In sensation literature, these ambiguities are perhaps less fraught because more starkly presented.

When her daughter asked if she had read *The Moonstone*, Queen Victoria admitted, "I have heard of but not read *The Moonstone*...I am not fond

5. Charlotte Brontë, *Villette* (Oxford: Oxford University Press, World's Classics, 2000), 386, 387.

of sensational ones."[6] Instead, she recommends Margaret Oliphant and Mrs. Craik. Oliphant also objected to many 'sensational ones.' In her essay on "Sensation Novels" written in 1862 for *Blackwood's*, she names the reasons for her critique, and then explains why she exempts Wilkie Collins from most of the charges she hurls at others. Sensation novels are composed of a "strange hybrid between French excitement and New England homeliness"; it is precisely the mix of the feverish with the phlegmatic which characterizes the genre which renders incident implausible, much as it inhibits the drawing of character. Turning to *The Woman in White* rather than *The Moonstone*, she praises Collins (opposing him to Dickens in *Great Expectations*) for both originality and execution. What makes the book exceptional is the portrait of its villain, the elderly Count Fosco: "He is intended to be an impersonation of evil, a representative of every diabolical wile: but Fosco is not detestable; on the contrary, he is more interesting, and seizes on our sympathies more warmly than any other character in the book." What appeals to her most is not his diabolical cunning, but his genial and unexceptional good nature: "what virtuous people would call his 'simple tastes,' his thorough enjoyment of life, and all the pleasant things within reach."[7] Characters in the novel, even his victims, initially share Oliphant's good opinion. Unwary, they admire the shock of extraordinary within the habits and inclinations visibly associated with this corpulent, aging impresario. Marian Halcombe describes how

> This fat, indolent, elderly man, whose nerves are so finely strung that he starts at chance noises, and winces when he sees a house-spaniel get a whipping, went into the stable-yard on the morning after his arrival, and put his hand on the head of a chained bloodhound—a beast so savage that the very groom who feeds him keeps out of his reach.[8]

His relentless pursuit of money drives him to persecute the three young women who stand in the way of his reward; but what captures the reader's imagination is his evident *pleasure* in devising ingenious plots which enfeeble each of the women by manipulating her thoughts. To be sure, 45-year-old Sir Percival bears responsibility for the attempts on the lives and sanity of the females too, but he is a mere lout: we prefer Fosco's aging calm, his cultivated grace and mature self-irony.

6. *Darling Child: Private Correspondence of Queen Victoria and the Crown Princess of Prussia 1871–1878*, ed. Roger Fulford (London: Evans Brothers, 1976), 43.
7. Margaret Oliphant, "Sensation Novels," *Blackwood's*, 91 (May 1862), 565, 567, 568.
8. Wilkie Collins, *The Woman in White* (New York: Modern Library, 2002), 222.

As we saw in the chapter on Dickens, lunacy laws were notoriously lax, and Collins exploited their vulnerability in several novels. Where Dickens notes the elision between the aging poor and the lunatic, Collins focuses on the easy manipulation of the legal system by the respectable classes. Cases of abuse are plentiful and well-documented. Recall for instance, the stories narrated by Louisa Lowe, secretary of the Lunacy Law Reform Association. Lowe describes the sorry tale of one old lady whose younger relatives arranged for her to be kidnapped and committed; they made her release conditional upon her transferring legal powers to a nephew whose control included the right to re-incarcerate her if she refused his advice. In another case, an old man was incarcerated by his second wife, despite the insistence by a daughter of the first wife that he was perfectly sane. Lowe addresses herself to William Gladstone, "an aged woman" appealing to an aged man for "Just and Safe" lunacy laws.[9]

Lunacy is frequently the means by which sensation literature exposes the fault lines indicating social failure—failure to deal with economic unrest, female agency, and marginal groups, including the aged. What makes Collins's treatment notable in *The Woman in White* is the decision to arm two fragile groups—young women and older people—each often the target of questionable incarceration, against each other. Madness can inflict its pain on anybody at any stage of life, but older people were considered more vulnerable because the mind lost its elasticity just like other organs, and even "the best constituted female mind is susceptible of being totally unhinged" at puberty, during the childbearing years, or at the onset of menopause.[10] A more conventionally transgressive plot would pitch the powerful against the weak, but Collins's insight here is that Fosco's power derives not so much from his gender (he is notably 'feminine' in many ways which he and other characters note), or his social position. His age provides the cunning and broad experience he exhibits, and his poverty provides the motive. Subjugation to the male plays a part, but not so great a part in this drama of vulnerabilities. Fosco even thrives on his inability to succeed: in 'The Count's Narrative,' his parting thrust is to exalt his desire for Marian even as he acknowledges its hopelessness:

9. Louisa Lowe, *The Bastilles of England; or, The Lunacy Laws at Work* (London; Crookenden & Co., 1883), 13–16, 46–7, 48.

10. Edward John Tilt, *The Change of Life in Health and Disease: A Practical Treatise on the Nervous and Other Afflictions Incidental to Women at the Decline of Life*, 2nd edn. (London: John Churchill, 1857), 266.

> We were received at the mansion by the magnificent creature who is inscribed on my heart as "Marian"—who is known in the colder atmosphere of Society, as "Miss Halcombe."
>
> Just Heaven! With what inconceivable rapidity I learn to adore that woman. At sixty, I worshipped [*sic*] her with the volcanic ardour of eighteen. All the gold of my rich nature was poured hopelessly at her feet. My wife—poor angel!—my wife who adores me, got nothing but the shillings and the pennies. Such is the World; such Man; such Love. What are we (I ask) but puppets in a show-box? Oh, omnipotent Destiny, pull our strings gently! Dance us mercifully off our miserable little stage! (*WW*, 616)

Two binaries, gender and age, circumscribe the sensation of this narrative: manly Marian, and womanly Fosco on the one hand; on the other, youthful Anne, Laura, and Marian, who together approximate the age of Count Fosco, their foil. The sensation of generational vulnerability and aged volatility is at least as thrilling as the more conventional, expected drama among the young.

Like Milton's devil, Fosco frequently draws interest away from the congress of the good. He attracts something deeper from the reader than sympathy and tears: he draws a complete fixation. When he is in the room no other character holds our attention; no scene, dialogue, or situation matters so much as the details of his person and predicament. We love to loathe him; we loathe to love him. But where others have focused on the manner in which Collins makes evil interesting, attractive, and erotic, I want to emphasize how he makes age and aging bold and appealing. "At the ripe age of sixty," Fosco commands in his concluding remarks, "I make this unparalleled confession. Youths! I invoke your sympathy. Maidens! I claim your tears" (*WW*, 629). Here as everywhere else, a grotesquely fat and aging figure makes youth seem paltry and insignificant.

Bewitched: styles for staging old age

In 1584 Reginald Scot published a treatise on witchcraft in which he describes "who they be that are called witches":

> One sort of such as are said to bee witches, are women which be commony old, lame, bleare-eied, pale, fowle, and full of wrinkles; poore, sullen, superstitious, and papists; or such as knowe no religion; in whose drousie minds the divell hath goten a fine seat; so as, what mischeefe, mischance, calamitie, or slaughter

> is brougth to passe, they are easilie persuaded the same is done by themselves; imprinting in their minds an earnest and constant imagination herof.[11]

He attributes the prominence of older women among witches to the ceasing of menses, at which time the uterus was dislodged and might migrate to the brain, where it could wreak havoc, causing the "melancholike humor" which "is the cause of all their strange, impossible, and incredible confessions of witchcraft."[12] By the age of 63, he claimed, women enter the final stage of life, known as "the crooked age," from which only death can follow. Lois Banner has commented on such cultural diagnostics by noting the humped back which results from spinal deterioration due to osteoporosis, and which has been long associated with other signs of aging that figure prominently in images of witches: especially wrinkles and the distension of such facial features as nose and ears.[13] To these attributes, Sona Rosa Burstein adds mumbling and mental distractability, finding cause to associate the habits of so-called witches with the common features of senile psychosis.[14] Why such animosity against older women? Banner explains that "there seems to have been a willingness to scapegoat European society's most vulnerable members—its aging women—as the cause of widespread social ills." She supports her claims statistically, pointing out that in parts of Switzerland (the Jura region), France, and England, "the median age of suspected witches was between fifty-five and sixty-five years of age. Witches in New England during the 17th century were somewhat younger (between forty-five and fifty)."[15] Lyndal Roper's recent book *Witch Craze* (Yale, 2005) similarly argues that the predominance of old women charged with witchcraft in Germany testifies to a perceptible fear among the populace that witchcraft was the expression of rage and jealousy towards fertile youth. Some critics have urged caution in the face of these strong claims. Alison Rowlands, author of her own book on witchcraft in Germany, takes issue with Roper, pointing out that "recent research puts the overall average of men executed for witchcraft in Germany [in the seventeenth century] at 24 per cent," a significant minority which

11. Reginald Scot, *The Discoverie of Witchcraft*, 1584; repr. 1886 (London: Elliot Stock), 5.
12. Ibid. 45.
13. Lois W. Banner, *In Full Flower: Aging Women, Power, and Sexuality: A History* (New York: Vintage, 1993), 189.
14. Sona Rosa Burstein, "Aspects of the Psychopathology of Old Age Revealed in Witchcraft Cases of the Sixteenth and Seventeenth Centuries," 65–70, referred to in E. Bever, "Old Age and Witchcraft in Early Modern Europe," in Peter Stearns, ed., *Old Age in Preindustrial Society* (New York: Holmes & Meier, 1982), 150–90.
15. Banner, *In Full Flower*, 190, 189.

she believes Roper's account "trivializes," as it does the other targets in the area, clerics and children, for example. Nor, as she emphasizes, can we assume that the supposed witches took their vengeance only on economically sound families in possession of enviably vibrant children.[16] Edward Bever provides the most comprehensive assessment of the connection between witchcraft, witch trials, and older women: on the basis of evidence drawn from a wide range of sources, he determines that "it seems safe to conclude that suspects over fifty constituted between half and three-quarters of the accused witches" whether in America or Europe.[17]

Outside of fairy tales, old women hold no majority in the literary portrait of witchery, although the features associated with them are drawn frequently from the same ghoulish costume-box. However, in the supernatural tales by Gaskell and Oliphant, elderly people, and especially elderly women, play a part well exceeding the statistical norm. They are not called witches (usually), though in feature and function they are often crones, hags, and are wrinkle-ridden, pale, ghost-like, or simply ghosts. In Gaskell, they may assume the role of narrator, whose account of some mysterious incident blends subtly with the speaking voice and living memory that has the power to communicate it. In the works below, the storyteller's age is part of the story; it becomes the context in which narrative events can unfold. The old man who narrates "The Poor Clare" (1856) explains that elderly people prefer reminiscence to "watching the events...immediately passing before their eyes."[18] In fact, the story he tells concerns the "old faith" (Catholicism) in an "old hall" like an "old keep" with trees so old "that the dead bark had peeled away from sapless old age" ("The Poor Clare," p. 50). Although he himself avoids the claim, we understand that age is a sign for gothic intrusion just as gothic modes often mark an attentiveness to age. In "Disappearances" (1851), the adult narrator records the story told her by "a very clever old lady, of one hundred and twenty—or, so I thought then; I now think she, perhaps, was only about seventy" ("Disappearances," pp. 3–4). The old lady's tale involves the disappearance of a paralytic old man, a mystery which is never solved, and which "left a painful impression on many

16. Alison Rowlands, "A Long Disenchantment: Witch belief and witch persecution across the centuries, and the world," *TLS* (June 3, 2005): 3–4. See also E. William Monter, "Patterns of Witchcraft in the Jura," *Journal of Social History*, 5 (1971), 1–25, who warns us that the scanty evidence left from the Jura trials may not be fully representative.

17. Edward Bever, "Old Age and Witchcraft in Early Modern Europe," ch. 7 of *Old Age in Preindustrial Society*, ed. Peter N. Stearns (New York: Holmes & Meier, 1982), 157.

18. Elizabeth Gaskell, *Gothic Tales* (Harmondsworth: Penguin, 2000) 45. Future references to Gaskell's stories are from this book; pages will be cited parenthetically within the text.

minds" ("Disappearances," p. 4). Significantly, the narrator's recollections of other disappearances involve younger characters whose absences are indeed subsequently explained. A tale which begins with an anecdote that continues to mystify, that leaves an indelible 'impression,' and that is powerfully bound to the witch-like clever lady whose age seemed far greater than was humanly possible—*this* story haunts while the several other anecdotes try to alleviate the haunting. The narrator tries to comfort the reader by praising the detective force, which nowadays makes use of science, technology, and rationality: but these seem scant devices against the unsettling disappearance of a paralyzed old man who is left "to bask in the sunshine" ("Disappearances," p. 4) only to be irrevocably gone in the evening without any evidence of wrongdoing. Would science tell us that the sun melted him? Would rationality prove that his paralysis was healed? Would new techniques discover old blasphemies? At the close, the story's impression continues to cause pain.

The aged Hester narrates "The Old Nurse's Story" (1852), which is situated in a "great, old rambling house" filled with "old pictures" and two ladies, almost octogenarians. The story itself—love, passion, betrayal—is instigated by the guilty party and means to offer youth an unsentimental lesson in the passage of generational time: "Alas! Alas! What is done in youth can never be undone in age! What is done in youth can never be undone in age!" The regret of old age and the hardness of youth explain the aged visages "with their grey, hard faces, and their dreamy eyes, looking back into the ghastly years that were gone" ("The Old Nurse's Story," p. 21). The story suggests an alternative to nostalgia as explanation for a preoccupying interest in a past typically associated with age. The aged do not regret the loss of a past; they regret the past. Neither is the present a comfort. In "The Crooked Branch" (1859) another Hester along with her husband Nathan advance into the horrors of an old age terrorized by their dastardly son. His persecutions are the expedients by which a gothic portrait discloses the vulnerabilities of the aged Benjamin Huntroyd (for such is the son's name) plays demon to his parents, who become "quiet and speechless" ("The Crooked Branch," p. 262), blind, and paralytic, and finally brought to traumatic death. The expressive reach of demonhood or witchery here releases fears and fantasies of the extremity of conflict, and it is significant that the gothic roles can appear on both sides of the generational divide. While the turn toward a supernaturalism is a rich imaginative resource, other narratives—with a stronger attachment to conventions of verisimilitude—bring the evil incarnation within the reach of ethical response, often to the point of introducing the toxin only to stimulate the production of a 'remedy.'

Margaret Oliphant was an apt pupil, and just slightly hurried enough as an author to leave obvious traces of influence in her works. Gaskell's gothic stories imprinted themselves on her consciousness; Oliphant repeats names of Gaskell's characters, refigures her plots, and like Gaskell, makes age an animating force in several illuminating tales. Three stories contribute substantively to our understanding of Victorian age, and particularly to the themes of this chapter: the heightened narrative forms associated with the conflict of generations and the frustrations which make aging fester. Oliphant's "Old Lady Mary: A Story of the Seen and the Unseen" (1884) makes age prominent at the start with the opening sentence standing as a full first paragraph: "She was very old, and therefore it was very hard for her to make up her mind to die."[19] The twist here, explained in a lengthy second paragraph, involves the fact that Lady Mary "had lived through almost everything that is to be found in life. ...She had not forgotten anything in her life—not the excitements and delights of her beauty, nor love, nor grief, nor the higher levels she had touched in her day" ("Old Lady Mary," pp. 163–4). The clue nestles in the ensuing explanation: "All these things were like pictures hung in the secret chambers of her mind, to which she could go back in silent moments. ...Sometimes at such moments there would be heard from her a faint sob, called forth, it was quite as likely, by the recollections of the triumph as by that of the deathbed" ("Old Lady Mary," p. 164).

Memories remind her that she has led a full life, and they stimulate the pleasures of an active present. Where then is the difficulty? Is the 'faint sob' simply a sentimental gesture of self-absorption, or does it signify more deeply? In fact, the story turns on Lady Mary's petulant 'joke,' which consists of a failure to tell anyone that she has made a will, leaving her fortune to the "very distant relation, with 'no claim'" who lives with her ("Old Lady Mary," p. 166). When she dies, the young woman, also Mary (though "little Mary"), is destitute, but out of love for her protector, defends her against all criticism and complaint. Guilt makes Lady Mary return to haunt the house until the will is discovered; more importantly and more eerily, the two Marys share a brief, single "moment" before the young girl faints and the old woman returns to the afterlife.

19. Margaret Oliphant, *A Beleagured City and Other Stories*, ed. Merryn Williams (Oxford: Oxford University Press, 1988), 163. References to other Oliphant stories come from this volume and will be cited by page parenthetically within the text.

The problem with Lady's Mary's comfortable old age, which on its surface conforms to a Ciceronian ideal of moderation, is that it produces death rather than life. A visitor to the pictures hung in the secret chambers of her mind, Lady Mary haunts her own life until in death she can discover the passion which drives old age quite as much as youth. No less than Wilde, who made the claim, Oliphant realizes that an "inordinate passion for pleasure...is the secret of remaining young," or in her case, the secret of remaining vital, attached to life.[20] No secret unhappiness should be posited here, no lingering regret or anticipatory dread: it is rather that Lady Mary's comfortable old age requires the quickening of sensation, an emotional register which here can animate death as well as life. Lady Mary has outlived all emotions: she finds her way back to vitality by finding cause for regret. It is not that she chose to err in order to provoke compunction, but rather that, having erred, she discovers a remorse drawing her to others. The narrative exploits the familiar convention that stipulates some unfinished business which recalls one to life, but more subversively, it implies that the unfinished business *is* life, that the ideal in which there is only smooth passage between will, desire and possibility is itself flawed, as it is based on a static aesthetic (the pictures in her memory) rather than a generative condition.

Lady Mary's death results in a change of consciousness: she realizes that she has become different in *kind* and not simply in degree from the rest of humanity: "she sat down upon the ground, a soul forlorn, outside of life, outside of all things, lost in a world which had no place for her" ("Old Lady Mary," p. 220). She cannot be seen, heard, or understood by any with whom she once engaged. Only a child has the imaginative capacity to perceive her presence, though Lady Mary cannot express herself to the girl. The story calls this death, but it might well represent the life of the aged which goes unseen, unrecognized, invisible. A remote spirit is the image for old age; haunting is its activity. The story concentrates on the living death of an old lady; it employs the supernatural conceit of an afterlife as a means for exploring the death-in-life of the aged.

"The Library Window" is the last piece of fiction Oliphant wrote, in January 1896. Here an older woman, now widowed, describes a visit to her elderly aunt when, as a young girl, she is recovering from a vague 'illness' or

20. Oscar Wilde, "Lord Arthur Saville's Crime," in Oscar Wilde, *The Picture of Dorian Gray and Three Stories* (New York: Signet, 1995), 266.

indisposition. Once again, the story proper is framed by concerns of aging, though it makes little enough of the subject—little enough of any subject—between the frames. A young girl spends her convalescence wondering whether the window she sees opposite her own is real or imagined. She feels certain it is real when she begins to see the shadow of a Scholar, and her Aunt confirms the belief at the close by reminding her of a friend's report that "women of our blood" ("The Library Window," p. 326) possess the ability for second sight. This special perception—visual or mental—is required to see the window and the man, but even then, only a glimpse is possible. In and out of the story, Oliphant weaves the thread of age, age intent to trouble the young, to disturb tranquillity and to frustrate satisfaction.

The unnamed girl (called "honey" by her aunt) brackets the tale with reference to age; however, what makes this story singular is that the Aunt feels only sympathy for youth, while Honey feels competition, resentment, and occasionally fear towards the aged. Her early response is indeed contempt for the tedium of age: "Her life went on in a routine never broken. . . . She said. . .that routine is a kind of salvation. It may be so; but it is a very dull salvation, and I used to feel that I would rather have incident, whatever kind of incident it might be. But then at that time I was not old, which makes all the difference" ("The Library Window," p. 289). Fair enough. But while the Aunt enjoys the rhythm of sociality, Honey enjoys nothing but sitting quietly in a recess, looking out the window, reading, and listening to the tones of animated conversation. She comes to prefer this life with Aunt Mary, who "because she was so old" was also "very tolerant," and leaves space for the life of reveries. The girl's mother, on the other hand, "liked to keep me running about," perhaps because our narrator is seen to be so "fantastic and fanciful and dreamy" ("The Library Window," p. 290).

In her nook within the drawing room recess, Honey "built myself up, with my books and my basket of work" ("The Library Window," p. 290), only to find the fortress permeable by the intrusions of the old: "They were all pressing into my recess, pressing upon me, a row of old faces. . .I had a sense in my mind how curious it was, the wall of old ladies in their old satin gowns all glazed with age" ("The Library Window," p. 292). One lady in particular frightens her, Lady Carnbee, enshrouded in black lace. Her "white, pale, bleached, and bloodless" hands are broken only by protruding veins and a great deal of jewelry, including "a big diamond in an ugly old claw setting" which "clutched at my half-terrified imagination" and made "as if it might clutch me with sharp claws, and the lurking, dazzling creature bit—with a sting that would go to the heart" ("The Library Window," p. 293). Not surprisingly, she compares Lady Carnbee to a witch (p. 294) only to be dumbfounded when her Aunt replies to this announcement only: "Is that what you think, honey? well: maybe she once was" ("The Library Window," p. 298). The old people offer a variety of explanations for the image in the window, and the girl sets all possibilities against her own, admitting that she "would have been better pleased to make out to myself that it was some superiority in me which made it [the window] so clear to me, if it were only the great superiority of young eyes over old" ("The Library Window," p. 302).

The *insight* conventionally assigned to age struggles with the *second sight* which the girl identifies with youth, though an ambivalence intrudes upon her convictions, making her aggression and her guilt equally visible:

> It would have been unkind to think it was because they were old and their faculties dimmed. It is so sad to think that the faculties grow dim, that such a woman as my Aunt Mary should fail in seeing, or hearing or feeling, that I would not have dwelt on it for a moment, it would have seemed so cruel! And then such a clever old lady as Lady Carnbee, who could see through a millstone, people said—and Mr. Pitmilly, such an old man of the world. It did indeed bring tears to my eyes to think that all those clever people, solely by reason of being no longer young as I was, should have the simplest things shut out from them; and for all their wisdom and their knowledge be unable to see what a girl like me could see so easily. I was too much grieved for them to dwell upon that thought, and half ashamed, though perhaps half proud too, to be so much better off than they. ("The Library Window," pp. 306–7)

Just as at the start of the tale, the narrator claims for herself a love of incident and contempt for the quiet life that we soon see she admires. But the attempt at textual fiat is plainly vulnerable here. Indeed part of the subtle work of the story is to unsteady the contrast of generations. From the perspective of aging narrative distance, Honey looks back to chide her younger self and warn the reader: "I was then young and very matter-of-fact. I had not found out that one may mean something, yet not half or a hundredth part of what one seems to mean; and even then probably hoping to be contradicted if it is anyhow against one's self." At one point she placates her "almost angry" Aunt by slyly moving from one 'meaning' to another; "how can your sight be as good as ever when you are in doubt about that window?" The girl knows and doesn't know, and 'it' remains obscure. That 'it' has something to do with creative imagination is clear ("it was like a country which one had discovered" "The Library Window," p. 306), but this is trite, and the story isn't. What gives bite is the contrast between the sympathy of the old for the young girl, and the girl's half-recognition that she yearns for the age that looks terrifying in its limitations and incapacities. Lady Carnbee pricks the girl repeatedly with the diamond tied to her pencil-thin finger—the telltale sign that the knowledge sought by Honey is well known to the old lady witches. "I canna tell you! How can I tell you?" her Aunt confesses, "It is a longing all your life after—it is a looking—for what never comes" ("The Library Window," p. 326). The girl thinks it is a man; critics have called it the creative spirit; the story however, returns to age. In the story's strange conclusion the girl's mother abruptly arrives and tells her to prepare for immediate departure abroad. The girl grows up, grows old, and realizes that "the imagination is a great deceiver, as Lady Carnbee said." When she is "an old, old woman" Lady Carnbee dies and bequeaths the diamond ring to the narrator, who wishes someone would steal it since "I am afraid of it still" and bewildered by its connection to the story of the window ("The Library Window," pp. 330–1). One thing is certain: she who possesses the ring possesses the story of old age. The young girl becomes old—this is the story: the narrator's present and not her recollected past. The child's fear of age does not give way to acceptance or calm; rather, it becomes the fear of an older widow who remembers staring at age and looking away, looking out the window, looking for another plot to tell which might mask the fear, and the desire which haunts the heart, pierces the eye, and rouses the mind.

These narratives allow youth and age to attribute supernatural power one to one other, as a means of representing the great expressive power which generational interaction characteristically involves. Like Carroll, these authors bring cross-age exchange into the substance of narrative; but they extend beyond Carrollian whimsey, making 'eerieness' more sinister than pleasurable, and more painful than sad. Even so, the effect tends to be rather homeopathic than dire; it depends on the inter-penetration and inter-animation of comfort and disease, youth and age. There is no blending of contrasts, nor is the 'mix' equal: the lingering effect is more disturbing than harmonic. One appreciates the relief produced through the recognition of a symptom. But a fully reformist discourse requires the beginning of social legislation, scientific discovery, cultural enlightenment. These are beyond the reach—either more fantastic or verisimilar—of the common witches and demons introduced in these tales.

One further story, "Mr. Sandford," contributes to the representation of aging through plots which depend on forms and forces of the extraordinary, although in this instance it is precisely the question of whether anything extraordinary *has* occurred which stands at issue. Written for *Cornhill* in 1888, the tale unfolds within late-century realist conventions, a kind of mild version of Tolstoy's excruciating tale *The Death of Ivan Ilych*, published two years earlier. Oliphant's story pursues the plight of a painter whose advancing age (he is 60) marks the death knell of his popularity. The point isn't simply that 'tastes change' over time. Like the other stories we have considered, this one insists that each generation inevitably supersedes the last, and that the process is neither pretty, polite, nor pleasant.

Like Ivan Ilych, who feels particularly fine just before his crisis engulfs him, Mr. Sandford first shows himself as confident, successful, prosperous: "a man of sixty who is in perfectly good health does not feel himself to be old though he may be so."[21] The realization that his style of painting no longer suits public taste heightens his awareness of other fragile elements in the picture of his life—such as the failure of family life, in which his wife devotes herself only to the children, who are pleasure-seekers glad to accept complete parental support without contributing anything beyond good cheer. The tale brings together material and psychological pressures in order to complete its picture of a man who suddenly *feels* what it is to be obsolescent. Considering one of his paintings, Sandford realizes that, despite its flawlessness, "there was no occasion for its existence at all" ("Mr. Sandford," p. 346): the remark clearly extends to himself as well. Late one night, in the solitude of his studio, he tries to paint in the new style, confident that he could "make a great success as an impressionist" (p. 354), only to realize the next morning that the work was unworthy.

Oliphant assures us that "such a tragic shock...was not prosaic" ("Mr. Sandford," p. 355). Age comes to everyone who stays alive, but to each with the intensities of ungeneralizable experience. Oliphant's story moves delicately between typification and singularity: "The same thing had happened before—but he had never been sixty before...a sharp and sudden realisation of age and what it means...gives at once a new character to the experience—a character never apprehended before" ("Mr. Sandford," pp. 356–7).

That future only gradually takes shape, as Sandford ages in the course of a few months. Although he renounces suicide, he longs for death, because it

21. Margaret Oliphant, "Mr Sandford," *Cornhill Magazine*, 58 (April 1888), 343.

at once marks his escape and material security (through life insurance) for his family. Here Oliphant points out the obvious, as a means of throwing dust in the reader's eyes: "A man cannot die when he wishes it," and "No one can make sure, however warmly such a decree might be wished for, or even prayed for, that it will be given. If only that would happen!" ("Mr. Sandford," pp. 502, 504). Feeling "on the edge of a precipice," he decides to join his dealer in the Yorkshire moors: the plot takes him to the area where the lights and shadows help define the last portions of a dark canvas ("Mr. Sandford," p. 501). Oliphant challenges the norms of her own realism, bringing her methods close to those of her character and allowing the prospect of death to move realist contingency toward allegorical necessity.

> now and then he would find himself on the moors in the sun-setting, when the western sky was still one blaze of yellow or orange light, varied by bands of cloudy red, with the low hills and sweeps of moor standing black against that waning brightness which...sent out little light. Mr. Sandford did not compare his own going out of practical life and possibility...with that show in the west. People seldom see allegories of their own disaster. But as he strayed along with the sense of dreariness in his heart which the dead and spectral aspect of hill and tree was so well calculated to give, his own circumstances came back to him in tragic glimpses. ...These things glided before him as he looked over all the inequalities of the moor standing black against the western sky. ("Mr. Sandford," pp. 508–9)

Whether he next jumps, is thrown from an upset carriage, or suffers a stroke or heart attack before the carriage overturns—all this is unclear. Still we do know that "The effect was wonderful; the orange growing intense, darker, the yellow light pervading the illuminated sky" ("Mr. Sandford," p. 511). Of course the narrative is obscure: this is its precise effect. The turn to the surreal, the tragic/sublime and the allegorical reflects Oliphant's ambitious attempt to register the force of age as superfluity, and superfluity as death.

Within the narrower terms of social comedy, "Mr. Sandford" ends by diminishing heightened affect in the service of a comfortable resolution, achieved through the breaking of an impasse. The family *is* rescued by his death, while Sandford escapes the bondage of old age. Ironically, though predictably, his reputation is also secured by his demise, and once again his paintings circulate. The romance concludes: "But it is not to everyone that it is given to die at the right moment, as Mr. Sandford had the happiness to do" ("Mr. Sandford," p. 519).

"Suicide" is a name for this death—and this despite the story's wilful abstention from naming the causes of Sandford's end. It qualifies as suicide, not on grounds of internal psychological motive, an *intention*, but as an act willed by a social narrative: the concatenation of circumstances that make death the right outcome at the "right moment." Here we should take note of Victor Bailey's important observation that "In England and Wales in the nineteenth century, the suicide rate rose in each successive age period, reaching its maximum between 55 and 64 years of age." Furthermore, in his study of suicide in the city of Hull, Bailey notes that "economic difficulties" are the primary motive, or at least the accelerating factor, which precipitates the event in this age group.[22] The crisis of confidence which makes Oliphant's Sandford hesitate to move on, his perception that appreciation of his art has dwindled, the loss of income and threat to his family's well-being—all converge in the network of emotions and perceptions commonly associated with age. These produce the paralysis and the panic that make suicide a 'solution' to besetting problems. The impeccable timing is also a register of aesthetic precision; in his last act, Sandford offers his death as a form of art worthy of appreciation; and within the wider contexts of Victorian aging, his self-assertive self-destruction would not have seemed presumptuous. Barbara Gates argues that in the last decades of the century a great relaxation of intolerance towards suicide can be found; indeed Gates claims that "self-destruction was on its way to becoming a central metaphor for *fin de siecle* England. Suicide took on the status of a trope quite easily," with many of the leading late-century journals publishing essays on the subject, while poets and novelists portrayed suicides with greater sympathy than condemnation.[23] Oliphant offers the possibility of suicide without naming it, not because her readers would have been horrified or shocked, but because the definite articulation would have compromised the delicate narrative potpourri she has 'painted.'

Years later, Oliphant would herself address the impasse of age that both incites and obstructs her story. "Faced with the problem of *living on*," she asks, "what is one to do? I confess that I have not had the courage to follow this question...to such depths of human discomfiture as may have been, or may yet be. A greater artist might have done so, and led the defeated man through

22. Victor Bailey, *"This Rash Act": Suicide Across the Life Cycle in the Victorian City*, (Stanford: Stanford University Press, 1998), 212, 223.

23. Barbara Gates, *Victorian Suicide: Mad Crimes and Sad Histories* (Princeton: Princeton University Press, 1988), 155 and 151–67.

all the depths of humiliation and dismay; but my hand is not strong or firm enough."[24] It is clear that she sees her conclusion as a turn towards romance, brought about through sleight of hand. Oliphant started the story a few months before turning 60: it began publication in April, the month of her birthday. She too had been sole provider for a family hopelessly unable to earn any money and wrote the tale "under the influence of the strange discovery which a man makes when he finds himself carried away by the retiring waters, no longer coming in upon the top of the wave, but going out" ("On the Ebb Tide," p. 7). And she too, of course, faced the challenge of generational change, when those who still produced "historical novel-writing" confronted younger writers committed to the "beauty of colour for itself and art for art" ("On the Ebb Tide," p. 347). The story mocks those who spout what Mrs. Sandford calls the doctrine of "new lights" ("On the Ebb Tide," p. 347), but it takes seriously the imperatives of change. No more than art can the body aspire to *stasis*, to a heavy persistence in the present tense. Under the pressure of time and history, the aging self (and the self as aging artist) can confront impossible demands that require unnatural responses in scenes of great strangeness.

Age probable, age speculative

In the middle of her story Oliphant distinguishes the Mr. Sandford who "called himself an old man with a laugh" from the same man at the same age but now in different circumstances, who "stood helpless" ("Mr. Sandford," p. 493). Perhaps an awareness of precipitous fall helps to explain the portrait of robust old age one finds in *Hester*, a novel published in 1883 when Oliphant was only slightly younger, but where we see the subject from a wholly "different aspect" ("Mr. Sandford," p. 493). And yet, for all her strength, the 65-year-old Catherine Vernon is similarly vanquished at the close of her novel. Placing her alongside Elizabeth Gaskell's Mathilda Jenkyns, of *Cranford*, will let us gauge the power, including the social power, of age, even as it acknowledges its surrender to youth. Writing of Gaskell's novella, Pauline Nestor reminds us of the great difference it makes when singleness rather than marriage is the norm.[25] Similarly, we can speak of

24. Margaret Oliphant, "A Preface: On the Ebb Tide," *The Ways of Life: Two Stories* (London: John Murray, 1919), 18.

25. Pauline Nestor, *Female Friendships and Communities: Charlotte Brontë, George Eliot, Elizabeth Gaskell* (Oxford: Clarendon Press, 1985), 51.

the readerly disorientation when the narrative medium shifts from simple to advanced maturity, from adulthood to a perspective incontestably linked to old age. Notoriously, Mary Smith's attitude towards the aging women of Cranford shifts from condescension to admiration; *Hester* is narrated from the start from a position not identical with, but near, its leading protagonist, the elderly Catherine Vernon. As these instances will let us see, there is a narrative *of* old age just as there are narratives *about* old age. In this respect, these works mark a distinction from the imaginative acts of Dickens, Trollope, and Carroll, but they also offer a contrast in the representation of *female* age, which will become as important in the realm of social policy as it does within the practice of narrative.

In Gaskell's *Cranford* and Oliphant's *Hester*, we find a rejection of the supernatural often employed in their shorter fiction, and a turn back toward the conventions of realism. But because both works look to provoking life of 'speculation' within the vagaries of the economic market, they engage their own forms of extremity. Mary Poovey has shown with great care how "the most important component of novelists' adaptation of financial themes to the formal conventions of realism is the way that novelists' control of narrative attention, which leads the reader to focus on some details and ignore others, reproduces for the reader the very dynamic of disclosure and secrecy that was also essential to the emergent culture of investment."[26] This commingling of 'disclosure and secrecy,' is captured in the terms 'investment' and 'speculation' themselves, which were everywhere in the air (*Little Dorrit*) from mid-century. Surely David Itzkowitz is right to point out the difficulty in fully distinguishing between the two, but Poovey's contrast between disclosure and secrecy helps us see how each term draws imaginatively on its own distinctive principles or procedures, even if they share a common source in the market and destination in profit.[27]

Gaskell's 1853 story of a small community of elderly women turns on the sudden failure of the Town and Country Bank into which the Jenkyns sisters had invested their tiny fortune. Much has been made of the high

26. Mary Poovey, "Writing about Finance in Victorian England: Disclosure and Secrecy in the Culture of Investment," *Victorian Studies*, 45 (Autumn 2002), 38.

27. Quoting W. W. Duncan, a speculative broker: "As a matter of fact...investment and speculation are words with but slightly different meanings...The investor receives his interest; the speculator his profit. Again a distinction without much difference." David C. Itzkowitz, "Fair Enterprise or Extravagant Speculation: Investment, Speculation, and Gamboling in Victorian England," *Victorian Studies*, 45 (Autumn 2002), 125.

ethical manner in which Mathilda Jenkyns ("Miss Matty") responds to the dramatic change, both as a response to the losses of other investors in the Joint Stock Company and to her own life of "retrenchment" which allows an annual income of only £13.[28] Written thirty years later, Oliphant's *Hester* narrates the history of Vernon's Bank, a country institution whose fortunes are twice compromised—first by the reckless expenditure of John Vernon and next by the reckless speculations of Edward Vernon—and twice saved by the indomitable Catherine Vernon, who successfully runs the bank herself for the many decades which separate the two incompetent men. The resourcefulness of these women in the face of economic crisis has dominated critical focus for good reason, but my own interest has less to do with the fact that *old women* deal admirably with economic crisis than that age itself is inscribed within the narratives in a manner extending well beyond the characters themselves. In these novels, age is an attitude, a disposition of the text. It has been my contention throughout that it is in this fashion that we best understand the inscription of Victoria's 'age' on her 'Age.'

We might begin with the claim that investment and speculation have narrative analogues which account for their potency within the text. The aging women of *Cranford* famously sustain their gentility through a system of "elegant economy," which allows the imaginative licence to ignore or deny all evidence of economic need, expansive sociality, or cultural broadness. It is crucial, however, that we know that they see what they do not say, and the discontinuity between the two—between what *is* and what is desired—captures just that generational distance between youth and age that makes possible commerce between what is separated. The genteel past of the once young women no longer exists in the present circumstances of their age: by preserving the illusion of gentility, however, they create the conditions for 'speculation,' the conditions by which limited interest from investments, limited annuities, indeed many other styles of limitation, that might come to seem 'sufficient,' 'enough,' or even slightly more. There is a curious Wonderland aspect to the town of Cranford which results from their elegant, 'speculative' economy. By adopting a method which adjusts to reality by fictionalizing it, the ladies of Cranford participate in the same *kind* of activity which, down the generic line, transforms the mundane into the extraordinary, and old women into witches, fairies or wicked stepmothers.

28. Elizabeth Gaskell, *Cranford* (Oxford: Oxford University Press, 1998), 138, 140. Future references from this edition will be cited parenthetically within the text.

Deborah and Matty Jenkyns uncannily resemble the Red and White Queens in their respective domineering and confused habits; the aged Mr. Brown and Mr. Holbrook are each in their own ways like Carroll's White Knight; and the "fat," "inert," "dull," "pompous and tiresome" Mrs. Jamieson could pass easily for Humpty Dumpty (*Cr*, 24, 116). From the perspective of Alice's youth, the creatures of Wonderland and Looking-Glass seem bizarre and otherworldly, as do the creatures of Cranford from the early descriptions of Mary Smith. We will see how age alters our perception of Carroll's creatures, and here too, as Mary adopts the attitudes of the characters she most admires—first Mathilda and then also Peter Jenkyns—the uncanny figures are re-cast in more familiar costume. In effect, the novel recapitulates in reverse the conversion of actuality into something less than ideal but more than 'real,' transforming reality into something which might be called "good enough." The phrase can be likened to Trollope's use of "old enough," which, we have seen, indicates a satisfying generational equilibrium. In Gaskell's story, 'good enough' marks the elusive social space where the possible meets the desirable.

More precisely, we might say that the work of character is to move from the actual to the desired condition, whereas the work of plot is to trouble that motion, so that unadorned reality can be accepted satisfactorily. For example, "the great Cranford panic" (*Cr*, 104) arises from the indulgence of fantasy stirred by the appearance of Signor Brunoni, an itinerant magician who performs in the town. The cluster of excited activity among the old women reaches a pitch when their fears and fantasies accelerate beyond their capacity for toleration. Self-proclaimed skeptic and cynic, but also the one "to have had adventures" (*Cr*, 82), Miss Pole becomes "the principal person to collect and arrange" rumors "so as to make them assume their most fearful aspect" (*Cr*, 89), and even "Miss Matty did not like to be outdone, and capped every story with one yet more horrible" (*Cr*, 92). "Conjuration, sleight of hand, magic, witchcraft" (*Cr*, 83)—the old ladies work themselves into a condition of near hysteria, and what begins as pleasure becomes, as the inimitable Sam Weller once ordained, "too excitin' to be pleasant" (*Pickwick Papers*, ch. 20). Here plot intervenes serendipitously: in search of "some old woman" who knits, Miss Pole rediscovers Signor Brunoni, only this time he is poor, sick, and reduced to his 'real' name, Samuel Brown. Amid the ensuing efforts to help the ailing man and his family, Mary Smith admits that "Somehow, we all forgot to be afraid"—but the "somehow" is a fictional 'feint' since she has just explained "how the great Cranford panic, which had been occasioned by his first coming in his Turkish dress, melted away into thin air on his second coming—pale and feeble" (*Cr*, 104). Mary Smith narrates what she does not 'see,' leaving us to join the cycle and, like the old ladies, to see without telling what transpires.

Non-working women and spinsters unburdened by family have archetypically—and often in cruel stereotype—been assigned leisure for fantasy. But women have no monopoly on the fantastic in Cranford. As many have noted, Mathilda's brother, Peter Jenkyns, eagerly places his restless imagination in the service of his sister at the close of the novel. Peter's gender is deliberately confused, but even more than his cross-dressing or his sympathy with women, he shares the narrative power of an absorptive age. Like them, he has learned that "a little credulity helps one on through life very smoothly,—better than always doubting and doubting, and seeing difficulties and disagreeables in everything" (*Cr*, 108). *Cranford* is a landmark text in the affirmation and celebration of old age, rejoicing in its labor of productivity; it manufactures a kind of safe speculation—which of course appears oxymoronic, but no more than 'elegant economy.' Again like Trollope, Gaskell makes paradox the means for achieving commerce between incompatibles, and thus to render unstable circumstances 'good enough.' "A kind of," "a sort of," and "like" are significant locutions which circulate freely among the aging Cranfordians. So, for instance, Lady Glenmire's poverty is considered of a piece with her marriage to a Scottish aristocrat, who is ineligible to sit in the House of Lords: an impoverished aristocrat "seemed a kind of swindling us out of our respect on false pretenses; a sort of 'A Lord and No Lord' business" (*Cr*, 76). But the situation only comically exposes an ability to employ creative paradox as a means for adjusting reality to desire.[29] Waiting excessively long for the butler to bring tea, Lady Glenmire "grew quite impatient, but it was a pretty kind of impatience after all" (*Cr*, 77) one which never upsets decorum or amiability. On another occasion, Mrs. Forrester is seated first, but in the second place of honor since her standing is not as prestigious as the sister-in-law to a (deceased) earl: her position is 'high,' but not 'high enough.' Mary Smith offers her own comparison to "a seat arranged something like Prince Albert's near the Queen's—good, but not so good" (*Cr*, 65). The language of approximation is what makes things

29. I am indebted to Tanya Stanciu for a class paper she wrote on the advantages of what she called "flexible phraseology," including paradox, employed by the ladies of Cranford.

'good enough' without making them ideal. The old speak a language of compromise and toleration without sinking into resignation. It is a language which permits a kind of regulated speculation: the ladies "speculate" about how Mrs. Jamieson will respond to a marriage which defies class distinctions (*Cr*, 115), and Mary describes her attempt to find the absent Peter as "this speculation"(*Cr*, 128). At the meeting where the aging Cranfordian spinsters—most of them like Mrs. Forrester "not poor exactly, but...[not] what you may call rich" (*Cr*, 138)—decide how much each can contribute secretly to Miss Matty's income, the outcome is an investment with no interest ("your father," they tell Mary, "knowing her investments, can fill up the blank" *Cr*, 137). The "secret" investment (an investment which is no investment) ends up producing a surprising return when Peter is able to restore the money, provide gifts, and reward all with his highest estimation. A 'kind of' investment or speculation, or a 'speculation but no speculation' is what the ladies of Cranford excel in most.

The linguistic pattern does not simply exploit an economic terminology: it suggests a model for financial exchange and for the currency of age. For Miss Matty trade is much more than a monetary transaction: she opposes the norm of profit and loss and replaces it with one of profit with no loss. Elizabeth Langland describes how Mathilda's brief but successful foray into Victorian business "supercedes the competitive business ethic with a cooperative social ethic": Matty offers "collaboration rather than competition" when she discusses how best to sell her tea without depriving Mr. Johnson's shop of any sales.[30] For my purposes, it is crucial to see that Matty's tea shop succeeds precisely because it is not quite a tea shop. If Mary Smith, who devised the plan in the first place, recognizes "The only thing against my plan was the buying and selling involved" (*Cr*, 133), it is because she understands that linguistic elasticity has a social concomitant, which resembles nothing so much as moral/economic reciprocity. Matty will give the children extra candy and her adult customers "good weight" for their tea (*Cr*, 148). In return she gains a devoted following among the young and receives many gifts from the adults. It is cliché now to say that 'it takes a village to raise a child,' but Gaskell shows that a community is necessary before old age can flourish, before it can contribute to social good by engaging in its own production of value. Miss Matty will always require Marthas, Peters, and Marys: the first to

30. Elizabeth Langland, *Nobody's Angels* (Ithaca, NY: Cornell University Press, 1995), 124.

tend her physical needs, the next to bring her gentle preferences and projects into the social realm, and the last to give these same a literary form, so that they can be communicated to a still wider audience. But if the aged require assistance, in Gaskell's version, they offer at least as much in return. It is not a case of loss and profit: it is not even a fair exchange. These old ladies ask for nothing though they graciously accept what others are willing to give, and they offer something priceless—not in return, but in any case.

The elderly women of Cranford 'speculate'—financially and imaginatively, by taking risks and by projecting wider possibilities—and in so doing, increase the value of meager investments. Out of small capital and large fancy, and through the liberal acceptance of paradox, they manufacture a community which is 'good enough.' If their peculiar circumstances supply the context for this transformation (few men live in Cranford, though they dominate the near, but not so near, Drumble), it is their age which furnishes not only knowledge, perspective, and imaginative reach, but also a medium of experience that creates its own habits and dispositions, vocal tones and language patterns, ethics and economics, its own distinctive form of life. Here again, the movement from Gaskell to Oliphant marks both a consolidation and a turn. Cranford's community of elderly women generated more than even Gaskell likely anticipated. It contributed to the narrative form of a 'medley'—of which Tennyson's long poem *The Princess* (first published in 1847, though revised after) is the prime example—but it also established a Literature of Age in the broadest sense: a thematic, a rhythm, a tonality, a new set of narrative possibilities.

In 1894 Margaret Oliphant wrote to her publisher, John Blackwood, to propose a book, *The Words of a Believer*, which would present "my own theories of the world and its management," but she worried about assigning gender to the narrator since "it would be more actually true to make a woman the speaker, but a generation ago it would have given the adversary an occasion to blaspheme against old women and their maunderings. I doubt whether this would be the case now; but it is a curious question, and one on which I should like to have your advice."[31] Gaskell's women of Cranford may well represent just the sort of old women whose "maundering" conversation might be denigrated by readers impatient for straightforward speech and strong actions. But the old people who populate Oliphant's

31. *The Autobiography and Letters of Mrs. M. O. W. Oliphant*, ed. Mrs. Harry Coghill (New York: Dodd, Mead and Co., 1899), 403–4. The book was published a year later in *Blackwood's*.

fiction tend towards a conversational style which is straightforward, even terse; often they express their deepest thoughts through smiles, laughter, tears, pauses, or other forms of insinuation or silence. Sarah Gamp aside (she is an exception to every rule), the garrulity often attributed to old people has little resonance in the works of those Victorian authors most attentive to their presence. In Oliphant chatter is distinctly a youthful affectation, and even reminiscence is more often asserted than enacted by the text. We have noted Oliphant's attempts to outline an aesthetics of old age, which Wilde will perfect in the next generation, but like Dickens, Gaskell, and Trollope, Oliphant conceives her literary charge as inseparable from the social and economic circumstances in which they grow. In *Hester* a historically specific generational discord both sharpens the portraits of age and provides a dynamics for aging. "They have one way of thinking, and we have another," a character puts the case starkly, "They are young and we are old" (*H*, 230).

The novel accepts that age is as likely to engender folly as wisdom, self-preoccupation as selflessness (to wit the Vernon hangers-on who populate the almshouses). But if age is no proof against speculation and profligacy in general, it nonetheless plays a crucial part in devising alternative patterns for communal discourse. These collective practices of mutual reliance differ, notably but not radically, from those achieved by Cranfordians at the close of Gaskell's novel. I introduce them here not to encumber the case, but to demonstrate the importance of slight differences, when each nuance illuminates new corners in which age has crouched.

Catherine Vernon is 65 at the novel's start, but her present position is largely defined by an economic crisis of over thirty years earlier, which demanded both her fortune and her expertise. Having saved the family's bank from the profligacy of its reckless chief, Catherine has managed it successfully for those decades. At her retirement, she appointed two young men—Vernons also—to assume her place, leaving her free to establish almshouses for the poor aged members of the family. The novel begins with the gathering of family, and the narrative divides between a romance centering upon three possible suitors for the young Hester Vernon, and a generational plot focusing on the tensions between youth and age. Both plots are complicated by the 'royal twist' with which, as we know, Oliphant typically endows her fictions. In this case, Catherine Vernon's wealth, position, and personality establish her as "more than the Queen"; she is compared to a Saint and even described as "almost like God" (*H*, 46, 23, 50). But while she is revered by the small county society, her standing breeds resistance among relatives—young and old—who feel acutely the "ungenerosity in the midst of her generosity" (*H*, 36) that sometimes takes the form of "ostentatious benevolence" (*H*, 58). Like Lady Mary, considered above, Catherine's life of good fortune renders her indifferent to the tensions stirring around her. She fails to comprehend signs of trouble at the bank, where Edward Vernon's weak ethics and Harry Vernon's abundant ineffectual good nature create an increasing instability. The aging Caroline can comprehend neither Harry's value, nor Edward's deceit, nor Hester's uncanny likeness to her (younger) self.

The heavy oppressive power of age is what stimulates an illustrative succession of events. Unable to return Catherine's exhausting and possessive love, Edward Vernon feels desperate to gain a fortune, so that he can flee the bank, the family, the county, and the woman who, even in her retirement, continues to control them all. His plotting creates no surprise: he takes the money of his customers and speculates recklessly with it, causing panic and the threat of another run on the bank. Once again, Catherine's resources and her management are required to save the bank, the family, and the people who have entrusted their resources to them. Again, the extremities of speculation put questions of age in sharp relief. Here, however, the valence suggested within *Cranford* is reversed. The speculative habit is a condition of youth and modernization, a reflex prompted by a refusal of an older woman and her traditions. In large measure, the change here reflects the changing circumstances of modernization between Gaskell's and Oliphant's work. *Cranford* reflects the hold of a provincial settlement, where age finds room to flourish outside the looming modernity of the nearby city. Oliphant's Catherine Vernon, however, lives within an inescapable modernity that has raised possibilities for speculative finance on a scale undreamed of in Cranford; now the work of age is to resist the lure of speculation and to preserve time-sanctioned habits of social and monetary exchange. Edward Vernon understands the economic precisely in terms of generational contrast. "'Aunt Catherine is—all very well; but she's an old woman. She may have understood business in her day. I suppose she did...But we cannot permit ourselves to be kept in the old jogtrot because of Aunt Catherine. She departed from her father's rule, no doubt. One generation can't mould itself upon another'" (*H*, 318). Indeed, "the headlong poetry of the money-market" derives from its novelty: "It was like an old woman's insane objection to anything daring...It would be like pouring in new blood to stagnant veins; it would be new life coming in, new energy, something that would stir the old fabric through and through" (*H*, 247, 249). But speculation is necessarily associated with secretiveness: Edward refuses to disclose his activities to the clients, his business associates, his family, or even to Hester, whom he claims to love. His half-hints and partial disclosures cause not only disease, but also an excitability that can best be described as a kind of speculation itself:

> But the most uneasy of all was Hester, who that day, for the first time, took upon her the most painful burden of women—the half knowledge which is torture, which the imagination endeavours to supplement in a thousand unreal ways, knowing them to be unreal, and dismissing them as quickly as they are formed—and the bitter suspense, the sensation that at any moment things may be happening, news coming which will bring triumph or misery, but which you cannot foresee or accelerate, or do anything but wait for. (*H*, 351)

Women are receptive to the 'dis-ease' of speculation because they are privy to half-truths. But in this case Hester's powerful likeness to Catherine mitigates against the spread of disease from Edward, and reinforces the sense that the relation between the girl and the older woman is stronger than that between the two young people. Indeed if the ending to *Hester* is exhilarating because it refuses to settle the question of Hester's marital choice—notoriously, she is left to consider the possibilities of no marriage or to choose between two very eligible suitors—it is more so because it refuses to subordinate the relations between youth and age to the marital plot. The deepest romance of this novel is that between old and young. Despite the usual snags and stumbles, nothing irregular obstructs the path of love between younger men and women. But the course of love (shared, withheld, denied)—and the range of love (tender, obsessive, eager, reserved, knowing, blind) between young and old unfold with great care and originality. Here the narrative is unsentimental and unpredictable.

"Love," it must be quickly said, is after all only one name for the ramifying connections across the lines of generation. Oliphant continually tests the variety of dispositions that cross-generational relationships excite. Mrs. John, Hester's mother, enters in the robes of a familiar conceit—the silly, frivolous girl grown into a pathetic, trivial old woman. But the daughter's presuppositions about her mother are constantly overturned, letting us glimpse the inner pain which gives dignity to the manifest follies all too easy to dismiss. Although she wishes Hester to accept Harry Vernon's proposal at least in part so as to establish her own comfortable position, Mrs. John shows herself fully conscious of her daughter's contempt for this desire. Hester is oblivious to her mother's attempt "to get rid of that plaintive tone which she was herself aware of, which she had so often tried to remedy" (*H*, 103), and is genuinely surprised to learn that she had felt their dependence on Catherine as "so bitter." To her daughter's exclamation "you never let me know that you felt it," Mrs. John replies "What would have been the good...when we could do nothing? The thing was to put the best face upon it" (*H*, 105). We realize that much of the seeming-folly lies in the work of "face," and if the best face is also the most conventional one, that simply lays out the demands of reading age. The very fact that Mrs. John remains known only as the appendage of her deceased, disgraced husband (he who initially caused the bank to fail) is enough to warn us that there is another woman—only partially developed—about whom we know next to nothing. She herself, on the other hand, offers surprising moments of knowledge, the knowledge for instance "that nothing a mother could say would please a child nowadays" (*H*, 108). For her part Hester is long in coming to recognize her mother's depths. In fact she cannot see that her eagerness to dismiss her mother serves her own purposes. In a wry narratorial aside, Oliphant confesses: "To feel your parent smaller and sillier than yourself is sad. A great many young people do it without any adequate reason, strong in their sense of being the reigning monarchs of the present, while their progenitors belong to the past. Perhaps indeed it is the nature of youth to take a pleasure in such superiority." She goes on to say that it is different when the parent fails to comprehend a child, but then confounds the additional insight once again by adding that "Mrs John was very well aware of it herself" (*H*, 99).

Much of the interest of *Hester* for our purposes lies in its determination to bring the aged out of the shadows and to suggest that life on the fringes of sociality can lead to the accumulation of social force. Captain and Mrs. Morgan, each over 80, are the two oldest characters in the novel, and while the Captain is the first to draw attention—in large measure because his relation to Catherine Vernon derives from the mother, and he is thus not a "true" Vernon—his wife is the another who is found first in a nest of platitudes, but steadily makes her way toward a gnomic resonance. She may be a poor, invalided outsider, but she speaks literal and figural truth when she says that "I see everything from my window" (*H*, 117). Hester speaks to the aged Morgans "as she never talked with her mother" (*H*, 100): it is no surprise when she discusses Harry Vernon's proposal with them instead of having that conversation—for which her mother yearned—at home. Mrs. Morgan's surprisingly measured advice not only raises her in our estimation, it also dignifies the mother, Mrs. John, as she could not have dignified herself. Both Hester and Captain Morgan are rebuked on the grounds of their youthfulness, for even though he is in his eighties, "you are so young, my dear; and my old man, bless him, he is very young." What age has to say to youth here is that dichotomies are easy: that is why youth grasps for them. "You are so young and so fierce," is Mrs. Morgan's recognition, and in response she teaches that "this world is a very strange place. Right and wrong, are like black and white; they are distinct and easy. The things that baffle us are those that perhaps are not quite right, but certainly are not wrong" (*H*, 119). Here we are close to the Cranfordian perception that language must be more nuanced if it is to capture the real conditions of ethics and social practice. The words are simple, the sentences direct, but, like the speech of the elderly ladies of Cranford, the language offers a release from semantic impoverishment and an opening to moral subtlety. The novel suggests that this is what Mrs. Morgan has learned by seeing everything through a window.

Oliphant, however, is staunchly resistant to a sentimental reading of the wisdom of age. Alongside the attractive portraits of insightful but forgotten women, she fully acknowledges the degradations of age. The pensioners who cling parasitically to Catherine Vernon, the crowd of Vernons, appear as the Looking-Glass opposites of the ladies of Cranford. Their version of 'elegant economy' is comic too, but it is made harsh through the display of resentment, greed, jealousy, and false pride. They are spiteful and hypocritical hangers-on who seize upon the fiction that Catherine has generously dangled, pretending that they condescend to stay in order to help Catherine out. Instead of gratitude, they offer contempt and disregard. Unlike Augusta Webster's almoner, who loses touch with the world entirely—"my world that has forgotten me, a waif | floated away from it on too rough tides left spoiled and stranded to drop piece by piece" ("In An Almshouse")—Oliphant's almoners retain their worldly connection only through the endless gossip they exchange and the bitterness they cultivate. There is no joy, no rest, no enlightened consciousness, despite their ability to see through and see widely.

The closed circle of conversation, in which aging disappointment turns and feeds upon itself, stands as an antithesis to the risky but productive relations between young and old. One thinks here of those 'cousins' to the Vernon parasites, the hangers-on who wait upon Miss Havisham in *Great Expectations*. In both cases, the self-enclosure of age generates frightful images of moral failure, as much to suggest that, left to themselves, the elderly will tend to refine the poison of selfishness, whereas social ties across generations—ties of the greatest variety—will encourage an entirely different trajectory of age.

Parents and children, sponsors and protégés, masters and apprentices, memory and anticipation—these connections across a distance of time, as well as across the distance of social position, invite (though surely do not guarantee) a flexible reciprocity founded on the acknowledgment of difference.

This last thought brings us back to the aging Catherine Vernon herself, whose eminence in the community owes everything to her intricate web of relations. And yet part of the challenge of this character—and her importance within a history of Victorian aging—is that she is both at the center of a network and separate from it, at once an exemplary social creature and, from her position of strength, a force of opposition. Her chief oppositional instrument, perhaps improbably, is laughter. But in *Hester* laughter and farce are no balm gently laced with irony, as we might find in Carroll; Oliphant employs these tones more aggressively. Humor is Catherine Vernon's leading response to the complex milieu that surrounds her. "I laugh. It is the best way," she explains (*H*, 172), and indeed her ability to keep herself amused marks her well-being as she ages. Eileen Gillooly has described the many instances in which women in Victorian fiction use laughter for violent ends: it is one of the few expressions open to women which might subversively transform the fixities of their lives.[32] Age, like gender, renders its 'victims' vulnerable, and the humor which Gillooly recognized as the means for a daughter's defense, or maternal sympathy, becomes also an instrument for the 'mother's'—or grandmother's—revenge. In her youth Catherine was denied love through marriage; as an adult her work supplied her with satisfactory relation; as an old woman, in the absence of more intimate feelings, she takes what remains—her power and clarity of vision—as the means to assemble a community whose antics can provide her with amusement, if not sympathy or love.

Laughter, after all, is a conspicuous trans-generational reflex, one that keeps the elderly within the wider human mix. It is also what allows the young to enter the web of sociality. Notably when Hester comes to maturity and finds the courage to break from the past, "She suddenly laughed out" (*H*, 395). But when Catherine faces the shock of Edward's infamy (for his willingness to abandon the bank is recognizably second to his eagerness to abandon her, to whom he owes everything) her own laughter fades, and for the first time she feels the isolation of age. "Her laughing cynicism" is no protection against his betrayal (*H*, 359), and although in

32. Eileen Gillooly, *Smile of Discontent: Humor, Gender, and Nineteenth-Century British Fiction* (Chicago: University of Chicago Press, 1999).

public she "laughed them to scorn," as soon as her coarse relatives depart, we are invited to see "how very little like laughter was her face" when the effects of the ordeal wash over her: "Catherine's face lengthened and darkened as if by a sudden effect of years; the sanguine life and confidence and force went out of it She looked an old woman in that moment" (*H*, 360). In her desperation, she tries to recover the power of amusement—"She would...teach herself to see the humour in this as in so many things. Was not seeing the humour of it the last thing that remained to the noble soul amid the wonder of life?" (*H*, 381)—but in the final phases, the eruptive power of laughter gives way to the slow force of patience. When the crisis comes (again) and she has no private fortune to contribute to the bank, Catherine's behavior is a rebuke to each of Edward's secretive steps. The counter of age to surreptitious, speculative youth is a forbearance and an openness seen as only possible within the broad sweep of a long life. She meets repeatedly with anxious people, listens to their worries and tries to assuage their doubts:

> She bore everything - the long hours of contention, of explanation, of censure, of excuse, of anxious pointing out again and again of the strong points in her case. She argued it all out with every individual, and again with every combination of them, when two or three together would return to the old objections, the difficulties they had originally started, and which again and again had been argued away, with no doubt the natural special pleading of all who speak in their own defence....She bore those repetitions of the old objections with composure. She did not get impatient, twisting and turning in her chair like Mr. Rule, or crushing her impatience under foot like Harry. (*H*, 424).

The young grow tired, whereas age "has a right to its dolorous triumph....The young can sleep, but not the old" (*H*, 419, 421). Or again: "Youth is more simple than age even when it is most self-willed" (*H*, 412). Age is not distressed by repetition; neither does it make a prize of novelty. Catherine's patient, inexhaustible attention breaks the narrative rhythm of eager cupidity; the ability not to come quickly to conclusion, not even to aim for conclusion, is a gift of the elderly; it marks a triumph over the feverish and monied desires of the young. Through Catherine's late long labor, the book endows age with a power of critique inseparable from the power of example: we learn that henceforth the bank will be run along the conservative lines that allowed it to flourish during the three decades of Catherine's rule.

And yet the force of the triumph depends on its being ultimately a lost cause. The second time around—that is, in the time of the present narrative—Vernon's Bank is saved by the old but returned to the hands of the young. Within the austere representation of this cold-eyed narrative, generational change is remorseless.

> If the young but held out, even the most unwise and the most cruel, they must win in the end. ... in the long run the battle was to the young ones. They had time and passion, and universal human sympathy, on their side, whereas the old people had none of all these, neither time to wait, nor passion to inspire, no sympathy anywhere in heaven or earth. (*H*, 380–1)

Hester offers one of the century's most sustained and subtle reflections on the life of the elderly, but it refuses to celebrate age at its close. Conscientious to the last, Catherine passes on her knowledge, while the young simply accept their inheritance. The ending is marked by a curious absence of romance: Catherine dies of a broken heart and it is uncertain whether Hester will choose to marry either of her eligible suitors. There is no exaltation, no devastation: we end on a note of suspension, poised among available tones and modes. Although Catherine has died and Hester is ready to assume the prominence to which she is titularly entitled, the voice and perspective at the close are distinctly old(er). We read that "Catherine had not been able to bear the grim mockery, the light of a farce upon that tragedy of her own" (*H*, 456). But the irony here is that the farce belongs as much to age as to the tragedy which she endures. Ultimately it is not the young who triumph but narrative itself, and the forms for narrative which have been associated with age: detachment, stamina, memory, observation, critique, forbearance.

Teresa Mangum notes that in many Victorian paintings the old stand outside the central foci of narrative interest.[33] It is an essential perception. But as we have begun to see already and will recognize in far more detail in the final chapter, when the elderly are excluded from the center, they often assume indispensable, even quite remarkable, powers. Frequently, in narrative as in painting, the old see, and are seen, from an angle. Commonly we find them at or near a window, on a bench, along the wall, or in a corner. From their relative positions, they may feel themselves large or small.

33. Teresa Mangum, "Little Women: the Aging Female Character in Nineteenth-Century British Children's Literature," in *Figuring Age: Women, Bodies, Generations*, ed. Kathleen Woodward (Bloomington: Indiana University Press, 1999), 60 (59–87).

According to J. W. Kay, writing in *Cornhill* in 1862, because age teaches perspective, it allows one to feel small once again. This is a Carrollian insight. Alice, it has been said, experiences all the changes of size which accompany childhood and adolescence. But old people also experience changes of size, both physically and, as it were, 'mentally.' Kay writes that as the elderly, "we learn to measure our own powers aright; to know how little we can do; how small the space we occupy in the world."[34] He even connects the diminution of the self with the enlargement of sympathy ("On Growing Old," p. 507). Certainly an older character's perspective may coincide more easily with the artist/narrator precisely because of a distance that is self- or socially imposed. Of course the angle may be so skewed as to create an eccentric, even, expressionist, effect rather than to encourage (the illusion of) impartiality. Oliphant's pensioners peep from windows, around walls, and from gardens, but their spite turns everything they see bitter while Catherine's humor—until the end—turns everything comic. The capacity to occupy extreme points on the spectra of modes and tones is part of what made the elderly often most significant when they are on the most distant margins.

Writing of the representation of the elderly in nineteenth-century painting, Susan Tamke has elaborated on social costs of estrangement from the focal center: "They are never viewed as a 'self' but as an 'other.' The only emotions they show are directed toward the young or toward heaven. They do not act, but are acted upon; they are objects rather than subjects. They are outside the human community except as they relate to the young."[35] As in paintings, the novel also traditionally reserves 'first place' for the young, who must answer the narrative questions of romance, vocation and self-definition. We have studied several challenges to this generic settlement, and Oliphant's novel *Hester* puts in stark perspective the difference generated by small adjustments of focus. Hester remains at the center of her novel, but she is not central to its concerns. That position is reserved for Catherine, and for the vexed relations between young and old which predominate because of the rich affective force of one old lady's experience. The insights of Mangum and Tamke into Victorian painting help us to 'see' what has been erased, but without challenging the power of their assessments, our

34. J. W. Kay, "On Growing Old," *Cornhill Magazine* 5 (April 1862), 502

35. Susan Tamke, "Human Values and Aging: The Perspective of the Victorian Nursery," in *Aging and the Elderly: Humanistic Perspectives in Gerontology*, ed. Stuart F Spicker, Kathleen M. Woodward, and David D. Van Tassel (Atlantic Heights, NJ: Humanities Press, 1978), 68.

movement through these narratives has suggested another dimension to marginality. It has suggested, first of all, that even youthful protagonists avail themselves of the resources of the peripheral. So, for instance, 'honey' in Oliphant's "The Library Window" chooses whenever possible to sit outside the circle of old people in her aunt's home. And Hester also prefers to sit "in the background, half hidden by the curtains and by the Captain's seat" (*H*, 80); we see her enshrined "in the shelter of the curtain, invisible from outside, hardly visible within" (*H*, 118). Brontë's young heroines—from Jane Eyre to Caroline Helstone and Lucy Snowe—all prefer Jane's ideal to "see without being seen" and not only because they prefer to choose what has been imposed as their destiny, but also because they understand the advantages of the fringe or perimeter.[36] These examples all suggest that the "marginalizing of the elderly," whether it is making the best of a bad lot or choosing one's destiny, is a complex fate and that it is compatible with central narrative interest. The works discussed have also suggested that while the old are indeed relegated to the outside and while they can rarely choose to alter their position, they retain surprising powers of agency.

One telling power—subtly congruent with the narrative forms that surround it—is the power of observation and interpretation. Even without moving from the fringe to the center, these aged figures perfect the instruments of knowledge.

> Catherine Vernon shared, with most sovereigns and the ruling class in general, the peculiarity, not indeed a very unusual one, of liking to know everything that went on within her sphere. It was not as gossip, nor, she would have said with some reason, from curiosity alone. She had for so long been all-powerful, and sure that the means were in her hand to help those that wanted help, and to regulate affairs in general for the benefit of the world, that it had become a necessity, almost a duty on her part, to keep herself informed of everything that went on. When an individual feels capable of performing the part of a visible Providence, it becomes incumbent upon that person, so far as possible, to know everything, to shut his eyes to no detail, to note every little incident, and to encourage not only the confidences of his possible clients and *protégés*, but the observations of all surrounding them, and every hint as to their motives, their intentions and purposes, that can be got at. . . . It was her wish that everything should be told to her, and she was perhaps too apt to think that those who were not willing or able to open their hearts, were people who had secrets in their life, and probably a good deal that would not bear the light. (*H*, 121)

36. Charlotte Brontë, *Jane Eyre* (New York: Norton, 2001), 141.

As we will see, Victoria expresses a similar desire, and like Catherine Vernon she came to feel her purpose often thwarted. It is hardly shocking to intimate that as sovereigns age, their powers decline. In many ways, Victoria's political powers began to decline from the moment she ascended the throne. But if it is too simple to chart the course of age as decline, it is too benign or sentimental to adopt the optimism of many Victorians who wrote about age as if it could, with slight modification, attain the harmony between desires and capacities which Cicero's Cato promised to the well-regulated man. Catherine Vernon's wish to know everything reflects a desire to remain the sovereign mistress of her world. But that hope is itself only the shadow of another—the wish to retain self-control. Retaining command over oneself and one's 'satellites' recapitulates the Trollopian fantasy of empire and age constructed in the last chapter. Trollope was one of many to depict the stealthy convergence of an expansion of space with the extension through time, and to represent this narratively as a problem of generational contest between youth and age on the one hand, empire and colony on the other. By the 1880s and 1890s many narratives exploited the analogy: one has only to think of Rider Haggard's astonishing late-century success to be reminded how imperial imagination intersects with fantasies of shape-shifting age. But, as we have seen through Trollope's example, the parent/child metaphor inscribed within the colonial paradigm is itself fractured and unstable. Throughout the nineteenth century, writers struggle to represent the precarious imbalance provoked by generational discord. But empire is only one way to describe the preoccupation with extension through time and space; it gives way to other forms for expressing the inexorable aging of self and society which this book charts.

Like claims of class throughout the nineteenth century, generational necessities are typically expressed as some form of 'need,' pressed on a society in which resources are held to be scarce. Under these conditions, the wants of the elderly appear as excessive demand, monstrous desire, or hopeless and inconceivable fantasy that should be contained through social regulation at home or through (forced or voluntary) emigration abroad. From the Dickensian perspective, there is little to choose between the young Oliver Twist or the old Fagin, the young David Copperfield or the aged Trotty Veck, when it comes to asking for "more." Young and old clamor for more food, more love, more money, even more information. The application for 'more' from a society reluctant to spend its collective capital helps to explain policies of regulation and containment at home as well as the attractions of empire. But if young and old alike require social nourishment to thrive, or at least not to die, what distinguishes youth from age is the nature of the claim. The young want what nature has already bestowed while the old often seem to want an extension to nature's bestowal. The old are embarrassed by their needs; the young are embarrassed only by the lack of means to fulfill them. We see this sharply and poignantly in Lewis Carroll's *Alice* books, where the White Queen apologetically enacts her confusion, the Red Queen's anger mounts in proportion to its futility, and young Alice perpetually revises strategies for reaching her goals. With these late thoughts in mind, we return to the 1860s, when Queen Victoria famously casts herself in the role of 'aged Queen' and initiates the long process of retrospection, which, as we shall see, became a central agon in the last third of the century, as well as a primary image by which the Victorians were characterized by future generations.

4

Victoria to Victorian: The Queen and her Age

In 1869 Lewis Carroll composed an invitation to himself from Queen Victoria for the purposes of amusing youngsters he had met on a train. The invitation stated: "Dear Mr. Dodgson, I hope you will be able to come to our garden party on Friday afternoon. Yours truly, Victoria R."[1] Victoria would have been gracious to have issued such an invitation, given that when Carroll saw her for the first time (on the occasion of her visit to her son at Christ Church in 1860), he was "shocked to find how short, not to say dumpy, and (with all loyalty be it spoken), how *plain* she is."[2] Elsewhere, he indulges in a fantasy of refusing the Queen his photograph on the grounds "'that his rule is never to give his photograph except to *young* ladies.' I am told [he writes] she was annoyed about it, and said, 'I'm not so old as all that comes to,' and one doesn't like to annoy Queens, but really I couldn't help it, you know."[3]

These playful daydreams conjuring a relation with the Queen are unexceptional for the times: an illusion of social fluidity incited fancies of unlikely, even ludicrous encounters. The reveries speak to an imaginative licence provoked by the relative oddity of a reigning female sovereign and encouraged by the illusion of familiarity made possible by the mass distribution of images (photographs, engravings, cartoons) circulated by an ambitious press. Margaret Homans argues that, in the decade after Albert's death, writers repeatedly re-created girls in the figure of the Queen, as a way of filling in the absence left by Victoria's grief-stricken withdrawal. Her suggestion is that as figures of the Queen proliferate, as they do in the Carroll stories, the power of royalty dwindles, and the name Queen comes to be an empty signifier. Homans

1. *Letters of Lewis Carroll*, ed. Morton N. Cohen, (London: Macmillan, 1979), i. 135.
2. Ibid. 44.
3. Ibid. 116.

cites, for instance, Carroll's Queen of Hearts, whose command "off with their heads" loses credibility as it is repeated.[4] Elaine Showalter remarks on the proliferation of Queens in the middle and later century, noting that the eminent physician and friend of Dodgson, Dr. Hugh Welch Diamond, "was struck by the great number of female lunatics who claimed to be queens" resident in the Surrey Asylum in which he was psychiatric consultant.[5] The abundance of Queens is indeed a significant feature of many texts and artifacts throughout the 1860s. But here I consider the preoccupation with royalty, manifest in the multiplication of girl Queens, as a process by which national character was endowed with a generational dimension and a chronological fluidity. Albert's death vastly accelerated the aging of his bereft spouse. The swift passage from wife to widow transformed the spectacle of both a girl queen and a happily domesticated matron into the unstable and agitating figure of an aged monarch desperately seeking to maintain her privilege. However, and crucially, the later images did not cancel the earlier ones. At any moment the Queen could now be figured as an innocent girl, a concerned and solicitous matron, a wise and experienced elder, or, alternatively, as an old woman either exhausted or engulfed by passions made grotesque by their intensity at her "age." Alice's sudden transformations from one size, condition, or space to another, oddly configure the abrupt, unsettled experiences with which Victoria contended in the period after Albert's death, and convey a sense of the nation's preoccupation with its own age as the century neared its close.

Victoria becomes Victorian

Many writers have analyzed the relation between Queen Victoria and the age which bears her name, realizing that, though the two are not neatly convergent, their relation is inescapable. Elizabeth Langland, for example, examines the extent to which English culture fashioned itself in the aspect of its Queen: as maternal, domestic, and socially (though obviously not economically) bourgeois.[6] W.E.H. Lecky had similarly characterized her in discussing "Queen Victoria as a Moral Force," where he concedes that

4. Margaret Homans, *Royal Representations: Queen Victoria and British Culture, 1837–1876* (Chicago: University of Chicago Press, 1998), 96.
5. Elaine Showalter, *The Female Malady: Women, Madness, and English Culture, 1830–1980* (New York: Pantheon 1985; repr. Penguin, 1987), 87.
6. Elizabeth Langland, "Nation and Nationality: Queen Victoria in the Developing Narrative of Englishness," in *Remaking Queen Victoria*, ed. Margaret Homans and Adrienne Munich (Cambridge: Cambridge University Press, 1997), 13–32.

> Lord Salisbury probably in no degree exaggerated when he said that if he wished to ascertain the feelings and opinions of the English people, and especially of the English middle classes, he knew no truer or more enlightening judgment than that of the Queen. She thought with them and she felt with them; she shared their ambitions; she knew by a kind of intuitive instinct the course of their judgments; she sympathized deeply with their trials and their sorrows.[7]

The Queen thought of herself in closely similar terms. In a letter to her eldest daughter in 1872 she wrote that "I always feel what a blessing and advantage it was for me to have lived in such very simple and restricted circumstances—almost humbly—and that is why I dislike so living in great Palaces. My tastes are simple and humble."[8] Modest, domestically inclined, and fertile: this was how Victoria's reign was depicted at mid-century. Her expanding family was a productive figure for England's expanding empire, as was the deliberate cultivation of her Elizabethan predecessor whose geographic expansionism prefigured (and validated) the imperial will of the Victorians. If Victoria was a second Elizabeth, she not only reflected her predecessor's luster, she augmented it by compounding the image of a Queen regnant with a second image of the devoted wife and mother. Reflections of Victoria as a composite of mother, wife, and empress are found pervasively within the text and imagery of the period. In *Queen Victoria's Secrets* (1996), Adrienne Munich points out the less decorous side of Victorian 'Englishness': the domestic familiarity coupled with increasing influence in foreign lands had its negative images in both the repressive and rapacious sexuality for which the Queen (and her age) came to be known.[9] In 1867, Walter Bagehot noted that the domestic Queen "brings down the pride of sovereignty to the level of petty life," something with which even common people might identify.[10] But at the same time, as Munich argues, familiarity made her vulnerable to cultural debasement, and indeed debasement of an evocatively specific kind: "her contemporaries could imagine

7. W. E. H. Lecky, *Biographical and Historical Papers*, 506–7, British Library W52.1155.
8. July 31, 1872; *Darling Child: Private Correspondence of Queen Victoria and the Crown Princess of Prussia 1871–1878*, ed. Roger Fulford (London: Evans Brothers, 1976), 56.
9. Adrienne Munich, *Queen Victoria's Secrets* (New York: Columbia University Press, 1996), 3.
10. Walter Bagehot, "The Monarchy", ed. *The English Constitution*, Miles Taylor (Oxford: Oxford University Press, 2001), 41. Not surprisingly, Thompson, Langland, and no doubt others writing about Queen Victoria also have found this quotation useful. Homans offers a splendid analysis of Bagehot's characterization of the monarchy. See *Royal Representations*, 101–15.

her as an erotic powerhouse."[11] Indeed, the press lost no time in hinting of the Queen's erotic liaisons with her gruff rustic equerry John Brown after 1864 and Prime Minister Benjamin Disraeli, who attributed his successful relations with the Queen to his manner: "Gladstone treats the Queen like a public department, I treat her like a woman."[12] Even when she was almost 70 years old, rumors flew about her passion for her youthful Indian servant Munshi Abdul Karim (in his twenties), to whom she awarded a variety of privileges that provoked scandalous gossip. Munich makes the daring judgment that "Her sexual passion singled her out as one of the world's famous lovers, comparable to Cleopatra, Helen of Troy, and George Sand."[13] And then apart from the explicit innuendo, the public showed itself keen on hints of Victoria's sexual command. If, in official portraits she appears as pure, regal, sweet, and untouchable, in more informal photographs and cartoons she appears under the iconic conventions of 'comely' and 'winsome.' John Plunkett, who has analyzed the royal *cartes de visite*, concludes that in contrast with formal portraiture, they "created an intimate familiarity with the royal family," that indeed, "Victoria's photographs were invested with a heavy ideological mixture of ordinariness and intimacy,"[14] where intimacy can be another softly coded name for desire.

Yet these reveries of a supple and yielding body intersect with images of strength and assertion, and the effect is of a divided cultural fantasy that incites daydream but resists determinacy. Dorothy Thompson (in "Queen Victoria: The Monarchy and Gender") has argued that the cultural work of Victoria derived from her institutional position, rather than her private and domestic life and that it encouraged the radicalization of women, even as it "tamed the radicalism it inspired."[15] This is the perspective adopted by most scholars writing about Victoria at the end of the twentieth century, but

11. Munich, *Queen Victoria's Secrets,* 156.
12. Quoted in Elizabeth Longford, *Victoria R.I.* (London: Weidenfeld & Nicolson, 1964; repr. 1998), 402; Robert Blake gives two reasons for Victoria's antipathy for Gladstone: "his Liberalism put her liberalism to shame"; and formality seemed like coldness. In contrast, "Disraeli never underestimated personality in politics"; he recognized Victoria's enormous ambitions and pandered to her fantasies. See Robert Blake, "Gladstone, Disraeli, and Queen Victoria," *The Centenary Romanes Lecture* (delivered November 10 1992, Oxford University) (Oxford: Clarendon Press, 1993), 10, 16.
13. Munich, *Queen Victoria's Secrets*, 211.
14. John Plunkett, *Queen Victoria: First Media Monarch* (Oxford: Oxford University Press, 2003), 163, 181.
15. Dorothy Thompson, "Queen Victoria: The Monarchy and Gender," in *Outsiders: Class Gender and Nation* (New York: Verso, 1993), 164–84.

Carroll too had offered the image of a queen fractured into several independent and mutually exclusive pieces: the Red Queen with her emasculated husband, the angry duchess, the fragile and helpless White Queen, and the ambivalent Alice Queen. In her essay "Queen Victoria, Empire, and Excess" Munich invokes Carroll, among others, who represent the Queen as excessive, over the top, massive, fit for an empire.

Lewis Carroll's Alice books capture the sense of a culture saturated with Queenliness, and one indication of the dominance of the Queen in the imaginative life of her people is the fantasy of likeness between them. Though she claimed royal prerogative, Victoria often figured herself as the embodiment of the ordinary. In this guise she believed she could understand her subjects as no one else could; she was fit to command, not simply because of her royal birth, but because of her thorough knowledge of the British people. In similar fashion, her subjects often felt they understood their Queen. Margaret Oliphant, for instance, whose works we have considered in the last chapter, returns here as a hard-pressed literary worker who plotted her own life alongside her neighbor from Windsor, the Queen, and often finds that the latter falls short by comparison. Here we examine the alternating transparency and opacity between Victoria and her people, the recognitions and mis-recognitions that gave surprising power to the relations between the aging queen and the multi-aged public

Of interest here is how the exuberant multiplicity of images come to reflect a cumulative, *retrospective* glance, a glance which perceives, say, the young queen through memory, regret, and nostalgia ('the Queen as she was') or the older queen with some of the attributes of her younger self, and finally the aged queen as the embodiment of an entire life experience. Each of these perspectives inserts momentary representations within the long narrative of age, providing what we may call an 'aged' context for all perception of the Queen. The nineteenth century became 'Victorian' when it became old, that is, when it described its attributes from the position of age. The present discussion, by extending the analyses of works by Carroll, Oliphant, and Gaskell begun in the last chapter, will explore the constructions of age in the later part of the century, which prepared the ground for public debates in the nineties and into the early years of the twentieth century.

Descriptions of the period frequently resemble those of a fond parent, 'touching up' the images which memory selects. Often, for example, we see a picture of social life modeled on small, domestic scenes. In 1884, Victoria herself writes that "[I] know perfectly well what my people like and appreciate and that is 'home life' and simplicity."[16] With nearly half a century of experience on her distinctive perch, she engraves her image with the favorite domestic maxims of the age. Munich characterizes the royal marriage as "staged" and Victoria's grief after Albert's death as "performed"; indeed, she claims that "the monarchy depended upon skillful exhibitions and heartfelt performances."[17] Here it is important to notice the convergence between deliberation or craft, and the spontaneous expression of genuine emotion; and also to recognize a variety of performances alongside the diversity of affective life. If the Queen stylized 'home life and simplicity' on the one hand, her experience also led her to express grave doubts about the pleasures that these forms generate. At 21, marriage seemed only bliss, but at 60, she briskly opines that "The longer I live the more I think marriages only rarely are a real happiness. The most are convenience—not real happiness."[18] Her early ambivalence about children becomes decidedly negative over time. She complains about her fertility and that of her own children, protesting "The family becomes too enormous," while she hopes that the "number [of grandchildren, especially the boys] won't increase."[19] Notoriously, the squirming bodies of infants repulsed her. Childbirth, she writes to her own daughter, made her feel uncomfortably like a cow and reminded her of the unseemly connections between animals and human beings. She attributes her disaffection from babies to a reaction against her own mother's enthusiasm: "I know dear Grandmama went into such ecstasies over them, so that I felt the reverse."[20] Older children may not be physically loathsome, but as she writes (again to her daughter): "you will find as the children grow up that as a rule children are a bitter disappointment—their greatest object being to do precisely what their parents do not wish and have anxiously tried to prevent."[21] All of this is not simply to say that, as she grew older, Victoria changed her mind about central life experiences: more important is the subtle revision that brings obscurities into startling focus and that made her age—and her Age—an ongoing construction and reconstruction.

Carroll, of course, knew nothing of Victoria's aversions towards the body or her suspicions of children. In earnest or jest, the Queen was publicly portrayed as a doting mother. Nonetheless he imagines a baby as a pig, and

16. February 27, 1884, *Beloved Mama: Private Correspondence of Queen Victoria and the German Crown Princess 1878–1885*, ed. Roger Fulford (London: Evans Brothers, 1981), 160.
17. Munich, *Queen Victoria's Secrets*, 84–5; 11.
18. January 10, 1879; *Beloved Mama*, 34.
19. April 23, 1873, *Darling Child*, 88.
20. July 31, 1880, *Beloved Mama*, 85.
21. January 5, 1876, *Darling Child*, 202.

as Alice releases her hold on the animal, calmly watching it trot into the woods, she offers this cool evaluation: "'If it had grown up,' she said to herself, 'it would have made a dreadfully ugly child: but it makes a rather handsome pig, I think.'"[22] Her assessment captures the older Queen's perception of the obverse side of bourgeois respectability, the mirror image generated and contained by its opposite. So too, Carroll uncannily captures the aging Queen in his portrait of the Duchess, who though in Tenniel's drawing is apparently modeled after a fourteenth-century duchess famed for her ugliness, also resembles some portraits of the Queen.[23] We need not press for the source of analogies between the material monarch and Carroll's extravagant fantasy in order to see what a productive pair they make.

Victoria considered herself old as soon as she became a widow in 1861. She was then 42 and would live another forty years. Like the Queen herself, the *Alice* books are about the Age, and about age. Furthermore, the popularity that both enjoyed from the 1870s forward reflects a public that was also aging, and, for the first time, in numbers and influence great enough to constitute a dominant perspective.

I have suggested that as we can identify the ways in which the monarch came to stand for the period of her reign, so too Carroll's *Alice* books participate in the cultural invention of Victorianism at a crucial moment of self-definition. We might even reflect that Dodgson's dates of birth and death (1832–1898) are more accurate indicators of the period than Victoria's (1819–1901). Carroll was born in the year of the First Reform Bill and died just before the Boer War. If Victoria was constructed (and constructed herself) as an image of the period's earnestness, we might say that Carroll was fashioned as the prince of nonsense, who gently undermined the architecture of earnestness. Carroll and the Queen both adopt the perspective of age (in both cases before their 'time') and the narrative of aging as essential instruments of understanding and self-understanding. Both points of view are detached from a determinate political program: Carroll was no radical (in fact he was a Tory), and Victoria's politics shift from Liberal to Conservative and never settle firmly. But his comic romance and her tragic romance illuminate what was distinctively

22. Lewis Carroll, *Alice in Wonderland and Through the Looking-Glass* (New York: Oxford University Press, 1998), 50.

23. Martin Gardner refers us to Quintin Matsys's portrait of Margaretha Maultasch in his *Annotated Alice* (New York: Meridian, 1960), 82 n.1. But the traits of 'ugliness' in this visage closely resemble those changes associated with an aging face.

"Victorian" about the nineteenth century and, for the purposes of this study, what makes Victoria and the "Victorian age" emblems for the aging process during the last quarter of the nineteenth century.

When she became Queen in 1837, Victoria entered the collective consciousness as a relative stranger, susceptible to the work of public fantasy. Her subjects (and the press) welcomed her as unstained, uncompromised, and unformed. Popular myth held that when she was told she was next in line to inherit the throne, she solemnly replied: 'I will be good.' The dominant emotion in 1837 was curiosity: who was this new Queen, and who could she be to her subjects? Like the caterpillar addressing Alice, the question of the day was "*Who* are *You*?"

By the time of her formal coronation, a year later, on June 28, 1838, the public greeted her in the fashion of Alice's welcome at the banquet dinner, "with ninety-times nine." The streets were bed to 400,000 people the night before the grand procession; in his diaries, Lord Greville describes it as "not a mob here or there, but the town all mob, thronging, bustling, gaping, and gazing at everything, at anything, or at nothing."[24] Victoria's account was equally hyperbolic, a characteristic of her diary writing in general: "many as there were the day I went to the City, it was nothing—nothing to the multitudes, the millions, of my loyal subjects who were assembled in every spot to witness the Procession. Their good-humour and excessive loyalty was beyond everything."[25] This initial acclamation and the subsequent popular embrace of the Queen as wife/mother/sovereign need to be kept well in mind, as we move to the later period which is the focus of this chapter, when Victoria became an early example of mass-mediated celebrity: her iconic presence became familiar and then debased—revived and declined and revived again. But the attention here will settle on the reinvention of Victoria in the last third of her reign, the revival of her reputation which had begun to suffer, and the ways in which the *Alice* books revealingly figure (even pre-figure) the transformation.

On June 20, 1837 Victoria's journal reads as follows.

> I was awoke at 6 o'clock by Mamma who told me that the Archbishop of Canterbury and Lord Conyngham [the Lord Chamberlain] were here and

24. *Greville's England: Selections from the Diaries of Charles Greville 1818–1860*, ed. Christopher Hibbert (London: Folio Society, 1981), 157.

25. *Queen Victoria in her Letters and Journals*, ed. Christopher Hibbert (London: John Murray, 1984), 34.

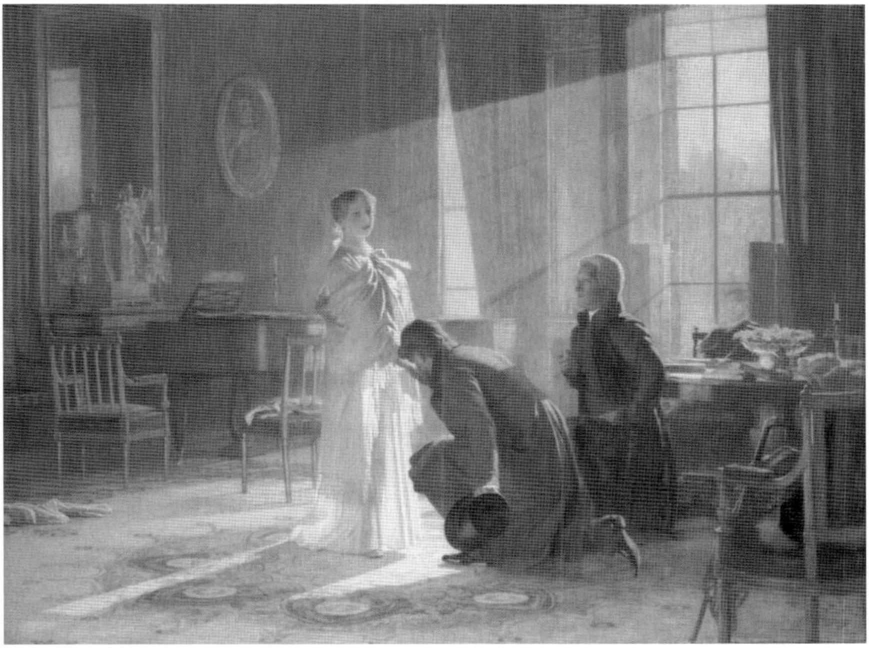

Figure 4 Henry Tanworth Wells, *Victoria Regina: Victoria Receiving the News of her Accession.* The Royal Collection ©2008 Her Majesty Queen Elizabeth II

> wished to see me. I got out of bed and went into my sitting room (only in my dressing gown) and *alone*, and saw them. Lord Conyngham then acquainted me that my poor Uncle, the King, was no more, and had expired at 12 minutes past 2 this morning and consequently that I am *Queen*.[26]

The occasion was most famously captured and commemorated not at the moment of occurrence, but fifty years later, when, following a period of some frustration with the monarch, the nation began again to embrace its queen sentimentally. A telling moment came with Henry Tanworth Wells's *Victoria Regina: Victoria Receiving the News of her Accession,* which was first exhibited at the Royal Academy in 1880, decades after the event, and repainted in greater detail in 1887 (See Fig.4). This was a widely circulating image, but it belongs to a broad current of reappraisal and re-imagining. Susan Casteras has argued that in the last two decades of her reign, and her life, Queen Victoria's pictorial image underwent what she calls "a reversal of ageing." In many significant paintings of the later period, the Queen was re-created

26. *Queen Victoria in her Letters and Journals*, ed. Christopher Hibbert (London: John Murray, 1984), 23.

in the guise of her youth. Only there was little pretense of representing her youth as it occurred; the artifacts plainly, and self-consciously, offered an image of the young queen that the culture wanted to remember, notably, Casteras claims, with "strong infusions of jingoism, nostalgia, wishful thinking, and fantasy."[27] In his corrosive modernist biography of Queen Victoria published in 1921, Lytton Strachey proposed a different explanation for the same phenomenon. He claims that from the late 1870s, "the nation's attitude toward her, critical and even hostile as it had been for so many years, altogether changed," the reason being precisely her "old age," which lent to her a 'serenity' she had never possessed before and caused the public to feel that "a gentle benignity flowed from the aged Queen."[28] My thought here has been to bring together these three moments of generational process—the jubilant reception of the young Queen Victoria, the waning of enthusiasm in the middle years, and the revival of her reputation which took the form of a fond reminiscence of her reign—and to connect them to the status of queenship in the *Alice* books.

The 1860s were a pivotal decade in which demands for reform in virtually every domain—the home, the workplace, education, welfare, elections, building and sanitation—far exceeded legislative attempts to respond. For the Queen, the early part of the decade was dominated by two deaths in quick succession; she lost both her mother and her husband between March and December 1861. Notoriously, the overwhelmed Victoria secluded herself, refusing public appearances although she continued to meet with her ministers and to tend to issues of state. Her public display of grief met with initial sympathy, then with growing incredulity and even irritation when the period of mourning seemed to be extending indefinitely, indeed to have become a life of mourning. Alice's tears which threaten to drown all of Wonderland provide a contemporary image for Victoria's sadness. If respectable opinion held that it was indecorous not to maintain the proper show of grief for at least a year after the death of a family member, it was also thought improper to display a passion and an appetite for grief unassuageable. Colin Matthew claims that the root objection arose from a suspicion that the Queen had ceased working, and that in the context of an entrenched bourgeois work ethic, such laxity was an unforgivable trans-

27. Susan Casteras, "The Wise Child and her "Offspring": Some Changing Faces of Queen Victoria," in *Remaking Queen Victoria*, ed. Homans and Munich 198.

28. Lytton Strachey, *Queen Victoria* (Harmondsworth: Penguin, 1978), 219, 228.

gression.[29] The "to let" sign which facetiously garnish Buckingham Palace provides a figure for the public's impatience at the Queen's seeming desertion (Posters were marked: "These commanding premises to be let or sold, in consequence of the late occupant's declining business").[30]

Evidence for the revival of Victoria's reputation in later years is conclusive, but Strachey's suggestion that the reconciliation was effected by the "aging Queen" requires amendment: it was not simply the Queen's *age*, her chronological span, which precipitated the response. As will become clear, aging was the half-conscious strategy by which the public explained and defused what it called the Queen's aggressive neglect. By many relevant measures, Victoria became an old woman in her forties, Albert's death marking its onset, and although far from making her "gentle"—at least insofar as *she* or those closest to her experienced her temperament—the change in status transformed her public aspect from one of unhealthy passion to one of still budding youth. What is eclipsed is old age itself, as if youth is succeeded by a second childhood which is not exactly old age, but a suppression of it. Carroll's three queens—the young girl alongside the angry and the helpless matrons—capture the crucial decades of this complex public/private development. *Alice in Wonderland* comes alive in the 1860s, but Carroll already shares with later generations the spirit of transformative retrospection. Although she is unnamed, the Queen's presence undeniably shadows through the associative images of Queen Alice and all the other female powers. They exemplify and perform the period's anxieties about power, about expansion, about families—great and small, and about growing—any and all kinds of growing, but especially about growing older and old. In the early 1850s, Thackeray's Pendennis (ostensible narrator of *The Newcomes*) laughingly derides his impulse to dwell on his hero's past, about which only a grandmother could be interested: "but shall we weary our kind readers by this infantile prattle, and set down the revered British public for an old woman?"[31] By the 1860s and 1870s, the question is no longer facetious: "the revered British public" began to recognize itself in the mirrored image of "an old woman."

The two volumes of Queen Victoria's *Highland Journals*, printed twenty years apart, will bring these issues into sharper focus, because the volumes

29. Colin Matthew, *The Nineteenth Century* (Oxford: Oxford University Press, 2000), 6.
30. Longford, *Victoria, R.I.*, 321.
31. William Thackeray, *The Newcomes* (London: J. M. Dent & Sons, 1952), i. 36.

bring the strains of aging near to the task of writing and help us to see how the experience of age can become so closely bound to its representation. *Leaves from the Journal of our Life in the Highlands* appeared in 1867 for private circulation, followed quickly by a second edition for public consumption in 1868. An immediate success, sales quickly exhausted the print run of 20,000 copies, and new editions briskly ensued. The Queen was gratified, appreciative, and vindicated, but also curious about her success. "What has she done to be so loved and liked?" she asks in a letter to Theodore Martin.[32] She would answer the question in various ways, often using the occasion to reflect on the reciprocity between herself and her subjects or on their delight in observing her own family happiness. A more detached observation appears following the success of her second volume of the *Leaves*. In February of 1884, she offers a revealing self-reflection (partly quoted earlier) in a letter to her daughter.

> I have been nearly 45 years on the throne, I have always been fully aware of what I was doing—and know perfectly well what my people like and appreciate and that is 'home life' and simplicity. I know the good, the great good it did in 68 and now again. . . . It is for others—and to show my affection for and gratitude towards those who history would perhaps not think of mentioning—as well as to describe habits and customs which are not known, that I have wished to publish these extracts.[33]

Living in time means living through time as well, and nothing has greater resonance in the journals than Victoria's attentiveness to the small activity and ongoing processes of age, aging, and the aged. In an essay entitled "Heroines and their Grandmothers," Anne Thackeray Ritchie claims that "Happiness remembered, is happiness always; but where would past happiness be if there was some one always standing by. . . to point with a sigh to future troubles long before they come, and to sadden and spoil all the pleasant of springtime, and all the sport and youth by dreary forebodings of old age, of autumn, and winter snow, and bitter winds that have not yet begun to blow?"[34] Queen Victoria assumes just such a stance of vigilant retrospection, and yet neither intention nor effect is precisely as Ritchie envisions. For Victoria the perpetual reminder that things do and have changed, that old age and troubles have succeeded youth, often heightens the glow of memory and occasionally brings unexpected pleasure to the more difficult years at hand.

32. January 16, 1868; *Queen Victoria in her Letters and Journals*, 202.
33. *Beloved Mama*, 160.
34. Anne Thackeray Ritchie, "Heroines and their Grandmothers," *Cornhill*, 1865, repr. *Prose by Victorian Women* (New York: Garland, 1996), 498.

As early as her first visit to Scotland in September 1842, Victoria's impressions of the difference between the two places are unconsciously rendered through the apprehension of two generations: "The country and people have quite different character from England and the English," she observes, noting as if by way of explanation that "The old women wear close caps". (By the next day she can elaborate "The old women with that kind of cap which they call a 'mutch.'"[35]) It seems ludicrous to relieve great difference with small annotation, but this not only sets the pattern, it does so by way of a significant example. Age resonates in these volumes through the specific introduction of old men and women, and through the things they handle and the names they use.

The first volume of the Queen's *Highland Journals* was written when she felt suddenly thrust into the aged condition of widowhood; the second—composed, as many have noted, as a eulogy to John Brown, just as the first was to Albert—bears the impress of impending decline, as Victoria closely registers her passage into her seventh decade. But in the second volume we find ramifying implications of the effects of age. Sometimes the excursions still luxuriate in their sense of novelty, but frequently they are new only to the reader. Victoria's sensations are those of recollection, as she revisits people and places she has known well before. She dwells, for example, on her conversation with Willie Duff, "an old acquaintance…who had formerly a very long black beard and hair, which are now quite grey."[36] The fisherman appears simultaneously as a young and an old man. The effect is slightly startling, as if within the confines of a conventionally managed verisimilitude, time might play cunning tricks. *The Saturday Review* found the tone of the second volume "melancholy," explaining that "the saddest associations are awakened when she revisits the most cherished scenes."[37] It is as if the illusion of transparency which characterized the first volume is now broken by the experience of age. A large number of those she describes are in fact elderly, and among the reasons is that Victoria now derives such pleasure from time spent with older people.[38] Here is an account of the death of a woman whom we met first, already an old woman, in the first volume of Victoria's *Leaves*:

35. Victoria, Queen, *Leaves from the Journal of our Life in the Highlands* (London: Smith, Elder and Co., 1868), 31, 32.
36. Victoria, Queen, *More Leaves From the Journal of A Life in the Highlands From 1862–1882* (Leipzig: Hernhard Tauchnitz, 1884), 45.
37. "Her Majesty's 'Leaves,'" *Saturday Review* 57 (Feb 16,1884), 218.
38. In the chapter on Dickens I discuss other reasons for the 'greying' of the rural population.

> On Sunday, August 22, 1869, I went to see old Mrs. Grant, whom I was grieved to see sitting in her chair supported by pillows, and her poor feet raised upon cushions, very much altered in her face, and, I fear, dying of dropsy.
>
> On August 26 I again saw her, and gave her a shawl and pair of socks, and found the poor old soul in bed, looking very weak and very ill, but bowing her head and thanking me in her usual way. I took her hand and held it.
>
> On the 27th she died.
>
> On the 28th I stopped at her cottage and went in with Louise and Leopold. We found all so clean and tidy, but all so silent. Mrs. Gordon, her daughter, was there, having arrived just in time to spend the last evening and night with her; and then she lifted the sheet, and there the poor old woman, whom we had known and seen from the first here twenty-one years, lay on a bier in her shroud, but with her usual cap on, peaceful and little altered, her dark skin taking away from the usual terrible pallor of death. She had on the socks I gave her the day before yesterday. She was in her eighty-ninth year.[39]

The rhetorically emphatic prose so characteristic of Victoria's letters and private journals gives way to this simplicity, much as the great distances between class and status, privilege and humility, fall away to reveal basic acts of human recognition, the reciprocity of two people bound by nothing stronger (or weaker) than their mortal fate.

Throughout the *Highland Journals* Victoria writes with little of the sentimentality that pervades her letters. Just as she enjoys expeditions where she can appear 'incognito,' she permits herself the relief of allowing others, for a time, to take center stage. In these volumes, the prose is spare, simple, and restrained, the effect being to dignify the people, to deflect notice from the Queen to those who are the object of her regard. Whether she is describing life or death, children or octogenarians, she offers the close observation and appreciation of an outsider. Attending a communion service in November 1871, she remarks on the readings and rituals, the visual aspect of the scene and the grave bearing of those who participated. Then she concludes: "It would indeed be impossible to say how deeply we were impressed by the grand simplicity of the service. It was all so truly earnest…It was most touching, and I longed much to join in it. To see all these simple good people in their nice plain dresses (including an old woman in her mutch), so many of whom I knew, and some of whom had walked far, old as they were, in the deep snow, was very striking."[40]

39. Victoria, Queen, *More Leaves*, 98.

40. Ibid. 127.

The mutch has become familiar, and it is possible to see the aging community as having something to teach, rather than simply possessing the picturesque qualities of an exotic northern strangeness.

The first volume of the journals includes a chapter on "Visits to the Old Women," which opens on an accidental encounter with a woman "who...was very poor, eighty-eight years old," to whom Victoria gives a petticoat. It proceeds to narrate visits to four other old women, including "old Kitty Kear's, who is eighty-six years old—quite erect, and who welcomed us with a great air of dignity"; old widow Symons ("who is 'past four-score', with a nice rosy face, but was bent quite double; she was most friendly, shaking hands with us all, asking which was I, and repeating many kind blessings"): then to another Mrs. Symons who is related "to the old widow living next door" and "then across a little burn to another old woman's," and finally to "old Mrs. Grant...who is so tidy and clean, and to whom I gave a dress and handkerchief, and she said, 'You're too kind to me, you're over kind to me, ye give me more every year, and I get older every year.'"[41] (See Fig. 5) The unaffected adulation may flatter, but what

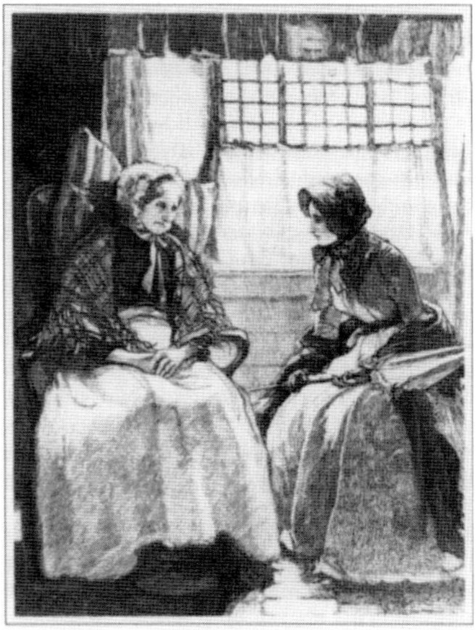

Queen Victoria at Balmoral: a morning call.

Figure 5 *Queen Victoria at Balmoral: A Morning Call.* Photo courtesy of David Duff

41. Victoria, Queen, *Leaves*, 154, 155

particularly moves her is the exemplary endurance and good nature, the ability to feel joy and exuberance, interest and affection. If Victoria was a model for bourgeois domesticity or majesty, she was also an apprentice, and these elderly Scots were for her, as well as her audience, important models of successful old age.

Of course as she looked at others, they returned the gaze. Through the late years of her life, she was more represented than representing, and she was as vulnerable to mockery as to reverence. John Plunkett has suggested that the public was suspicious of the obvious doctoring of photographs of Victoria's old age, noting that "Complaints against the manipulation of Victoria's photographs can be found intermittently in the 1880s and 1890s."[42] The marks of age may not have been interpreted as beauty, but neither were they necessarily intimidating. The historical record suggests that images of the Queen remained irreconcilably multivalent, with as much connotation of dignified (or at least stubborn) persistence as inevitable decline. Steven Katz has argued that with the medicalization of the body at mid-century, the Victorians began to dissociate disease from old age, and one result of this is the liberation of age from the necessity of death:

> By the mid-nineteenth century, the study of old age and the aging process had become increasingly distinct from traditional ideas about the life-span. Modern medicine had reconstructed the body in terms of pathological anatomy, displacing degenerative processes to micro-levels of tissues and cells, and gradually separating old age as a special part of the life course, one marked by systematic signs of senescence[43]

Katz's claim is that at this rather determinate historical moment people began to distinguish between old age and the diseases which one may suffer at that time: instead of avoiding old age itself, the idea was to avoid the ailments, which old people only display more regularly and conspicuously.[44] Certainly, few signs of fear show themselves in Victoria's eager visits to the elderly cottagers in Scotland. In her letters one finds a longing for companions in old age rather than an aversion to them.

42. John Plunkett, *Queen Victoria*, 190–1.
43. Steven Katz, "Imagining the Life-Span; From Premodern Miracles to Postmodern Fantasies," in *Images of Aging: Cultural Representations of Later Life*, ed. Mike Featherstone and Andrew Wernick, (London: Routledge, 1995), 66.
44. Steven Katz, "Imagining the Life-Span," 66.

A focus on Alice

In the last chapter we recognized a notable difference for the aged between center and centrality, and saw that occupation of one did not ensure possession of the other. This is crucial to an understanding of age in a century in which, with a few important exceptions, the elderly were swept to the edges, until their numbers and their needs began to swell into a conspicuous mass, impossible to ignore. In Carroll, the questions of frame and center, margin and core, undergo striking elaboration and refinement. One of the recurrent issues in textual criticism of the *Alice* books has been the relation of the sentimental frames to the unsentimental narratives which they enclose. The interior stories have been variously characterized as playful, humorous, anxious, threatening, or cold, but interpretation of the frames is consistent. Yet it seems as if, however one interprets the inner core of the *Alice* stories, there is little question as to how to read the frames themselves: they are frankly and unabashedly sentimental. I agree. But they are nonetheless complex, and complex precisely in the manner in which they express emotion and engage with the narratives that they surround. Carroll's photographic vocation provides a gloss on Alice's adventures.

Carroll's reputation as a photographer is as strong if not as universal as his literary fame. As Charles Lutwidge Dodgson, rather than Lewis Carroll, he was quickly drawn to the camera and purchased one as early as 1856. Until recently, he was more likely to be remembered for the pictures he took of naked little girls, but in the last decade a serious reconsideration of his entire *oeuvre* has placed those pictures in a much wider context.[45] Unlike the commercial photographers of the period, but similar to photographic artists such as Julia Cameron and Oscar Rejlander,[46] Dodgson aimed for a distinctive visual atmosphere which complemented the expression he found and produced in the bodies of his subjects. He avoided the quickly conventionalized smiles and aimed rather for a more ambitious

45. There have been several exhibitions of his photography in London and in major American cities in the last decade, including Austin, San Francisco, Manhattan and Washington. There are also several books now available with excellent reproductions of Carroll's photography. The most recent is *Lewis Carroll, Photographer: The Princeton University Library Albums*, Roger Taylor and Edward Wakeling, eds. (Princeton: Princeton University Press, 2002).

46. Although their styles are very different, and Carroll was no fan of hers despite the joint exhibit of their works held in 1864, Julia Cameron is the artist to whom he is most often compared.

expressiveness.[47] Most immediately relevant, several of his portraits elucidate the relation between the frames in the *Alice* books and the question of age. A first example is that of Ethel and Lilian Brodie, taken in June 1861, a year before the momentous occasion of the boat ride where Dodgson first told the Liddell children some form of the story of *Alice in Wonderland*. The second is of the famous author of *The Princess and the Goblin*, George MacDonald and one of his daughters, Lily, another child friend of Carroll's (see Figs. 6 and 7). This image was produced in 1863, a year after the boat ride. Jan Gordon, Edward Guiliano and Uli Knoepflmacher have reproduced these prints and have each offered strong insight into their relevance

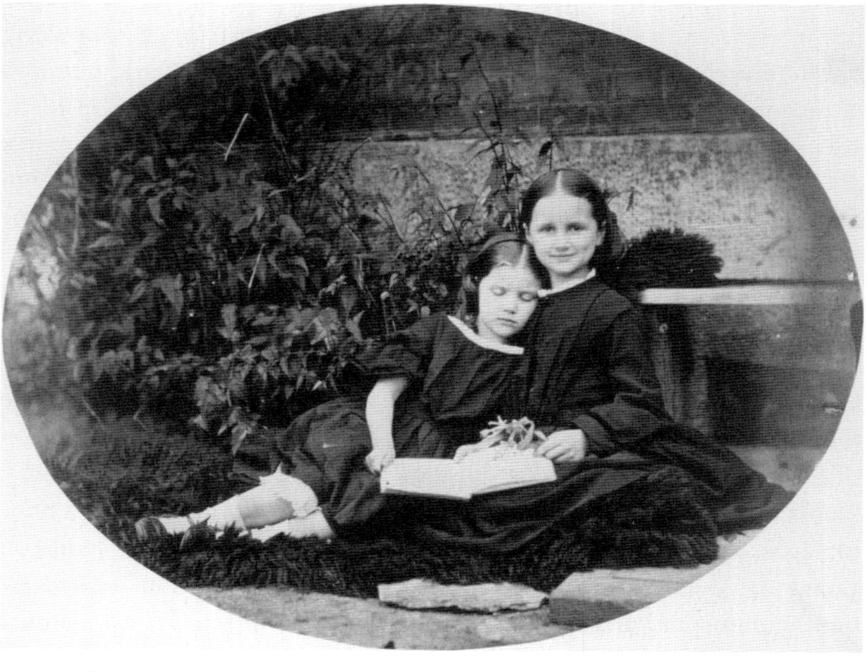

Figure 6 Ethel and Lilian Brodie. Courtesy of Morris L. Parrish Collection of Victorian Novelists, Princeton University

47. Figures are no less 'posed' though they seem less rigid. Helen Groth aptly refers to "the inherent romanticism of Carroll's own photographic practice," and she associates his work with the manufacture of nostalgia throughout the period. See *Victorian Photography and Literary Nostalgia* (New York: Oxford University Press, 2003), 34.

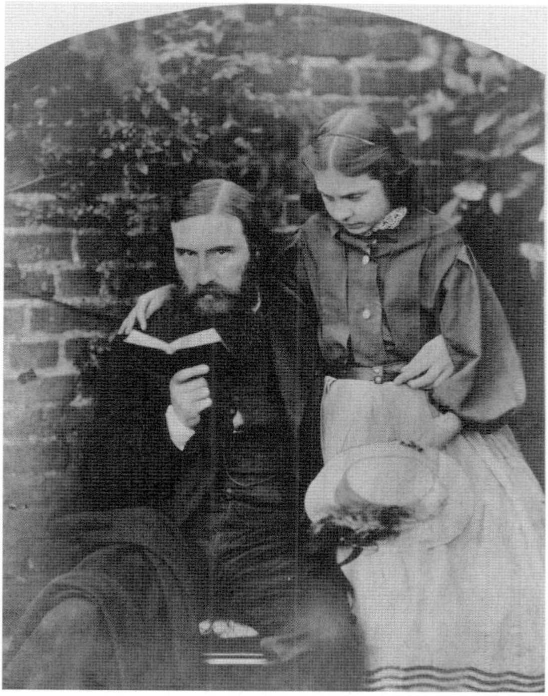

Figure 7 George MacDonald and Lily Scott MacDonald. Gernsheim Collection, Harry Ransom Humanities Research Center, University of Texas at Austin

to the *Alice* books.[48] Here, however, the interest lies in specific formal structure of visual representation.

As a first point it is worth emphasizing that the viewer's eyes are drawn *not* to the sleeping child or the young girl with downcast eyes. The primary focus falls on the wide-awake older sister in one case and the figure of the man in the second. In the first, the dream world is suggested by the blurring of the edges of the garden and the sleeping child, but the clarity and sharpness of the older sister are provocative. Like Alice, she disregards the book on her lap, but her gaze directly engages the viewer; her slight smile and the dimple on her right cheek give her an air of intrigue and I find

48. Uli Knoepflmacher, *Ventures into Childland: Victorians, Fairy Tales and Femininity* (Chicago: University of Chicago Press, 1998), 162; *Soaring With the Dodo: Essays on Lewis Carroll's Life and Art*, Edward Guiliano and James R. Kincaid, eds. (Charlottesville: Lewis Carroll Society of North America, University Press of Virginia, 1982), 19; *Lewis Carroll Observed*, ed. Edward Guiliano (New York: Lewis Carroll Society of North America Clarkson N. Potter, Inc , 1976), 52.

myself wondering more what she is *thinking* than what her sister is *dreaming*. In the second photo, the girl has a more compelling expression on her face, but even so, the father's gaze claims our initial attention. From the viewer's perspective here, imagination is attractive just *insofar* as it is filtered through the lens of maturity, or consciousness.

With this in mind we turn to the frames to the *Alice* books. At the start of *Wonderland*, Alice attributes her boredom to her sister's preoccupation with a book which contains no "pictures or conversations."[49] Of course the dream world which follows is constituted by those missing elements (pictures and conversations), but what it lacks is precisely what the sister's book presumably possesses—that is, commentary. And what is commentary, after all, but the narrative counterpart to the frame? Commentary offers precisely a frame of judgment, or a frame of context, or the frame of another level of fictive ontology. One way, then, to think about the frames of the *Alice* books is to ask what stands as the place of commentary. As I'll argue later, commentary is not simply abolished, even from within the dream vision. But an obvious first point is that, however much they flatten the experiences within, the frames provide both entrance to and exit from the dream-thoughts. Critics have generally argued that the narrative frames provide a disciplinary counter to the wild internal disorder and that the frames diminish the stories' power by containing them through facile explanation and pedestrian response. At *Wonderland*'s close we may cringe at Alice's sister's attempt to explain the dream by providing farm-yard equivalents to the sights and sounds of the fantastic creatures and at the taming of the story, so that nightmare turns into pleasant reverie. But I want to explore another possibility, namely that under the guise of rationalizing the thoughts and sentimentalizing the emotions of the story, the frame performs another, more subversive task. Consider the final paragraph of *Alice in Wonderland*:

> Lastly, she pictured to herself how this same little sister of hers would, in the after-time, be herself a grown woman; and how she would keep, through all her riper years, the simple and loving heart of her childhood; and how she would gather about her other little children, and make *their* eyes bright and eager with many a strange tale, perhaps even with the dream of Wonderland of long ago; and how she would feel with all their simple sorrows, and find a pleasure in all their simple joys, remembering her own child-life, and the happy summer days. (p. 111)

49. Lewis Carroll, *Alice's Adventures in Wonderland and Through the Looking Glass and What Alice Found There* (Oxford: Oxford University Press, 1971), 9. Further references to this edition will be cited parenthetically within the text.

"First," we had been told, "First, she dreamed about little Alice herself" (p.110)—first and last indicating the process by which the dream is produced and transmitted. First there is Alice, bored and sleepy; then there is the dream, which we read too, followed by Alice's re-telling of it, which we don't hear, and which the sister appropriates for her own reverie; and last there is the transmission, not directly, but by way of the sister's imagining Alice as the teller.

If we lend a spatial dimension to 'first' and 'last' along with the chronological dimension, we achieve another perspective on the frame. Prior to 'first'—that is, prior to Alice—we have the sister, now seen as the instigator of the dream insofar as she produces the boredom by which the dream gets dreamt. Consider the two photographs where the viewer's open eyes seek open eyes, before resting on the more elusive younger subject. In *Wonderland*, Alice has the dream, but in *Through the Looking-Glass* Carroll offers the possibility that the dream has Alice—which (without claiming that the sister is the Red King, who offers the idea) might suggest that the dreamer produces the character whose dream is a means of distancing herself from it. In other words, Alice is conjured by the sister as preamble and part of the dream itself. And "Lastly" Alice is re-imagined, this time not as the dreamer but as the storyteller, perhaps again by way of distancing the teller of the tale from the tale itself. A complex series of displacements folds back upon itself: from Carroll (or Dodgson to Carroll) to the sister, from the sister to Alice, from Alice back to the sister and finally, again by way of the sister, from Alice to her children. The elaborate layering, distance upon distance, separates author from audience, and author as dreamer from the wish that the dream contains. *Alice's* dream-wishes are in the stories themselves, but *Carroll's* dream-wish is embedded in the frames: his wish, which the frames conceal, can be seen as an appeal to the child to admit the tremble of old age, to admit just that 'commentary' which the child would banish, with the hope that by drawing near, the distance between youth and age might collapse and make possible connection between the two. Youth will not abolish age; age will not corrupt or diminish youth: the two will find a way to remain mutually entangled, much like Alice and the faun, whose fragile union lasts only so long as they are unconscious of their relation to each other.

The poem which Carroll attaches to the start of *Looking-Glass* extends the range of implication. He calls his work a "love-gift" (p.116), which was how many of his child-friends described the stories and anecdotes he used to narrate, when he asked them to sit still for photos or, as in the Wonderland story, when he looked to fill the time. The stories are gifts to the hearer/reader. But the poem isn't really about the gift, or even about children; it's about the gift-giver, the author, and about aging:

Come, hearken then, ere voice of dread,
With bitter tidings laden,
Shall summon to unwelcome bed
A melancholy maiden!
We are but older children, dear,
Who fret to find our bedtime near.

And the last stanza:

And, Though the shadow of a sigh
May tremble through the story,
For "happy summer days" gone by,
And vanish'd summer glory—
It shall not touch, with breath of bale,
The pleasance of our fairy-tale. (p. 116)

Here is the unpalatable certainty which provokes the author's sentiment: although "the magic words shall hold thee fast," it is the *story* that will excite the child rather than the *sigh within*. This is not simple regret—hard youth set against sentimental age, as critics often describe figures such as the White Knight in relation to Alice. Our interpretation changes if, as I am suggesting, we attend to the desire behind the acknowledgment of a painful reality. The 'love-gift' carries age to youth, but the story declines to imitate the child's world. The author wants not simply the child's "pictures or conversation": *the author wants commentary*. He wants reflection on the state of things. Alice asks 'who am I,' but the author asks 'does it matter who you are?' Carroll uses his stories as a photographic *carte-de-visite*: they are his calling cards, his admittance to the world of the child. He wants access because age introduces space between image and reflection; it creates distance between thoughts and emotions, or actions and thoughts.

Experience is one name we give to the distance which age imposes on the adult sensibility. In the *Alice* books the formal, tonal expression of experience, distance, or age, is through irony, regret, and sentiment. Thus, although no chronological age is specified, we know the gnat in Wonderland is 'old'—we know because of its attempt to provide just that commentary which Alice wants to avoid. The persistent comments annoy Alice, but his whispered tone is so slight that a strong rebuke is unthinkable. Like many of the other 'old' creatures in the *Looking-Glass* world or in *Wonderland*, the gnat sighs often, and his sighs mingle with tears. Notably, he employs the same strategy of displacement that Carroll attempts more successfully: "That's a joke," he tells Alice, "I wish *you* had made it" (p. 155). So Carroll 'makes' Alice tell his (the author's) dream: his story becomes—by way of Alice's sister—Alice's story.

Wonderland's Mock Turtle is also aged, in the peculiar Carrollian sense of possessing the awareness of living through time—and living past one's own emotions. Carroll makes a portmanteau word out of 'mock' because the turtle used to be 'real,' but now, apparently is no longer; and his present is characterized by his need to 'mock,' that is to perform the function of age in his parodies of song, dance and education.[50] The turtle's sobs and sighs, his sadness and regret, linger long after the encounter ends. they are among the sounds the sister recalls in the final paragraphs. Alice's parodies are as yet unconscious, but nonetheless marks of her aging.

Along with parody, we have instances of narratorial intrusion, frequently in an ironic mode, standing in the place of commentary. In *Wonderland* this happens most often through asides, sometimes parenthetical, which serve various purposes, but among them, the establishment of the space of distance within the body of the text, bringing the frame into the story at the same time that it remains fenced off. For example, in the process of her long fall, Alice comforts herself with the fantasy, "After such a fall as this, I shall think nothing of tumbling down-stairs! How brave they'll all think me at home! Why, I wouldn't say anything about it, even if I fell off the top of the house!" and the narrator adds in parentheses, "Which was very likely true" (p.10). Several critics have noted the number of such jokes about Alice's death; James Kincaid argues that, rather than suggesting her death, the jokes attempt to keep Alice young, to prevent her from aging.[51] Alice herself notes with some satisfaction that if she can't grow any larger, she can't grow any older and, as she puts it "That'll be a comfort, one way—never to be an old woman" (p.33). What Knoepflmacher refers to as the "photographic freeze,"[52] the containment of the subject by the frame around the image is comparable to the literary strategy of telling and re-telling the story of the youthful Alice's adventures. But there is also another dimension. The effect of growth through time is age, and extension through space results in changes in size or distance. Narration in Carroll grows too. It grows partly by increasing the distance between story and plot, tale and telling, but still more notably, by devising other forms of ramification and exfoliation. The episodic plotting releases a

50. Humpty Dumpty explains to Alice that in a 'portmanteau word' "there are two meanings packed up into one word" (*Alice*, 192).
51. James Kincaid, *Child-Loving: The Erotic Child and Victorian Culture* (New York: Routledge, 1992), 277–9.
52. Uli Knoepflmacher, *Ventures into Childland*, 167.

range of metonymies, displacements from thing to word, from words to other words, all moving along a frictionless surface of association. One thinks, for instance, of the habit of unraveling a thought or a sound—as when the bleeding pinprick becomes the bleating of sheep in the shop Alice discovers in the seventh square. These are narratological counterparts to aging. And we should include also the subordination of cause to the pursuit of consequences, and the tendency of all moods to move towards irony, parody, or satire, as they gather distance through time, and as they are displaced from one teller to the next.

Like Dickens and Thackeray, Carroll joins the harshness of irony to the softness of sentimentality. To enquire which mode is primary is to engage farcically in the attempt to decide which kitten instigated Alice's *Looking-Glass* adventure. For our purposes it is enough to say that irony and sentimentality are mutually dependent and reciprocally justifying. They come together in the figure of the White Knight, who is himself wholly sentimental, but who is represented ironically by the narrator, who of course realizes that the Knight is a figure for the author. Alice betrays youthful naiveté when she assumes that experience results in mastery. She thinks the White Knight is an inexperienced rider because he lacks proficiency, but in Carroll's world experience guarantees nothing beyond a life in time, a discrete distance, and a tendency towards regret. The White Knight has trouble making progress because experience clots, rather than smooths, our movement through the world. Alice assumes, when he offers to sing his song, that the relation between intention and performance will be straightforward. But the White Knight understands the arduous life of metonymy: what a song is called may differ from what it is named; the title of a song may not be the same thing as what the song *is*. In any case, it is both ironic *and* sentimental that the name of his song "really is" *The Aged Aged Man*. Of course it is only one way to describe the song, but so too, age is only one way to describe him or anything else for that matter.

Aging is not all regret, disappointment, sighs, and sobs. To the child's active curiosity, we find the older person's active 'invention.' Here is the paradigmatic situation of the frame once again: youth situated against age in the form of curiosity encircled by invention. If we understand by curiosity the *desire for narrative*, and by invention, the *generating of narrative*, we can recognize the circuit of exchange between youth and age in the situation of the older storyteller (older by virtue of his experience rather than his years) and his eager audience. This is the wish the frames express: not to diminish the distance between youth and age, but to tease it into phantasmagoria, to exploit it so that this story might be told.

The anxiety of superfluity

It has been useful to see the sharp outlines of age through the conflict of generations. But royalty brings to this conflict the peculiar effect of making regal age simultaneously exceptional and representative. Ruskin assured his readers that the erosions of time would be suspended for women who could maintain a balance between "majestic peace" and "majestic childishness," claiming that "There is no old age where there is still that promise." A more practical Mrs. Craik characterizes old age as "sovereignty deposed," and ruefully advises a voluntary abdication of influence in favor of more youthful queenly maidens.[53] Margaret Oliphant, whose 98 novels and over 400 essays cast her among the most prolific writers in the nineteenth century, aggressively pursued the analogy between women and royalty.[54] Unlike Mrs. Craik's womanly ideal, Oliphant allows the female sovereign to endure the passage of years, and unlike Ruskin's queenly woman, she *does* age.[55] Although readings of her fiction tend to focus on the youthful heroines who make comely queens, much remains to be said about Oliphant's treatment of older women, whose monarchies are neither in the making, nor so firmly settled, that they are impervious to other pressures.[56] Here we do well to turn to her *Autobiography*, where she is so openly preoccupied with the circumstances of her aging and so canny in her reading of its effects.

53. John Ruskin, "Of Queens Gardens," *Sesame and Lilies*, ed. Debora Epstein Nord, (New Haven: Yale University Press, 2002), 80; Mrs. Craik, *A Woman's Thoughts about Women* (London: Hurst & Blackett, 1858), 320.
54. For reference to the full productive output, see "Introduction," in *The Autobiography of Margaret Oliphant: The Complete Text*, ed. Elisabeth Jay (New York: Oxford University Press, 1990), p. vii.
55. Gail Turley Houston contrasts Oliphant's use of the queenly metaphor with Ruskin's. She claims that Oliphant returns to the queenly woman the material substantiality which Ruskin denies her: "Drastically rewriting the abstract representation of woman as queen found in *Of Queen's Gardens*, Oliphant analyzes the political power of the real queens of England. Rather than focusing on the spiritual powers of women as metaphorical queens submissive to *a priori* masculine authority, Oliphant forces the reader to look at the material conditions of women's lives." *Royalties: The Queen and Victorian Writers* (Charlottesville: University Press of Virginia, 1999), 143.
56. See e.g. Elisabeth Jay, introduction to Margaret Oliphant, *Miss Marjoribanks*, ed. Jay (Harmondsworth: Penguin, 1998), Elizabeth Langland, *Nobody's Angels: Middle-Class Women and Domestic Ideology in Victorian Culture* (Ithaca, NY: Cornell University Press 1995), 158, and Melissa Schaub, "Queen of the Air or Constitutional Monarch?: Idealism, Irony, and Narrative Power in Miss Marjoribanks" *Nineteenth-Century Literature*, 55 (2000), 195–225.

Although decidedly modest and clear-headed, Oliphant kept mental company with those majestic women whose works or lives served as a template against which her own life could be measured. George Eliot, she acknowledges, is a greater writer than her, and Brontë more powerful. She often referred to Queen Victoria by way of comparison to her own struggles and griefs, although, if her occasional journalism displays marked praise of Victoria, her letters and fictions often release crisp ironies. The sudden shocking confrontation with the death of loved ones, which Oliphant no less than Victoria faced within the same five-year period, consolidated their association in the writer's mind. Oliphant's husband died in 1859, and her eldest child and only daughter died in January 1864, the latter event wounding Oliphant in a manner comparable to the effect of Prince Albert's death on Victoria. I have suggested how Victoria's mourning (and melancholia) transformed her into an old woman—both in her self-understanding and in the eyes of her subjects. Oliphant, also barely middle-aged at the time of trauma, writes as the first anniversary of her daughter's death approaches that "I have grown an old woman all at once."[57] She both sympathized with, and disengaged from, the Queen's intensely public display of grief. Her early response is to urge attention away from the Prince, away even from the more generous view of him that emerged after his death. In *Blackwood's* of January 1862 she addresses the memory of "The Prince Consort," but tellingly returns to Victoria, writing that "Now, when the suddenness of the shock has passed...we have time to think and say, 'What a loss to England!' But the cry of that Sunday was the spark struck out at heat from the heart of the nation—'the poor Queen!'"[58] Decades later she recalls the convulsive collective reaction, when the passionate love in the royal marriage became clear to the public: "Understanding for the first time all that he had been to her, a flood of pity and terror burst forth, which was stronger than grief in the sensations of the moment. How was she to bear it?"[59] The pity and terror belong to the public; they are emotions inspired by startled recognition of the Queen's passions. Against this background Oliphant defends Victoria

57. To Mrs. Tullock, January 22, 1865, *The Autobiography and Letters of Mrs. M. O. W. Oliphant*, ed. Mrs. Harry Coghill (New York: Dodd, Mead & Co., 1899), 196.
58. Margaret Oliphant, "The Prince Consort," *Blackwood's*, 91 (January 1862), 132. (131–6).
59. Repr. of "Queen Victoria: A Personal Sketch" [1880] re-titled "The Domestic Life of the Queen" in *The Life and Times of Queen Victoria*, 2 vols., ed. Robert Wilson (London: Cassell, 1900), 112.

from the charge that her "grief was excessive, and indulged in beyond the legitimate duration of natural grief" ("Domestic Life," 115). Privately, she was less generous, departing from the view that the Queen was exceptional by virtue of her passion no less than by her position. To John Blackwood, she carps that

> If any of us ordinary people were to treat our friends and visitors and society in general in the same way we should simply put ourselves out of the pale of society, and lose both visitors and friends. I doubt whether *nous autres* poor women who have had to fight with the world all alone without much sympathy, can quite enter into the "unprecedented" character of the Queen's sufferings. A woman is surely a poor creature if with a large and happy affectionate family of children around her, she can't take heart to do her duty whether she likes it or not. We have to do it, with very little solace.[60]

In Oliphant's own illuminating case, old age initially meant the absence of solace after the devastating loss of her child. That event generated the start to the *Autobiography*, which is a hybrid of diary, journal, and memoir begun in 1864, and then resumed twenty-one years later, in February 1885. It loosely follows the peripatetic wanderings of the widow and her brood until, one by one, her children each are lost. Oliphant begins as a sad woman, grieving for the loss of her cherished daughter; she resumes as an old woman, not in years, but in manner, tone, and self-presentation.

> Twenty-one years have passed since I wrote what is on the opposite page. I have just been reading it all with tears; sorry, very sorry for that poor soul who has lived through so much since. Twenty-one years is a little lifetime. It is curious to think that I was not very young, nearly thirty-six, at that time, and that I am not very old, nearly fifty-seven, now. Life though it is short, is very long, and contains so much. (*Autobiography*, 13)

The *Autobiography* is framed by the death of Oliphant's oldest and youngest children: the rest (the three others) die in between, along with her mother, husband, and brother. Like so many Victorians, and Queen Victoria herself, Margaret Oliphant's life was haunted by scenes of dying and death. And yet it is not death as such that shapes the perspective dominant in many of her late narratives, including *Hester* (1883), "Mr. Sandford" (1888), "The Library Window" (1896), and the *Autobiography*. The death of loved ones transformed her life, but it was age which, towards the close of her life,

60. Quoted in Elisabeth Jay, *Mrs. Oliphant: A Fiction to Herself* (Oxford: Clarendon Press, 1995), 194.

renewed her writing. When she turns her maturing theme to a rendering of her own life, she brings old age to a late-century self-consciousness that will have profound effects on social policy as well as imaginative life. It is not too much to say that from her standpoint as a prolific, middle-class popular woman writer Margaret Oliphant represented nineteenth-century age knowing itself more fully as well as more painfully than before.

In contrast to the imaginative force of Charlotte Brontë, Oliphant considers herself to "have had far more experience and, I think, a fuller conception of life" (*Autobiography*, 10). Chronologically and functionally, her age is no index of her experience, but of course an essential dimension of old age must be the consciousness of feeling old, however able-bodied and youthful one may be. When life feels "long," one can call oneself old. Who can contest the self-assignment? And when life has indeed been, and felt, "very long," one is *very old*. But the gradations are subject to context, for Oliphant acknowledges that "sixty-five and eighty-five are very different, [but] nobody can doubt that sixty-five is old," even as she makes precisely such distinctions: "Catherine Vernon, who was sixty-five, and knew herself to be an old woman, looked at the other, who was over eighty, as a girl looks at her mother—wondering at her strange experiences, feeling herself a child in presence of a knowledge which is not hers" (*Hester*, 83, 158–9). It is a perception such as this that creates a sense of age not as a characteristic of temperament, still less as a mark on a calendar, but as a milieu of experience, which can extend and vary and deepen.

Old age may be as calm or fraught as youth, but neither loneliness nor lovelessness makes one feel more intensely aged than the sense of superfluity. This is precisely what Oliphant studies so intently in the later writings, the experience of having lived beyond one's due time and therefore beyond any justified place within the social web. She feels herself to be of no interest to anyone: others may show some care for her, but to none is she 'beloved.' "No one belonging to me has energy enough" to write her biography "or even to gather the fragments" so that a detached observer might do so (*Hester*, 17). And why should they?—in her own estimate, she has been but "a fat, little, commonplace woman, rather tongue-tied" (*Hester*, 17). Feeling that she is unfit to be a biographical subject is partly a painful self-assessment of her literary standing, but more significantly it is a figure for a broader recession into insignificance, her disappearance from the circles of love and fascination. As we saw in the last chapter, Oliphant's fiction represented the power of the elderly on the margins, even as it dramatized the relentless passage of generations. The *Autobiography* often plays out its aging tones in a key of resignation that can become despair, but part of its power as a cultural document is that it is willing to refuse sentimentality and mystification and to risk plain speech: fat, little, commonplace.

Those who have died—and again, it is well to remember that the list includes her mother, her older brother, her husband, and several of her children—are less to be pitied than those whose attainment of old age makes a mockery of life.[61] Oliphant offers a Victorian summa of the anxiety of superfluity, comparing herself to her brother Willie, because both have "outlived everything" (*Autobiography*, 19). At the same time, much of her bewilderment lies in her survival, her ability to carry on, well beyond her due time. "I am sixty-two," she writes, "older than Sir Walter was when he died. I am a wonder to myself, a sort of machine, so little out of order, able to endure all things, always fit for work whatever has happened to me" (*Autobiography*, 56). While some of her children still live, she feels the stir of life; their need is no salvation, but it is a *raison d'être*: "Cecco does need me and my poor girls to whom I mean home" (*Autobiography*, 56). But on October 2, 1894, Oliphant writes the words which enforce the cold superfluity: "I am a mother childless" (*Autobiography*, 79). The last of her own children, Cecco, had died as all the rest had before him. Despite the nieces who survive, "My work is over, my house is desolate. I am empty of all things" (*Autobiography*, 81). She fears she cannot die. "I am as strong as an elephant. All this misery does not give me even a headache. I neither eat nor sleep for days together and I am as well at the end of them as at the beginning. What is to become of me, shall I never die?" (*Autobiography*, 81). And a week later, "my body is well, well, the horrible thing" (*Autobiography*, 86). After Cecco's death Oliphant changes the tone and the focus of her autobiography. First it had been for him, "but now that I am doing it consciously for the public, with the aim (no evil aim) of leaving a little more money for Denny [her niece]" (*Autobiography*, 95), her writing becomes less personal though no less personable.

61. Superfluity is a pervasive cultural anxiety, well-reflected in Victorian literature and letters. For example, shortly before his death, a disconsolate Lord Holland wrote to his son: "One prays for long life but what is it but outliving what one values most in it, those one esteems and loves." Quoted in Patricia Jalland, *Death in the Victorian Family* (Oxford: Oxford University Press, 1996), 145. Tennyson's *Tithonus* utters the wrenching *cri de coeur* of the superfluous: "Why should a man desire in any way | To vary from the kindly race of men | Or pass beyond the goal of ordinance | Where all should pause, as is most met for all?" (lines 28–31).

Like Heathcliff, for whom "the entire world is a dreadful collection of memoranda that she [Catherine Earnshaw] did exist, and that I have lost her," Oliphant continually interrupts the chronological flow of her narrative, moving between the 1860s, when the children were alive, to the present, when she has lost them all.[62] For example, the small garden which gave her young children so much pleasure "lies under my windows now, but I can't trust myself to go into it" (*Autobiography*, 123). The past does not encroach on the present so much as the present, like a high tide, washes over the past and the future, making each as bleak as itself. One has the uncanny experience of successive eras, with the later ones shading rather than cancelling those which came before. Explaining that at one period she typically worked until 2:00 a.m., she parenthetically adds "it is past three at this moment, 18th, nay, 19th April 1895, but this is no longer usual with me" (*Autobiography*, 134), the reader imagines her simultaneously awake and asleep, engaged and disaffected, one habit already fading into the next even as it is described. She alternates between the figure of a detached narrator gathering her memoirs and a private diarist, reliving the experiences she transcribes. "I am of all ages," says the aged Captain Morgan in *Hester*, "for I can remember all" (*Autobiography*, 83), but Oliphant's sharp memories only accentuate her feeling of living on as an ancient in a world of strangers.

When the possibilities for fulfillment dwindle, the absurdity of one's continued existence makes finding a motive for getting through each day imperative. Victoria's call to duty was at least that, and Oliphant found her own in perpetually rehearsing the financial worries which made her feel that those about her could not survive without her ongoing economic support. The material need of the others—even the now more distant others—forced, or justified, her decision to be a 'hack' writer instead of aiming for the glory of the highest writerly art. She became dependent on their need. In the fall of 1896, Oliphant notes that, through excessive writing, she has worked a hole in her finger: if it is a sign of physical disintegration, it is also the mark of dogged determination, the manifestation of a will to live and

62. Emily Brontë, *Wuthering Heights* (Oxford: Clarendon Press, 1976), 394. Margaret Homans makes equally good use of the quotation in order to describe Queen Victoria's reading of Tennyson's *Idylls of the King* "as a poem for and about the Prince and the Queen." See Homans, *Queen Victoria*, 183.

to work for as long as possible.[63] Oliphant's tone is proud rather than self-pitying; she does not share our horror or ask for our pity. When she *cannot* work, she feels her age most. The *Autobiography* abruptly ends with a passage devastating in its curtailment of the most intense pleasure in reciprocity. Speaking of Cecco, of what they shared before his death, she writes:

> I cannot tell what he was to me—consulting me about everything, desiring to have me with him, to walk with me and talk to me, only put out of humour when I was drawn away or occupied by other things. When he was absent he wrote to me every day. I never went out but he was there to give me his arm. I seem to feel it now—the dear, thin, but firm arm. In the last four years after Cyril was taken from us, we were nearer and nearer. I can hear myself saying 'Cecco and I.' It was the constant phrase. But all through he was getting weaker; and I knew it, and tried not to know.
>
> And now here I am all alone.
>
> I cannot write anymore. (*Autobiography*, 154)

Loss of love makes one old; loss of the capacity to work makes one older; loss of the power to contribute productively to others makes one aged. Now when Oliphant considers her failure to make "a truer artist of myself... instead of [aiming only for] the mere necessities of living," she checks both criticism and regret:

> What does it matter? Nothing at all now—never anything to speak of. At my most ambitious of times I would rather my children had remembered me as their mother than in any other way, and my friends as their friend. I never cared for anything else. And now that there are no children to whom to leave any memory; and the friends drop day by day, what is the reputation of a circulating library to me? Nothing, and less than nothing.

But then she fantasizes that perhaps in an afterlife, "the little faculty may grow a bigger one" and she could become a greater artist (*Autobiography*, 136). Without an outlet for work, her aging accelerates and becomes senescence.

If in her *Autobiography* Oliphant expresses her old age largely as an experience of superfluity and emptiness, in her fiction and journalism she sustains other possibilities, all of which gleam briefly in the personal portrait as well. The prospect of an old age that never lost its intimacy with significant social labor—this is a leading nineteenth-century ideal that Oliphant never

63. To Blackwood, October 6, 1896: "I have worked a hole in my right forefinger—with the pen, I suppose!—and can't get it to heal,—also from excessive use of that little implement." *The Autobiography and Letters of M. O. W. Oliphant* 427.

deserts, even in the midst of her despondency. In a review of works by the Duke of Argyll and William Gladstone at the end of the century, she stages her discussion as a problem of age; indeed the title of her essay is "The Verdict of Old Age" (1896).[64] These two men have enjoyed the privilege of a reflective old age, because "Happy are the old men who can give themselves to this noble work" since most "have neither the learning nor the fine seclusion, the remoteness from common care and labour" nor the "experiences which include the larger cares of a statesman and such a knowledge of life as only the rulers of the world can acquire" ("The Verdict of Old Age," 555, 558). From this "highest pinnacle," in which experience and reflection are but aspects of maturity, the "verdict of old age" assumes a scriptural authority ("The Verdict of Old Age," 571) which lays out the austere conditions of a meaningful existence to the very end of life. In less exalted fashion, we find Mr. Rule in *Hester*, a bank clerk who rose to be manager before retiring at nearly 70. Rule scorns Catherine Vernon's complacency in accepting that "We are all in the Sunday period of our lives, all of us here." "Not I," rejoins the intrepid Mr. Rule, "I have had my Sunday and I am ready to begin again, if there should be any want of me" (*Hester*, 81). It is a thought that rhymes with Mary Somerville's Victorian pride in working a good five hours a day at her mathematics, even though, "I am now in my ninety-second year."[65] For those fortunate few, work was more than livelihood: it was life. Oliphant preferred to work her own fingers to the bone rather than be deprived of a motive to work at all. Labor did not keep her young, but it made old age just bearable. Such convictions explain her impatience with Queen Victoria's withdrawal into premature old age without the solace of productivity, as well as her great relief when the Queen resumed her public life. Of course we are talking about meaningful work, fulfilling work, work which dignified the worker and helped to sustain an otherwise vacant old age. If, then as now, this kind of work was available to only a small minority, it was nonetheless the dream of many. Oliphant's complex of attitudes—a demand for socially significant work, a longing for the recognition of others until it is time to mourn their deaths, a fear of superfluity, a clinging to daily routine—is distinctive and exemplary.

64. Margaret Oliphant, "The Verdict of Old Age," *Blackwood's*, 160 (October 1896), 555–71.
65. Mary Somerville, *Personal Recollections, From Early Life to Old Age, of Mary Somerville. With Selections from her Correspondence. By Her Daughter, Martha Somerville* (Boston: Roberts Brothers, 1874), 364.

'New' age and 'old' age

For Carroll, age constructs life in scenes or passages, performative vignettes which make possible an "intensity of *thought*—a concentrated attention" necessary to the highest "enjoyment" of each moment (*S&B*, 470, 664). As he puts it in *Sylvie and Bruno Concluded*, "Thought supersedes the work of the fingers," so that when one can no longer be active, one need not ask despondently, "What can an old man do but die?"(*S&B*, 665). The aging earl, who puts the corrosive question, keeps probing: "With nothing more to learn, can one rest content on *knowledge*, for the eternity yet to be lived through? it has been a very wearying thought to me. I have sometimes fancied one *might*, in that event, say 'It is better *not* to be,' and pray for personal *annihilation*—the Nirvana of the Buddhists" (*S&B*, 667). The narrator, an elderly man too, roundly rejects this view, claiming refuge first, like Oliphant, in the relief of thinking of others, and next in the belief that the prospects of age are comprehensible only to others in the same condition. Lack of knowledge and failure of imagination are what let one deny that old age provides nurture and substance—'food' for thought—appropriate to its time and experience. Experience generates the language necessary to describe itself: asking one to understand age prematurely is like asking a child to comprehend maturity, or a living person to understand death. The earl, who *is* old, and thus ought to understand, reiterates the note of melancholy: "One gets tired as night draws on…one gets to long for bed! For those welcome words 'Come, child, 'tis bed-time!'" (*S&B*, 668–9). We should not read this as a longing for death so much as a longing for parents. For Carroll, if not for Oliphant, age does not dispense with the yearning for someone even older to nurture and protect, to guide and inform.

When Alice discovers there is to be a feast in honor of her Queenship, she protests against an infringement of her rights: "I didn't know I was to have a party at all…but if there *is* to be one, I think I ought to invite the guests," she chides, though later she admits "I should never have known who were the right people to invite" (*AW*, 225, 234). The emotional coordinates to each of these remarks are similarly contrasted: annoyance and anger on the one hand, meekness and insecurity on the other. In the *Alice* books, female adults generally exhibit the first, while most others—men animals, servants, and children—display the second. There are notable exceptions. Humpty-Dumpty ignores gender, age, and other categories to state the case bluntly:

"The question is...which is to be master—that's all" (*AW*, 190). We know that as the century approached its last third, a collective self-assurance characteristic of mid-century was more actively contested by competing voices. To be sure, there remain tones of strident authority, but the civic medium of ongoing controversy makes them more precarious, like Humpty-Dumpty's bold asseverations blasted as he perches on a wall from which he is about to fall. Within a rising din of multi-vocality was also the sound of heightened division between youth and age which plays itself out most visibly in the conflict between parents and children, and with special force in the form that battle assumed in the shape of mothers and daughters. While 'age' remained synonymous with 'old,' youth found expression through the epitaph "new."

We can call this period the great age of the New, and that's how people often knew themselves: *New Woman, New Hedonism, New Realism*. Journalism of the period employs the language of rupture, break, and liberation. The rhetoric of discontinuity was refined and indulged until, in the nineties, the very chanting of the term "New, New, New" led to many cynical reflections on the fakery and the self-promotion inside the latest cult of novelty. But even among those who scorned the reliance on the magic word, there lurked the uneasy recognition that something had changed. In the sober words of *Blackwood's*: "Things are discussed freely and easily which it would a few years ago have been a shame to mention or to think of."[66] For the partisans of the New, the rhetoric was that of a revolutionary break, a world-historical transformation. Grant Allen, celebrating the New Hedonism in an essay of 1894, wrote that "for the first time in the history of the race" it would now be possible to have healthy love, responsible parents. This is a characteristic locution: once there was a past—strange, obscure, cramped, and constrained—and now "for the first time in the history of the race," liberation will be here, in the nineties, in London.[67] This chapter has attempted to recover the generational disturbance in the last decades of the century that confused the terms of liberation and troubled the concept of change. What was it to be young or old? What was it to dream of transformation? And what to brandish, flourish, and parade, as if 'for the first time in history?'

"The Plaint of the Old" is the title to another essay of 1894 that directs us to the neglected conflict. Its author, Blanche Crackanthorpe, one of the conspicuous opinion-makers of the fin-de-siècle, acknowledges that

66. Margaret Oliphant, "The Anti-Marriage League," *Blackwood's*, 159 (January 1896), 149.
67. Grant Allen, "The New Hedonism," *Fortnightly Review* NS 55 (March 1, 1894), 377.

now is the time of the young, in their "temple of youth," "ablaze with light."[68] But she conjures a foreign visitor, who makes this accusation: "your old, they never leave off complaining...they live apart and alone... Old age is happy everywhere save in England." The English elderly are given only "good-humoured non-recognition" by those "self-engrossed moderns, eager, rushing, torrential." In the epoch of Grant Allen's New Hedonism and the gleaming youth of culture, the old are told to "get on with the dying."[69] This is what Queen Victoria was so evidently slow to do—and it is the Queen who did much to disturb the unfurled banner of novelty.

We have noted the abundance of pictures and illustrations of the Queen which flooded the market from the time of her accession, which occurred just as the first ventures into photography were making mass production a daily possibility. By the century's end, there were images circulating everywhere of her intact, corpulent persistence, her heavy refusal to die. The Queen was configured as the permanent matriarch, the eternal widow. She was of course not the only one to age: by the end of the century more people than ever were living past 50. The question of old age pensions was becoming pointed and difficult; within this context the Queen became an even more resonant node of attention. She herself identified as an icon of the elderly. We have seen that she felt forcibly thrown into a premature old age immediately after Albert's death, when she was only 42, and her pronounced and lengthy mourning included grief for the passing of her youth and the promise of her marriage. But when old age gradually did advance, the old age of years rather than experience, the issues with which Victoria contended were different from those she had confronted in her forties and fifties. Then she felt a need for solitude against the pressure to engage, but later she felt fully engaged with others and the world, without enjoying the secure conditions of reciprocity. Increasingly, Victoria felt as if her voice were no longer heeded; she became sensitive to small slights and occasionally bitter about speaking into the air. Her opinions no longer shaped political or even familial destiny: neither the intensity of her feelings nor the clarity of her thought convinced, persuaded, or compelled others to act as she desired.

68. Blanche Crackanthorpe, "The Plaint of the Old," *Contemporary Review* (1894) 278.
69. Ibid. 277, 278, 284.

But when a Queen feels marginalized, she does not sink gently into a resignation. From Windsor Castle, she writes in June of 1885 that "It's hopeless for me now to have people my age.... All my Ministers, who don't look young, are... younger than me... How old I feel and I am old."[70] Furthermore, those ministers, especially when they are Gladstone, remind her that her physical weakening corresponds to the weakening of sovereign privilege. Gladstone rejoiced in this as little as she, though she imagined their relations in terms of personal triumph and defeat. As early as 1870 he writes with a heavy heart: "For our time as a Government, and my time as a politician, Royalty will do well enough in this country, because it has a large fund to draw upon.... But the fund of credit is diminishing, and I do not see from whence it is to be replenished... the outlook for 10, 20, 30, 40 years hence is a very melancholy one."[71] Victoria has grown weak in body, and weak in constitutional power: "It is a miserable thing," she sighs, "to be a constitutional Queen and to be unable to do what is right."[72] She dislikes the drift of liberal policies, what she calls the "strange, ungrateful love of change,"[73]—as she sharply puts it to the Earl of Granville, in the royal third person:

> The Queen herself can *never* have *any confidence* in the men who encourage *reform* for the *sake of the alteration and pulling down what exists* and what is *essential* to the *stability* of a Constitutional Monarchy. A *Democratic Monarchy*... she will not *consent to belong to*. *Others* must be found *if* that is to be and she *thinks* we are on a dangerous and doubtful slope which may become too rapid for us to stop.[74]

Apart from the policies, she simply dislikes the dominant mood, its tone and manner, which resemble those of younger people who regularly provoke criticism in her letters. In the 1890s the husband of one of her favorite ladies in waiting noted in his diary: "Marie told me of a talk with the Q. about modern manners of children to parents..., she had heard dreadful stories of modern children".[75] In her essay "The Plaint of the Old" Crackenthorpe warned that if the young have to learn to make a "quiet corner" for the old so that they

70. *Beloved Mama,* 192.
71. Quoted in Robert Blake, "Gladstone, Disraeli, and Queen Victoria," 12.
72. February 15, 1878, *Darling Child*, 282.
73. April 5, 1880, *Beloved Mama*, 73.
74. August 8, 1880, *The Letters of Queen Victoria 1879–1885,* second series, III, ed. George Earle Buckle, (London: John Murray, 1928) 130–1.
75. *Life with Queen Victoria; Marie Mallet's letters from Court 1887–1901*, ed. Victor Mallet, (Boston: Houghton Mifflin Company, 1968), 128.

are not left "wholly to themselves," the old in turn are responsible for "casting out...the demon of pessimism" ("Plaint", 278, 279). But in the seventies and eighties, Victoria forecasts a grim personal future—"I can only foresee that my declining years will be very trying ones"—and a disastrous public one: "I warn constantly—but it is of no use whatsoever. Lord Granville would I think do what is right...but he is weak and much aged, and Mr. Gladstone don't care for foreign affairs or the power of England beyond Europe at all." She is tersely dismissive of the government that formally serves her: "To be a sovereign and to be unable to prevent grievous mistakes is a very hard and ungrateful task. This government is the worst I have ever had to do with. They never listen to anything I say and commit grievous errors."[76] She is repelled by the optimism of the liberals. They are like children.

And so are *her* children. So many of them survived and reproduced: there were more than forty grandchildren by the end of the century, and in the besieged consciousness of the Queen, they darted and swooped and refused to stay still. Within the popular imagination, the Royal Family, so large and so varied in character, its future so uncertain, could serve as an image for the nation as a whole: growing, dividing, marrying or cavorting, sometimes obedient but too often insubordinate. The Queen's endless worry over Prince Edward was not only a popular fascination, but also a figure for generational strife. Thackeray's Marquis of Steyne in *Vanity Fair* cynically conjures Shakespeare's Prince Hal, "trying on his father's coronet," as the archetype of generational insurgency: "The Crown Prince is always in opposition to the crown or hankering after it." Thackeray's old cynic finds this natural: "If you were heir to a dukedom and a thousand pounds a day, do you mean to say you would not wish for possession?" And whatever the child feels, the parent (he assumes masculinity) projects *his* past onto his son: "it stands to reason that every great man, having experienced this feeling towards his father, must be aware that his son entertains it towards himself; and so they can't but be suspicious and hostile."[77] In Victoria's case, the suspicion centered on her son's inadequacy, his unfitness to assume the responsibilities that one day would be his. No matter how old he got, as long as his mother lived, Edward played the part of the perpetually disappointing adolescent. And he was only one of many, as the public closely noticed, and

76. May 25, 1881, *Beloved Mama*, 109; June 13, 1882, ibid. 121; June 10, 1884, ibid. 168.
77. William Thackeray, *Vanity Fair* (Harmondsworth: Penguin, 2003) 512.

the Queen never forgot. "More and more unable to bear noise and high spirits of young people," her querulousness is openly displayed.[78] Her letters frequently turn on the failures of the young and reflect her own 'plaint of the old.'

In the early years of Victoria's reign, the discourse of etiquette books and domestic manuals focused on the obligation of mature women to form the characters of the next generation: a symmetry was implied between capacities on one side and needs on the other, with the expectation that this balance of tendencies could produce the much-desired comforts of home. There is always discrepancy between private stories and public messages, and in the lives of generations, the work of interpretation must choose carefully between signs of gentle pressure through suasion and active coercion through punishment. But in this chapter I have meant to pursue a quite different public story in the latter years of the nineteenth century, when private turmoil is reflected in public discourse, and the commerce between the two undeniably exposes sharp generational discord.

In her letters to her eldest daughter, Victoria speaks of "the constant struggles of one's children to oppose what parents do solely for their good"; she calls it a "sad thing" to "see how ungrateful [they] are…how little they will take good advice." Clearly attempting to placate and soothe her disgruntled mother, Princess Victoria reassures her that such generational strife has always plagued families, that it is "natural" and universal because "young people chafe at all restraint, and older ones at all opposition." But the Queen is unmoved and persistent in her denunciations: "You say older people can't bear opposition which is not true but what they do really feel acutely is when merely from opposition and often without any real pleasure and enjoyment therefrom—they [the children] do precisely the contrary to what they know is right and to what they have been brought up to and accustomed to look up to and respect."[79] As the children are in their "opposition and ingratitude," so was Gladstone as Prime Minister: her offspring and liberal democracy appear to her in much the same aspect.[80] Their images met, melted, and grew confused: between a pleasure-seeking

78. October 2, 1883, *Beloved Mama*, 147.
79. May 17, 1872, *Darling Child* 42; May 22, 1872, ibid. 43; May 28, 1872, ibid. 45.
80. May 28, 1872, ibid. 45.

Prince and a Prime Minister who refused to consult his sovereign, Victoria saw little to choose.

When Palmerston was Prime Minister she chided him for not responding to her queries soon enough, and for failing to keep her apprised of cabinet discussions.[81] And in the spring of 1894, during heated debate about whether to abolish the Lords, Victoria's impatience takes the aspect of a parent towards squabbling siblings: there are bad members in the Commons *and* among the Peers, she tells Marie Mallet.[82] Of course the governments of Europe *are* often made up of her relatives, and her worries about European stability are often strictly indistinguishable from her familial concerns. In her letters from the 1870s on, she repeatedly requests her children and grandchildren to tell her *everything*, as she will be happy both to know and to send advice in return. As will shortly become clear, Victoria's aspirations towards authorship reflect the wish shared by many of the writers considered in this study, to bring young and old into relation through the resources of narrative: stories heard and tales transmitted.

Here, though, we should complete the picture of the Queen's old age gleaned from her own reports and from others, and situate her lived experience within the cultural crisis between 'new' and old. Early in this chapter I referred to Lytton Strachey's biography of the Queen in 1921, which casts over the final years a glow of general approbation—an assessment which, while not simply *untrue*, is nonetheless only a partial truth obscured by the nostalgia that Strachey located in reactions to her death. "A gentle benignity flowed from the aged Queen," he reports, attributing it to her inevitable withdrawal from political interests, the centering of her focus on her self, and her large family, "over... [whom] she ruled with a most potent sway."[83] But of course we have just seen Victoria's impassioned interest in political affairs alongside her acute perception of attempts to marginalize her both politically and domestically. Strachey's attribution of the Queen's prestige to her growing old is more accurate; he finds age "an almost indispensable qualification for popularity in England."[84] Perhaps so, but it is an

81. See e.g. the famous exchange of messages regarding his duties as Prime Minister in *Regina vs. Palmerston: The Correspondence between Queen Victoria and her Foreign and Prime Minister 1837–1865*, ed. Brian Connell (London: Evans Brothers, 1962), 124.

82. Mallet, *Life With Queen Victoria*, 384.

83. Strachey, *Queen Victoria*, 228, 225.

84. Ibid. 240.

unstable popularity which depends equally on her powerlessness: "by the end of the reign the power of the Sovereign had appreciably diminished, the prestige of the sovereign had enormously grown."[85]

To the extent that his estimate of her later years rests on a brisk and detached view of aging, Strachey's account fairly reconstructs the Queen's popularity at the time of her last two jubilees. But when we contrast his report with her own, or even with reports of those who knew her well, a poignant breach opens between the aging Queen's sorrow and the public affirmation, a contrast that vividly displays the problem of aging in a society which adulates the new, even more than it manufactures nostalgia for the old. "I am very rheumatic. I am generally weak and much shaken. My troubles and sorrows I know well I must bear alone," the Queen writes in May 1883.[86] Strachey's bracing description reads as a retort: "Endowed by nature with a robust constitution, Victoria, though in periods of depression she had sometimes supposed herself an invalid, had in reality throughout her life enjoyed remarkably good health. In her old days, she had suffered from a rheumatic stiffness of the joints,...but no other ailments attacked her, until, in 1898, her eyesight began to be affected by incipient cataract."[87] Marie Mallet, Victoria's friend and lady in waiting for many years, provides both confirmation and rebuttal of Strachey's estimate. Her praise of the Queen's good health often seems an effect of her own fatigue and chill, but a succession of representative comments gives a richer portrayal of Victoria's last years. In 1891 Marie is writing that "She enjoys everything as if she were 17 instead of 72"; in 1896 she notes that "The Queen is looking better than she has done for years." But in 1898 she includes this extract from her husband's private account: "Bernard's diary. December 28th 'She [Victoria] spoke pathetically and for the first time of her old age, blindness and lameness, of her losses this year...which had saddened this great Jubilee year.'" And yet, no comment can be definitive, because each day brings new sensations. In May 1899, for example, Marie notes that "The Queen is in excellent spirits and most amusing, commenting on the wretched health

85. Ibid. 240. David Cannadine elaborates on the claim, arguing that the two are mutually dependent, and especially that Victoria's prestige is inconceivable without the lack of sovereign power. See "The Context, Performance and Meaning of Ritual: The British Monarchy and the 'Invention of Tradition,' c.1820–1977," in *The Invention of Tradition*, ed. Eric Hobsbawm and Terence Ranger (Cambridge: Cambridge University Press, 1983), 101–64.

86. *Beloved Mama*, 139.

87. Strachey, *Queen Victoria*, 244.

of the Prince of Wales and his children with evident pride in her own strength." When the Boer War ends, Victoria is still jubilant and strong, but shortly thereafter, Marie notes a swift disintegration: in one of her final notes she refers to herself, but the reflection of Victoria's old age could not be clearer (October 27, 1900): "The dear little Queen makes heroic efforts to be cheerful but her face in repose is terribly sad; I do not want to live to be very old; the penalties are too great."[88] (See Fig. 8.) Just a few months earlier, on her birthday, Victoria writes "Balmoral, 24th May 1900.—Again my old birthday returns, my eighty-first! God has been very merciful and supported me, but my trials and anxieties have been manifold, and I feel tired and upset by all I have gone through this winter and spring."[89] Here is age in all its fullness: its tedium, miseries, pleasures, and pains. If Victoria grows large in Strachey's account, it is at the sacrifice of her humanity; if she grows small in Marie Mallet's record, it is at the sacrifice of her majesty. In one portrait we see the way an impersonal public may assess the Age; in the other we see an aging Queen.

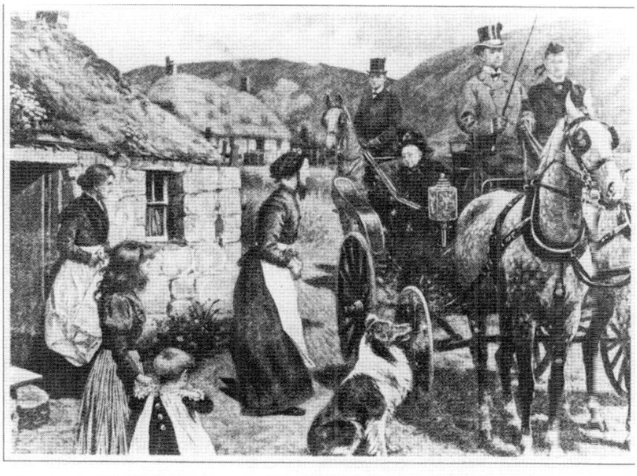

The Queen's goodbye. Visiting the cottages, October 1900. S. Begg.

Figure 8 *The Queen's Goodbye: Visiting the cottages, October 1900.* S. Begg. Photo courtesy of David Duff

88. Mallet, *Life with Queen Victoria*, 47, 91, 128, 167, 211.
89. Duff cites in *Victoria in the Highlands: The Personal Journal of Her Majesty Queen Victoria*, ed. David Duff (notes, introduction, description of acquisition and building of Balmoral) (London: Frederick Muller, 1968), 370.

Writing in the nineties, George Gissing makes Strachey seem naive and Marie Mallet sentimental. When Gissing published *In the Year of the Jubilee* in 1894, he gave sharp representation to Regina abscondita, *the* shrunken queen, aging into insignificance. Victoria is nowhere in this novel of her first Jubilee year 1887. The great night of celebration sets the plot in motion, but no thought is given to its object. "What have I to do with the Queen?" one character remarks. In Gissing's view, the distance of the monarch gives license to insurgent desire, and his protagonist, young Nancy Lord, must suffer "the impulse of lawless imagination which had first possessed her on the evening of Jubilee Day."[90] The Queen recedes and leaves appetite behind.

In the Year of the Jubilee records the triumphalism of the New—the pervasive cultural acquiescence in the great game of Novelty. For Gissing, as for so many others, what is precisely new is a New Woman: the woman who asks to be educated; who demands to vote; who longs to be modern; who seeks an end to the sexual double standard, desires a marriage built on fairness, wears rational dress. And even though these demands were parried, called utopian or anarchic, they created the great spectacle of change. In the waspish words of the *Quarterly Review*, "a change has come over society during the last fifteen or twenty years.... Women are now graduates in half-a-dozen professions and disciples in all. They practise medicine as well as novel-writing; the forceps is familiar to them no less than the bicycle."[91] Margaret Oliphant was more terse: "it is now the woman who seduces—it is no longer the man."[92]

And yet, even the New has a history: novelty, too, lives in time. Over a period of fifteen years or more, women had been contesting property laws, election laws, marriage laws, the Contagious Diseases Act, and yet the coining of the phrase, New Woman, marked a next stage in the conflict. Part of the challenge was now exactly in the epithet itself, "The New Woman." Sarah Grand claimed to have invented it in 1894, and whether or not she was first, it is clear that this was the moment when it began to circulate everywhere: newspapers, novels, breakfast tables—a handy conversational counter, a lozenge for debate. But what is so striking is that at this moment

90. George Gissing, *In the Year of the Jubilee* (Cranbury, NJ: Associated University Presses, 1976), 27, 113.
91. William Barry, "The Strike of a Sex," *Quarterly Review*, 179 358 (1894), 294.
92. Margaret Oliphant, "The Anti-Marriage League," *Blackwood's*, 159 (January 1896), 141.

of verbal crystallization, another phrase is there to describe the agent of disturbance: not the New Woman, but the Revolting Daughter. In the space of a few months in late 1893 and early 1894, just as the New Woman was taking on linguistic reality, even indeed slightly before, the Daughter emerges as the figure of transformation and the embodiment of insurrection—not the resisting Adult Woman, New or otherwise, but the Daughter, the rabid girl, who refuses the parental canon and threatens to trounce propriety. One of the suppressed conflicts of the middle nineties was a struggle between two epithets—New Woman/Revolting Daughter—that epitomized contesting ways of representing challenge.

Everywhere in the periodical press, the Daughter storms and prances. The older figures of resistance—the brazen suffragette, the smoking freethinker, the briskly professional doctor—these incarnations of the New Woman do not disappear, but at a decisive moment in the middle of the decade they give way to the character who in principle contains them all: the middle-class daughter who reads Ibsen and *The Heavenly Twins* and *Dodo*, who asks to visit the music hall, who demands freedom to dress as she pleases. Will she liberate culture? Or will she grow into monstrosity? In the middle of the decade, pages of journals are given over to the emergency of the hour: the insurrection within the household, the great refusal of the unashamed, unmarried daughter.

And there on cue, they suddenly appear, those daughters recruited for the generational drama. All through this period of journalistic spectacle, daughters are found, who gladly tease, taunt and—on demand—they demand. Alys Pearsall Smith, soon to marry Bertrand Russell, writes that the daughter is rebelling "against a bondage that enslaves her whole life. In the past she has belonged to other people, now she demands to belong to herself."[93] Kathleen Cuffe, another daughter, is obligingly pert, promising to "disentangle the things we do want from the things we are supposed to want." And "what [the daughter] wants, first of all, is the abolition of chaperons on all possible occasions."[94] As one commentator (Mary Haweis) put it, "daughters are 'revolting' all over the place, some for one reason, some for another."[95] Blanche Crackanthorpe

93. Alys Pearsall Smith, "A Reply from the Daughters", *Nineteenth Century*, 35 (March 1894), 450.
94. Kathleen Cuffe, "A Reply from the Daughters,", *Nineteenth Century* 35 (March 1894), 440.
95. Mary Haweis, "The Revolt of the Daughters: II Daughters and Mothers," *Nineteenth Century*, 35 (March 1894), 430.

names it the latest strike in these days of strikes: "we will call the mothers the employers, and the daughters the operatives," (the workers). And she goes on: "For inner barrenness of spirit, manifesting itself in ugly outside action, few things can match the ruthless young daughter." In the spring, the press reports that "a meeting of mothers [was] lately held to discuss the situation."[96]

Gissing's Jubilee novel belongs to this surprising conjuncture. His Nancy Lord is not a figure of feminist revolt in general, but of daughterly rebellion in particular, one who mocks the thought that she needs a parent's permission to walk the Jubilee streets. In this respect *In the Year of the Jubilee* is close cousin to Shaw's *Mrs. Warren's Profession*, which, though it would not be performed publicly for close to thirty years, was conceived and largely written in 1893–4, exactly at this moment of the daughters. "I have made the daughter the heroine," wrote Shaw in the flush of composition, "and the mother a most deplorable old rip." "The great scene will be the crushing of the mother by the daughter."[97]

"Because I made my daughter a good woman," says Mrs. Warren, "she turns me out as if I was a leper." And then she gives her curse: "may you live to have your own daughter tear and trample on you as you have trampled on me."—to which her Vivie coolly responds, "You are a conventional woman at heart. That is why I am bidding you goodbye now."[98] What gives special power to Vivie Warren and agitates a nineties culture that never saw her was the provocation of University training, the daughter educated not only beyond the reach of her mother, but educated out of the obligation to marry. During this roaring spring of 1894 there appeared a study of the first generation to attend Girton College, Cambridge: it showed that of 720 graduates, only 120 had married. To opponents of the New Daughter, this seemed the bitter truth: to know too much was to marry too little. As the journal *Nineteenth Century* queried, "Is it gain for our daughters to know more than their mothers, if they feel less?"[99]

96. Blanche Crackanthorpe, "The Revolt of the Daughters," *Nineteenth Century* 35 (January 1894), 23, 24, 26; Vacken Doyce, "The Revolt of the Daughters: I The Last Word on 'the Revolt,'" *Nineteenth Century*, 35 (March 1894), 427.
97. G. B. Shaw to Janet Achurch, September 4, 1893, *Bernard Shaw Collected Letters: 1874–1897*, ed. Dan H. Laurence, (London: Max Reinhardt, 1965), 404.
98. G. B. Shaw, *Plays: Pleasant and Unpleasant*, vol. vii of *The Complete Works of G. B. Shaw* (London: Constable, 1930) Act IV, p. 252.
99. "In the Days of Her Youth," *Nineteenth Century*, 37 (June 1895), 940.

The Diamond Jubilee

Still the Queen was not dead yet. The moment of 1894 brought out the revolting daughter, but even as she strutted through so many pages of anxious periodicals, the prospect of a second royal jubilee changed the terms of the generational reverie. Cicero had identified the riddle long before: there is a boundary to all periods of life except an old age that can confound all limits.[100] By the time of the Diamond Jubilee of 1897, the Queen had not only outlived her husband by nearly four decades; had not only outlasted her ministers, her Melbourne, Peel, her Palmerston, her Disraeli; but had lived past her own Silver apotheosis ten years earlier.

As the whole empire organized for celebration, the still surviving Victoria heightened the consciousness of senescence within the Epoch of the New, Victoria continuing to age, until almost none of her subjects could recall a time when she was not there. As Margaret Oliphant uncannily put it, "When Queen Victoria ascended the throne, the Dark Continent had not even begun to be called the Dark Continent"—as much to say that before Victoria, our modern things lacked names, our empire an imagery.[101]

"If ever old age could be in fashion," this is still Oliphant, "it would be now, when all of our thoughts are concentrated on the celebration of a great life [the Queen], which has already passed the limits traced for mankind." The "sight of an old Queen" in "the pageant of the ending century"—the fact that the Diamond Jubilee nearly converged with the year 1900—this created a compelling zone of daydream, rival to the phantasm of novelty. Sixty years of sovereignty merged with a hundred years of the calendar—together they activated a massive will to remembrance. Everywhere there was Jubilee retrospection, Jubilee nostalgia, rehearsing the same set of marvels: Railways, Telegraph, Anesthetics, Lighting, Sanitation, Empire. The length of the reign gave form to a world picture, a self-definition. Who are we? We are the sort of beings conceived in the age of Victoria. "We are the children of one Mother," proclaimed *Blackwood's*, "this is the meaning of the shout that

100. Marcus Cicero, "Treatise on Old Age," in *Select Orations of Marcus T. Cicero*, trans. Rev. Dr. M'Kay, 2nd edn (Dublin: University Press, 1855), 163. Gabriele Zerba echoes the observation in his famous *Gerontocomia* (1489). He points out that, unlike youth, old age "has no certain terminous"; its beginning and duration are inevitably different—*Gerontocomia: On the Care of the Aged and Maximianus, Elegies on Old Age and Love*, trans. L. R. Lind (Philadelphia: American Philosophical Society, 1988), 71–2.

101. Margaret Oliphant, "'Tis Sixty Years Since," 616.

will go round the earth on the approaching day of triumph."[102] Victoria is the antidote to novelty and speed. As Emily Crawford put it, "The Queen was appointed to help a slow work of evolution."[103]

The New Woman and the Old Queen, the Quick Insurgent Daughter and the Great Slow Mother, these converging conceits produced a confusion of generations. On the one side, the aging of the Queen and the ending century created an ambiguous past. When precisely was that previous generation, from which we know ourselves to have fallen? Twenty years ago in the 1870s, when today's mothers were daughters—that was one familiar and unsurprising proposal. But the approaching term of a hundred years also brought a reflex memory of mid-century, the robust moment of 1851, the Crystal Palace and the Great Exhibition, some forty-odd years before. And then Victoria's own reign excited yearning images of its beginning, the world of 1837. Twenty, forty, sixty, one hundred years ago, what exactly was nostalgia supposed to remember? No one was sure, and all those retrospective essays lurched toward wildly different points of origin, different pasts.

On the other side, youth was as unsteady as age. In the wake of the great sexual procurement scandal of the 1880s, the so-called "Maiden Tribute of Modern Babylon," parliament and the press had twitched over the question of the legal age of sexual consent. Thirteen was no longer thinkable. Some now wanted eighteen, some wanted twenty, but sixteen was the hard-won compromise. Within the less sensational confines of the middle class, the ambiguity was also chronic. Oliphant mocks the emancipated daughter "with her glib arguments and logic of three-and-twenty (that, I think, is her usual age: unless when she is eighteen, which the girl of my time preferred…)."[104] And many others struggled to name the time when callow youth ends and independence begins, when a daughter can safely leave her mother. Is that age 20? Is it 25? Without any settled narrative of adolescence, youth fluttered, disturbingly indeterminate. In short, within a brief period, Queenly retrospection met daughterly anticipation, and this meeting brought a heightening of generational discourse, only incited further by the unstable definitions: When *are* we old? When *are* we no longer young?

102. Margaret Oliphant, "'Tis Sixty Years Since," 599, 600, 615.
103. Emily Crawford, "Victoria, Princess and Queen," *Contemporary Review*, 71 (June 1897), 796.
104. Oliphant, "The Anti-Marriage League," 143.

The Great Mother and the Revolting Daughter—this is the conspicuous pattern of generational conflict that confuses the pursuit of novelty. The tormented resolution of *In the Year of the Jubilee* exposes the difficulty. Poised between the youth of 18 and the maturity of 26, 23-year-old Nancy Lord revolts her way into a secret marriage, and when the revolt is done, she finds herself a secret mother. She looks back on her own daughterly insurgence "in the stern spirit of a woman judging another's frailty." Now, motherly, mature, "I feel revolt to be silly."[105]

"All women become like their mothers," remarked Wilde, "that is their tragedy. No man does. That is his." This piece of timely wit captures the impasse embedded in the prevailing domestic figure: for all the vehemence of the daughter's assertion, she is ever liable to become a mother, and then to regret the "headstrong folly" of her youth. In place of Grant Allen's ringing call, "for the first time in the history of the race," the dream of rupture, we find the repetition of generations.[106] As that anti-feminist Eliza Lynn Linton curtly put it, "Things repeat themselves, and the Revolt of Women has been seen in the world before now."[107]

The figures of an aging Queen and the rebellious daughters provide us with a paradigm of diminishment: on the one hand, a loss of political, familial, and physical power, and on the other, the reduction of the New Woman into the Revolting Daughter, an adult act of resistance into an adolescent tantrum. "Youth" and "Age" show themselves not only as phases of life: at the end of the nineteenth century, they become tactics in the definition of culture. Just over a hundred years ago *those* large generational markers threatened to absorb challenge within the cadence of repetition: demand and regret, assertion and apology, daughter and mother. Thrashing novelty flailed within the web of Queenly remembrance. As a century and a royal life came to their end, the clash of generations sets the context for the last phase in our account, when the conundrum of senescence flares at the center without ever leaving the margins, and when the cultural iconography of age meets its politics.

105. Gissing, *Year of the Jubilee*, Part V, 290; Part VI, 404.

106. Oscar Wilde, *The Importance of Being Earnest* (Harmondsworth: Penguin, 2000), I, 312. Allen, "The New Hedonism," 392.

107. Eliza Lynn Linton, "The Partisans of the Wild Woman," *Nineteenth Century*, 31 (March 1892), 464.

5

Artistic Investigations and the Elderly Subject

The early modernists' repudiation of the Victorian 'heritage' simplifies a generational portrait, drawing stark lines between the youthful insurgence and an aged decrepitude clinging to the forms and figures of Victorian culture. But, as we have seen, to those who lived through the late century the picture was never so clear: already generational agitations confused the categories of youth and age. Amid the unclarities, however, one significant change deserves particular attention: the aging population became newly visible.

These last two chapters will engage with the startling new prominence of the elderly, as they became the focus for diverse though inter-animating investigations: literary, artistic, and social. I first collect this miscellany under the rubric of 'portraiture,' and the pictures which emerge—whether in analytic or narrative prose, in the fine arts, or in popular representation—raise difficult but evocative questions for the representation and collective self-understanding of age. Wilde's *Picture of Dorian Gray* offers an opening into the question of portraiture, and in surprising ways it displays the fate of age as a moral/political provocation. From Wilde's narrativized portrait we turn to the visual arts, where the career of Herbert von Herkomer, so long concerned with representation of the elderly, will serve as an opening to reflections on the visual design of generational life. The next, and final, chapter turns to the place where systematic political engagement with the elderly converges with the most immediate afflictions of the aging subject. The chapter begins with the place of age in William Morris's utopian fiction *News from Nowhere*, continues with the social investigation and political program of Charles Booth so central to the movement to pass an Old Age Pensions Bill, and concludes with an account of Beatrice Webb's encounter with old age, her own as well as that of her intimates, and with the frightful, revelatory anguish of Herbert Spencer, whose aging became an agony and a misery.

The face of age

Published within a year of one another, Oscar Wilde's *Picture of Dorian Gray* provoked a public flurry more sensational than William Morris's frankly socialist fiction *News From Nowhere*. Wilde's book was said (strangely) to have no moral, whereas the revolutionary politics of Morris's work were unconcealed in the socialist journal *The Commonweal* where it first appeared. Wilde was only 35 when he wrote *Dorian Gray*, but in many ways he (and his work) straddled the generations. As an artist he was impatient with entrenched conventions of realism which had been habit for so long that they threatened to obstruct the path of a new self-conscious, ironic, and refined art. And yet Wilde had recently become a father twice over and so had seen embodied evidence of the next generation which one day would supplant his own, and he had recently acknowledged a sexual orientation which prized the figure of male youthfulness. Of course he did not know then that his span of life was already approaching its term (he died at 45), but he too felt the pressure of time, personally and acutely.

It is customary to see Lord Henry as Wilde's representative in this novel, although Wilde found aspects of himself in each of the major figures: "Basil Hallward is what I think I am: Lord Henry what the world thinks me: Dorian what I would like to be."[1] But there is yet another character with whom Wilde has much in common. This is Mr. Erkskine of Treadley, an old gentleman of considerable charm and culture, who, however, had fallen into bad habits of silence, having, "as he explained once to Lady Agatha, said everything that he had to say before he was thirty" (*DG*, 54). Wilde of course had much more to say after he was 35; but at the time, he already had the reputation of repetition, repetition of his and others' words. From the perspective of youth, silence or repetition seem the terrible temptations of old age: from the vantage of age, youthful indifference to elderly voices dooms one to choose between silence or repetition. The public treated Wilde as a pert innovator,

1. Oscar Wilde, *The Picture of Dorian Gray and Selected Stories* (New York: Signet, 1962), introduction by Gary Schmidgall (1995), p. xxvii.

but among avant-garde artists, he often assumed the place of an aging parrot cast in a scene of exotic birds. Frequently accused of possessing cleverness rather than originality, his appropriation of others' words was legendary. Gary Schmidgall calls him a "consummate thieving magpie" in his use of the plots of others, while Jerusha McCormack claims that "It is hard to say anything original about *The Picture of Dorian Gray*, largely because there is so little that is original in it."[2] For McCormack this is no criticism; indeed, he says that Wilde intends to write a mythic story, composed from and for a common culture.[3] Wilde himself was very sensitive to the charge that his wit merely gave edge to the insights of others. No one can be certain whether Whistler's pithy response to Wilde's wish to have spoken a certain phrase—"You, will, Oscar, you will"—was in fact uttered by Whistler or by Wilde (being clever even at his own expense). Mr. Erkskine of Treadley listens closely to others and speaks in characteristic Wildean phrases. It is he who utters the famous lines: "the way of paradoxes is the way of truth. To test reality we must see it on the tight rope. When the verities become acrobats, we can judge them" (*DG*, 56). He confesses to Lord Henry that "I myself used to have literary ambitions, but I gave them up long ago," perhaps because "The generation into which I was born was tedious" (*DG*, 59). Erkskine accepts with irony the 'giving up' from which Dorian shrinks in horror. But he assigns tedium, that other characteristic of old age, to his times, nursing the image of a young maverick too outrageous for the tired habits of an aged period.

Much of Wilde's adult life was similarly a contest between an artist struggling for expression and a generation that he saw as "tedious." Even so, the world was as willing to be amused by his art as it was ready to be outraged by his conduct. We have no reason to suppose that Wilde felt old when he wrote *Dorian Gray*, but we can recognize his acute sense of living in an outdated, an obsolete century. There is a paradox: where Wilde is concerned there is always a paradox. The modern world, about which he had so many critical insights, was outdated but also, in comparison with ages past, it was naive, insipid, and unworldly. *The Picture of Dorian Gray* is also the picture of an age, the Victorian age, as it settled into its final decade and the final years of the century. The story itself is 'old' in

2. Oscar Wilde, p. xv. McCormack, *Cambridge Companion to Wilde* (Cambridge: Cambridge University Press, 1997), 110.

3. For a good summary of the novel's literary pedigree see Schmidgall's introduction to the Signet edition (1995), p. xv–xix.

the sense of having several antecedents which Wilde may or may not have read or recalled. Poe, of course, but another story with resonant overtones which has gone largely unnoted is Mary Shelley's "The Mortal Immortal." This story, published in the 1833 *Keepsake*, takes a 123-year-old man for its narrator, a man who drank the alchemic mixture his master had prepared, thinking the effect would 'cure' him 'of love,' and so it does, only not in the fashion he expected. The drink makes him immortal, and as his wife ages, he remains forever "as untarnished as in my twentieth year," doomed to remain suspiciously young while those around him age and eventually die.[4] Despite his handsome visage, the narrator ages internally. He characterizes his marriage in its final years with this image: "We sat by our lone fireside—the old-hearted youth and his antiquated wife" (Shelley, "The Mortal Immortal," 55). Like Dorian, what makes his heart 'old' is the accumulation of negative affects that are stored there. He despises his jealous wife's attempts to appear young as well, even though he realizes that the cosmetic mask she dons is simply "less successful" than his (Shelley, "The Mortal Immortal," 56). The experience of old age consists of outliving his former feelings, even the certainty that his love for his wife would be unalterable. Similar aging passions motivate the emotional arc of *Dorian Gray*. Dorian's 'conscience' is called into existence by the awareness that his 'love' for Sybil could not endure. His guilt is not primarily for the neglect which drove her to suicide but for his own negative emotions that tarnish his innocence and disturb the purity of his portrait.

As Dorian moves through time without aging, he becomes fascinated as much with the aging of the portrait as with its ever-growing evidence of moral decay. Kay Heath argues that the picture educates Dorian without imposing experience as the means, even though at the close Dorian 'embraces' the repellent age he resisted throughout.[5] The plot expresses an ambivalence towards age by taking pains alternately to associate and then to separate crime, conscience, and age. It is as if Wilde were straining to comprehend how society, psychology, and physiology each expresses itself as aging, and aged. People are initially charmed by Dorian Gray, but "They wondered how one so charming and graceful as he was could have

4. Mary Shelley, "The Mortal Immortal," in *The Broadview Anthology of Victorian Short Stories*, ed. Dennis Denisoff (Ontario: Broadview Press, 2004), 55.

5. Kay Heath, "In the Eye of the Beholder: Victorian Age Construction and the Specular Self," *Victorian Literature and Culture* 34/1 (2006), 33, 35.

escaped the stain of an age that was at once sordid and sensual" (*DG*, 142). "An age that was at once sordid and sensual"—here we see clearly the conflation between Dorian's age and his Age, or period. And the portrait, we realize too, is the picture of him just as it is the portrait of an age, and of Age itself.

What makes his age sordid and sensual? What makes age itself sordid and sensual? And if Dorian merely *reflects* these aspects of his age and of age itself, then surely he is in harmony with both: physical nature, personality, and historical period converge and begin to seem interchangeable. As Lord Henry says tellingly towards the close, "You are the type of what the age is searching for, and what it is afraid it has found" (*DG*, 228). Dorian is like Yeats's "rough beast"; he has been summoned by the very Age (or Period) that would shrink in horror at its work. But in the final paradox, the 'art' of Dorian Gray is to recapture his early youth and beauty and thus replace modern discord with classical harmony. The portrait of age, it is worth emphasizing, is before all else a physical portrait:

> Hour by hour, and week by week, the thing upon the canvas was growing old. It might escape the hideousness of sin, but the hideousness of age was in store for it. The cheeks would become hollow or flaccid. Yellow crow's feet would creep round the fading eyes and make them horrible. The hair would lose its brightness, the mouth would gape or droop, would be foolish or gross, as the mouths of old men are. There would be the wrinkled throat, the cold, blue-veined hands, the twisted body, that he remembered in the grandfather who had been so stern to him in his boyhood. (*DG*, 136–7)

Dorian is both attracted to and repulsed by sin, but he is unequivocally appalled by age. And the most disturbing feature of age is its visibility. The Countess of Blessington had written that "Youth resembles a Claude Lorrain glass, which imparts to all objects its own beautiful tints; but age is like a magnifying lens, which leaves no defect unseen." Attempts to cover it up only make it more grotesque: "When age is seen moving through scenes of gaiety and pleasure, its wrinkles concealed beneath a mask of paint, and its wig wreathed with flowers, it reminds one of the death's heads which the ancients introduced at their festivals, to recall to their memories the brevity of life, and make them enjoy the present with more zest."[6] We might apply Lawrence's phrase about sex to Wilde's treatment of age: for Dorian,

6. Marguerite Gardiner, Countess of Blessington, *Desultory Thoughts and Reflections*, 2nd edn. (London: Orme, Brown, Green & Longmans, 1839), 8, 121.

if not for Wilde, age rather than sin is the "dirty little secret" which civilization would repress. It is a secret which constantly threatens exposure and humiliation. We assume it is Dorian's sins that upset other characters as well as the first readers of this novel. But however coarse, decadent, or forbidden the sins—whether they refer to sex, drugs, or crime—none of them is as frightening as the most inevitable and ordinary process of aging. As Turgenev once noted, "Do you know the worst of all vices? It is being over fifty-five."[7] There may be social reasons for aligning sin, or crime with aging, and these we will consider in due time, but the novel asks us to take seriously the conjunction of crime with the physical signs of age. Wilde was hardly the first to associate the two, and yet his doing so helps to explain why his novel triggered such a sensational response among readers from many walks of life and of widely different dispositions. Here, from a funeral sermon preached in 1841, is the remark of an Evangelical preacher on the subject: "The decay of age, as of death, is the sinner's accomplishment. Every old man, therefore, presents in his body the testimony of nature to SIN and DEATH. Two dread realities!"[8] A body flecked with age is marked with sin. Far from constructing an elaborate metaphor, Wilde takes literally this presumption, and then asks, Can age, like crime, have a life of its own, or are the two inextricably bound? The youthful Dorian would like to believe in their separation, but the narrative, itself assuming the perspective of age, insists on their connection.

A few years before Wilde wrote the novel, the display of Joseph Merrick, 'the Elephant Man', shook and shocked the public. Merrick never lived to be an old man, of course, but the changes in his body during the later 1880s made him a figure of horror and repellent fascination. That he couldn't live long was always clear, and as the dignitaries of London came to visit him—including Princess Alexandra and the Duke of Cambridge—he became, like death itself, difficult to look at directly. After he was exhibited at the Pathological Society in 1884, his disease "rapidly advanced," a speedy movement of decay, charted through every stage.[9] Merrick, you might say,

7. Quoted in Simone de Beauvoir, *The Coming of Age* (New York: Warner Paperback Library, 1973), 421.
8. Cortlandt Van Rensselaer, *Old Age; A Funeral Sermon* (Washington: n.p. 1841), 7. Quoted in Thomas R. Cole, "The Dualism of Aging in Victorian America," in *The Journey of Life; A Cultural History of Aging in America* (Cambridge: Cambridge University Press, 1992), 88.
9. "Death of the 'Elephant Man,'" *British Medical Journal*, 1 (April 19, 1890), 916.

wore the inside of his body on the outside: and the faster it grew in its distortions, the more he became a figure for the pathos of age.

More particularly, Merrick was a figure of premature aging, a complement to the dread of living well beyond a satisfactory life span. All through the period you find the anxiety that age will either last too long or come too quickly, that the stresses of commerce, the afflictions of the city will furrow the young brow and bend the middle-aged back. The physician George Day spoke of the "premature decrepitude, to which civilized man is almost necessarily exposed."[10] And one of the most common diagnoses in the asylums was "prematurely aged": the wasted body racing through the stages of decline. Joseph Merrick played the part of Elephant Man, not only because of the dreadful distensions of his flesh, but because he seemed already as old as an elephant; at twenty-seven he already contained the misery of age. Still more striking is the way that the Elephant Man looms behind Dorian Gray, giving reason to believe that the ghastly sensation of Joseph Merrick was a prod to Wilde's own grotesquerie. The fascination with repellent age is apparent as Dorian enjoys looking at his own body next to the decayed flesh rendered on the canvas:

> The very sharpness of the contrast used to quicken his sense of pleasure...He would examine with minute care, and sometimes with monstrous and terrible delight, the hideous lines that seared the wrinkling forehead or crawled around the heavy sensual mouth, wondering sometimes which were the more horrible, the signs of sin or the signs of age. He would place his white hands beside the coarse bloated hands of the picture, and smile. He mocked the misshapen body and the failing limbs. (*DG*, 142)

Dorian is yet another who suffers the prematurity of age, the headlong hastening through all the phases of decline. The fact that the horror is kept secret is a richly melodramatic device; it is also a revelatory sign within the culture of aging.

And in this connection, I reintroduce the subject of cremation, which was so pertinent to Trollope's *The Fixed Period* of the previous decade. Few may remember the cremation in Dorian Gray. But after the murder of Basil Hallward, Dorian needs to remove the incriminating corpse, and so decides to change him "into a handful of ashes that I may scatter in the air"

10. George Day, *A Practical Treatise on the Domestic Management and Most Important Diseases of Advanced Life* (London: T. and W. Boone, 1849), 5.

(*DG*, 180). He summons and coerces Alan Campbell to perform the off-stage procedure involving fire and nitric acid. When Dorian returns there is a "horrible smell" but no corpse (*DG*, 186). Wilde in effect offers a camp perspective on the new public policy of death: a kind of cremation for home use, a sanitary reform that even a murderer can love. In the present context we might see cremation as the acceleration of the bodily process, a spectacular kind of premature aging. The proponents of cremation liked to contrast the slowly decomposing body with the brevity of fire and the antiseptic cleanliness of ashes. Trollope's Neverbend insists that "The actual clay will evaporate into the air, without leaving a trace either for the eye to see or the nose to smell" (*FP*, 86). When Mr. Graybody, "a slow decrepit old gentleman" who is curator for the college grounds, says that "when you tried the furnaces [using pigs] there was a savour of burnt pork.... They say that men and women would not have quite the same smell," Neverbend furiously replies "There won't be any smell at all—not the least; and the smoke will all consume itself, so that even you, living just where you are, will not know when cremation is going on" (*FP*, 86–7). Henry Thompson, leader for the cause of cremation, was even more explicit, and less humorous than Trollope. In his articles, printed in the *Contemporary Review* in the 1870s and 1880s, vivid description of bodily decomposition in the ground is set against the pristine beauty of the instant disposal assured by cremation. He describes the body as "a marvellously complex machine" which, after death, retraces its steps in order to reduce the body to carbonic acid, water, ammonia, and a few mineral compounds. Without the vitality of life to warm the body with its glow, decomposition appears as ruthless, degrading, and dangerous: "could I paint in its true colours the ghastly picture of that which happens to the mortal remains of the dearest we have lost, the page would be too deeply stained for publication."[11] Then beyond what it means for the dead self, the decomposing body is a blight upon the living. It continues to exert an influence in the world even though it is no longer present. Thompson warns "that the placing of the dead body in a grave and covering it with a few feet of earth does not prevent the gases generated by decomposition, together with putrescent matters which they hold in suspension, from permeating the surrounding soil, and escaping into the air above and the water beneath." The unburnt

11. Henry Thompson, "The Treatment of the Body after Death," *Contemporary Review*, 23 (January 1874), 319, 326.

corpse is represented as a putrid vessel of diseases (including tuberculosis, smallpox, typhoid, diphtheria, and cholera).[12]

It should be clear that this transitional state of the body, the decomposing corpse, stands in the place of decrepit age, or, to reverse the equation, decrepit age reminds others of the direction in which their bodies are tending. Wilde's novel makes age exciting by forbidding it, concealing it, denying it. It is not primarily the fantasy of living on which inflames desire and provokes repression. The desire is to defy nature and perpetuate youth, and to re-draw the map of age. "You must have some secret," Lord Henry charges Dorian towards the novel's close, "I am only ten years older than you are, and I am wrinkled, and worn, and yellow" (*DG*, 227). Youth may not possess wisdom, but it purchases novelty instead, and who is to say in the end which has greater appeal? Certainly Lord Henry has no doubt: "Youth!" he exclaims,

> There is nothing like it. It's absurd to talk of the ignorance of youth. The only people to whose opinions I listen now with any respect are people much younger than myself. They seem in front of me. Life has revealed to them her latest wonder. As for the aged, I always contradict the aged. I do it on principle. If you ask them their opinion on something that happened yesterday, they solemnly give you the opinions current in 1820, when people wore high stocks, believed in everything, and knew absolutely nothing (*DG*, 227).

I have argued that in Wilde's novel age is a punishment: the accumulation of experience weathers and soils. It takes its toll on the body, the mind, the pleasures, and the expectations. As Jeff Nunokawa contends in a splendid essay on the secret of *ennui* in *Dorian Gray*, exhaustion is the novel's dominant subject and mode. Nunokawa understands this general tedium as the result of cultural oppression, the cruel banishment of homosexual desire which is countered by its continual reappearance in displaced forms.[13] For every blasé and languid response there is an assertion of new desire. Nunokawa's insight captures the anguished realization of one's solitary march through time. Wilde's Dorian rejects tedium for sensation; he associates the former with age just as he associates the latter with youth. Age, then, is always

12. Henry Thompson, "A Reply to Critics and an Exposition of the Process," *Contemporary Review*, 23 (March 1874), 557; "The Progress of Cremation," *Nineteenth Century*, 23(January–June 1888), 10.
13. Jeffrey Nunokawa, "The Importance of Being Bored: The Dividends of Ennui in *The Picture of Dorian Gray*," in *Novel Gazing: Queer Readings in Fiction*, ed. Eve Kosofsky Sedgwick (Durham, NC: Duke University Press, 1997), 151–66.

in the future while the moment's sensation becomes a symbol of youth. On the level of plot, there is nothing to retard the unending succession of moments which Dorian adopts as a way of life. This rhythm of plot instructs us not to read closure into its conclusion. Just as Dorian understands, when he inspects the picture, that his final "renunciation" was no retraction of desire—it was the cunning assertion of a new desire, so too we might say that his impulse to destroy the picture expresses no final rejection but only another cunningly disguised pleasure. It is as if to say, 'Death? I will experience that too.' And of course, consciously Dorian doesn't even acknowledge that he seeks death; he claims he is destroying the picture as a repetition of the way he destroyed its artist, thinking that he might free himself from conscience altogether and so enjoy the undisturbed proliferation of desires.

It is important that Dorian really "be" young, that he is not simply posing. There is something illicit and grotesque about an older man who dons the mask of youth. Dorian is no Gustav Aschenbach, of Mann's *Death in Venice*, whose painted lips defy the youth he intends them to suggest. Nor is he Bertha, the wife in Mary Shelley's story, who pathetically uses cosmetics to hide the contrast between her husband's persistent youth and her advancing age. By the end of the century it was not unusual for a woman to rouge when her natural bloom disappeared, but in literature the cosmetic mask of youth typically accentuates the fact of age, and there is something repugnant in the prospect of grasping age hiding behind the disguise of youth. What else is Red Riding Hood's wolf but an old man whose age makes appetite beastly?

Convention made ordinary the denial or disguise of age on the part of women. For men, there were fewer conventions available in part because the marks of age were less socially consequential. There are not many scenes depicting men estimating the physical marks of time on other men or inspecting their own bodies for the same. In 1899, the author of an article on male aging writes this in *Blackwood's*:

> We cannot...picture to ourselves a male being who will deliberately and out of malice prepense go up-stairs, lock his dressing-room door, and sitting down in front of his looking-glass study his features in the glass and note the havoc which length of days has wrought on a countenance once, in somebody's eyes at all events, pleasing to behold. Beau Brummell may, for all we know or care to know to the contrary, have done something of the sort; but we think of Beau Brummell rather as a "very, very pajock," than a man of bones and sinews.[14]

14. "*Anno Domini*", *Blackwood's Edinburgh Magazine*, 165 (January 1899), 354.

Wilde's characters liberate age from the secrecy and disguise in which it had been hidden. A woman may boldly declare her age along with her delight in reaching it, and a man can speak frankly about his anxieties with regard to the bodily effects of age.

Here we come to a source of that anxiety, perhaps the animating force behind the horror, repugnance, and fear of old age. After the publication of *Dorian Gray* Wilde admitted the one "error" of the novel, that it did in fact contain a moral. And that moral is nothing other than the principle that "all excess...brings its own punishment."[15] Desire, any desire, is not itself suspect. It is the extension and ramification of desire, the excess of desire, the prospect of a glut of desire, more desire than the world, or even art can satisfy—this is the scandal, the horror, the 'dirty little secret.' What Dorian's "ethical" situation demonstrates is that desire is not necessarily diminished by gratification, that in fact, some passions are inflamed, leading towards addiction rather than extinction. "He had mad hungers that grew more ravenous as he fed them," we are told (*DG*, 143). Youth, like sin, would be perpetual if it could: and if age only brings with it an increase of appetite along with a decrease in the probability of gratification, then indeed the prospect of old age is unseemly and terrifying. Thus if the plot (Dorian's agelessness) tends towards an endless repetition of youth, the theme (his various and successive preoccupations) tells a different story which the form (repetition) ironically endorses. The movement from sensation to sensation announces Dorian's age by the consistency of form which underlies the novelty of each moment. He chooses the very means to undercut his enterprise when he selects repetition as a method for securing novelty.

Still, Dorian Gray clearly represents an unconventional portrait of old age, perhaps reflecting a specifically fin-de-siècle dread which goes unwritten, unspoken, itself figured as a secret vice. Indeed, in his vivid picture, Wilde reverses the more harmonious model of old age that had been passed down from Cicero and Seneca. We have noted before that in his famous *Treatise on Old Age* Cicero describes a complementary process whereby the desire for pleasure decreases as the ability to satisfy it diminishes. "It is not only no disparagement, but even the highest praise of old age, that it does not greatly long for any pleasures," he writes. "Doth it lack feasts, and heaped up tables,

15. Quoted in Schmidgall, introduction, p. xxii.

and numerous goblets? It lacks also intoxication, and dyspepsia, and sleeplessness."[16] Seneca, in one of his *Letters to Lucilius*, written when he was 61, declares "One might say that no longer feeling the need for pleasure takes the place of pleasure itself."[17]

Wilde tells a different story. It is full of irregularities and dark spaces: it is the gothic rejoinder to Ciceronian classicism. In Wilde's nightmare the appetite neither diminishes nor keeps pace with the possibilities for satisfaction. Rather, appetites proliferate as soon as they have been gratified. As Lord Henry tells Dorian, "The tragedy of old age is not that one is old, but that one is young" (*DG*, 228). If youth is desire anticipating fulfillment, old age is appetite dreading renunciation. Because the old cannot satisfy their voracious appetites, desire inevitably exceeds satisfaction. This inharmonious structure ensures that old age will be a period of instability, imbalance—in Wildean aesthetic terms, inartistic. You should not desire what you cannot have: this is the crux of the matter. And this surprisingly conservative dictum animates the novel. But it is less a moral adage than a practical observation. And if youth is the simple wish-fulfillment of an aging culture, Wilde offers another solution to the problem of age in his depiction of class.

Class, or really class difference, is what generates the question of style in the text—because style governs how the privileged classes satisfy aging appetites. Like Dorian Gray, the upper classes are already old, old in comparison to the working classes, who had achieved class identity only in the nineteenth century. And old in the sense of assuming the parent role in relation to the workers. Even if titles of nobility were disappearing steadily, the upper classes maintained their privileges, the most notable of which, for Wilde, was the privilege of taste. Wilde explicitly describes style as an attribute of class:

> Society—civilized society, at least—is never very ready to believe anything to the detriment of those who are both rich and fascinating. It feels instinctively that manners are of more importance than morals, and, in its opinion, the highest respectability is of much less value than the possession of a good chef. The canons of good society are, or should be the same as the canons of art. Form is absolutely essential to it. (*DG*, 155)

16. *Select Orations of Marcus T. Cicero*, trans. Rev. Dr. M'Kay, 2nd edn., (Dublin: University Press, 1855), 155.
17. Letter 12, quoted in Simone de Beauvoir, *The Coming of Age*, 180.

According to Wilde the dispossessed classes commit crimes because the only forms of expression available to them are coarse and vulgar. The upper classes possess the wealth necessary to obtain culture—education, travel, wide experience, and distance from the material wants which necessarily dominate lower-class life. Their wants can be more refined—or, and it is an important difference, they can *appear* to be more refined. Style is the look of desire made acceptable. It makes lovely raw appetite. Unlike wrinkles and veins which obtrude through a thin cosmetic coat, style can claim to transform the essence; in style one may hope to find the fountain of youth. In the portrait itself style makes lovely the deep current of Basil Hallward's homoerotic attraction. In Lord Henry it makes lovely the language that separates meaning from action or action from consequence. In the figure of Dorian Gray it makes lovely the solipsistic desire to remake the world as self, to appropriate all experience, all history, all form, color, and sound into the confines of a single consciousness and for the purposes of a simple pleasure.

My most recent claim is that Wilde exploits two dominant strategies in his encounter with the problem of aging, that trans-historical problem that took on special urgency at the end of the nineteenth century—in significant part, I have suggested, because of the aging queen. In Wilde aging is figured as a condition of ever-increasing desire without the hope of satisfaction. One way to confront the problem is represented in terms of the wild wish-fulfillment of eternal youth, the perpetuation of the period during which desire is commensurate with the capacity for fulfillment. In his magical youth, Dorian chooses—unwisely as it turns out—this path of resistance to the turning clock. The other mode, characteristically Wildean, is opposition to age through art, form, and the artifice of style. It is less satisfactory to the lower senses, but more reliable (if you are of the upper or artistic classes) as well as less private and phantasmagoric. Dorian's "error" is to settle for a bad bargain: he purchased the right to satisfy all desires, when he might have satisfied them less exuberantly but at much less cost, simply through the exercise of his birthright: his possession of the power of wealth, status, class, and taste.

But it is just here that the problem of egotism interposes, introducing that tendency towards moralism which Wilde regretted, and throwing into disarray Dorian's well-plotted efforts to avoid the effects of age by separating the quest for sensation from its gratification. For as antithetical as George Eliot and Wilde may appear, both are uneasy about nothing so much as the terrors of self-preoccupation. Unlike Sibyl Vane, whose character alters with each evening's performance, Dorian never plays a second role; he simply plays himself in different styles: a change of color, scent, or tone. For example, at one point we're told that "in his search for sensations that would be at once new and delightful, and possess that element of strangeness that is so essential to romance, he would often adopt certain modes of thought that he knew to be really alien to his nature" (*DG*, 146). He aims to produce pleasures for himself and to this end he plays to each character a seductive tune. To others he becomes an addiction: youth, beauty, congeniality, philanthropy—his seeming compliance masks the aggressive intention. Vampire-like, he leaves the world strewn with victims who once fed his devouring curiosity. The listless and weary Adrian Singleton, whom Dorian encounters at the Opium den, is a good example of the living shell of one of Dorian's victims: 'he would often adopt certain modes of thought that he knew to be really alien to his nature, abandon himself to their subtle influences, and then, having as it were, caught their colour and satisfied his intellectual curiosity, leave them with that curious indifference" (*DG*, 146). 'Catching their color' vividly captures the cannibalistic nature of Dorian's method. His youth is composed of the youth that belongs to others, to history, to anyone and anything still possessing 'color.'

We can see how within the frame of age desire, class, style, and solipsism come together in this reading of the novel. But they also come together *in* the novel. And when they do, when aging desire (addictive, intense), meets with upper-class taste and the solipsism it permits, then the plot comes to a crisis. For a time, it is paralyzed. It quite literally stops in place. While Dorian exchanges one pleasure for another—perfume, tapestries, music and so on—readers are expected to find pleasure in his pleasures. Most do not. Many long for the reintroduction of the temporality of plot, for the release of character from the maw of one man's unlimited, unceasing desire, for a new balance between the constituents of narrative. It arrives only when Basil Hallward's visit stirs the action once again, just as his portrait of Dorian initiates the plot at the start.

Dorian seeks to transcend his (chronological) age, his historical moment, and the biology of Age itself, but he finds himself trapped by the confines of egotism. The self as fetish is the refusal of age. And in his recognition, as I have suggested, Wilde betrays his moralism. Releasing Dorian to the license of the pleasure-seeking ego, Wilde composes a narrative which finally reveals excessive pleasure to be a prison of subjectivity. Dorian never became other selves; he merely absorbed others into his own experience; savored their taste, color, and sound and then discarded them when familiarity replaced novelty. As in all neuroses, what initially feels like mastery reveals itself as bondage. One cannot resist time by stopping it. The paradox is paradoxically Wildean. The best way to master age is to live in time. Feeling middle-aged in a period dominated by middle-class prejudices, Wilde felt stuck in the wrong historical moment. Finding himself at the end of a century rather than in the vanguard of the new must have seemed an absurdity. But the obligation to age, and the difficulties of aging gracefully, with ease and style, these are the lessons one learns from the languor of Henry, the death of Basil, and the *failure* of Dorian Gray.

There is one more point worth pursuing before widening the field of discussion; it is broached at the novel's supreme moment of solipsism, where one reads that "There were times when it appeared to Dorian Gray that the whole history was merely the record of his own life, not as he had lived it in act and circumstance, but as his imagination had created it for him, as it had been in his brain and in his passions" (*DG*, 157). We have seen that Lord Henry advises us to consider Dorian as a product of his age, an emanation of the twilight years of a century during which the world was changing from rural to urban, agricultural to industrialized, national to imperial, faithful to skeptical—some would say from innocence to experience. It is an old age. And in his sharp, witty, critical, and theatrical vision, Wilde dangles the ornamental challenge of the ever-young upper-class amoralist. In its long record of Dorian's career, the novel offers an aesthetic refusal of what passes for bourgeois responsibility, seriousness, *earnestness*—a refusal which depends on repudiating the aged society with the artifice of youth and style.

Yet, as I have just suggested, in the very act of carrying out this program, the novel involuntarily generates its own serious morality. Through the extremism of its ghostly pursuit of youth, it uncovers the power of old things. We should not forget that Dorian's most prized objects are always old if not antique. Textiles, instruments, embroideries—all of his collections glorify the old and rare specimens. People follow suit. Ultimately, the most interesting characters in the novel are not young: and this is a paradox realized even within the narrative. Dorian himself comes to despise his youth: "What was youth at best?" he asks, "A green, an unripe time, a time of shallow moods, and sickly thoughts. Why had he worn its livery?" (*DG*, 232).

One can imagine a scenario in which Dorian desperately leaps back into the picture because he cannot bear for another second to be merely young and beautiful. His old, decrepit self may be loathsome, but in possessing age it also possesses character—it is a kind of ultimate ghastly accumulation of character. In a minor key, one thinks of Lady Narborough, who finds her young guests "tedious" and admits that when she visits her daughter's family "I really wake them up" (*DG*, 188). Dorian's favorite is the enticing

Madame de Ferrol, who "is really wonderful, and full of surprises"—this according to Lord Henry, who explains, "Her capacity for family affection is extraordinary. When her third husband died, her hair turned quite gold from grief" (*DG*, 190). (Wilde liked the passage so much he used it again in *The Importance of Being Ernest.*) Madame de Ferrol is now married to her fourth husband and, according to Lady Narborough, "she is audacious enough for anything" (*DG*, 190). Finally there is Lord Henry himself, and until Dorian kills him, Basil Hallward, both middle-aged and growing older.

Notably, however, even when the novel of youth returns to old values and to ethics, it still resists coinciding with its age. This is the endless subversive challenge of Wilde: the infinite mobility of paradox. He carries Dorian all the way to an extremity of egotistic desire that explodes in self-annihilation, but even as the novel takes its distance from the gothic horror, even as it allows time to pass and character to age, it keeps alive the dream of style. The dead decrepit body of Dorian Gray lies beneath the portrait that has recovered its image of youth. At the last the novel measures the destruction of desire unbound, but still preserves the memory of its transgression.

Narrative paintings of age

So long as the body provokes fascination—admiration or horror is in a deep sense irrelevant—the question of age will obtrude. In his commentary on Victorian 'ageism,' Thomas Cole usefully collects the anxieties that cluster around images of the Victorian elderly:

> The primary virtues of Victorian morality—independence, health, success—required constant control over one's body and physical energies. The decaying body in old age, a constant reminder of the limits of self-control, came to signify precisely what bourgeois culture hoped to avoid: dependence, disease, failure, and sin.[18]

Wilde's 'portrait' of age makes a moral map of the decaying body. Once again, recall that Lord Henry, a mere decade older than Dorian, describes himself as "wrinkled, and worn, and yellow" (*DG* 227), though no reader imagines him with repugnance. By transferring the negative affect from

18. Thomas R. Cole, "The 'Enlightened' view of Aging; Victorian Morality in a New Key," in *What Does it Mean to Grow Old? Reflections from the Humanities*, ed. Thomas R. Cole and Sally A. Gadow (Durham), NC Duke University Press, 1986), 121.

the aging body to the aging portrait, Wilde allows us to 'forget,' temporarily, what the body has in store. The drama of Dorian's violent attack on the portrait and his subsequent death obscures the subtle mark of preference, for though death and age converge at the last, death also stands in the place of age. The gothic climax suggests, among much else, that one prefers a ghastly death to the grotesque comedy of living beyond one's due time.

Such displacements help explain a notable subordination of the elderly in visual representation. In Chapter 3, I referred to Teresa Mangum's claim that, in the bourgeois culture of the nineteenth century, typically "the youthful or middle-aged heterosexual couple occupies the center of the canvas while the elderly woman is relegated to the frame with her child counterparts."[19] Often, as we shall see, such subordination has peculiar advantages, but the denial of center stage does mark an anxiety if not an antipathy. Portraiture, of course, amply represents the elderly, primarily because the long history of patronage assured representation of the rich and influential—as well as the historical incidents, heroic exploits, or mythic fantasies associated with their wealth and power. But the portraits of the elderly more frequently illuminate prestige than they do age. Hubert Herkomer's description of painting his earliest portrait, of Lord Stratford de Redcliffe, in his nineties at the time of the painting, testifies to the difference. The commission was extended through King's College, Cambridge, where the picture still hangs. Thus the setting and the atmosphere were alike exalted. But the subject was an invalid confined to his chair and unable to adjust easily to the conditions of sitting. Herkomer explains:

> His Lordship was to be painted in a black coat, and wearing his special orders; but as an invalid he could not endure that coat for any length of time, and I did not dare to hand him down to posterity in a dressing-gown. I remember that more than half my time was taken up by attending to him as a nurse. Every now and again I would put a touch on the canvas, which I had to lay flat on the floor, in order to get some kind of light by which I could see what I was doing.[20]

The portrait which emerged—imposing, collected and refined—is not an inaccurate portrait of age, but it achieves its effects through a division of attention between age and status, time and money.

19. Teresa Mangum, "Little Women; The Aging Female Character in Nineteenth-Century British Children's Literature," in *Figuring Age: Women, Bodies, Generations*, ed. Kathleen Woodward (Bloomington: Indiana UP, 1999), 60.
20. Sir Hubert von Herkomer, *The Herkomers*, 2 vols. (London: Macmillan, 1910), i, 218.

Many of the most imposing portraits of old age are found in individual portraits or group portraits, in which the powers of decision, choice, and judgement fall to the elderly. The distinguished portraits of the Victorian poets and sages come instantly to mind: among them, those of Carlyle, Ruskin, Tennyson, and Cardinal Manning. The art world itself was governed by elderly boards and individuals, as seen in pictures such as Charles West Cope's *The Council of the Royal Academy Selecting Pictures for Exhibition in 1876*. (see Fig. 9).

But power and prestige may easily coexist with the debility and dependence of age. The official public face can unwarily disclose the course of private and bodily life that unfolds beneath the signifiers of status. Age may be asked to enact a social allegory of wisdom, compassion, stoicism, or resignation, but it may also alter the balance of shape, space, and color by introducing disruptive tones. Herkomer warns of the risk that portraiture will expose "disease and not character" (*The Herkomers*, ii. 115).

> I have seen symptoms of senility creep over the face of an aged sitter, before his family or his medical advisers suspected its near approach.... I might have selected the look of senility which I saw pass over the face of my aged sitter: I might have thought it gave more pathos, or was artistically more interesting, had I not instantly recognized that it was pathological, and not psychological. (*The Herkomers*, ii. 115, 116)

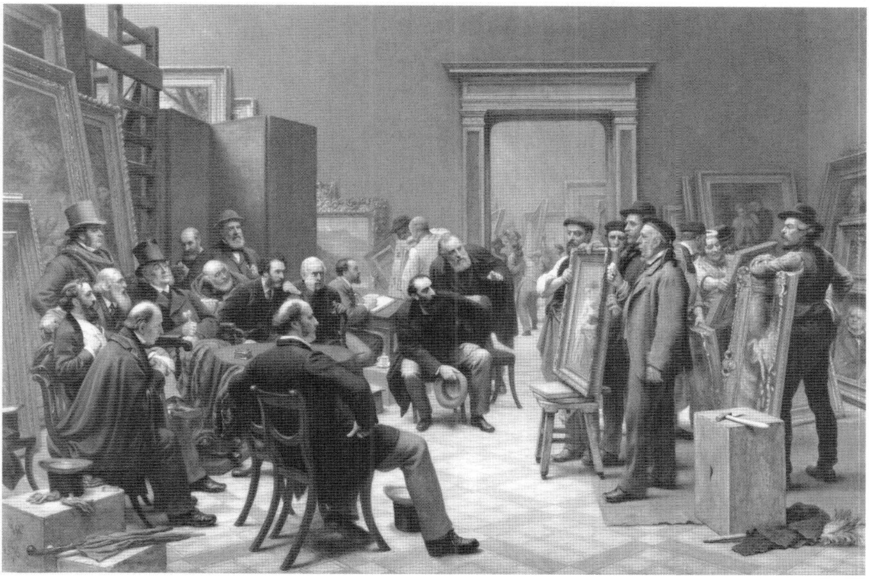

Figure 9 Charles West Cope, *The Council of the Royal Academy Selecting Pictures for the Exhibition in 1876*. Royal Academy of Arts, London

In a more subtle and less fully conscious manner, age remains as a pressure that is always potentially destabilizing. Consider Whistler's famous portrait of his mother (1872), which was conceived by the artist first as an image for age: the picture was originally entitled *Arrangement in Gray and Black no. 1: The Artist's Mother.* The colors with which he works summon the figure of age, quite as much as the maternal age—composed of stoicism and reserve, independence and endurance—seems to require somber hues. From the perspective of prose fiction, Dinah Craik also describes old age in terms of colors; for Craik, old age smooths angles and harmonizes hues, which are "softening and darkening in colour, until black, white, and grey alone remain, as the suitable garb for old age."[21]

Seldom do the narrative paintings for which the Victorians are renowned take elderly characters as principal subjects or centers of concern. The exceptions, however, are illuminating, primarily because, in striking ways, they participate in the depiction and suppression of the aged body. Probably the most notable exception is the career of Herbert von Herkomer, one of the few Victorian painters whose fame arose from the narratives of old age. In his autobiography, Herkomer explains that until he had managed to "find my subject," instead of imitating or being told what to paint, he could not consider himself a genuine artist. He recalls being struck by a group of peasants working in a field when "a little girl approached the oldest man of the group, and handed him some refreshments. He stiffly and slowly straightened his back, and remained standing whilst the others were in various attitudes at their work" (*The Herkomers*, i. 139). Herkomer recognizes subject which had eluded him, though he does not yet identify it precisely as 'old age,' or even 'generational amity.' But shortly after drawing this first picture, "the starting-point of my career" (*The Herkomers*, i. 141), he finds himself again in search of a 'subject' in order to submit an illustration to W. L. Thomas, founder of *The Graphic.* After two days of fruitless search, he describes how

> I wandered in a sort of aimless way, perhaps for want of something better to do, into the Chapel of the Royal Hospital, which was situated at the end of my street. I was put into one of the side pews allotted to visitors, for the whole body of the chapel was occupied by the old pensioners, wearing their red coats. What grand old heads! *here* was a subject of the first water! The service, the sermon and the music were non-existent for me. I was alone with my subject. (*The Herkomers*, i. 149)

21. Dinah Craik, *A Woman's Thoughts about Women* (London: Hurst and Blackett, 1859), 326.

This image became the *Chelsea Pensioners in Church*, first completed as a wood engraving, published in *The Graphic*, and later made into the famous oil *The Last Muster*. Before this latter transformation, however, on a trip to the Bavarian Alps, Herkomer consciously realizes what draws him to his subject, namely "the pathos of old age" (*The Herkomers*, i. 169). And several years later, when deciding upon a painting to submit to the Royal Academy, he dares to pursue his subject against the advice of colleagues:

> I had set my heart on a large and amplified version of my "Chelsea Pensioners in Church." All my artist-friends, however, tried to dissuade me from the venture, declaring that I could make nothing of those red coats, and further, that the public would not be interested in a lot of old men. This opposition rather strengthened than weakened my resolution. (*The Herkomers*, i. 195)

Then when he completes the oil painting, he worries "that so curious a picture would never be hung" (*The Herkomers*, i. 202). But in the event his anxiety, and that of his friends, were equally unfounded. The picture sold immediately for £1200, and upon its being submitted to the Royal Academy, both George Richmond and Edward Leighton wrote enthusiastic endorsements, the former telling Herkomer that "when the picture came before them the whole Council clapped their hands enthusiastically." Fellow artists were joined by the general public.

> On the opening of the exhibition practically the whole press burst forth in a unanimous chorus of praise; and my name and work was on the lips of all who had seen the picture. The question seemed to float in the air—"Who was this Herkomer, who had thus leapt into ripe work with a bound?" (*The Herkomers*, i. 203)

The picture was a sensation both at home and abroad; in 1878 it won the prestigious Medal of Honour from the International Exhibition in Paris. Although he was dismayed to find himself 'ticketed' as "the painter of old men" (*The Herkomers*, i. 217), and his later works are varied in subject, Herkomer clearly had 'found his subject,' and his paintings of the elderly are signal events in the representation of Victorian age. He himself singled out "the pathetic side of life…a sympathy for the old, and for suffering mankind" as the "real bent" of his personality and his aesthetic interest (*Autobiography*, i. 130).

The Last Muster narrates the scene of a Sunday service at the Chelsea Hospital, the hall crowded with aged veterans all dressed in bright red military garb and sitting in multiple rows. The parquet floor beneath reinforces a norm of regularity. One man at the end of a row disturbs the uniformity of the scene as he slumps slightly forward and allows his cane to rest at an angle. Only by these small signs do we realize that a fellow soldier seated by his side cannot rouse his attention because the man has died (see Fig. 10). What is it about this painting that garnered so much enthusiasm and praise? If we set it alongside his other studies of old age, some details emerge which help us get beyond the suggestion of mere sentimentality.

In 1898, Herkomer exhibited *The Guards' Cheer*, "ostensibly a companion picture to my *Last Muster*, representing Crimean veterans of the Guards standing on the stage erected in front of their own monument in Waterloo Palace, to view the Jubilee Procession of 1897." The subject of the painting is historical, the "bitter and almost useless struggle" of the famous battles of

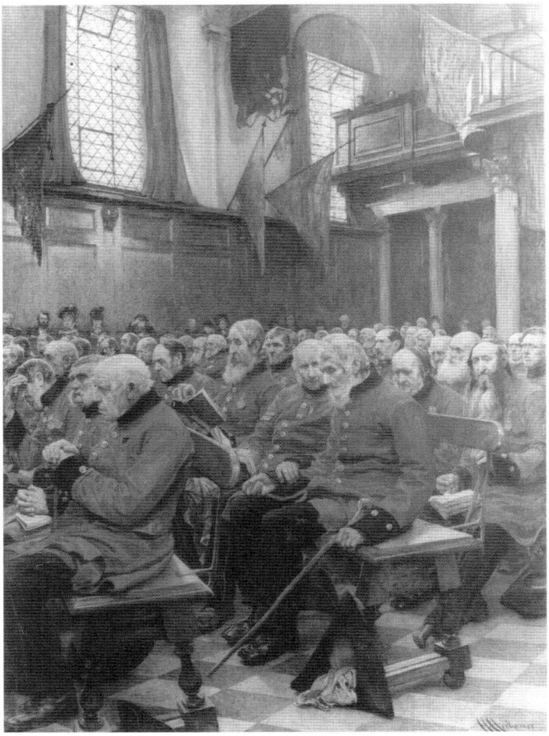

Figure 10 Hubert von Herkomer, *The Last Muster*. Photo © National Museums Liverpool, Lady Lever Art Gallery, UK

the Crimean War, but the context is "a great event in the reign of a beloved sovereign"—the great event referring to the War, but also, of course that of the Jubilee itself (*The Herkomers*, ii. 170, 171). Forty years and more have passed since the young Queen sent her love and pity to the ill-equipped, ill-prepared soldiers of that sorry war. And like the Queen, they have survived, unlike the multitudes who were slaughtered in battle. The picture offers a somber reminder of the tenacity of life rather than its fragility. The group of men cheer their Queen as she advances in the procession; there is praise and hallelujah instead of recrimination (see Fig. 11). Once again the group which might have been a mob is reassuringly supportive, not this time with passivity or resignation, but with ardent support and earnest good wishes.[22]

Within this context should be placed Herkomer's *Sunday at Chelsea Hospital* (Fig. 12), and representations of female old age, including his sketch entitled *Study of Old Age*, which became *Eventide*, and *Christmas*

22. One of the most notable painters of Crimean War scenes was Elizabeth Thompson (who became Lady Butler). Thompson and Herkomer competed for the position of Associate member of the Royal Institute of Art in 1879, with the latter narrowly winning the position by two votes. Wryly, Herkomer attributes his success to the vagaries of chance: "One of these two precious votes was given by a member who asked his neighbour on the night of the election, 'Who is this Herkomer, anyway; he is a foreigner, isn't he?' He got for answer: 'Well, whatever he is, his art is thoroughly British. He's all right; you vote for him'" (*Herkomers*, i. 219). Mary Anne Stevens, on the other hand, suggests that gender was at issue, and notes that the first female Associate wasn't elected until 1922 ("The Royal Academy in the Age of Queen Victoria," in *Art in the Age of Queen Victoria: Treasures from the Royal Academy of Arts Permanent Collection*, ed. Helen Valentine (New Haven and London: Royal Academy of Arts in association with Yale University Press, 1999), 36. It should be noted, however, that female *students* were accepted from 1860 on—(Helen Valentine, "The Royal Academy Schools in the Victorian Period," in Valentine, *Art in the Age of Queen Victoria* 45). No doubt these are each reliable accounts, but another cause may have been the greater sentimental appeal of Herkomer's military paintings. Thompson's three paintings of the Crimean War (*The Roll Call* (1874), *Balaclava* (1876), *The Return from Inkerman* (1877)) *recall* the battles; they delineate bearing up under harsh circumstances and great suffering, but they do not associate these aspects with age. Doubtless it is true that, as she put it, "The fact that counts is the power of touching the people's heart," but in her paintings, what touches the heart is the sad memory of a tragic war (quoted in Julian Treuherz, *Victorian Painting* (London: Thames and Hudson, 1993), 179). Herkomer's soldiers are not on the battlefield: they survived that *and* the decades which now make them all old men. A great part of our sympathy derives from their aged broken bodies, which still bear the scars as well as the discipline and patriotism associated with the military regimen. Thompson's subject is historical and about the war; Herkomer's is contemporary and about age. When the council of judges all 'clapped their hands,' it was in appreciation of the contemporary subject—age. We know this because of his immediate 'ticketing' as 'the painter of old people,' something he dreaded, admitted, and exploited.

Figure 11 Hubert von Herkomer, *The Guard's Cheer.* © City of Bristol Museum and Art Gallery

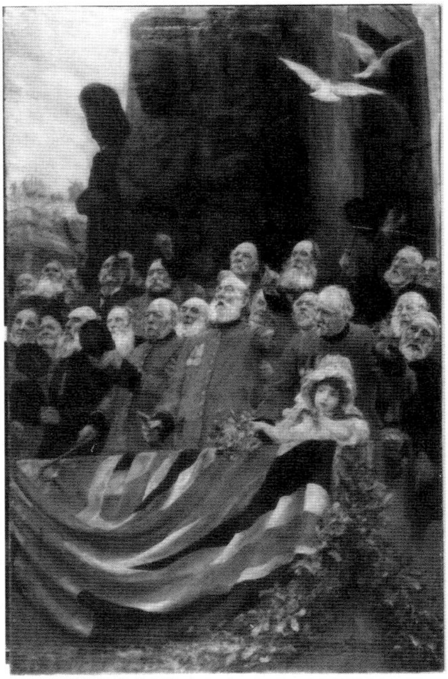

Figure 12 Hubert von Herkomer, *Sunday at Chelsea Hospital. The Graphic*, February 18, 1871, p.152. Butler Library, Columbia University, New York

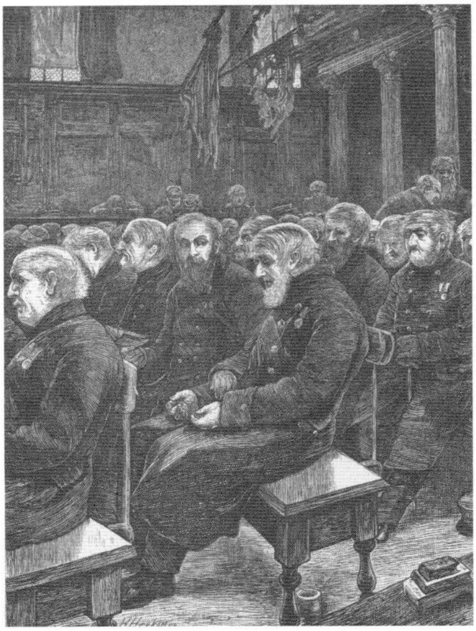

in a Workhouse (see Figs. 13 and 14). In these paintings one again finds the relationship between foregrounded individuals and a background mass as a device for rendering the conditions of age. The architectural space divides between a vast encompassing structure, and the particular bodies easily contained within it. In each canvas, the drama is self-consciously subdued; gestures and activities are muted, as are the emotions.

Although the old are the subject, and in the foreground, the visual context swallows the ostensible focus and provokes an appeal far more powerful than the individual fates. We might say that the foreground of each painting is a template, instructive of how to cope with the background. The foreground displays a manageable instance of some human extremity—death, poverty, fragility—while the background displays a threat already contained.

The threat lies in numbers, in the sheer quantity of people whose needs, thus compounded, challenge the capability of the viewer to feel, the society to acknowledge, and the state to tend. But the very recognition that the economically needy aged now exist in numbers requiring large-scale social and systematic assistance conveys the glimpsed prospect that age itself will deliver the solution which policy had yet to resolve. Herkomer's pictorial vision contains nothing inflammatory, nothing to suggest the threat of

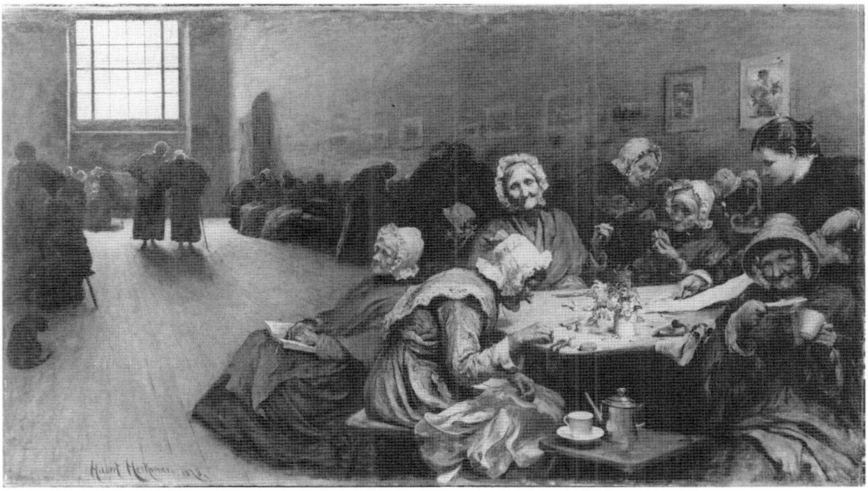

Figure 13 Hubert von Herkomer, *Eventide—A Scene in the Westminster Union.* Photo © National Museums Liverpool, Walker Art Gallery, UK

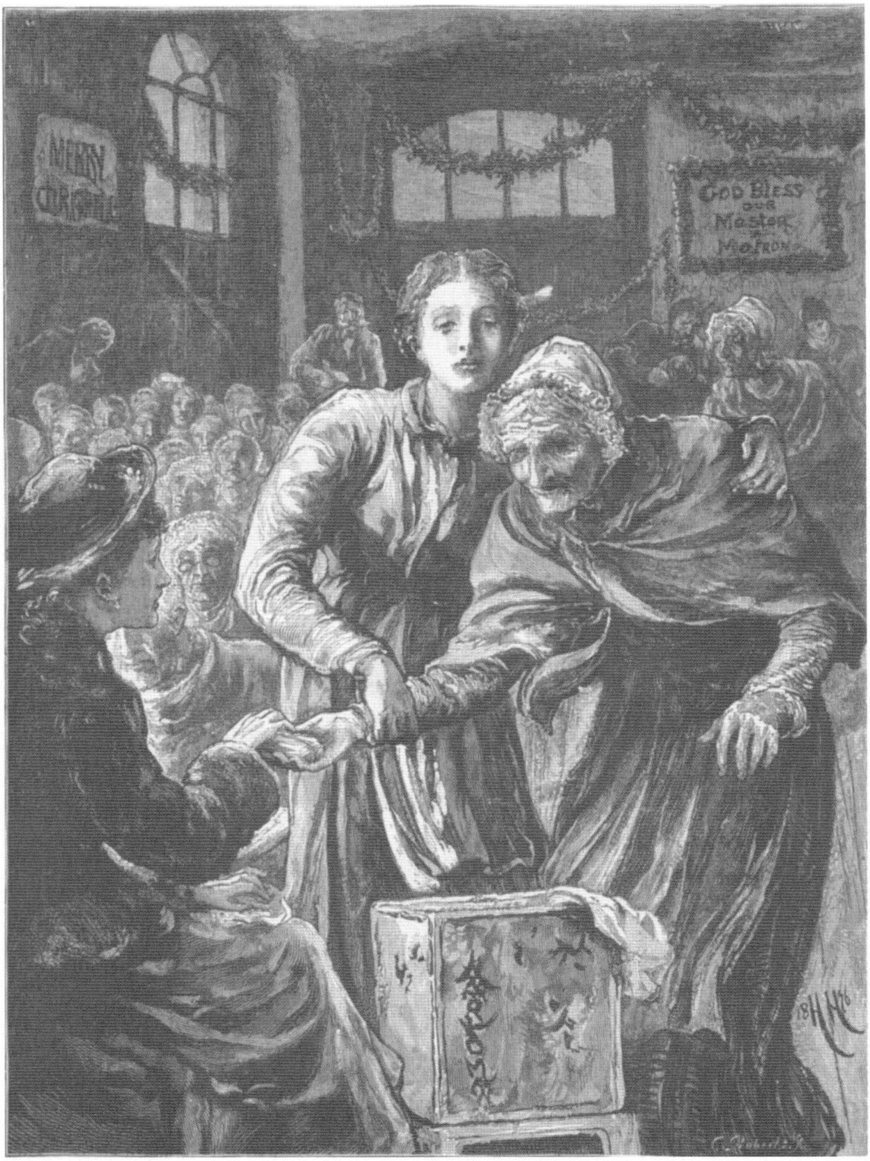

Figure 14 Hubert von Herkomer, *Christmas in the Workhouse. The Graphic*, 25 December 1876, p.30. Butler Library, Columbia University, New York

discontent, insurrection, overwhelming need, or expectation. Speaking of *The Last Muster* and *The Guards' Cheer* specifically, Joseph Kestner remarks, "In both Herkomer's canvases...the veterans are aged, too old or too penurious to pose any threat to the culture or become involved in radical politics."[23] Either death or feeble decrepitude will defer or defeat the need for a concerted response: that is the wistful fancy. Death and incapacity only increase the urgency for social action: that is the painful reality. The images convey both sentiments.

To the old pensioners the death of one is an old story, a common fate, which invites and requires forbearance. The old man quietly dies without calling attention to himself, without demanding from others either feelings or actions which might exceed their capacity to perform. The old women who hover in the background of the workhouse are similarly sedate. They linger, like inoffensive barnacles, along the walls; they sit or stand quietly, patiently, glad for relief when it is their turn to receive, but unobtrusive and still when it is not. Like Dickens, Herkomer addresses the social emergency by treating it as a problem of scale and perspective. The problem is massive, but the way to address it is through local and visually restrictive intervention. In some pictures the foreground offers a model for social policy: youth will comfort or provide for age. Just as he realized the potential for his early picture in the image of the young peasant girl offering refreshment to the oldest man, so when he came to paint *The Guards' Cheer* his eye caught the scene which prompted the picture: "One of the Pensioners had brought his little grandchild, in her brightest frock and hat, and had placed her by his side in the front row. This happy incident I at once grasped, as it gave me a touch of 'sentiment' very dear to the artist who had been trained in the best of the Victorian period" (*The Herkomers*, ii. 173). In pairing youth with age, Herkomer suggests that there can be exchange and mutuality, not simply the acceptance of responsibility in the face of need. Surely this is what animates John P. Burr's picture of *The Village Barber* (1881), in which the ancient barber engages in his task of trimming a young boy's hair. John Leech offered a version of this generational trope as early as 1843, in his depiction of old Mrs. Greenhill's entrance to the workhouse in Frances Trollope's novel *Jessie Phillips*. The passage which inspires the illustration describes Mrs. Greenhill waiting to hear if her appeal for out-relief will be granted (it is denied):

> Round the walls of this small chamber, and firmly fixed to them, were wooden benches, as narrow as it was well possible for an adult human being to sit upon. On these benches of little ease were seated, when Mrs. Greenhill entered the room, seven or eight aged females—the youngest among them must have been considerably past sixty, and one or two of the oldest appeared to touch the very last stage of human life.[24]

23. Joseph Kestner, *Masculinities in Victorian Painting* (Aldershot, Hants: Scolar Press, 1995), 270.
24. Frances Trollope, *Jessie Phillips: A Tale of the Present Day*, 3 vols. (London: Henry Colburn, 1843), i. 224.

The 'idiot-girl' Sally enters the room and addresses her old friend. In Leech's picture, only the women directly engaged with the young girl express animation; the others have withdrawn entirely into their own thoughts, or into their own mental vacuity. Even without supervision or restraint, there will be no hazardous 'combining' here. Herkomer introduces numbers, and though there is little exchange among the aged, there is the suggestion of common emotions, shared habits and practices, the bond between those who have endured similar experiences. But again the crowd of the aged do not ignite terror or exert the pressure of conscience. Their vulnerability leaves the viewer's power intact: thus they inspire pity rather than fear.

A small tension hovers over *Christmas in the Workhouse*, where the iconography of folk tale summons images of an old crone handing poisoned fruit to a young woman. Here, the fruit passes from young to old, and within the contemporary context, this reverse gesture can suggest a subterranean fantasy that the Victorians only rarely acknowledged: namely a wish to do away with the growing 'problem' of old age, just as in the tales, age would do away with the beauty of youth. But this flicker of cruelty only emphasizes the will to generosity that lives on the surface of consciousness and canvas. Scarcity has not been replaced by plentitude, but acceptance overcomes the hint of competition. Herkomer characteristically channels charged social emotion through discrete personal encounters instead of allowing them to accumulate communal and pictorial force. The vast spaces, which seem to empty at the top, provide room for emotions to fly, bat-like, and dissipate the anxiety that they might otherwise bring to compact focus. These pictures imply that problems might be addressed on the small scale, so that they never occupy the large scale of social crisis. Within the canon of such imagery, the elderly can be given what they need and they can be given the means to help themselves. They sew, they read, they discipline themselves: there is no unruly mob, the overwhelming need resolves into small units, with the largest problem most distant and the immediate problem addressed satisfactorily by the tableau before one's eyes.

Though they do not constitute the main plot of most Victorian narrative paintings, old people are amply represented in sub-plots, where they often assume crucial functions, visually and socially. Frequently, they stand as the stern arbiters of a situation or scene, as in Emily Mary Osborne's 1857 *Nameless and Friendless*, in which the elderly art dealer assesses the value of a painting, which will mean everything to the widow and her young son who wait to hear the price.

Similarly, in Robert Braithwaite Martineau's *The Last Day in the Old Home* (1862), the foreground focuses on the reckless irresponsibility of the thoughtless young man, whose behavior has destroyed the nuclear family, but of equal importance is the transaction occurring off to the side, where the heir's mother sorrowfully relinquishes the keys of Hardham Court to the agent. Like the old home, the old mother is negligible: but the agent and the young grand-daughter both gaze at her, and her action contributes decisively to this narrative (see Figs. 15 and 16).

Stanhope Alexander Forbes's *The Health of the Bride* (1889) gives an interesting turn to this style of figuration. Here the subject of the painting is delicately challenged (though not usurped) by the little drama displayed in the foreground, where the elderly grandfather, seen only from the back, with his bald head catching part of the light, hugs his grand-daughter affectionately while he helps his grandson to some of his ale. Most eyes are turned to the bride, but the subject is not the romantic couple so much as generational plentitude. The grandmother raises her glass in one hand, but the

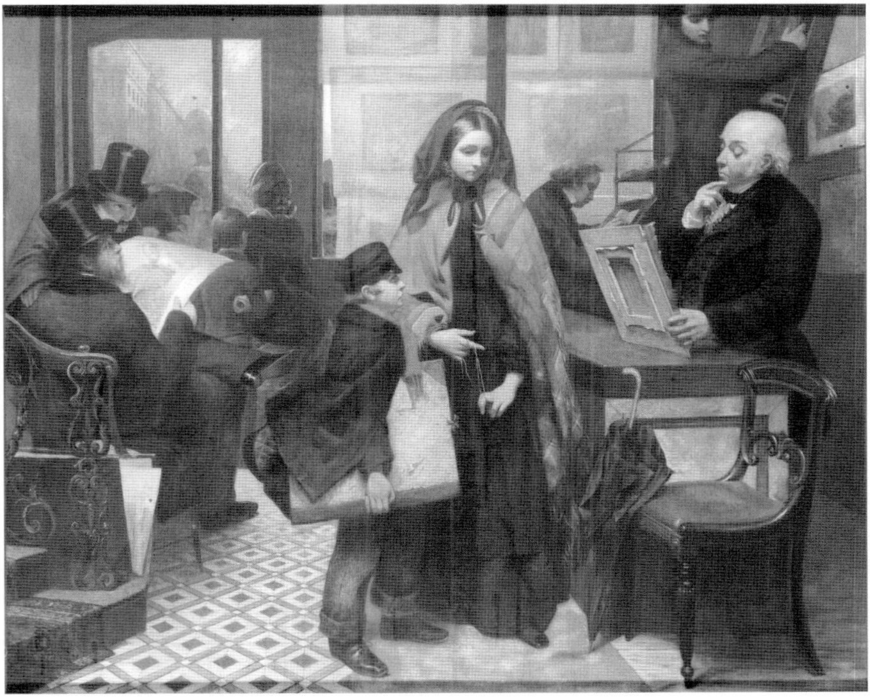

Figure 15 Emily May Osborn, *Nameless and Friendless.* Private Collection. Photograph: Photographic Survey, Courtauld Institute of Art

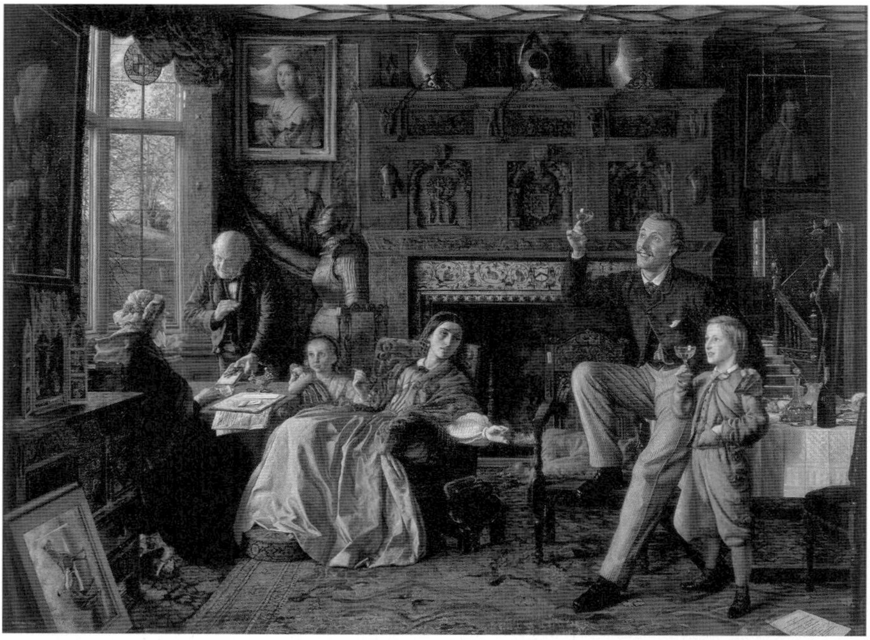

Figure 16 Robert Braithwaite Martineau, *The Last Day in the Old Home.* © Tate, London (2008)

other allows her to rest her head thoughtfully, and her closed eyes suggest that her mind is far away from the present occasion. The young boy is more interested in his drink, and his sister gazes at the fruit she holds with both hands, as if contemplating where to place the first bite. The grandfather who oversees their induction to conviviality (fruit and wine) must watch as he helps the boy drink from his own glass. Their diversion is not disrespectful, but it amplifies the social scene, marking marriage as a social and familial occasion more than a romantic occasion (see Fig. 17).

Frith's *Many Happy Returns of the Day* (Fig. 18) requires the presence of grandparents to complete a child's birthday celebration. In an early version of the painting, only the grandmother appears, but in revising the work, Frith added the figure of the grandfather. The painting carefully locates the child in the human march through time which is framed by the genial figures of age at either end of the scene.[25] Even Frank Bramley's *After Fifty Years* (1893), which represents the anniversary of an older couple, renders

25. This change is strikingly apparent in the 2007 Frith exhibition at London's Guildhall, where the two versions were hung side-by-side ("William Powell Frith: Painting the Victorian Age," November 6, 2006–March 4, 2007).

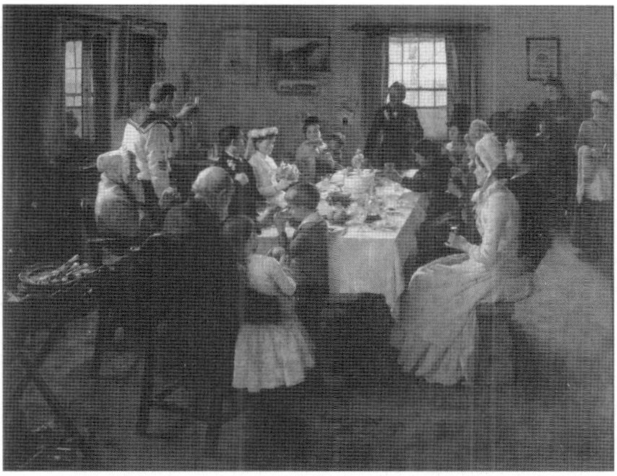

Figure 17 Stanhope Forbes, *Health of the Bride.* © Tate, London (2008) and the Bridgeman Art Library

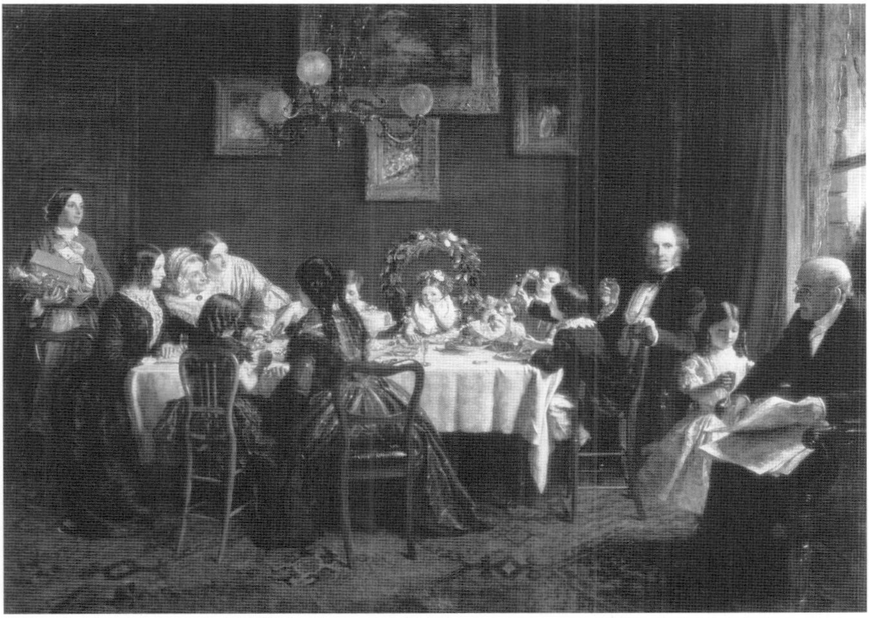

Figure 18 William Powell Frith, *Many Happy Returns of the Day.* © Harrogate Museums and Art Gallery, North Yorkshire, UK, and the Bridgeman Art Library

the scene of celebration as an intergenerational affair (see Fig. 19). Once again we might turn to Herkomer, who, in writing about his picture entitled *Back to Life*, describes why the recovering child and her nurse "had to be supported by other figures, not only to make a 'composition,' but to draw

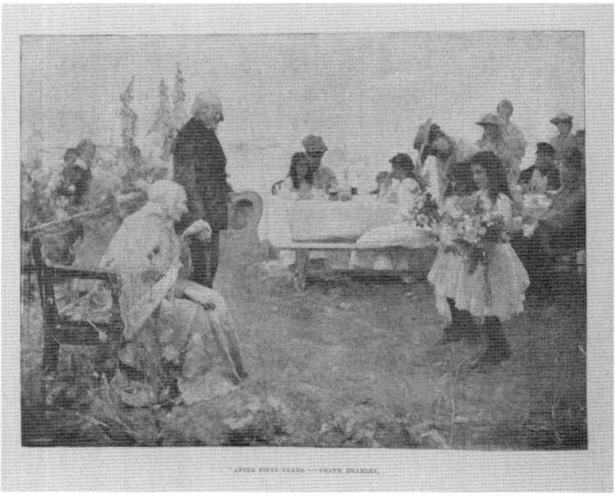

Figure 19 Frank Bramley, *After Fifty Years.* Courtesy Special Collections, University of Virginia Library

the eye even more to the figures of central interest. Sympathy, and pleasure at seeing the child once more out of her sick-room had to be expressed, and that by figures (mostly women) *of all ages*" (*The Herkomers*, ii. 98, my emphasis).

The last phrase, "of all ages," has special bearing on the depiction of the oldest ages, since they are the ones most often forgotten by narrative painting. I have been arguing that the old do not distract from the focal concentration on younger subjects; nor do they attract focus to themselves. Rather, they perform essential tasks for the *narration*, which depends precisely on breaking the hold of *focus*, on broaching the temporality of individual lives and public history and on opening the hopeful sociality of intergenerational life. The elderly, then, are neither marginalized nor absorbed by the central points of visual attention. They may properly be called peripheral, but their angle of perspective is often essential to work of social representation. They are perhaps integrated most effectively, then, when the scene depicts an occasion at which all generations are represented: celebrations or regrets, holidays, services, and performances. Frequently, they play a significant role whether integrated in the scene or not, and no matter how subordinate their position is in relation to others. Sometimes the most striking manner of representation is an effect of *looking away* rather than *looking at*—as much to suggest the world beyond the private ceremony at the focal center.

Much of the satisfaction imparted by paintings of mixed social groups—such as choirs—derives from the generational amplitude. Young, middle-aged, and elderly engage in common activities of reciprocity and affection that suggest how tension among the sexes, classes, and generations might be overcome. The elderly play a part in this representation that is as subtle as it is significant. The signifiers of their age are marks of time and mortality; in this respect they are bearers of a "realist" fate that resists the mystification of nostalgia. At the same time their integration into social ceremony carries a utopic possibility: if the very old can be welcomed by even the very young, then a flourishing society might one day preside over the marriage of all such deep differences. The "ideal" is in general stronger than the "real" in these works, and sentimentality erases many of the lines of mortal age. And yet in the last years of the century the social pressure of aged reality overcame even the most energetic acts of sentiment.

6

The Politics and Personality of Age at the Fin de Siècle

The nineteenth century ends in a long-deferred encounter with the politics of age. This chapter moves toward an encounter with that encounter, and it does so at its start by way of William Morris's *News from Nowhere*. No more than Oscar Wilde did Morris see himself as engaged in self-conscious reflection on the subject, but as with those visual artists who depict the elderly by looking away from them, both writers are most illuminating on the conditions of the aged when they mean to illuminate something else. To bring the names of Morris and Wilde together must not be to flatten the former's socialism or to inflate the latter's, but the shared consciousness is more than incidental. In the 1880s and 1890s both figures bore the weight of their Ruskinian inheritance, and both struggled to connect art and material life within the politically aroused milieu of the fin-de-siècle. To be sure, if Wilde supported socialism, it was in order to elevate art and the individual, but although Morris engaged more fully and directly in radical politics, and sought to elevate art for the sake of the community, nonetheless he shared a foundational insight with Wilde: namely that, until the failures of capitalism were overcome and were surpassed by the new life of socialism, there could be no full human flourishing–aesthetic, social, personal, political. But the political turn had another and more immediately decisive result, the government-sponsored social investigations led by Charles Booth, which would lead to a passage of the Old Age Pensions Act, which serve as one summa of the narrative lines followed here. This chapter concludes, however, by encountering the difficult combination of public policy and the lived experience of old age—the agonizing doubleness of an "objective" social rationality and the failing powers of a subjectivity.

Youth in age, a utopia?

What makes Morris's politics a portal for this investigation into old age is the explicit convergence of a transformational social vision with artistic practice. Like many other late Victorians, Morris felt distaste for the burden of the recent past, the past of his own century: the record of industrialism accompanied by the rise of vulgarity. Dorian Gray wished "that our eyelids might open some morning upon a world that had been refashioned anew in the darkness...a world in which the past would have little or no place, or survive, at any rate, in no conscious form of obligation or regret" (*DG*, 145). The 'old' past survives in just this manner, and as I have argued above, Dorian's fascination with 'old ages' (the distant past) is woven into his present pleasures. Medievalism is for Morris what Hellenism is for Wilde, the historical milieu in which he locates the virtues conspicuously lacking in the sordid present. For Morris, the Middle Ages understood what the modern Victorians have almost entirely forgotten: how to make ordinary objects beautiful, how to sustain the tie between beauty and use, and how to take pleasure in work. He saw a return to such history as the reverse of nostalgia; it was a revival of the past, not for its own sake, but for the sake of those caught within a corrupt and moribund present. As Shaw neatly put it, Morris "started from the 13th century simply because he wished to start from the most advanced point instead of from the most backward one—say 1850 or thereabout."[1] What complicates the picture is the ambitious temporality of *News from Nowhere*: the projection of a *future* utopia drawn from precedents in the distant *past*, an image of social desire intended to generate a *present* political praxis. Past and future appear as worlds both older and younger, and certainly more authentically human than the mechanistic and over-elaborated world of late Victorianism. For our purposes here, the striking complication is provoked by the prominence of aging characters within the utopic life of Nowhere. The 56-year-old narrator, whose dream, or vision, forms the basis of the story, stands as both an arresting elderly visitor to this transformed society and as a goad to the surprising problems of the aged.

Once he arrives in the London of the twenty-first century, William "Guest," for so he is called and calls himself, extends his curiosity to all that

1. *Shaw: An Autobiography, 1856–1898*, ed. Stanley Weintraub (New York: Weybright & Talley, 1969), 152.

is new and different, but he reserves emotional attachments for those who express great interest in, and preference for, precisely the wretched period of two hundred years ago, that is, the aged nineteenth century. And with one important exception, to be considered shortly, these emotional referents centrally include the elders of 'Nowhere.' These relics, antiquarians, and 'grumblers' suggest that if the rejection of decrepit, degraded Victorian values led to the present happiness, it simultaneously created a loss, a lack of creative vitality, which had been an unexpected artistic byproduct of the frantic, uncontrolled growth through industrial capitalism.

At first glance it might appear that the calm, contemplative, deeply satisfying 'rest' characteristic of Nowhere-ians is a figure for easeful age. Indeed, there is an abundance of aged people, places, and things in their flourishing England. The story begins in the city, but traces the "exodus of people from the town to the country" which occurred once the mania for modernization had been overcome, making possible a respect for process rather than production, and for the association of beauty with use.[2] Indeed the successful incorporation of the aged into productive social life depends on the fact that "the difference between town and country grew less and less." Country life is "vivified by the thought and briskness of town-bred folk" while town life is "happy and leisurely" (*NN*, 61). The aging of the countryside, so marked throughout the nineteenth century as the young departed for the cities, is replaced here by a thoroughly integrated, intergenerational community. Furthermore, there is no long premature aging in Nowhere once the debilitating conditions of capitalism have been obliterated: "How long-lived your people must be!" exclaims Guest at one point. "Yes," notes his interlocutor, "we certainly have beaten the three-score-and-ten of the old Jewish proverb-book" (*NN*, 41).

Age looks different in Nowhere, however, and no longer takes on the characteristics, conventional and national, of old-ness in 'past' times. Its aspect alters in man and beast. Carried by an 'old' horse called "Greylocks," who is nonetheless vigorous and able, Guest and his guide Dick repeatedly come across young and old people who often seem indistinguishable. At one point, a nameless elderly man accompanies Guest, chatting, as all the old folks do, about the nineteenth century, and when it is time for him to

2. William Morris, *News from Nowhere, or, An Epoch of Rest* (London: Routledge & Kegan Paul, 1970), 152.

leave, "he jumped down and strode away vigorously, like a young man." The following conversation appears just before these words.

> "How old should you say that neighbour will be?" said I to Dick as we lost sight of him; for I saw that he was old, and yet he looked dry and sturdy like a piece of old oak; a type of old man I was not used to seeing.
> "O, about ninety, I should say," said Dick. (*NN*, 41)

The aged maintain their youth because the debilitating conditions of capitalism do not inhibit their well-being, and because they bring resources of indispensable value to the community. Not only do they possess greater knowledge of 'what came before' in the history of Nowhere; they also promote collective flourishing through recognition of the dignity of labor: "the old men amongst the labourers managed to teach the younger ones gradually a little artisanship" so that the supreme virtue—that of taking pleasure from one's work—could be realized (*NN*, 153). The transition from the 'machine age' to the 'handicraft period' is accomplished not simply through the recollection of earlier forms of social organization, but crucially through a generational transmission that prepares for an authentically blooming modernity.

Though 'only' 56, Guest belongs among the much older people in Nowhere. "You look rather old for your age," he is told early on, the explanation being that "one ages very quickly if one lives amongst unhappy people" (*NN*, 15). One of the female servers at Guest House, whom he takes for 20 (though she is apparently 42), thinks *he* is 80. Clara, soon to be reunited with her husband Dick, expresses the wish to see a younger Guest, without the wrinkles of age: "Don't you think," she asks, "he will look younger after a little time with us?" (*NN*, 116). Happiness may smooth wrinkles, but if Guest is associated with the aged Nowhere-ians, it is not only because as a nineteenth-century man he has aged more quickly than his twenty-first century counterparts. It is also because the older people consistently express appreciation for the century he would reject. When it is time to conclude his discussion of the past with 'old Hammond,' Guest notes that "I should like to have gone on talking with the older man, who could understand something at least of my wonted ways of looking at life, whereas, with the younger people, in spite of all their kindness, I really was a being from another planet" (*NN*, 115). Guest finds a way to be *of* this society only to the extent that he finds counterparts, in looks and in temperament, as if the natural counterpart to a Victorian gentleman of 56 would be a Nowhere-ian centenarian. When he looks at Hammond, who is said to be "getting old" at 105, "his face, dried-apple-like as it was, seemed strangely familiar to me; as if I had seen it before—in a looking glass it might be, I said to myself" (*NN*, 44). Hammond himself confirms the link, referring to himself and Guest as "we two oldsters" (*NN*, 45).

But none of the other old people straddle the two ages as our narrator does; they have no more experience of the nineteenth century than the younger generation. Their interest in the past reflects no familiarity. It remains unclear whether it is wisdom, distance, or some other aspect of old age which stirs their appreciation for the Victorians. The young Clara unconsciously suggests a possibility when she wistfully remarks, "I wish we were interesting enough to be written or painted about" (*NN*, 87). Indeed, the novel is a nineteenth-century achievement that can neither be replicated nor surpassed in the felicity of Nowhere. When the 'old grumbler' praises *Vanity Fair*, asking "Why don't you write books like that now?" (*NN*, 136), no answer emerges to challenge his own earlier comment that "good sound unlimited competition was the condition under which they [Victorian novels] were written" (*NN*, 28). His grand-daughter, Ellen, points out that had he lived in those times he praises, he would have been poor and miserable: "you, grandfather, would have had to work hard after you were old; and would have been always afraid of having to be shut up in a kind of prison along with other old men, half-starved and without amusement" (*NN*, 136). Morris displays the contradiction without resolving it. Paradise has its paradoxes, which most often display themselves within the frame of age.

When old age remains hale and when the aged are agile and alert, intergenerational sexual ties become clouded and complicated. Indeed one of the unexpected (and largely unelaborated) features of life in Nowhere are the erotic possibilities between old men and young women. Personal relations, no longer motivated by insecurities, economic or emotional, are the 'natural' extension of fully realized lives within a healthy environment. Attraction between men and women is just one of many pleasurable events: it is neither romanticized nor exaggerated. As old Hammond tells Guest, "we are no more inclined to eke out our sentimental sorrows than to cherish our bodily pains; and we recognize that there are other pleasures besides love-making" (*NN*, 49). The pleasures of art—which has no name beyond 'creation' in Nowhere, since it is the product of all that its citizens do, rather than a specialized activity set off from the rest—and the fulfillment of work are at least as powerful as the preference of one human being for another. No coyness hangs about sexuality; nor are romance and sexuality necessarily linked. When Guest awakes after his first night at the Inn, the attendant Annie greets him with a kiss and "reddened as she did it, not from shyness, but from friendly pleasure"; as he sets off on his up-river journey again, "She kissed me in her frank friendly way" (*NN*, 121, 123). Guest, still accustomed to the old-fashioned ways of sexual competition, has to remind himself that no doubt she possesses a lover her own age. Similarly, when the newly re-united Clara and Dick take leave of old Hammond, in order to accompany Guest on the river, Clara "went up to old Hammond, threw her arms about his neck and kissed him heartily." On another occasion, when she meets an elderly man, Guest observes that "Clara took his hand in a coaxing way which I noticed she used with old men" (*NN*, 118, 126). Finally, Ellen, the woman with whom Guest himself falls in love, enjoys a teasing, almost flirtatious relation with her own grandfather: "leaning on the old man's shoulder, and caressing his healthy apple-red cheek" (*NN*, 137). The 'couple'—a pairing of two on the basis of mutual attraction—is just one form for romance, and although Morris imagines sexuality among older people exclusively through a middle-aged man's fantasy of young women with older men, he is determined to show that erotic life belongs within the rich amplitude of a healthy old age.[3]

He is less confident about romantic intimacy—for old or young—and the provocations of romantic love help to precipitate Guest's return to the nineteenth century. When it becomes clear that Ellen returns Guest's feelings, the tide of narrative turns, causing Guest to make emotional preparation for his retreat. He gives no reply when Ellen bluntly proposes that he remain with them and that they live together, and concedes the point when she concludes, "'I begin to suspect you of wanting to nurse a sham sorrow, like the ridiculous characters in some of those queer old novels that I have come across now and then.' I really had almost begun to suspect it myself, but I refused to admit so much" (*NN*, 171). Is the problem that romantic love destroys the idyll, or is it that, in accepting utopia, Guest would no longer be aged, aged in the Victorian sense of the word, angry, disappointed, frustrated, and rebellious? Would the loss of the perspective of age diminish the power of the utopic vision?

3. For a female version of this story, see Oliphant's "An Elderly Romance," *Cornhill*, 40 (November 1879), 549–72—in which the happily ensconced family, headed by the brother–sister couple of 60-year-old General George Stamford and 57-year-old Ursula, who share a house called 'Brothers-and-Sisters,' is broken apart by the president of the board of directors for the railway. Mr. Oakley comes to visit Stamford, falls in love with Ursula, and, despite Stamford's outrage, runs off with her. They live happily ever after.

In choosing conflict rather than rest, Guest dooms himself to fretful last years. The sputter of language enacts the trauma of return—"Clara's face turned full upon me...I turned to Ellen...then turned and went out of the porch...but as I turned round the corner"—when Guest runs full tilt into the self-image that displaces the youth of Nowhere with Victorian age: "It was a man who looked old, but whom I knew from habit, now half-forgotten, was really not much more than fifty. His face was rugged, and grimed rather than dirty; his eyes dull and bleared; his body bent, his calves thin and spindly, his feet dragging and limping" (*NN*, 181). But must this be read as a rejection of visionary politics or the romance it generates? In the simplest terms, one could say that Guest will use his vision much as Morris uses the fictional narrative: as a tableau at a distance, an image of desire that must remain out of reach until collective political action brings it to hand. But there is another sense in which Guest's choice reaffirms the importance of age and the crucial role it plays in political imagination at the end of the century.

Throughout his visit, Guest is ambivalent about the pervasive serenity that presides in Nowhere. As we have seen, he and the other elderly figures attribute the attainments of the novel to the unrest of the Victorian life. To be sure, Nowhere-ians produce beautiful art, but their talents are not literary. Boffin, named for Dickens's elderly dust collector who loves books, tries unsuccessfully to write novels of the sort published in the nineteenth century. If social plenitude lets the decorative arts flourish, it evidently retards the literary muse. But it would be too simple to assume that Guest returns because he prefers the literature of his own age. If we look at the constituents of his dream vision, we find a notable analogy to the circumstances of old age. Here too, we can recognize an illuminating convergence between Morris's narrative and Wilde's.

Guest's ambivalence is plainly the necessary condition for Morris's narrative. His arrival and departure create the story: without this *difference* in their lives, the difference of his arrival, his divergent point of view, and his alien presence, this world not only lacks narrative force; it lacks the temporality on which the consciousness of history depends. Precisely in his bearing as the Man of Age, the one who spans centuries through dream-vision, Guest generates the contrastive terms of past and present which can give a trajectory, an *end*, to politics. The achievement of Nowhere requires the long memory of the age. Furthermore, the perfection of a social idyll—that is, Nowhere without Old Hammond, without the old Grumblers, or even Ellen's temporary fear that they had better learn the past in order to avoid recreating it—risks the narrative tedium that is an embedded risk of utopian thought.

News from Nowhere consists largely of a Socratic inquiry, a discursive dialogue built upon question and answer that exposes the grotesque failure of the past (that is, the present tense of Morris and his first readers) and characterizes the advent of Nowhere, not merely as good in itself, but as liberation from the failure of the past (present). "Contrast is necessary for this explanation," Hammond avers in a remark that might stand as epigraph to *News from Nowhere*. At the center of the work is a sustained act of commentary, a judicious and synoptic account in the form of "explanation," whose social counterpart is the smooth life described. Both are largely without disturbance, and verge on monotony. No laws, courts, military, or police are to be found in Nowhere, which does without any formal institutions, including schools or government. Citizens of the country choose their work, their pleasure, their place of residence. They exchange goods and services without cash payment. The community thrives because individuals willingly accept responsibility for themselves, others, and the social whole.

Yet, while mutual dependence is the social norm of Nowhere, individual desire remains the basis for the actions of its citizens. Inheriting conventions of narrative conflict, the fictional domain is ripe for dissension, struggle, and discord, but what the novel insists upon is a state of peace. To the extent that there is regulation, it is internal, and the conditions of economic plenty—ample work, eager workers, plenty of goods—ensure that the citizens of Nowhere can allow desire, whim, and fancy to govern their activity. But the political romance cancels the possibility for chaos, or even noteworthy unruliness, among the hopeful denizens of a new world.

For although the utopic liberation of Nowhere releases desire from its restraints, the narrative itself depends on the plural forms—we, you, they—in its explanations and descriptions. Historical generalizations generate only more of the same; they do not generate particulars. Here, for example, is Old Hammond's account of Bloody Sunday, November 13, 1887:

> I have read a muddled account in a book. ... Some people, says this story, were going to hold a ward-mote here, or some such thing, and the Government of London, or the Council, or the Commission, or what not other barbarous half-hatched body of fools, fell upon these citizens (as they were then called) with the armed hand.

Guest affirms that "it *is* true; except that there was no fighting, merely unarmed and peaceable people attacked by ruffians armed with bludgeons" (*NN*, 35). We have two accounts here, one historical commentary (Hammond summarizing from a book he has read), and the other personal testimony. But the eyewitness account differs only slightly from the history encompassing it. It is no more vivid; it merely validates the historian's description, proves the case; it adds nothing to the *experience* of political struggle. Even Guest's private thoughts are impersonal; his memories consist of images and scenes that might have been similarly described by anyone else. All this, of course, is because History, not the individual, is the subject and agent of *News from Nowhere*. Guest confirms the story of the past for Old Hammond just as Dick and his friends illustrate the truth of Hammond's descriptions of life in Nowhere. And yet, the work remains haunted by its memories of a Victorian narrative embedded in a world in which individual struggle is the condition of social vision.

Though he has traveled a very different route and employed a style as plain as cotton is to Wilde's brocade, Morris's narrative arrives at the same crisis as *The Picture of Dorian Gray*. Nowhere carries with it an ominous 'no time.' Summoning an end to a conflict in social space—the bitter, debilitating struggle between classes—Morris has also magically ended the passage of time. In conjuring one thing, another quite different effect is achieved. It is not simply that the nineteenth century exists in time and possesses historical consciousness while the twenty-first century is timeless and yearns for that very historical consciousness for which it no longer has a need. Morris's narrative suggests that the aged find a home with the Victorians, however unruly, unfair, dirty, and disgusting the shelter might be. The only real manifestation of age among Nowhere-ians is a yearning for the Victorian era which they condemn outright—and for good reason. Guest could have a rich life if he chose to stay: he would look and feel young again, and enjoy the romance to which youth is entitled (at least in narratives). Why does he cling to age? Perhaps the best answer is that the Man of Age is the one who most vividly sees the change that history can bring and that this recognition emerges from both his own need and his consciousness of past and present. Guest returns to life in time, so that he can be the bearer of historical promise.

Charles Booth and the Pensions Bill: the enumeration of the elderly

The concern to find a home for the aged, to provide material succor and moral dignity during the declining time of life, to take responsibility not only for one elderly relative at a time but for the great conspicuous mass unable to tend to themselves—these preoccupations became a national as well as narrative concern at the end of the nineteenth century. In retrospect, the passage of an Old Age Pension plan seems inevitable, but at the time the path to state aid for the elderly was uncertain, and even those strongly in support of government intervention were divided. The history of this landmark event has been well tilled: the excellent studies of the movement by John Macnicol and Pat Thane provide learned accounts of central issues and personalities.[4] Suffice to say here that opposition arose from those who resisted state intervention on political or economic grounds, and also from those who were in favor of a nationalized plan but who had competing considerations and other, more self-interested concerns to protect. The boards of Friendly Societies and various Trade Unions, for example, worried that mandatory contribution would divert funds from their own coffers. And many of the most vociferous agitators for and against a pension plan had as their primary concern a desire to distinguish aid for the elderly from the stigmatized Poor Laws, which notoriously provoked the antipathy of providers and horror of the poor who received provision.[5]

The existence of a problem was uncontested and incontestable, but the ways toward remedy were obscure. Charles Booth was by no means the only tabulator of the need or the only proponent of a legislative solution; indeed, his own proposals were repeatedly reviewed and rejected by government committees. But though his specific plans were never adopted, Booth's representation of the conditions of poverty among the elderly were vital documents in both the political and imaginative life of the fin-de-siècle. Booth thought of himself—and others have followed his lead—as the epitome of a scientific investigator whose trust in numbers and visible 'facts' kept him far from the imaginative undertakings of those in the literary and fine arts. But

4. John Macnicol, *The Politics of Retirement in Britain, 1878–1948* (Cambridge: Cambridge University Press, 1998), Introduction and the six chapters which make up Part I, pp. 3–163; Pat Thane, *Old Age in English History: Past Experiences, Present Issues* (Oxford: Oxford University Press, 2000), esp. chs. 9–11 (pp. 165–235).

5. Macnicol, *The Politics of Retirement in Britain,* 63. He contends that Booth was precisely one of those for whom renovation of the Poor Law rather than old age pensions was of primary concern (see below, n. 13). The Simeys also note Booth's primary concern with abolishing out-relief. See T. S. Simey and M. B. Simey, *Charles Booth: Social Scientist* (Oxford: Oxford University Press, 1960), 161. However, even if the subject arose as a secondary concern, Booth was not content simply to separate the elderly from other inmates of the workhouse, and leave their welfare to some other agency. Whatever was his initial reason for addressing the subject, he *pursued* his research and made specific recommendations because of the legitimacy of the problem. With regard to the Friendly Societies, see P. H. J. H. Gosden, *The Friendly Societies in England: 1815–1875* (Manchester: Manchester University Press, 1961), 219.

as we shall see, the 'portrait' he drew of the aged was as provocative as those created by Wilde or Herkomer, Oliphant or Gaskell or Morris.

Booth's work on the elderly and his campaign for the pension grew from his studies of the London poor. And the fact that, as a focus of inquiry and policy, age was *subsequent* to poverty is indeed a significant aspect of its history. The poor had attained the status of a social 'sub-culture' but the elderly are then revealed as a sub-culture within a sub-culture. At a crucial turn in his analysis Charles Booth writes that "on the whole people are poor because they are old."[6] It is a fairly startling remark, but it reflects an understanding that only became possible in the second half of the nineteenth century when new categories and statistical methods were brought to bear on the massed poor. Only then was it possible to see that poverty had become overwhelmingly a problem for the last years of life. By the end of the century one in two inmates in the London workhouses was a poor old woman. What Dickens described as the "groves" of aged women should stand as the antithetic social figure to Queen Victoria as the aging exemplar of her Golden Jubilee. That Charles Booth attended the Jubilee and brought away an image of "a dumpy little black-clad lady in her carriage" suggests the political charge often muted in his neutral prose.[7]

Judith Walkowitz points to the continuity between Booth's and earlier documentary narratives, beginning with Mayhew and Engels, and extending through Greenwood, Sims, and Mearns. Like Mayhew in particular, whose *London Labour and the London Poor* (1861–2) was based on interviews initially carried out in 1849–50, Booth and his collaborators relied on data about the poor collected from first-hand accounts. Indeed, some investigators on his 'team' moved into the areas to which they were assigned in order to engage more closely with those whose lives they documented—though as Walkowitz reminds us, unlike charity reformers, they made no effort to intervene directly in the lives they observed.[8] Rather the goals of Booth's investigators were wide-scale and long-term, with an aim of providing rigorous empirical foundations for legislative policy. Many critics, of course, have discussed how such apparently 'objective reports' inevitably shape the

6. Charles Booth, *The Aged Poor in England and Wales* (London: Macmillan, 1894), 54.
7. Belinda Norman-Butler, *Victorian Aspirations: The Life and Labour of Charles and Mary Booth* (Lr Allen and Unwin, 1972), 150–1.
8. Judith Walkowitz, *City of Dreadful Delight: Narratives of Sexual Danger in Late Victorian London* (Chicago: University of Chicago Press, 1992), 36.

material they seek to describe, and Walkowitz notes that the force of such empirical and 'ethnographic' study depends on fashioning a social mask for the investigator: "As a detached, scientific explorer of the 'terra incognita' of the London poor, Booth assumed a carefully constructed persona of a male narrator whose scientific knowledge of a class would shed light on 'darkness.'" And as the 'story' unfolds, it implies that "Whether victims of environmental or biological determinism, the poor would remain the poor, unless extricated from their fate by the transforming power of heroic investigators and reformers."[9] A central burden of this chapter will be the relationship between statistical investigation and the lived experience of the elderly, including the experience of those who understand themselves as rational, impersonal observers of a public problem.

It took Booth so long, seventeen years, to complete his project, that he repeatedly had to revise statistics in order to keep up with the changing data. He was initially surprised (he claimed) to discover that Henry Hyndman's figure of a 25% poverty rate in the London of 1885 had grown to 31% in 1886 and that by 1896 the number had risen to 35%.[10] Still, these statistics, as 'hard' as they may appear, often represent a mere dream of clarity. What is most distinctive in Booth's projects, as Ben Gidley has well observed, is the heterogeneity of method and the sheer un-tameable diversity of evidence: "a mass of detail, moving from maps and statistics to house by house depictions of streets and moving biographies of ordinary people."[11] The great armature of representation appeared in handsomely published volumes, but it could not conceal the ideological investments which appear so glaring a century later. Gidley points to the discrepancy between Booth's heterogenous representations of the poor with the struggles toward self-representation among the poor themselves. Walkowitz emphasizes how the very identification of the poor depends on presuppositions of a "visual semiotics to identify the social character of streets as rough or respectable." Neighborhoods are characterized as 'rough' if they exhibit noisy or

9. Judith Walkowitz, 37, 30.

10. In their study of Booth, the Simeys quote Hyndman's description of an encounter in which Booth expressed his belief that the case had been "grossly overstated"; they imply that this conviction provoked him to embark on his own statistical survey. Macnicol rejects the romantic simplicity of such a claim and lists many compelling reasons for Booth's interest in the subject at this time. See Simey and Simey, *Charles Booth* 69–70; and Macnicol, *The Politics of Retirement in Britain*, 76.

11. Ben Gidley, *The Proletarian Other: Charles Booth and the Politics of Representation* (London: Goldsmith's University of London 2000), 2.

boisterous behavior, including women gossiping or children playing, open doors and broken windows, or the appearance of undesirable markers such as prostitutes. Respectability, on the other hand, is associated with the urban iconography of neat, clean, quiet, and sparsely populated streets, doors closed and windows curtained, flower pots, and birdcages.[12]

The invisible work of categories, often many of the *same* categories, extends from the analysis of poverty to the study of the aged. Macnicol points to the oddity of choosing the poor working classes to represent the elderly. The effect is to direct attention almost exclusively to the male, working population, and the further result, suggests Macnicol, is to promote two underlying goals of Booth's project: (1) to socialize young men into habits of thrift and responsibility suitable to a modernizing workforce; and (2) to distinguish the elderly from other impoverished people as a way to separate the Poor Law and the proposed Old Age Pensions.

> These twin concerns made the discourse on old age a highly masculinist one. Despite the fact that women outnumbered men in old age—and were to do so by nearly two to one in the post-1908 pensioner population—the male pronoun was repeatedly used to describe the aged, and the 'problem' was constructed in terms of a masculinist, military metaphor of the 'worn-out worker' deserving to be 'de-mobilised' from the 'industrial army'. ... This was more than a sexist convention: it revealed the crucial paradox that the late nineteenth-century debate about old age poverty was always a debate about older male workers, yet the highest rates of poverty in old age were suffered by women.[13]

Alongside this trenchant claim, one might note that much argument about provision turned on distinguishing among those who had been improvident, those who had been in no position to save during their long service in some humble occupation, and those who were widowed and without any means for self-support. Discussion of means-testing, still anathema to critics of the 1834 New Poor Law, was often overwrought, and it was accentuated in the case of the elderly, who simply could not be told to care for themselves. Furthermore, since one of the *causes* of poverty was old age, the 'cure' had somehow to relieve conditions—conditions of infirmity and the inability to work—that could not be substantially altered or eradicated. In America, according to Tamara Hareven, the discussion of old age shifted

12. Walkowitz, *City of Dreadful Delight*, 34–5.
13. Macnicol, *The Politics of Retirement in Britain*, 30–1.

in the last third of the nineteenth century, moving from a focus on how to increase longevity to an interest in the physiological changes of senescence.[14] In Britain too one detects an interest in making old age healthy, not so much to extend life, but to encourage the elderly to care for themselves for as long as possible. Medical discussions of old age enter the political arena, and the emerging questions revealed how much was at stake: if people were healthier longer, could the debilities of old age be postponed? What would a healthy old age look like—physically, socially, economically, politically? De Beauvoir claims that the reliance on iatrophysics was greatest in the nineteenth century, when the aging body was considered comparable to the erosion of mechanical devices.[15] Images of old age were never consistent with this model, but certainly by the end of the century people were asking if old age and deterioration were inextricably bound, and if the failure of bodily organs ought to be considered a remediable regression. Some wondered to what extent theories of degeneration might apply to the aged; sociological investigators and economic advisors asked whether or to what extent the numbers of healthy aged people would produce a strain on younger generations. These are all questions which the austere statistical presentation quickly aroused, making Booth's work as agitating and enveloping as Darwin's had been at mid-century.

The two books Booth wrote on the aged were published separately, though both were completed during the period of his larger study of the London poor. The first, *Pauperism: A Picture and the Endowment of Old Age: An Argument* appeared in 1892, the elaboration of a speech he had given to the Statistical Society on December 15, 1891. This work situates his proposal for pensions among a variety of rivals. But the times were not right or the conditions not pressing enough for parliamentary action. He had already started to write a second book on the subject, *The Aged Poor in England and Wales* (1894), when he was invited to be a member of the Old Age Commission, and he was careful to separate the tasks. The purpose of the second monograph was to provide a detailed and close-grained picture of the circumstances of the aged throughout the country; the aim of the Royal Commission was to suggest a picture of what could be done

14. Tamara K. Hareven, "Changing Images of Aging and the Social Construction of the Life Course," in *Images of Aging: Cultural Representations of Later Life*, ed. Mike Featherstone and Andrew Wernick (London: Routledge, 1995), 120.
15. Simone de Beauvoir, *The Coming of Age* (New York: Warner Paperback Library, 1973), 32.

through legislative remedy. But if one was descriptive and the other prescriptive, they relied on the same data collected from a variety of sources, including institutional and individual reports. In neither work did Booth consult the old themselves. Nowadays, our temptation is to resist such empiricism as naive and unselfconscious, but another response might be simply to weigh the force of the empirical ideal at this particular historical conjuncture. Booth and his team of investigators immersed themselves in the lives of the poor, counted them, placed them into categories, fitted them into tables of data, and presented them as arguments for a reform of social policy.

Part of my effort is to make strange this activity, so that we can feel the force of its novelty and also its provocation. A maturing social science confronted a multitude of the aged—this newly defined category that invited but also baffled understanding. Put then before the mind's historical eye the spectacle of two communities: the team of brisk investigators moving through London and the aggregation of the aged. To engage the Booth materials is to encounter the formidable problems within this attempt to comprehend the terms of a new problem, a new object for policy. The goal, in effect, was to compose a group portrait of the elderly, a rationally articulated design of a recently discovered mass.

Much of the difficulty in this arduous venture came from the varying conditions in which the aged poor were to be found—in the workhouse, on outdoor relief, tended by providential and benefit societies, insurance and thrift agencies, assisted by religious bodies or helped by relatives. Of the 648 Workhouse Unions, 285 returned usable surveys from which Booth derived much of his information. Beyond these documents, he drew on the Parliamentary report submitted by the Local Government Board in June 1893, as well as data from the 1891 Census. The numbers have the power of abstract generality, but they too alter as the angle of vision changes. We meet a particular district, and then we meet it again in relation to other districts of its kind, and then again in relation to all other districts. As Booth himself puts it in his introductory remarks, we must distinguish "first, between groups which yield an average wide enough to eliminate individual peculiarities; next between those which emphasize common peculiarities; and lastly, those which distinguish individuality to the utmost extent." Specific workhouses are described and then organized into regions, with London, the great particular, granted separate regionality because of its perpetually anomalous standing. The language sustains the tones of impersonality, but it struggles to accommodate these shifting perspectives. We move constantly from generalizations, "Life for old people is easier in the country" to slightly more generalized particulars: "The part played in the country by neighbourly knowledge must in towns be supplied by elaborate organization of charity, very apt to err on this side or that; to sympathize too readily or distrust too suspiciously," and then elsewhere to patient committee-conducted interviews with individuals who endure, or administer, old age.[16] The project depends on mustering an irresistible corpus of data that yet remains responsive to the irreducible experience of aged bodies, failing one at a time.

Amid the accumulating mass of information, a central perception recurs: namely, that poverty does not simply accelerate the debilities of old age, but that age *produces* poverty. Booth's figures register a 2.8% rate of pauperism among children under 16, 3.8% between 16 and 60, 8.1% between 60 and 65, and then an astonishing 25.9% among those older than 65. The recognition that merely to age was to increase vastly the chances of poverty forced the late Victorians to question entrenched attitudes towards the poor. The New Poor Law (1834) had proved how difficult it was to distinguish between the "deserving" and the "undeserving" poor; even so, officials were reluctant to promise universal aid. But old age was not something anyone could have avoided through greater prudence or stronger self-discipline. To address the predicament of the elderly within the Poor Law was to moralize (and demoralize) old age and to miss its distinctive exigencies. Booth ratifies efforts to encourage, even demand, thrift for those approaching seniority, but enjoins a policy that will always place thrift alongside the need to eat. He represents an impoverished end of life not as weakness of will but as the predictable outcome of a new chain of circumstances. Industrialization has outstripped the capacity of the elderly; the demands of competition have inevitable generational effects:

> Old age fares hardly in our times. Life runs more intensely than it did, and the old tend to be thrown out. Not only does work on the whole go faster and require more perfect nerve, but it changes its character more frequently, and new men—young men—are needed to take hold of the new machines or new methods employed. The community gains by this, but the old suffer. They suffer beyond any measure of actual incapacity, for the fact that a man is old is often in itself enough to debar him from obtaining work, and it is in vain he makes pretense by dyeing his hair or wearing false teeth.[17]

16. Booth, *Aged Poor*, 47.
17. Charles Booth, *Pauperism: A Picture, and the Endowment of Old Age: An Argument* (London: Macmillan, 1892), 167–8.

It is a picture of systematic necessity that challenges a still prevailing discourse of strong and weak character, the prudent and the profligate.

This context of data and categories, empirical methodologies and political strategies, yielded Booth's ambitious proposal for a "universal pension plan" divorced fully from the moral distinctions embedded in the Poor Law system: "We must...disregard the idea that any old man would be above drawing his pension, as it is of the essence of the proposal that the pensions would be paid in an honourable way, so as to be absolutely free from any poverty qualification or stigma whatever."[18] To achieve that end, he relied on the austerity of numbers, calculating that "To take a lower age than 65, or a larger amount than 5*s*. a week, would be dangerous, and increasingly dangerous for every year deducted or every shilling added....Sixty-five years of age and 5*s*. a week are as far as it would be safe to go."[19] Booth estimated the cost of universal provision at £17,000,000 (lowered to £16,000,000 once he excludes Poor Law relief for the elderly and the number of people who would not collect the pensions for which they were eligible). The inevitable consequence is that younger generations must provide support for those who approach a weakened age. Macnicol sees this as an attempt to discipline younger generations as they move into the modern industrial system, to oblige them to develop a conservative temperament that we call "far-sighted" and "responsible." No doubt such images circulated within the composite ideology of the reformers, but it was accompanied by another and progressive body of imagery. Through their contributions to the health and flourishing of the elderly, the young would develop habits of solidarity and consciousness of an intergenerational community—and, in a similar spirit of social reciprocity, would come to anticipate their own dependence on future generations.

Booth's political success, slow though it was, no doubt came through this tactical balancing of values and interests. Unlike Morris, who was a committed socialist, or Wilde, whose left-tending politics grew out of his aesthetic, Booth was a political conservative who nevertheless advocated a landmark program of national welfare. His rhetorical self-presentation always maintained at least an illusion of symmetry: in a telling comment he indicates the terms of equilibrium: "State action with regard to any pension scheme would be fatal if it in any way disturbed the basis of work and ages, discour-

18. Charles Booth, *Pauperism: A Picture, and the Endowment of Old Age: An Argument* (London: Macmillan, 1892) Ibid. 200. 19. Ibid. 204.

aged thrift, or undermined even in the slightest degree self-respect, or the forces of individuality upon which morality as well as industry depends."[20] The exchange between young and old is re-enacted in this fable of political balance—the power of the State weighed against individuality, collective provision against self-respect. Further, if both rich and poor receive the same 5*s*. each week, it will be a sign that even distinctions of class can be countered by the common fate of aging. Booth was himself a wealthy man, and the force of his universalizing gesture can be felt through these words of his granddaughter: "He himself had assured the 1893 Royal Commission on the Aged Poor that were his proposals to be implemented, he would certainly apply in person for his pension each week. I often think of him as I collect mine."[21]

Booth's proposals were unrealized when the Queen enjoyed her Jubilee in 1897, and still unrealized as the century turned. He served again on a Royal Commission in 1906–7, but after suffering from a heart attack, he resigned on the advice of his physician. A bill (not his) was finally passed in 1908, with the first pensions issued in January of 1909. In honor of his role in the passage of the legislation, the House of Commons presented Booth with an illuminated address. "The half million aged persons who now draw free pensions from the State, are the first of a great multitude whose declining years will be made peaceful and honourable by your high souled initiative, and whose increasing infirmities will be sweetened and hallowed by gratitude to Almighty God for what you have done."[22]

These are deservedly warm words, but they should not mask the agitation within, and without, Booth's great endeavor—an agitation that is as revealing as the political resolution of 1908. We can best approach this point through another instance of Boothian calculation. Throughout the published volumes the reader finds sentences such as the following two: "In England and Wales there are at present about 733,000 women and 590,000 men over 65 years of age, or in all about 1,323,000 (estimated pending full returns for 1891). We may...say that about half of the pauperism from 60 to 65, and five-sixths of that from 65 upwards, must be accounted old-age pauperism."[23] It is a scene worth invoking: the indefatigable Booth delivering his statistics and charts in the hearing room of the Royal Commission, making the case year after year—with new large numbers or old large numbers re-calibrated. It is also worth seeing such

20. Ibid. 182. 21. Norman-Butler, *Victorian Aspirations*, 127.
22. Ibid., appendix F, "Text of the Illuminated Address presented to Charles Booth in the House of Commons, 1909," 207–8. 23. Booth, *Endowment of Old Age*, 196, 165.

a passage as a typographical event, those many digits interrupting the alphabet, almost as interjections—400,000!—numbers straining for transparent interpretation. We can see this strain as a cultural symptom as well as social diagnosis.

It is Beatrice Webb, who worked alongside Booth for so many years, who will let us pursue this last point. As she began her career, she announced, with her usual directness, that "Social questions are the vital questions of today. They take the place of religion," and they do so precisely by offering the vision of the human totality, the one worthy object of devotion—the one worthy vocation, as described in the next passage.

> To me, "a million sick" have always seemed actually more worthy of self-sacrificing devotion than the "child sick in a fever," preferred by Mrs. Browning's *Aurora Leigh*. And why not? The medical officer of health, who, made aware by statistical investigation of the presence of malaria in his district, spends toilsome days and troubled nights in devising schemes for draining stagnant pools and providing for the wholesale distribution of quinine, has a compassion for human misery as deep-rooted as, and certainly more effective than that of the devoted nurse who soothes the fever-stricken patient in the last hours of life...the impulse of pity for the needless misery of men, as distinguished from the suffering of those individuals whom you happen to know, can be as operative in the study of human nature in society as it is in that of the pestilential poisons besetting the human body.[24]

The sheer vivid act of will in such a passage, indeed in such a life, is always worth acknowledging, the rational demand for generality, for the fairness of a utilitarian calculus that will maximize human flourishing, the demand for a universality that can never be achieved with rare acts of individual attention. That we have Old Age Pensions today is only due to this act of universalizing will.

And yet one reason it took so very long to achieve the Pensions and a reason that age and retirement continue to be vexing, unresolved problems, is that the experience of age confounded the category invented to understand it. The elderly looked like another problem susceptible to the statistical methods of a modern social science, but that was just another ruse of Age.

Here I turn more directly too persons, disregarding Beatrice Webb's own dictum, but then she too turned to persons, both because her long life and strenuous career became tangled with the trauma of senescence, and because her life writings are essential documents in the study of late-century rationalism (the social scientific mind) and the trauma of decline through her

24. Beatrice Webb, *My Apprenticeship* (1926; repr. Cambridge: Cambridge University Press, 1979), 258–9.

age. Even as she began her social vocation in the early 1880s, her father, Richard Potter, suffered a stroke and brought her to this difficult recognition: "There is a deep sadness in decaying power, more terrible to me than death itself. And all who have passed the prime of life, who have lived those few golden years for work, must exhibit this decline in the power for persistent work."[25] But the more striking and suggestive case is that of another person, namely Webb's revered model and friend, Herbert Spencer, who gives to us, as he gave to Webb, the most difficult image of the collision between the rationalist and the aging body, because in this case the aging body was his own.

Spencer played a formative role in Webb's emotional and intellectual development. As "the oldest and most intimate friend of the family, the incessantly ratiocinating philosopher," Spencer first "appeared in the guise of a liberator" to the Potter children. He urged them to resist convention, to defy submission, to venerate the realm of fact: "What he taught me to discern was not the truth, but the relevance of all facts; a gift said to be rare in a woman and of untold importance to the social investigator confronted with masses of data, whether in documents or in the observed behaviour of men—ascertained facts significant and insignificant, relevant and irrelevant."[26] Beatrice would read his works thoroughly, and reports that she learned "to look on all social institutions exactly as if they were plants or animals—things that could be observed, classified and explained." Her indebtedness endears him to her and stirs a lifelong commitment, but it does not stop her from applying to his own example the analytic scrutiny he taught her. His "unique life" becomes for her "no less...a warning than...a model."[27]

The interest, really the terrible interest, of Spencer to us here is the spectacle of his turn to himself, with all the rigor and austerity that he brought to the study of social life. After suffering from heart palpitations in 1853, he began to monitor his habits closely: in 1855 he set strict limits to the number of hours he could work; a year later, he reduced hours to minutes. He came to consider birthday greetings an affront to which he caustically replied, "I feel now that the prolongation of a feeble old age is not a matter for congratulation; rather for condolence"[28]—and describes his days in terms of the number of heartbeats he uses up, each one diminishing the total that remains, and leaving him so much closer to death:

25. *The Diary of Beatrice Webb*, ii. *All The Good Things of Life: 1892–1905*, ed. Norman and Jeanne MacKenzie (London: Virago, 1983), 76.

26. Webb, *My Apprenticeship*, 21–2, 26.

27. Ibid. 29.

28. David Duncan, *Life and Letters of Herbert Spencer*, ii (New York: Appleton and Co., 1908), 217.

> I dictate for ten minutes and then rest awhile...I do not usually repeat this process more than five times, making a total of fifty minutes. Very frequently...I dare not do more than three times ten minutes or twice ten minutes; and often I dare do nothing....Walking has to be restricted to two or three hundred yards when at my best, and occasionally has to be given up altogether. A drive of an hour and a quarter or an hour and a half, in a carriage with india-rubber tyres, is all the further exercise practicable; and continually a little excess in this produces injurious effects, now and then demanding entire desistence. Reading, even of the lightest kind, is almost as injurious as working. Everyday the temptation to reading has to be resisted: a few pages at once being alone practicable....So is it with conversation. When I am below my average, this has to be given up altogether, and when at my best has to be kept within narrow bounds.[29]

Webb encountered this extraordinary conduct at the closest range. She often visited Spencer, taking some pains to travel to Brighton to spend a few days with him, only to find that once there he refused to speak with her for fear of exhausting his precious minutes. "Poor old man! shall I ever be as lonely as that? God grant that I may die in my working days. His life is one continual touching of his pulse to see how it fares with himself; a torturing self-analysis of all his physical feelings."[30] Intensely preoccupied with his decline, she diagnosed the problem as "excessive self-consciousness," which makes him certain that exertion would kill him. In his own writing, Spencer concurs, accounting for the calamity of his old age by citing "forty years of brain-work."[31] On a visit in January 1896, Webb complains that

> At every hour of the day you feel his presence in the house; you may be sent for or sent away according to whether his pulse goes a little quicker or slower. When you do get a chance of talking to him you feel instinctively that you must either amuse or flatter him; anything else will produce sleeplessness. So he lives on with so many slaves about him, a seedy discontented secretary, a decayed gentlewoman or two to read or play [piano] to him, and three other servants; any friends who come have to assume the same position. Poor old man. For all that he is a noble wreck.[32]

The "noble wreck" would live on until December 1903, while Webb continued to describe her visits in tones that capture exasperation, clinical detachment, pity, and fondness for the tie. "Poor old man; the last ten or

29. Herbert Spencer, *An Autobiography*, 2 vols. (New York: D. Appleton and Co., 1904), ii. 528.
30. *The Diary of Beatrice Webb*, i. *1873–1892 "Glitter around and Darkness within"*, ed. Norman and Jeanne MacKenzie (London: Virago, 1982), 180 (October 18, 1886).
31. Spencer, *Autobiography*, ii. 531.
32. Webb, *Diary*, ii. 89–90 (January 19(?), 1896).

even twenty years he has been the prey to demons of egotism and self-deception, demons bred by an utterly false and inadequate conception of human conduct. The last quarter of his life has been a tragic parody of a Theory of Personal Rights."[33] Webb's Spencer is a living, dying contradiction, one whose experience of age contradicts the ethics of his youth, who succumbs finally to a failing, self-involved subjectivity. For all her old affection, Webb cannot disguise her disappointment to herself and wishes that he could be the philosophic self he constructed in his writing and not the decaying self he can no longer hide.

Peter Laslett has briskly remarked that "To dislike the old is hatred of the self, rejection of what you yourself must inevitably become." Those who despise the old are inevitably "despising themselves."[34] In light of this thought, it is worth recalling the relationship between the study of age and the study of the poor. To those who did not share their dispossession, the poor remained external and other, almost entirely "other" to the social investigators, the makers of policy, the journalists, the painters, the writers of fiction. As specimens of social science, they were secured as objects for an objectifying eye. But no matter how rationalist the disposition, no matter how empirical the methodology, the aging body is a possible future for everyone. This is what Webb's Spencer and then Webb herself were obliged to recognize.

And Laslett's stern words may miss the dislocations on which the representation of age depended (and still depends). Especially at that moment of post-Darwinian bewilderment, the decrepit body is bound to seem like the body of someone else, a detached artifact in some unthinkable future. The aged are objects not subjects, and it seems painfully right to say that this is something they know about themselves. The worst losses of age include finally a loss of the power to constitute subjectivity—when the self surrenders and becomes a specimen.

The picture of Dorian Gray concealed in the attic is a figure of generational distance—not just spatially, but ethically: the distance of all subjectivity from the object that is the decayed body. Within its tease and its taunt, the force of the narrative, *Dorian Gray*, its own peculiar terror, lies with Dorian finally and fatally taking the object onto himself, becoming that wrinkled throat, those bloated hands. What was a spectacle of mockery becomes the self: this is the terror of age.

33. Webb, *Diary*, ii. 269 (February 2, 1903).

34. Peter Laslett, *A Fresh Map of Life: The Emergence of the Third Age* (London: Weidenfeld & Nicoloson, 1989), 97.

7
Gravestones, Obituaries, Epitaphs

Death, the limit of life, has a special imaginative resonance for the elderly and for those whom the elderly leave behind. The last years of an old age, often unwillingly, make death the aim of existence, an approaching telos indicated in every mark of decline. Here, I look at another set of marks: not those written onto the aging, finally failing body, but those left in memory of the departed elderly. We have studied some of the intricate passages as the course of old age moved towards the modernity of institutionalization, social 'security' and an increasingly prolonged period of senescence. There is no happy resolution. There can be only one end to the narrative of old age. But like many Victorian endings, closure is as complex as initiation, and sometimes it stirs a reopening. In this brief chapter, I ask what we might learn about the elderly when they are seen from the other side of a grave.

Prompted by a *Times* obituary, Elizabeth Barrett Browning composed a poem in 1862 opening with the lines "What shall we add now? He is dead."[1] Three years after publication of Darwin's *Origin of Species*, the question and its answer take on a newly agitating force. Whether being 'first' or 'last' earned one 'fame' or 'shame,' both—all—level to the same insignificance. After life, genres change: "The epitaph's an epigram" (line 25). As Barrett Browning neatly suggests, the attempt to extract an essence and to summarize a life is one task of burial inscription and obituary. Since living and dying for the elderly were experienced (and perceived) differently from that of younger people, we might expect that the afterlife of the aged would also produce its own forms and styles. If death erases good and bad, "first...or last and worse," it nonetheless continues to mark age (lines 116–17). The span of years typically inscribed on a tomb, even when no

1. Elizabeth Barrett Browning, "Died..." in *Victorian Verse*, ed. Christopher Ricks (Oxford: Oxford University Press, 1990), 107–8.

words follow, makes clear the significance of life as chronos. After the sudden death of his beloved sister-in-law, Mary Hogarth, Dickens composed a brief epitaph for her grave in Kensal Green Cemetery: "Young, beautiful and good. God in His mercy numbered her among His angels at the early age of seventeen." The inscription begins and ends with age. Gravestone iconography similarly distinguishes young from old through such images as buds (child), halved or broken columns (adult), or garnered wheat (aged). If there is one thing we should know about a person who once lived, it is, evidently, her or his age.

Thackeray muses on the difference between the death of an infant and that of a young woman in his novel *The Newcomes*, where Pendennis writes that:

> Yet two more days passed, and I had to take two advertisements to the *Times* newspaper on the part of poor Clive [Clive Newcome]. Among the announcements of Births was printed, "On the 28th, in Howland Street, Mrs. Clive Newcome of a son, still-born." And a little lower, in the third division of the same column, appeared the words, "On the 29th, in Howland Street, aged 26, Rosalind, wife of Clive Newcome, Esq." So, one day, shall the names of all of us be written there; to be deplored by how many?—to be remembered how long?—to occasion what tears, praises, sympathy, censure?—yet for a day or two, while the busy world has time to recollect us who have passed beyond it. So this poor little flower had bloomed for its little day, and pined, and withered, and perished. There was only one friend by Clive's side following the humble procession which laid poor Rosey and her child out of sight of a world that had been but unkind to her. Not many tears were there to water her lonely little grave. A grief that was akin to shame and remorse humbled him as he knelt over her. Poor little harmless lady! No more childish triumphs and vanities, no more hidden griefs are you to enjoy or suffer; and earth closes over your simple pleasures and tears! The snow was falling and whitening the coffin as they lowered it into the ground. It was at the same cemetery in which Lady Kew was buried. I dare say the same clergyman read the same service over the two graves, as he will read it for you or any of us to-morrow; and until his own turn comes.[2]

The baby and the adult each receive one line, but the child, whose entire life is encompassed in the simultaneous act of birth and death, has no record of life between. The epitaph for Rose Newcome, on the other hand, suggests not only a personality ("childish triumphs and vanities…hidden

2. William Thackeray, *The Newcomes* (London: J.M. Dent & Sons, 1952), II, 416–417.

griefs"), but also collective humanity and a tradition. The reminder that life is short, and can be *very* brief, defies the slow processes of deterioration which a lengthy old age imposes. But there can be no hasty generalizations in this regard. Florence Nightingale, for example, was singular in many ways, but not in her instruction to include only her initials along with the dates of birth and death as the memorial inscription on her grave: 'F.N. Born 1820. Died 1910.' Like the very young, who have yet to accumulate the experiences which fill a life, the very old often sift and simplify. Life resolves not into its particulars, but into the general outline. It begins; it ends. All the rest is for the living.

Two issues, intertwined, are at stake here. The first concerns the nature of narrative inscription (image or word). The second bears on the specific associations which these forms have to older people. Inevitably, some remarks of a general nature are in order since the elderly, in addition to being old, are also just people. Age, however, provides a ceremonial entrance to the complexities of the genre of memorialization. Dickens's Christmas story *The Chimes* intones:

> The Year was Old that day. The patient Year had lived through the reproaches and misuses of its slanderers, and faithfully performed its work. Spring, summer, autumn, winter. It had laboured through the destined round, and now laid down its weary head to die. Shut out from hope, high impulse, active happiness, itself, but messenger of many joys to others, it made appeal in its decline to have its toiling days and patient hours remembered, and to die in peace. (ch. 2, "The Second Quarter")

Memorial narratives respond to this appeal; they attempt to 'set in stone' the attributes by which a dead person might wish to be remembered (Thomas Jefferson, for example, who stipulated what should be written on his gravestone), or they impose those qualities which others choose to inscribe. Sometimes they do one or the other; sometimes both. Even brief inscriptions memorialize: a mere set of dates testifies to the significance of those years among all other years. Obituaries, of course, are often more impersonal than other forms of narrative devoted to remembering the dead; especially if they recall well-known public figures, who may be more or less controversial, they can take up less affirmative, or even delicately corrosive, tones. It is important, then, to distinguish between memorialization and inscription, even though the bulk of narrative inscription does memorialize. Death offers the opportunity to memorialize, but often enough, under the guise of remembering the dead, the compositor testifies rather to the emotions of the living. Someone is marked 'loving' often enough, but as frequently people are described as 'beloved' rather than loving. Memorialization is an invitation to inflate, whether from an excess of grief or in an attempt to focus only on the good rather than the 'whole' character of the deceased. The room for slippage between subject and author, and between representing whole or partial estimates of a life make the genre less stable than it might at first appear. Dickens wrote the obituary for Thackeray in *The Cornhill*, which must take precedence over obituaries appearing elsewhere both because of the matching fame of living and dead authors and because of Thackeray's special connection, as its first editor, to the journal. Throughout the piece, Dickens tries to resurrect a non-satiric Thackeray, not the one who "too much feigned a want of earnestness," but the "softened and serious" man.[3] As if the satire were mere veneer, Dickens peels it back to reveal a man who "was charming with children" possessed "natural gentleness" and "unaffected manly sympathy with the weak and lowly"(p. 328). He goes so far as to evoke an image of the young writer regretting "his satirical pen" and offering a "petition for forgiveness" (p. 329) should his satire have caused offense or pain. What fun Thackeray might have had with this image of himself, and how he might have returned the favor, by evoking a Dickens desperately trying to quench the fire of his own satire with the waters of sentiment. With far less ambivalence, Dickens characterized the obituary he wrote for his friend, the painter Clarkson Stanfield, as a "little wreath upon that dear friend's grave."[4] And though he begins with the admonition that for all artists one must distinguish between "private sorrows" and "public pursuit" (p. 331), he tries to bridge the two by recalling intimate personal exchanges alongside reference to the paintings by which the artist would be remembered. His fame will be carried in "the roar of the sea," but Dickens will think of him always by his "pet name" and his unique smile (p. 333). Obituaries thus negotiate between public and private, social and personal; they offer a composite image of the dead, something for everyone. The effect, however, is to divide the person into so many memorable elements rather than to suggest a whole as a synthesis of its parts. Obituaries often create aggregates rather than harmonious unities.

3. *Cornhill*, February 1864, repr. in Dickens's Journalism, 4: *The Uncommercial Traveller and Other Papers*, ed. Michael Slater and John Drew (London: J. M. Dent, 2000), 328, 327.
4. "The Late Mr. Stanfield," *All the Year Round*, June 1, 1867, ibid. 332.

Though it might seem to be the least susceptible to manipulation, the genre of memorialization offers as much room for play as other literary genres. We cannot simply reduce all death to tragedy, nor soften all memory to accomplishment and praise. Dickens, for one, presses the sentimental/ tragic conventions of the genre until it releases comedy. In *The Mystery of Edwin Drood*, the bombastic auctioneer Thomas Sapsea composes this inscription for the monument over his wife's grave.

ETHELINDA,
Reverential Wife of
MR. THOMAS SAPSEA
AUCTIONEER, VALUER, ESTATE AGENT, &C.,
OF THIS CITY.
Whose Knowledge of the World,
Though somewhat extensive,
Never brought him acquainted with
A SPIRIT
More capable of
LOOKING UP TO HIM.
STRANGER PAUSE
And ask thyself the Question,
CANST THOU DO LIKEWISE?
If Not,
WITH A BLUSH RETIRE. (*MED*, ch.4)

Whose epitaph has Sapsea composed, his wife's or his own, or is there a difference? By inflating himself at her expense, he reveals her self-immolation at the altar of his egoism, and handily supplies us with a description of his character and his wife's. Her absence reflects the vacancy she 'filled' in life, and through the caricatured discourse of the epitaph Mrs. Sapsea's personality has found accurate (though hardly adequate) expression.

Inflation, of course, is more commonly put to earnest purposes, often straining toward emotional effect that will condense sentiments accumulated over long duration. The inscription that John Stuart Mill composed for his wife Harriet Taylor's grave is in its way as inflated as Sapsea's, though to opposite effect. In addition to her "great and loving heart…loving soul, clear, powerful, original and comprehensive intellect," Harriet was also "the guide and support, the instructor in wisdom and the example in goodness, as she was the sole earthly delight of those who had the happiness to belong to her." She was "as earnest for all public good | As she was generous and devoted | to all who surrounded her." And finally, "Her influence has been felt in many of the greatest improvements of the age | and will be in those still to come | Were there even a few hearts and intellects like hers | this earth would already become the hoped for heaven." This, from one of the most dedicated and selfless legislators and philosophers of the century, is high praise indeed, and few 'retire without a blush' from the grave site in Avignon, at the evidence of such devotion to another. His exaggerated praise reflects his own modesty, but viewers inevitably apply the praise to the man who wrote the words rather than to the woman he loved. Mill was in his early fifties when Harriet Taylor died; for the remaining fifteen years of his life he continued to speak and write of his dead wife in these glowing terms. We learn many things from narrative inscriptions, but in few other modes is the distance between intent and effect so vast, the shifts in tone or mode so unstable, or the movement between subject and object so vacillating.

Kathleen Woodward reminds us of Walter Benjamin's insight, that life assumes the shape of a story precisely at the moment of death. Woodward connects this thought to the psychiatrist Robert Butler's concept of the 'life review'—a dying person's effort to bring life (at last) to coherence.[5] Obituaries, epitaphs, eulogies, and gravestones also attempt an act of biographic unification through the resources of truncated syntax. An individual's own life review may or may not be unbiased, but it is in principle more comprehensive than what we may call memorial narratives. Furthermore, the autobiographic life review tends toward an orderly progression which rarely constrains the memorial. Memorial narratives may have formal beginnings and endings, but neither need correspond chronologically to the life span of the subject. Tennyson's *In Memoriam* offers an extended reminiscence, but its moments reflect the conditions of the speaker's mourning, its alternating moods and longings, rather than the life-course of Henry Hallam. Although a richly evocative picture of Hallam emerges, we achieve no full grasp of his life, nor do we expect one.

Matthew Arnold's chronic nostalgia results in a wide variety of memorializing narratives. "Stanzas in Memory of Edward Quillinan" extols the gentle 60-year-old man, and confesses that the success and fortune the poet might have wished Quillinan in life would have compromised the very

5. Kathleen Woodward, "Reminiscence and the Life Review: Prospects and Retrospects," in *What Does it Mean to Grow Old? Reflections From the Humanities*, ed. Thomas R. Cole and Sally A. Gadow (Durham, NC Duke University Press, 1986), 144–5.

qualities he most prizes: "Alive, we would have changed his lot, | We would not change it now" (lines 19–20).[6] Here is the illuminating paradox: the poet's belated intervention preserves more accurately the life which *in life* he would have altered. Yet the aim of the poem is not to record the life for the purposes of preservation so much as to create effects among the still living, those whom he 'touches' by example. The poet, speaking through the old man, or the epitaph, speaking through the poet (the obituary, speaking through the journalist), create the influence that is the expression of 'life' which persists beyond death. It may have little or much to do with the actual person who once lived, though it *represents* that person once s/he is beyond self-expression. For so many Victorians learning to doubt immortality, memory after death constitutes a kind of after-life. What we "add" cannot signify to the dead, but it forms the basis of an 'influence' which the dead continue to exert on the living.

Authorial manipulation is as important to inscriptions as to other forms of writing, and Mr. Sapsea explains that the effect of such narratives must be to make visitors to a tomb "monumentally directed" (*MED*, ch. 12). But there is friction between the two objectives, accurate preservation and active persuasion, and sometimes in order to achieve the latter, the former must be altered substantially. Here is a good example of the problem. Arnold Bennett claimed to have found the germ for his novel *The Old Wives' Tale* in an incident involving the entrance of an old woman into a restaurant where he was dining:

> She was fat, shapeless, ugly, and grotesque. She had a ridiculous voice, and ridiculous gestures. It was easy to see that she lived alone, and that in the long lapse of years she had developed the kind of peculiarity which induces guffaws among the thoughtless. She was burdened with a lot of small parcels, which she kept dropping. She chose one seat; and then, not liking it, chose another; and then another. In a few moments she had the whole restaurant laughing at her…
>
> I reflected, concerning the grotesque diner: "The woman was once young, slim, perhaps beautiful; certainly free from these ridiculous mannerisms. Very probably she is unconscious of her singularities. Her case is a tragedy. One ought to be able to make a heart-rending novel out of the history of a woman such as she." Every stout, ageing woman is not grotesque—far from it!—but

6. *Matthew Arnold*, ed. Miriam Allot and Robert H. Super (Oxford: Oxford University Press, 1992), 137.

> there is an extreme pathos in the mere fact that every stout ageing woman was once a young girl with the unique charm of youth in her form and movements and in her mind. And the fact that the change from the young girl to the stout ageing woman is made up of an infinite number of infinitesimal changes, each unperceived by her, only intensifies the pathos.
>
> It was at this instant that I was visited by the idea of writing the book which ultimately became *The Old Wives' Tale*. Of course I felt that the woman who caused the ignoble mirth in the restaurant would not serve me as a type of heroine. For she was much too old and obviously unsympathetic. It is an absolute rule that the principal character of a novel must not be unsympathetic, and the whole modern tendency of realistic fiction is against oddness in a prominent figure. I knew that I must choose the sort of woman who would pass unnoticed in a crowd.[7]

When we read of someone that 'she was a fond wife, good mother, and kind friend,' we assume that this is a summary of vignettes which constitute a life and capture something of its process and fruition in old age. Inevitably, the epitaph reflects the compositor at least as much as the person it describes, unless, like Hardy's Michael Henchard (*The Mayor of Casterbridge*), whose will dictates his own epitaph, one provides his/her own before dying. Bennett's assumption that this woman was once 'young, free, beautiful, free from mannerisms' reveals his generous sympathy but robs the woman of her unique history. The relation of past to present is vexed at best, and whether consistency or inconsistency predominates may never accurately be assessed. But despite the distortions of the present—he describes her in terms of the way she is perceived by others—and the fancies of a past, we have a fleeting sense of this old woman as she enters the public world, a colossal reminder of the privacies of old age (whether or to what extent self-imposed or inflicted), the indifference and even intolerance of younger generations to the aged, and the fraught relations which are both intimate and cool, knowing and unknown, which characterize the aged in relation to all generations before it.

The Old Wives' Tale is a wonderful story indeed, and relevant in many ways to this study, pre-eminently as an example of the 'old' nineteenth century living on and into the twentieth century. But it is *not* the story of the old woman who was its source. Just as Bennett's novel might be seen as an 'epitaph' on the figure of age in the nineteenth century, so too the Preface

7. Arnold Bennett, *The Old Wives' Tale* (Harmondsworth: Penguin, 1983), Preface, 31–2.

to the novel functions as an epitaph to the lady whose predicament stirred Bennett's imagination. The Victorian epitaph characteristically looked to summarize an entire life through a few resonant characteristics. Bennett, on the other hand, places the expansion narrative against the painful simplicities of the epitaph. Still, like the epitaph, his preface considers the end first, and then invites us to ask, 'what was life such that *this* was its end?' At the close of Book II, Constance Povey states the case in her own terms: "I'm a lonely old woman now. I've nothing to live for any more, and I'm no use to anybody. Once I was young and proud. And this is what my life has come to! This is the end!" (*OWT*, 310). Only it isn't the end, for there are two more books detailing the slow advance in age, towards death.

When the life has been very long, there is often a particular resonance to the life review. In Bennett's novel, Constance (*constance*) performs the task of reflecting over the life span first after her sister Sophia dies, and then again, shortly thereafter, in the moments before her own death. As she stares at her sister's dead body, Constance sums up: "And she had ended—thus! This was the piteous, ignominious end of Sophia's wondrous gifts of body and soul. Hers had not been a life at all" (*OWT*, 585). The pathos of a life unable to realize its possibilities overcomes her, its futility manifest in the physical remains: "But look at her now, with her twisted face, her sightless orbs, her worn skin—she did not seem sixty, but seventy! She was like something used, exhausted, and thrown aside! Yes, Constance's heart melted in an anguished pity for that stormy creature" (*OWT*, 586). It is just this look of age in death that had shocked Sophia and precipitated the stroke which ended her life. Sophia had gazed at the body of her husband, whom she had not seen for thirty-six years.

> It was a genuine unforeseen shock, the most violent that she had ever had. In her mind she had not pictured Gerald as a very old man. She knew that he was old; she had said to herself that he must be very old, well over seventy. But she had not pictured him. This face on the bed was painfully, pitiably old. A withered face, with the shiny skin all drawn into wrinkles! The stretched skin under the jaw was like the skin of a plucked fowl. The cheek-bones stood up, and below them were deep hollows, almost like egg-cups. A short, scraggy white beard covered the lower part of the face. The hair was scanty, irregular, and quite white; a little white hair grew in the ears. The shut mouth obviously hid toothless gums, for the lips were sucked in. The eyelids were as if pasted down over the eyes, fitting them like kid. All the skin was extremely pallid; it seemed brittle. The body, whose outlines were clear under the sheet, was very small, thin, shrunk, pitiable as the face. (*OWT*, 576–7)

What strikes her is not death; it is age: "The manner of his life was of no importance. What affected her was that he had once been young, and that he had grown old, and was now dead. That was all. Youth and vigour had come to that." It is this "riddle of life that was puzzling and killing her," not the waste, but the fact that in *whatever* "manner" one lives a life, it comes to this, to age and then to death. Catching her image in the mirror, "she glimpsed a tall, forlorn woman, who had once been young and now was old"; she who had "exulted in strength... | now was old"—what else is left for her but to die? (*OWT*, 577–8). For Bennett, old age is the negation rather than the summation of a life. After Sophia's death, her heir and nephew, an artist, designs a tombstone; but though we learn that Cyril constructs it to be sturdy and solid, and that Constance thinks the lettering "affected and finicking," we hear nothing about what he has inscribed. The epitaph has come before, in the impressions of her sister as she contemplates the meaninglessness which age impresses upon life. For Constance there is a little variety, but only by way of arriving at the same point from a different direction. The townspeople look at Constance as she makes her last walk through the town square: "Mrs. Povey and her sciatica again! Poor thing, she really is a little tedious!" they think (*OWT*, 612). Adopting her own point of view for a moment, we contrast their assessment with Constance's own life review: "She had lived in honesty and kindliness for a fair number of years, and she had tasted triumphant hours.... When she surveyed her life, and life in general, she would think, with a sort of tart but not sour cheerfulness: '*Well, that is what life is!*'" (*OWT*, 613). There is no more detail to add, for as the narrator reminds us "No one but Constance could realize all that Constance had been through, and all that life had meant to her" (*OWT*, 615). This doesn't mean that all attempts to (re)capture the life experience are futile, only that they are partial, liable to distortion, and almost never focused solely on a single subject. The deceased person is only the occasion for reflection, the centerpiece upon a table set for many.

We have seen the variety of ways that the gravestone, the epitaph, and the obituary are attempts to assuage the emotions of those left behind: they are composed (usually) by and (always) for the living; they mark the effort to revive, not the dead, but valued attributes of the dead, which are also threatened with extinction. They are frequently, however, composed *before* rather than *after* death has occurred. In Patrick Marber's play *Closer* (1997), the character Dan reveals the dark comedy behind writing obituaries of notables in preparation for their demise. And Dickens's John Chivery, spoony son of the lock keeper of the Marshalsea Prison in *Little Dorrit*, composes inscriptions for his grave endlessly in an attempt to freeze forever each moment of exquisite misery as he endures Amy Dorrit's indifference. As these examples make clear, narrative inscriptions not only anticipate the death, they also anticipate the emotions associated with death. They revive memory before memory has itself departed and replenish emotion before it has been bereaved. If we can 'guess' when someone will die and what others will feel, we acknowledge the free play of narrative inscriptions, the humor and invention in the midst of grief, and the fiction-making behind the somber purposes of the genre.

Dickens's Pip demonstrates another instability of the genre, the vagaries, often involuntarily comic, in the interpretations of inscriptatory legends. All readers will recall the opening of *Great Expectations*, as Pip describes his impressions of his family, based on "the authority" of their tombstones:

> The shape of the letters on my father's, gave me an odd idea that he was a square, stout, dark man, with curly black hair. From the character and turn of the inscription, "*Also Georgiana Wife of the Above*," I drew a childish conclusion that my mother was freckled and sickly. To five little stone lozenges, each about a foot and a half long, which were arranged in a neat row beside their grave, and were sacred to the memory of five little brothers of mine—who gave up trying to get a living, exceedingly early in that universal struggle—I am indebted for a belief I religiously entertained that they had all been born on their backs with their hands in their trousers-pockets, and had never taken them out in this state of existence. (*GE*, ch. 1)

The polite reference—"Also Georgiana"—so common to family grave sites—carries with it special significance within the nineteenth-century context. We begin with a single grave, and conclude with a society of seven. As we have seen, the massive growth in population throughout the century did not stop with the living: overpopulation below ground was as urgent a problem as was the overcrowded city above. But here the point is to examine the openness of interpretive possibility within a genre that lays claim to scriptural authority even in its dependence on archaic forms of speech and in its use of traditional and religious symbolism. Dickens, richly and ruthlessly, exploits all the flexibility embedded in the form. David Copperfield is strangely moved by "my first childish associations with [his father's] white grave-stone in the churchyard, and of the indefinable compassion I used to feel for it lying out alone there in the dark night, when our little parlor was warm and bright with fire and candle, and the doors of our house were—almost cruelly, it seemed to me sometimes—bolted and locked against it" (*DC*, ch. 1). In *Barnaby Rudge*, Barnaby and his mother refresh themselves in a graveyard while they wait for a coach to depart for London. The writing that they find on Mr. Rudge's grave contains "a brief inscription recording how and when he had lost his life," when in fact, we discover much, much later, he is still alive. Barnaby's pet raven inspects the inscriptions with greater perspicacity: he walks on the gravestones, "appearing to read the tombstones with a very critical taste. Sometimes, after a long inspection of an epitaph, he would strop his beak upon the grave to which it referred, and cry in his hoarse tones, 'I'm a devil, I'm a devil, I'm a devil!' but whether he addressed his observations to any supposed person below, or merely threw them off as a general remark, is matter of uncertainty" (*BR*, ch. 25). The challenges to the "monumental direction" of the epitaph should by now be clear. The brevity of life, however short or long the span of the deceased, and the analogous brevity of the inscription meet in instabilities of tone, ranging broadly from ironic (evoking life's irrelevance) to romantic (in nostalgic recapitulation) on the way to spiritual (suggesting life's 'meaning' or its 'rewards' hereafter). These tonal slippages are matched by the interpretive uncertainties that at once inform and surround any attempt to summarize a life.

What this suggests is that the will to monumentality reflects an attempt to create consistency of emotions among disparate groups—mourners, visitors, the deceased, compositors of memorializing narratives. In the face of inevitable gaps between the living and the dead, the young and the old, 'insiders' and strangers, the inscription will offer a bridging discourse. Such truncated narratives ease the dread that there can be no exchange between those in radically contrasting states. Surely this is one implicit meaning of Henry Alexander Bowler's painting *The Doubt: "Can These Dry Bones Live?"*, (Fig. 20), in which a young woman leans over the back of a gravestone to study the bones of the deceased. Can there be *any* commerce across the chasm, and if so, how can inscription (which, in the picture, she cannot see, though it is present) function as conversation between the opposing states or conditions? If the in-scripted emotions seem trite (beloved/loving), the traits conventionally approved (generous, kind) and the accomplishments fairly predictable (awards, offices) this is no doubt because the mundane is so reassuring in the face of the ultramundane. Helplessness before narrative is part of the appeal of memorialization. If nothing more *can* be said, one must speak all the same. This is the urgent demand and the compelling reaction to memorializing narrative. We must

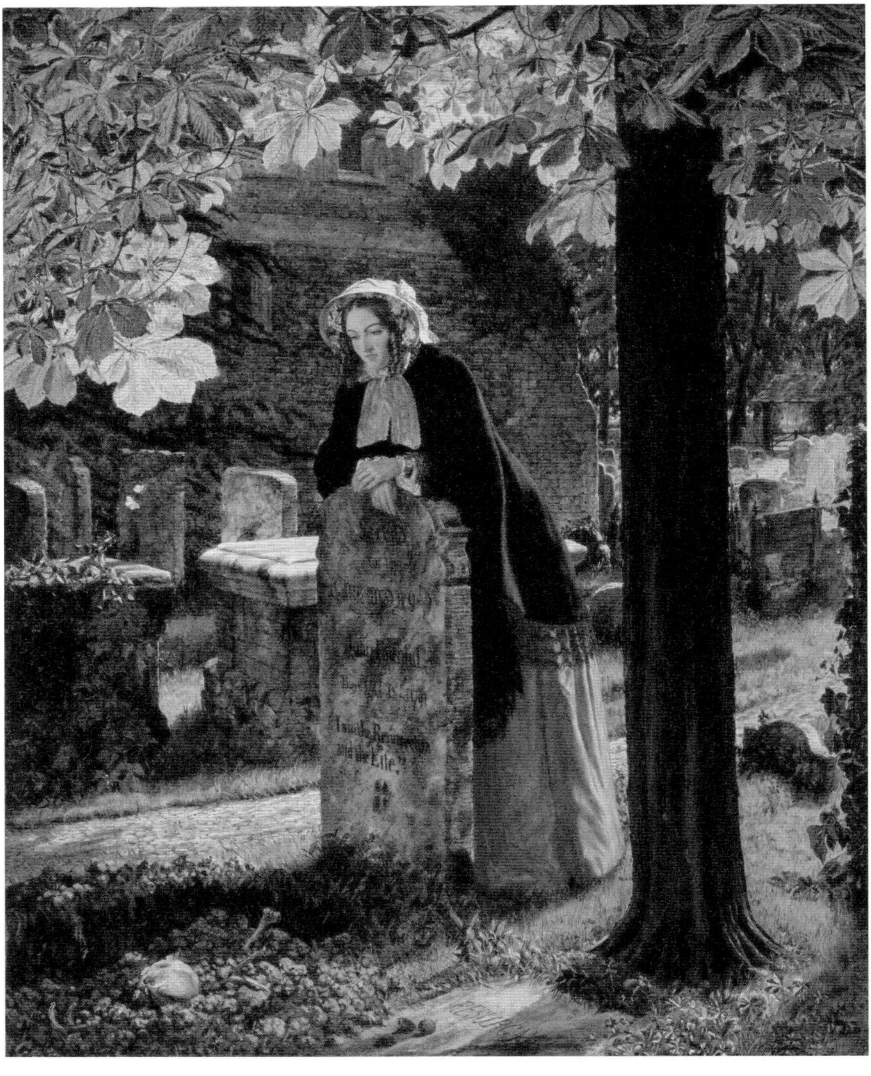

Figure 20 Henry Alexander Bowler, *The Doubt: Can These Dry Bones Live?* © Tate, London (2008)

resist the temptation to conclude that narrative inscriptions simply promise the consolations of transition, and thus contact, between unbearable contrasts. We have seen all too often how the desire for emotional and narrative coherence remains in ongoing relation to a textual/interpretive abyss of uncertainty.

In 1842 there appeared a curious book called *The Seven Ages of Human Life: Old Age*. It consists largely of quotations from eighteenth- and nineteenth-century literature, a list of people who lived to a very old age, and an attempt to associate longevity with profession. Interspersed throughout are the author's musings and observations, including this little insight: "The pleasures of memory in Old People may be thought, in a great measure, to counterbalance those of hope in the young."[8] If memory is the most valuable possession of the elderly, then the death of an older person is clearly a threat to the community. Certainly a much-remarked aspect of the social significance of the death is the loss of a collective past, disappearing one corpse at a time. Against the background of such loss, those elderly who 'forget' before they die seem to be failures at the one task society assigns to them.

If the attribution of memory to age and hope to youth can seem banal and hardly contestable, evidence from life reviews casts a disturbing light on the innocuous observation. An example from the fine arts makes the point vividly. Arthur Hughes's *Silver and Gold* (1864; Fig. 21) offers easily accessible contrasts, but Susan Casteras also detects an identity of interests: "The old woman and her *protégée*...perambulate...the latter, judging from her dreamy expression, probably ruminating about love while her caretaker harbors protective instincts."[9] Yet, rather than focus on the contrast—the one imagines a romantic tryst, the other imagines how to prevent such an encounter, we might identify the current of similarity between the two figures. Using Casteras's terms we would point to the common ground of preoccupation with the young lady's romantic life. And if we pursue explanation along these structural lines, we might say that the women are paired as contrasts in the present only: in time, the picture suggests, the old woman may be the face and habit of the once-young. The relaxed hands will become clasped and crabbed; the open eyes, dewy with anticipation, will become closed, as if to concentrate on the memory of a love that once was; the ornamental necklace will become a cross (suggesting a union only in death) or a locket containing a relic of the past; the rich colors will give way to deep black, and so on. In other words, the viewer is asked to see youth and age as bound together even in spite of themselves, much as the two figures, though each lost in thought about 'another,' are visually united through their mutually inclined heads and interlinked arms. The picture also suggests the possibility that memory may be no more sure than anticipation; each is a projection toward an absence that wavers as it recedes into either time past or time future.

8. Anon., *The Seven Ages of Human Life: Old Age* (Calcutta: the Baptist Mission Press, 1842), 151.
9. Susan Casteras, *Images of Victorian Womanhood in English Art* (Rutherford Fairleigh Dickinson University Press, 1987), 127.

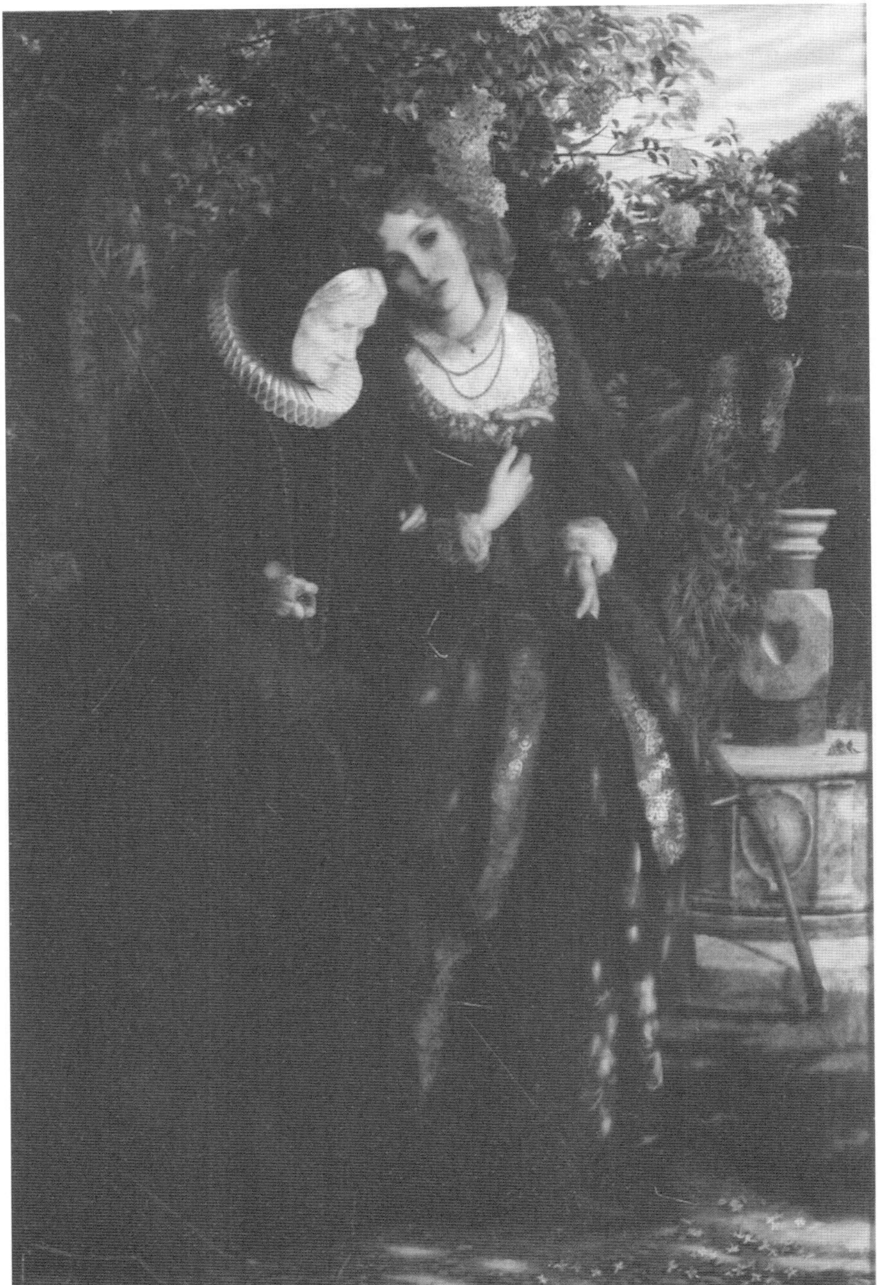

Figure 21 Arthur Hughes, *Silver and Gold*. Courtesy of Lord Lloyd-Webber

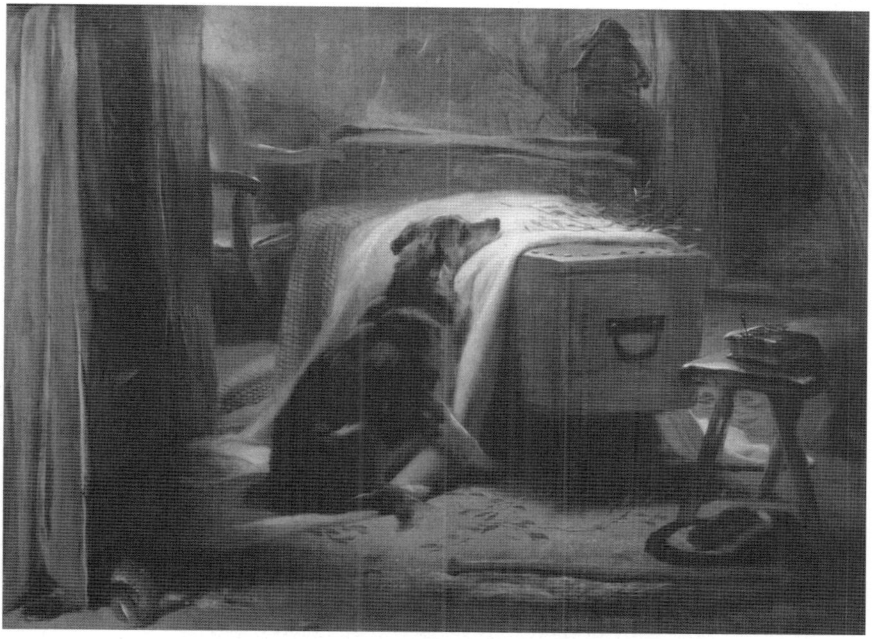

Figure 22 Edwin Landseer, *The Old Shepherd's Chief Mourner*. © Victoria and Albert Museum, London

Narrative inscriptions try to revive the missing person, but, as we have seen from a diversity of perspectives, the viewer/reader always shares the subject-position. In painting, this emphasis on the still-living subject often is displayed through the conspicuous absence of the deceased. Edwin Landseer's early painting *The Old Shepherd's Chief Mourner* (1834; Fig. 22) is an early case in point. The work transformed the artist into a celebrity, enjoying great popular approval, as well as royal esteem. And when Landseer himself died, it was this painting, among his multitude of works, that was etched in stone at his burial in St. Paul's.[10] The picture shows a dog resting his head on the grave of his master: there are no people to share the grief. The sentimentality is obvious: a dog's loyalty is set against the indifference of the world. But though obvious, the picture is not simple. Notice, for example, what would happen if another figure enters the tableau. Briton Rivière's painting *Sympathy* (1877; Fig. 23) does just that. In this image a dog shapes itself to the contours of a thoughtfully yearning young child who sits disconsolately on a stairwell.

10. Hallman B. Bryan, "Edwin Landseer," in *Victorian Britain: An Encyclopedia*, ed. Sally Mitchell (New York: Garland, 1988), 433.

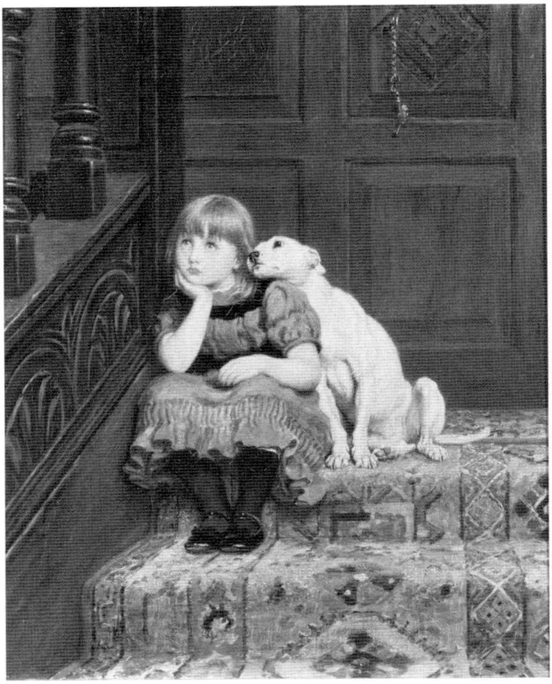

Figure 23 Briton Rivière, *Sympathy*. © Tate, London (2008)

There is an unmixed story to read here, a determinate way to read it, and a sentimentally coherent emotion to indulge: a sad girl, a sympathetic and loyal dog. Landseer's painting subtly breaks open the coherence, the sentimentality, and the simplicity. Reading 'with' the picture, we might say that the aged take their memories with them, that the young have no memory (only 'hope') and cannot preserve the passing lives of ordinary folk. C'est la vie (C'est la mort). But the picture invites an alternative reading which emerges when it is set alongside Thomas Hardy's poem "Friends Beyond" (1898). Here the speaker recalls those who lie buried in Mellstock churchyard—"William Dewy, Tranter Reuben, Farmer Ledlow late and plough, | Robert's kin, and John's, and Ned's, | And the Squire, and Lady Susan, lie in Mellstock churchyard now!" Though recalled to memory, the message they "murmur mildly" to him is not comforting. "We've no wish to hear the tidings" they tell him, "Curious not the least are we if our intents you make or mar, | If you quire to our old tune, | If the City stage still passes, if the weirs still roar afar."[11]

11. Thomas Hardy, "Friends Beyond," *The New Oxford Book of Victorian Verse*, ed. Christopher Ricks (Oxford: Oxford University Press, 1990), 367–8.

What if in death the old cease to be old? What if they no longer remember? What if it is *they* who no longer care? Landseer's picture details the memory of the living; it makes preservation a sentimental superfluity. What is strikingly absent in the painting is not the presence of mourners—no one could mourn as eloquently as the soulful-eyed dog. What is missing is the old man. The box which stands in his place is a relic of the living, a visual substitute for the man, who has left behind all ties, all connections, all memories. In an essay on the Paris morgue (*All the Year Round*, May 16, 1863), Dickens notes the fascination of the crowd as the body of an old man, somewhere between 65 and 90 (p. 221), who had been strolling when struck and killed by the fall of a building stone, is produced for public viewing. However various the responses to the corpse, "all these expressions concurred in possessing the one under-lying expression of *looking at something that could not return a look*."[12] So too, the power of the epitaph is that there can be no reciprocity. However modest the report, the tone must be always emphatic without appeal. Life assessments recall the dead so that the living will be remembered; they offer a testament to the life which included others, which made a world, which, if obliterated, would efface also the world in which we, too, have lived and continue to live. The fear beneath the sentiment is that *we* will be forgotten even as we are forsaken.

Charles Perugini's picture "*Faithful*" puts the case in a slightly different aspect (see Fig. 24). An old lady sits by a grave on a low wall with eyes closed and hands loosely folded as if what began as a prayer has become more personal reverie. It is clear that her mind dwells on whoever was buried in the grave upon which her flowers rest. The departed one is the subject of *her* thoughts just as *she* is the subject of ours: her isolation is the most striking aspect of the painting. She does not forget, but the absence of signifiers indicating her presence in the lives of others accentuates a mood of forgetfulness rather than that of memory. That vital part of us which has lived through relation with another is extinguished after death. The Other One is gone; that may be tragic: I am alone, and that is a living agony. Casteras sees "resignation" in the face of this woman and in her mien: I see remarkable potency in her figure, which is almost (and oddly) manly, with broad shoulders, spread knees, and unlined, youthful hands and forearms, notably bare and strong.[13] The bodily abundance is set against a scarcity of emotional

12. Charles Dickens, "Some Recollections of Mortality," *Uncommercial Traveller*, 223.
13. Casteras, *Images of Victorian Womanhood in English Art*, 127.

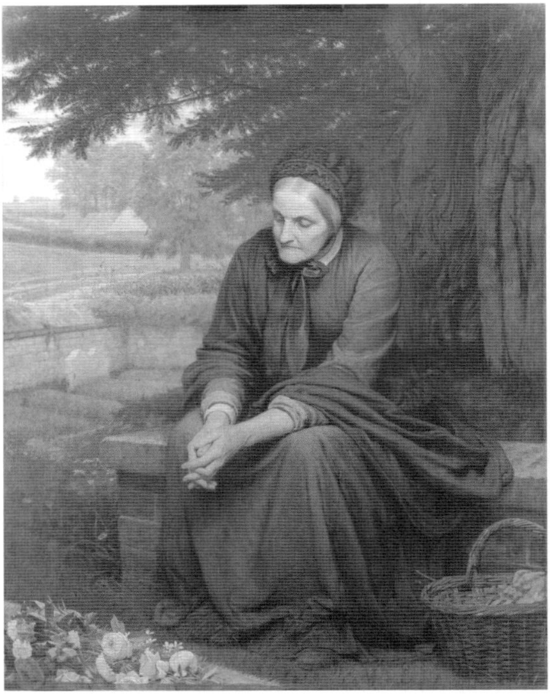

Figure 24 Charles Perugini, *Faithful.* Photo © National Museums Liverpool, Walker Art Gallery, UK

nourishment, as if the death has engendered a vital ruin. There is no satisfactory social integration of the bereaved just as there is no adequate personal relation left to her. (A compensating act of visual imagination appears in Frank Holl's painting *Her Firstborn* (1876), where the grave site of a young child attracts a social scene, with young and old sharing their grief for the child.) In Perugini's painting we cannot be certain that the woman mourns for an elderly person, but the very anonymity of the deceased suggests that it was partner rather than youth who passed away. Conventional images suggest a funeral service crowded with affiliations accumulated over a long period of time, but all too often friends of the elderly have already died, or are ailing; they drift away or avoid contact with those who remind them of their own mortality. A rich life doesn't always result in a comparable death.

The time-honored ascription of memory to the old, I have suggested, is complicated by the worry that the living will be forgotten by the loved one who has died. And if there is some comfort in assigning to the elderly the task of memory, there is an analogous exasperation when the old cannot or will not perform that function. Belaboring the past is as bad as forgetting it entirely: these are the twin excesses of the elderly vocation. Once again we evoke William Dorrit's display of old Nandy's supposed incapacities before Arthur Clennam. He asks the plasterer the age of his youngest grandchild, and while the old man thinks, Dorrit "tapped his forehead" and with theatrical condescension, informs Arthur "Memory weak" (*LD*, I, ch. 31). Here the reassuring joke is that old Nandy's memory is not failing, and the disturbing element is Mr. Dorrit's own anxiety about aging. But to let go of memory may also be seen as a blessing sometimes, as we witness from Herkomer's surprising admission, within the autobiography, that "If the power *to forget* had not been stronger in me than the power *to remember*, I might, in Pope's words, have referred to my life as 'that long disease'" (*The Herkomers*, ii. 233–4). Even Little Nell, whose spotless love and early death creates the pathos of Dickens's *Old Curiosity Shop*, in death inspires nothing so remarkable as the image of her old grandfather, "lying dead upon the stone" under which she lay. Not an act of memory but the immediacy of the visual gesture of death beyond memory—"the child and the old man slept together" (ch. 72)—gives the scene its force. No one weeps for old grandfather Trent though they do (or did) for Nell. But it is the prostrate figure of the old man, dead but still bent in devotion, that enacts the most powerful work of mourning. The scene lingers in Dickens, and he will draw on it again in *Little Dorrit*, where he imagines not one, but two old men, one dying for grief of his brother. Here is the narrative epitaph:

> One figure reposed upon the bed. The other, kneeling on the floor, drooped over it; the arms easily and peacefully resting on the coverlet; the face bowed down, so that the lips touched the hand over which with its last breath it had bent. The two brothers were before their Father; far beyond the twilight judgments of this world; high above its mists and obscurities. (*LD*, II, ch. 19)

For Dickens, there is no higher mark of esteem than to have lived through the irritations and misadventures of a difficult life, and still to be remembered with love. In *Martin Chuzzlewit* Mr. Mould, the undertaker, reminds Sairey Gamp that "Hearts want binding, and spirits want balming when people die: not when people are born" (*MC*, ch. 19), but as these last examples suggest, the balm and binding at the end of life take on extravagant aspects under the pressure of modernity. Ceremonies of religion and social rituals, iconographic conventions and traditions of narrative possess neither transparency nor universal assent. Painters, obituary writers, novelists, and the everyday composers of epitaphs, all strain to find images for the end of life and beyond. The elderly at the point of death, old age at the very limit of age, force human bafflement into strange forms of self-illumination.

Without careful preservation, most images and inscriptions fade. For the great mass of humanity, post-burial remarks prolong 'life' temporarily, perhaps at best for a few generations. Unless they designate famous personages or appear on exceptionally well-tended graves, most nineteenth-century inscriptions have themselves by now become blurred and illegible, hardly recognizable as words and references. Cemeteries became in the nineteenth century (and continue today) places for social encounters or private reveries which only tangentially (if at all) refer to those whose bones reside below ground.

The problem of 'what to do with the dead' was not only a pressing social issue for the Victorians, involving the construction of burial grounds, especially within the metropolitan space of London, but also a problem for narrative. The massive increase in population in the nineteenth century did not reflect a comparable decrease in the death-toll. On the contrary, mortality rates were as alarming as birth rates, and in London, 'housing' was a problem for the living and the dead. In the 1830s and 1840s, seven new cemeteries were constructed on the periphery of the city: Kensal Green (1832), West Norwood (1837), Highgate (1839), Nunhead (1840), Brompton (1840), Abney Park (1840), and Tower Hamlets (1841). Each had a 'personality' of its own, detectable even today, marked by its resident 'population.' The class spectrum of the burial grounds ranges from the prestigious Highgate Cemetery, where George Eliot, Michael Faraday, Karl Marx, and Radclyffe Hall (among others) are buried, to Tower Hamlets, long associated with the poor of the East End of London. The ambitious construction of cemeteries relieved but did not solve the problem of overcrowding: burial plots within London are considered a luxury. While I was writing this book, for instance, a Canadian woman, inheritor of empty places in a family plot in Highgate Cemetery, created local uproar by offering to sell the plots at an inflated fee over the internet.

As churchyards ceded to large open burial grounds, they began to function as public gardens or parks, grounds for meeting, strolling, riding, places for meditation or conversation. Long before the twentieth century, cemeteries offered spaces for leisurely excursions, appealing to those seeking quiet gardens and contemplative settings. In 1863 Dickens wrote an article for *All the Year Round* called "The City of the Absent," where he described the varied character of city churchyards, and the kinds of people who frequent them. In one, which he names "Saint Ghastly Grim," he finds that the "attraction of repulsion" compels him to visit it at midnight in a thunderstorm; in another he describes two very old people who resemble "Time and his wife." Inevitably, he observes, old men released from the workhouse for an afternoon scout out these haunts, where they may be found "leaning with both hands on their sticks and asthmatically gasping."[14] The aged are drawn to the place beyond age.

In *Our Mutual Friend* the desperate Bradley Headstone proposes to Lizzie in a churchyard near Leadenhall Street: "Here, conveniently and healthfully elevated above the level of the living, were the dead, and the tombstones; some of the latter droopingly inclined from the perpendicular, as if they were ashamed of the lies they told." (*OMF*, II, ch. 15). This is a crux for us, because here in the graveyard is where age and inscription meet. The "lies" refer to the inflated rhetoric of narrative inscriptions, but in another sense, they refer to a higher truth, just as the image before us 'elevates' the dead above the living. We have discussed the *difference* between youth and age in the ways each are evoked in the inscriptions which recall them, and we have also noted the futility of all attempts to 'add' anything to lives which have ended. Now we bring together these two strands which we have pursued separately. For in a 'higher' sense there is no difference between youth and age at all, and not because they are ageless. The dead may be ageless, but the graves, even freshly laid graves after just a month or so, are all in various stages of 'old.' Some are still in 'green' old age, whereas others are decrepit. The stroller in Dickens's essay carefully observes that "The illegible tombstones are all lopsided, the grave-mounds lost their shape in the rains of a hundred years ago, the Lombardy Poplar or Plane-Tree that was once a drysalter's daughter and several common councilmen, has withered like those worthies, and its departed leaves are dust beneath it" ("The City of the Absent," 262). The dead become ageless, the remains of the dead become, and remain, old.

14. Charles Dickens, "The City of the Absent"—"Some Recollections of Mortality" in *Uncommercial Traveller,* 223.

Coda

The legislative movement toward the Pensions Act, the aging and then the death of the Queen, the sociological investigations conducted by Charles Booth, the maturing of gerontology as a medical discipline, the increasing perception of a generational divide, the proliferating images of aging bodies—all these brought the ripening consciousness of age that I have spoken of as the invention of the elderly subject. It was not of course a datable event; indeed part of the complexity of old age, as we have seen, is that its elusiveness was a leading part of its condition. Secluded in remote parts of the household, assigned to the borders of paintings, caricatured in cartoons, caught in clichés, the elderly were near at hand, long before they came into visual, literary, or political focus. That they did win close attention by the end of the century is in large part due to their gradual but looming physical presence. I have emphasized the significance of institutional life, the massing of the poor in workhouses and asylums, which ultimately brought recognition of the aged poor as a subculture among a subculture. Even those more modest institutions the almshouses brought the elderly into a perceptible collective, a visible assembly that could be described and diagnosed, counted and catalogued, regulated and normalized.

But there is a second, less immediate effect of the growing prominence of the elderly. This was the tendency of individuals to look more intimately at their ongoing experience of aging, to mark it and to weigh it, and to make it a theme of self-understanding, even from a relatively early age.

Human beings have always pondered and dreaded the prospect of old age; the place of Cicero's reflections are one sign of the persistence of concern. But it is clear that in the last third of the nineteenth century, as age became such a conspicuous public topic and problem, it also became an intensely private preoccupation. The social formation of old age created terms, images, and narratives that lone individuals used to fashion the stories of their lives.

A large part of my aim has been to respect the specificity of aging: not only the wide diversities of circumstance (rich and poor, urban and rural, watched and forgotten, powerful and dispossessed) but also the distinct acts of representation by novelists, painters, journalists, sociologists and diary-keepers. The broad historical arc—the recognition of the elderly subject—was an uneven and varied development. It unfolded as a discontinuous episode of threshold moments and periods of quiescence. The method here has been to acknowledge the discontinuity and to narrate the arc of change by way of case study. The singular inventions of Dickens (a Gamp, a Higden, a Nandy), the particularity of lives in an almshouse and Trollope's particular Mr Harding, the letters (and images) of Queen Victoria, the reports (and revisions) of Charles Booth, Wilde's Dorian Gray, Morris's William Guest, the autobiography of Margaret Oliphant, the diary of Beatrice Webb—my assumption has been that these radiant cases are at once illuminating in themselves and also contributions to the discontinuous narrative of Victorian old age.

The precedent of the Pensions Act irrevocably changed old age. Details would be elaborated; provisions would alter; the age of eligibility would be adjusted. But the central principles of the Act have been enduring, and they brought to an end much of the uncertainty and indeterminacy that pervaded the condition of age in the nineteenth century. We need only cast a thought back to the lives, real and fictional, that have moved through this study to appreciate the force of the change. Betty Higden would not have strayed through the countryside, peddling her meager wares until she died from exhaustion; the workhouses would not have been the inevitable receptacle for so many urban elderly poor; Trollope's pensioners would not have depended on alms bestowed by an ancient will; the degraded men and women interviewed by Charles Booth's commission would not have been left picking oakum until they got "so mad that they began throwing it at each other." After long debate and confusions, the resolve to designate a population of the elderly, to fix an age (however arbitrary), and to ensure a basic level of provision for all represents a culminating moment in the history we have followed here.

Old age, of course, never ends, no matter how solicitous the degree of care. This study has worked to sustain its double view: aging as an increasingly focused object of social concern and aging as a phenomenology, an experience lived from the inside, which endures its own history through the nineteenth century and beyond. If the Pensions Act marked a clear threshold in the treatment of aging populations, no act could alter the inward agon of age. The Ciceronian image of self-respect, acceptance, and serenity continued—and continues—to be an animating ideal, which has been attained often enough to maintain its power of attraction. Yet the biographic and historical record, as well as our own encounters with those we know and love, shows clearly that Ciceronian serenity has been as much a cruel taunt as a guide to the last years of life.

The passage of the Pensions Act could not remove the terrors of age. On the principle that the double perspective sustaining this study should sustain it to the end, I turn back to Beatrice Webb at the close. In her long life that lasted nearly half of two centuries (1858–1943), she marked the landmark of the 1908 Act, and as Charles Booth's collaborator and friend, she could take (mixed) pleasure from the political compromises that brought the long-deferred legislative victory. But it was her fortune and misfortune to live beyond the public achievement and to carry the experience of aging long past the Victorian milieu that had formed her temperament and convictions. Earlier I recalled the stern impersonality of Webb's social ethics, her commitment to the "million sick" rather than Barrett Browning's one "child sick in fever," and her interest in "the needless misery of men as distinguished from the suffering of those individuals whom you happen to know." We met earlier her agonizing encounters with the frightful decline of her father and Herbert Spencer, encounters that brought the immediacy of particular failing lives hard against her will to impersonality. At Spencer's death in 1903, Webb put a question to herself, "Did the light that was in him survive even for himself? To me he seemed in these last years to be stumbling in total darkness, hurting himself and then crying aloud in his lonely distress, clinging to his dogmas but without confident faith, with an almost despairing and defiant pride of intellect."[1] Later and still harder was Beatrice Webb's encounter with herself.

On the eve of the publication of *My Apprenticeship* (1926), as Webb approached her seventieth year, she made a characteristically self-rousing demand. "Courage, old woman, courage: be game to the end and don't give way to the egotism of old age; live up to what old age *ought to be*, the impersonal beneficence of the Ancient unmoved by the opinion of a world he or she is about to leave."[2]

1. *The Diary of Beatrice Webb*, ii. *All the Good Things of Life: 1892–1905*, ed. Norman and Jeanne Mackenzie (London: Virago, 1983), 307–8 (December 8, 1903).
2. The Diary of Beatrice Webb, iv. *The Wheel of Life: 1924–1943*, ed. Norman and Jeanne Mackenzie (London: Virago, 1985), 68 (February 18, 1926).

Again in 1928, she summons equanimity: "There is not much to complain of in this slow and painless decline of energy. But it means that we must learn 'the habit of resignation.'"[3] Even when she comes to believe that she has become an elderly relic of a previous century, she remains stern with herself. In the face of debilitating depression, she calls herself to order with the reminder that "we have no reason for discouragement except the coming of old age, which being inevitable and universal it is cowardly to resent." And, even earlier, as she feels her generosity narrowing, she admonishes herself "don't give way to the egotism of old age; live up to what old age ought to be, the impersonal beneficence of the Ancient."[4] Cicero again, but the Ciceronian ideal turned back against the writer, and it is Webb's formal address to herself—her self-scrutiny and self-estrangement, her appeal to herself from the standpoint of universality and impersonality—that makes her case so rich and troubling.

All the more troubling because it was for Webb to live on, past this hard-won poise and psychic balance. "A sense of sadness in old age," she writes in 1929, "is watching one's contemporaries tumbling into senility—pity being intensified by self-pity. 'There, in a few months or years, shall I be,' is one's reflection." There indeed she was. As her husband Sidney and she declined together, they lost the self-will that had carried them into their final years; they saw themselves as "ghosts of our former selves haunting this mad century with its tragic happenings"; they remembered, without feeling, their former convictions. The "'Religion of Humanity,'" the creed that had animated a lifetime's vocation, has "vanished from the public eye in my lifetime." As Webb comes to her end, she records a "longing for the eternal sleep of death dominating my consciousness by day and by night." When she asks Sidney, "'Do you wish to go on living?' He sat silent, surprised at the question, then slowly said 'No.'" In April 1943, the last month of her life, she writes that "When he is dead I shall at once disappear gladly and by my own act."[5]

A dignified old age as an object of rational collective concern, an index of enlightenment, a focus of public policy, and a desolate old age of waning power, of self-doubt and loss of faith, of fatigue and melancholy that no policy or rationality can relieve—Beatrice Webb knew both extremities.

3. Ibid. 137 (January 21, 1928). 4. Ibid. 120–1, 68 (April 14, 1927; February 18, 1926).
5. Ibid. 197 (October 7, 1929); 399 (December 14, 1937); 152–3 (October 26, 1928); 475 (October 6, 1941).

A Victorian outliving herself into a next century, she endured a historical obsolescence, a comic/tragic belatedness, that converged with the most immediate experience of outliving will and purpose and joy. Yet if she lives on for us, in all her determination and trouble, it is because her example is also a parable. It teaches that old age defies the concern that it solicits. It shows how it belongs to the public commissioner and the individual and the commissioner-as-individual. It reveals how an old age can get older still, until it exceeds and surprises itself; how it swamps impersonality; how it is the fate of others up to the very moment that it becomes our own.

Index